Jean Piaget

Titles in the *Bloomsbury Library of Educational Thought* Series:

St Thomas Aquinas, *Vivian Boland OP*
Aristotle, *Alexander Moseley*
St Augustine, *Ryan N. S. Topping*
Pierre Bourdieu, *Michael James Grenfell*
Jerome Bruner, *David R. Olson*
Confucius, *Charlene Tan*
John Dewey, *Richard Pring*
Michel Foucault, *Lynn Fendler*
Paulo Freire, *Daniel Schugurensky*
John Holt, *Roland Meighan*
John Locke, *Alexander Moseley*
Loris Malaguzzi and the Reggio Emilia Experience, *Kathy Hall, Mary Horgan, Anna Ridgway, Rosaleen Murphy, Maura Cunneen and Denice Cunningham*

Maria Montessori, *Marion O'Donnell*
A. S. Neill, *Richard Bailey*
John Henry Newman, *James Arthur and Guy Nicholls*
Robert Owen, *Robert A. Davis and Frank O'Hagan*
R. S. Peters, *Stefaan E. Cuypers and Christopher Martin*
Jean Piaget, *Richard Kohler*
Plato, *Robin Barrow*
Jean-Jacques Rousseau, *Jürgen Oelkers*
Rudolf Steiner, *Heiner Ullrich*
Leo Tolstoy, *Daniel Moulin*
Lev Vygotsky, *René van der Veer*
E. G. West, *James Tooley*
Mary Wollstonecraft, *Susan Laird*

Series Editor: Richard Bailey is a writer and researcher in education and sport. A former teacher in both primary and secondary schools and a teacher trainer, he has been Professor at a number of leading Universities in the UK. He now lives and works in Germany.

Members of the Advisory Board

Jean Piaget

RICHARD KOHLER

Bloomsbury Library of Educational Thought

Series Editor: Richard Bailey

B L O O M S B U R Y

LONDON · NEW DELHI · NEW YORK · SYDNEY

KH

Bloomsbury Academic
An imprint of Bloomsbury Publishing Plc

50 Bedford Square	1385 Broadway
London	New York
WC1B 3DP	NY 10018
UK	USA

www.bloomsbury.com

First published 2008 by Continuum International Publishing Group
Paperback edition first published 2014 by Bloomsbury Academic

British Library Cataloguing-in-Publication Data
A catalogue record for this book is available from the British Library.

ISBN: PB: 978-1-4725-1888-0
ePUB: 978-1-4411-4444-7

Library of Congress Cataloguing-in-Publication Data
Kohler, Richard.
Jean Piaget/Richard Kohler.
p.   cm. – (Continuum Library of educational thought)
Includes bibliographical references.
ISBN-13: 978-0-8264-8411-6 (hardcover)
ISBN-10: 0-8264-8411-5 (hardcover)
1. Piaget, Jean, 1896–1980.   2. Education–Philosophy.   I. Title.   II. Series.

LB775.P492K64   2008
155.4'13092–dc22
[B]
                                            2007030629

Typeset by Aptara Books Ltd.
Printed and bound in Great Britain

10/18/17

Contents

Series Editor's Preface   vii

Foreword   ix

Introduction   1

Part 1   Intellectual Biography   3

  1   Piaget s Background   5

  2   Piaget s Career as a Naturalist   13

  3   Perturbations of Puberty   25

  4   The Reconstruction of Identity   40

Part 2   Critical Exposition of Piaget's Work   61

  5   Early Psychological Work   63

  6   Theological Foundations   99

  7   The Social-psychological Work   109

  8   The Pedagogic Work   128

  9   The Biological Work   156

10   The Main Psychological Work   163

11   The Epistemological Work   220

12   Neither Retirement nor Resignation   234

Part 3   The Reception and Influence of Piaget's Work   241

13   The Reception   243

14   The In uence   254

Part 4   The Relevance of Piaget's Work Today   261

15   The Relevance of Piaget s Work Today   263

Bibliography   267

Name Index   309

Subject Index   315

Series Editor s Preface

Education is sometimes presented as an essentially practical activity. It is, it seems, about teaching and learning, curriculum and what goes on in schools. It is about achieving certain ends, using certain methods, and these ends and methods are often prescribed for teachers, whose duty it is to deliver them with vigor and delity . With such a clear purpose, what is the value of theory?

Recent years have seen politicians and policy makers in different countries explicitly denying *any* value or need for educational theory. A clue to why this might be is offered by a remarkable comment by a British Secretary of State for Education in the 1990s: having any ideas about how children learn, or develop, or feel, should be seen as subversive activity. This pithy phrase captures the problem with theory: it subverts, challenges and undermines the very assumptions on which the practice of education is based.

Educational theorists, then, are troublemakers in the realm of ideas. They pose a threat to the *status quo* and lead us to question the common sense presumptions of educational practices. But this is precisely what they should do because the seemingly simple language of schools and schooling hides numerous contestable concepts that in their different usages re ect fundamental disagreements about the aims, values and activities of education.

Implicit within the *Bloomsbury Library of Educational Thought* is an assertion that theories and theorizing are vitally important for education. By gathering together the ideas of some of the most in uential, important and interesting educational thinkers, from the Ancient Greeks to contemporary scholars, the series has the ambitious task of providing an accessible yet authoritative resource for a generation of students and practitioners. Volumes within the series are written by acknowledged leaders in the eld, who were selected both for their scholarship and their ability to make often complex ideas accessible to a diverse audience.

It will always be possible to question the list of key thinkers that are represented in this series. Some may question the inclusion of certain thinkers; some may disagree with the exclusion of others. That is inevitably going to be the case. There is no suggestion that the list of thinkers represented within the *Bloomsbury Library of Educational Thought* is in any way de nitive. What is incontestable is that these thinkers have fascinating ideas about education, and that taken together, the *Library* can act as a powerful source of information and inspiration for those committed to the study of education.

Richard Bailey
Roehampton University, London

Foreword

In the international eld of education in the twentieth century two names towered above all others, namely John Dewey and Jean Piaget. If one compares frequency of citations, the reception in very different countries and contexts and the importance of their educational theories, Dewey and Piaget outperform all others by far. This is remarkable insofar as John Dewey was a philosopher and Jean Piaget was received mainly as a developmental psychologist. In the eld of education both came to be associated with progressive education, although considerable differences exist.

Jean Piaget s career is related to his beginnings as a biologist, his psychoanalysis and, most of all, his experiences in Geneva. In the reception of his work today, Piaget s developmental psychology and his later genetic epistemology predominate. Piaget is almost always understood from his middle and late works, whereas his own development itself shows strong references to progressive education. Geneva and not Paris was the undisputed center of the francophone *éducation nouvelle*. This direction of international progressive education is strongly rooted in Calvinism and it found a welcome test eld in Geneva, starting in the late nineteenth century.

Richard Kohler s work undertakes a reconstruction of Piaget s educational theory from its beginnings and in this way differs from so many other works, which derive an educational theory from Piaget s developmental psychology. Jean Piaget participated actively in the progressive education movement for decades; he organized innumerable conferences, gave lectures on topics in progressive education time and time again, and up to World War II he was considered to be one of the most important representatives of *éducation nouvelle*.

As this connection is often overlooked today, the present volume lls a gap. What comes to light is the educationalist Jean Piaget, who wanted to change educational practice and the schools beyond the context of the Canton of Geneva. This historical connection was largely forgotten also because in his later years Piaget did retreat from his activities in progressive education, while not distancing himself from them entirely.

The history of progressive education in Geneva and in the larger context of the French-speaking regions has not yet been written. Richard Kohler s work reveals clearly that Jean Piaget gures eminently in this history. Without his decades-long work for progressive education committees and associations, the focus of Piaget s psychological theories on the development of the child would probably not have come about or would have had a very different outlook. This relation to praxis distinguishes Piaget from one of the few educationalists that he accepted, namely Jean-Jacques Rousseau, who was, not by chance, also a Genevan.

Prof. Dr Jürgen Oelkers

Introduction

Jean Piaget (1896–1980) was a landmark in the history of ideas during the twentieth century. Without him, the history of psychology, especially developmental psychology, and the history of pedagogy would have taken a different course. Both the quantity and the breadth of his work are striking. He wrote and lectured in zoology, evolution theory, philosophy, psychology, pedagogy, sociology, theology, mathematics, logic, epistemology, and science history. These contributions form an entire system in the universalistic tradition of the Enlightenment and are intended to help improve the world. Piaget did not become a child psychologist because he was particularly interested in children but his research into cognitive development helped him to establish a theory that would explain our ways of thinking and thus explain the world. This project with its holistic claim fascinated many of his contemporaries and fuelled ideas for further exploration in various disciplines.

This book pursues three objectives. First, it is meant to be a concise but comprehensive introduction to Piaget's work. Pedagogical aspects are discussed at greater depth within the framework of this series, so Piaget's early work, which is often neglected, will receive greater attention. Second, it will identify the continuities and breaks in the development of his theory, as well as the reasons behind them. In my opinion, the logic and the specific problems of Piaget's system can only be understood if his religious convictions are taken into account. Third, it attempts to provide a biography that systematically incorporates philosophical, religious, scientific and institutional contexts.

To write a biography of Piaget is, however, a tricky task. His autobiographical writings are clever constructions, which, by means of a particular chronology and omissions of essential facts, create or obscure connections that do not reflect the true situation. False testimony is rare but tendentious arrangements of conflicts and glorifying interpretations of episodes are the rule. In addition, very few documents are available to shed light upon the details of Piaget's life. He wrote and answered only very few letters because, according to his son Laurent, Piaget considered this to be a waste of time. In order to obtain a credible portrait the available documents must be supported by biographical conclusions drawn from his theoretical writings.

This account has been structured chronologically for the first 30 years of his life, so that the development of his theory can be understood easily. After his first appointment as professor in 1925, Piaget often worked on several different projects simultaneously. A chronological account of these research topics would, therefore, be unsuitable. After the presentation of Piaget's early work in psychology, this book will focus on the systematic discussion of his various disciplines, with regular reference to biographical data.

Part 1

Intellectual Biography

1

Piaget's Background

Neuchâtel

Jean William Fritz Piaget was born in Neuchâtel on 9 August 1896, the first child of Arthur and Rebecca-Suzanne Piaget. Neuchâtel, where Piaget grew up with his two sisters Madeleine (1899–1976) and Marthe (1903–1985), is the capital of the canton of the same name in west Switzerland. The canton, which at the time had 134,000 inhabitants, is situated in the Jura, a mountain range along the border with France. Piaget was to pursue his career as a developmental psychologist and cognitive theorist 120 km away in Geneva. His other places of work were at Lausanne and Paris, at distances of 75 km and 500 km respectively.

The Piagets are an old family from Neuchâtel. In the mid-seventeenth century, one branch of this family settled in the small village of La Côte-aux-Fée, in the Val de Travers, near the French border. After the failed Royalist Rebellion of 1856, however, Jean's grandfather Frédéric (1830–1884) left the canton of Neuchâtel and moved to nearby Yverdon in the canton of Vaud. In the eighteenth century, Neuchâtel was officially a principality of Prussia but, in practice, it was almost autonomous. After French rule, from 1806 to 1814, the principality once more came under the control of the Prussian Hohenzollern family yet, paradoxically, at the same time it became a canton of the Helvetic Confederation. An initial revolution by the Democrats failed in 1831, but after the peaceful revolution of 1848, the Republic was declared. When a Royalist counter-revolution was defeated in 1856, the Prussian king Friedrich Wilhelm IV renounced his claim to power, and the Treaty of Paris guaranteed independence. Ever since, the republican system and the integration of Neuchâtel into the Swiss Confederation have remained largely undisputed (Barrelet 1996).

Around the turn of the century, the French-speaking part of Switzerland (the Romandy) was "a haven for intellectuals with high moral behavior, who were open to the world and to universal questions, as well as being sufficiently confined to this corner of the country, so that every utterance reverberated there and produced multiple effects" (Robert-Grandpierre 1996: 122). The intellectual climate was characterized by a free and scientifically oriented exchange, by a patriotic attitude and by the omnipresence of religious-moral discourses.

Neuchâtel with its 20,000 inhabitants was considered conservative and provincial compared with the larger and more fashionable La Chaux-de-Fonds. Wealth and political power were concentrated in Neuchâtel and in the lower part of the canton, near Lake Neuchâtel. The watch- and clock-making, machinery and jewelry industries had made the town wealthy, and some merchants and bankers owed their wealth to the slave trade (Fässler 2005: 207–219). From the mid-eighteenth century, the growing clock-making industry in Le Locle and La Chaux-de-Fonds, in the upper part of the valley, allowed peasants and herdsmen to work and earn from home during the hard winter months. Industrialization, especially the modernization of clock production, led to renewed social tension during the second half of the nineteenth century. 'The Mountains' became a center of socialist, anarchist, communist and Christian-socialist movements (Perrenoud 1990). The Radical Party, which arose from the revolutionary republican environment, represented progressive, laicist, bourgeois forces (62 mandates in the canton parliament in 1904); the conservative Liberal Party, with 30 seats, united the more federalist and traditional thinking citizens. Due to the majority system these two parties had been dominating the political scene since 1888 and joined forces against the rising socialists who, in 1904, sent 15 representatives to the parliament. Despite its election successes in the workers' regions, the pacifist Socialist Party remained a marginal political force until the introduction of proportional communal representation in 1912. In the town of Neuchâtel, the Liberals now gained 15 seats, the Radicals 14 and the Socialists 11, while La Chaux-de-Fonds was run by a left-wing council.

In the last quarter of the nineteenth century and in the early twentieth century, due to industrialization and a growing population, Neuchâtel invested considerable sums in the expansion of its educational system by building six primary schools, the canton grammar school, a museum of art and one of natural history. One of the most influential figures in Neuchâtel's system of science and education was Piaget's father.

Arthur Piaget

Arthur Piaget (1865–1952) was born in Yverdon, where his parents Frédéric and Marie-Adèle produced the Piaget-Allisson clocks. His prosperous family background allowed him to study philology, Modern Greek and medieval literature in Leipzig, London, and Paris. One of his professors in the French capital was Gaston Pâris (1839–1903), a champion of critical source-based historiography. At the same time, Arthur Piaget studied in Neuchâtel, and in late 1888 he received his doctorate from the University of Geneva for work on Martin Le Franc. From 1891 to 1894 he taught courses in fourteenth- and fifteenth-century French literature at the Ecole Pratique des Hautes Etudes in Paris, where he met the primary teacher Rebecca-Suzanne Jackson (1872–1942). Thanks to their marriage, he was introduced to the Protestant upper class society of Paris, because the Jacksons were an English immigrant family of industrialists whose wealth was based on English steel.

In 1895, Arthur Piaget was appointed lecturer for Romance languages and literature at Neuchâtel Academy. In his opening lecture, he exposed the *Canons' Chronicle*, which had been the most important document to prove the affinity and cooperation of Neuchâtel with the Swiss Confederation since mediaeval times, as an eighteenth-century fake. This historiographic dismantling of Neuchâtel's patriotic myth was seen as an attack on the political identity of the young canton and caused such strong polemics that Piaget considered leaving the town. Yet in 1898, despite opposition from conservatives, the critical historian was appointed manager of the state archives. In 1906, Piaget breached a further historic taboo of Neuchâtel canton by painting a more balanced picture of Prussian politics before the revolution of 1848. This is why Jean Piaget admired his father as "a man of a painstaking and critical mind, who dislikes hastily improvised generalizations, and is not afraid of starting a fight when he finds historic truth twisted to fit respectable traditions" (Piaget 1952/1: 106). At the same time, the pugnacious historian took over the editorial office of the canton's history journal, *Neuchâtel Museum*, which allowed him to reach out his scientific standards to interested amateurs. In 1909, Arthur Piaget was appointed founding rector of Neuchâtel University, where during his first year 39 professors and 11 associate professors, as well as 11 private lecturers, taught 169 matriculated students and 156 non-matriculated listeners (Schaer 1996: 70). Despite his senior position, he remained excluded from the aristocratic circle of traditionalists who dominated Neuchâtel because he had destroyed local myths. Among the intellectuals, however, Piaget counted as a philologist of international repute, whose unbiased and meticulous attitude impressed students and colleagues alike. His far-reaching network of connections was to allow his son access to specialists, academic societies and publishers.

According to witnesses, Arthur Piaget was "a fantastic father, broadminded and full of understanding for his son's vocation" (Tribolet 1996: 48). The uniting element between father and son was intellectual achievement, as the father taught his son "the value of systematic work, even in small matters" (Piaget 1952/1: 106). The only conflict Piaget described in his autobiographical writings arose in connection with the first work that he produced as a 10-year-old. His strict father devalued the roughly 100-page-long book with the title *Our Birds* "as a mere compilation" (Piaget 1952/1: 107). One can imagine how proud the boy must have been to have written a scientific work, like his father, and how disappointed and hurt he must have felt when he was accused of eclecticism. The father's reaction was in line with Protestantism that educates man to be "his own slave-driver" (Fromm 1941: 86). Although Arthur Piaget was not a practicing believer he had nonetheless internalized the Protestant ethics of achievement. The "inner world asceticism" of Protestantism is expressed above all in the duty to lead a rational lifestyle. In order to fulfil this duty, a Protestant is "urged to use the excellent means of working relentlessly. Work, and work alone, is supposed to dispel religious doubt, and to guarantee the state of grace" (Weber 1905: 105f.).

Jean copied his father's attitude to such an extent that he "was considered slightly abnormal" because he "did not move around much" and that he later had "not a single memory of play" (Piaget 1973/17). He even assigned therapeutic functions to work. "I simply have to get back to work, then all the anger of life will disappear!" (Piaget and Bringuier 1977: 89). The identification with his father's expectations of achievement and truth probably constituted the most important motivational factors for his immense work. Apparently, this identification was interspersed with resentment and feelings of rivalry. In his account of psychoanalysis, Piaget uncritically adopted the Oedipus situation. The

father, when he first appears, is a stranger. Therefore he is hostile. He does not nourish, and he is incapable of maternal warmth. Also, the mother seems to be a different person when he is not around, at least in the little one's fears and suspicions it appears to be so. Thus, the father falls into the category of things that cause distance from the mother. Moreover, he will soon prove his authority, he'll demonstrate a terrifying voice if the little one cries too long, even if these cries—above all, so it seems when these cries are calls for the mother. The father, therefore, must be removed; the father is despised as much as the mother is loved. It is difficult to contest this psychology [...] It will certainly not take long until the father, too, is loved. He will form a true unit with his wife in the baby's mind. Yet he will be the object of a new sensation, which is not like the elementary tenderness the mother enjoyed, but will be a secondary fondness into which enters the fear that is still active. This sensation is respect, composed of love, but also of fear and distrust. (Piaget 1920/2: 36f.)

Father and son had an ambivalent relationship: Jean admired his father and was fond of him, but fear and distrust marred this fondness. Anxiety was to dominate Piaget's life: "Fundamentally I am a worrier that only work can relieve" (Piaget 1952/1: 138). By concentrating on his work he was able to suppress his nagging self-doubts, his feelings of loneliness and insecurity, and in addition he could hope for social acclaim. "His restless temperament and [...] his almost pathological need of security" (Hameline 1996: 251) seemed to be the consequence of the exaggerated demands and of the humiliations that had been inflicted upon him. Young Jean hoped to gain his father's recognition by even surpassing his father's expectation and scientific achievements. It would not be far-fetched to define Piaget as a workaholic, who derived his identity almost exclusively from his professional success.

The Mother

Piaget described Rebecca-Suzanne Piaget-Jackson as "very intelligent, energetic, and fundamentally a very kind person" (Piaget 1952/1: 106). Thus, her kindness was hidden, and "her rather neurotic temperament [...] made our family life somewhat troublesome" (Piaget 1952/1: 106). The instability of her state of mind and her fits of temper were not conducive to a home environment that would have offered the children care and support. Piaget's sister Marthe characterized her mother as "an authoritarian woman who made their childhood unhappy" (in Vidal 1994a: 14). Even if Dr Henri Bersot's diagnosis of alienation and paranoia should be taken with a pinch of salt (because in those days women used to be very quickly seen as pathologically nervous or hysterical when they displayed spontaneous or nonconforming behavior), her mental illness seemed to be the main reason why young Jean spent part of his childhood with his grandmother in Paris.

Trying to escape from his mother's fits of temper and to do justice to his father's expectations Piaget took "refuge in both a private and a non-fictitious world" (Piaget 1952/1: 106): the collection and classification of pond and land snails. "Piaget explored the marshes for his malacology at a very early age, basically a lonely search, and when he returned, his social relationships remained tense" (Muller, oral communication cited in Perret-Clermont 1996: 263). Evidently, Piaget suppressed his feelings of loneliness by occupying himself with scientific activities and philosophical rationalization. In his autobiographical novel *Recherche*, he complained that his life was only taking place on an intellectual, abstract, and unreal level, and that he was craving an intensive life (Piaget 1918: 96, 104, 114). Sébastien, the protagonist and Piaget's alter ego (Piaget and Bringuier 1977: 32) suffered from manic and depressive conditions, from anxiety, phases of depersonalization and loneliness, which he wished to control and neutralize by means of reason. Indeed, Piaget's descriptions of family situations frequently contained an ambivalent and hostile atmosphere:

> At a very early age, even before speech develops, the child is constantly either punished or rewarded. Depending on the circumstances, the infant's behavior is either approved of and one smiles at him, or one frowns at him and leaves him to cry. Even the tone of the voices that surround him is enough to create an atmosphere of permanent retribution. During the following years, the child is under constant surveillance. Everything he says or does is supervised. (Piaget 1932: 364)

Experience of restrictive supervision, punishing educational measures and affective coldness led him to conclude that the parent–child relationship could only be determined by constraint and heteronomy. "The adult is both very superior to the child and very close. He dominates everything, yet still penetrates into the innermost core of every wish or thought" (Piaget and Leuzinger-Schuler 1947/9: 71). Piaget appeared to have felt powerless and at the mercy of both parents. The picture of the mother, which Piaget painted in his psychoanalytical writings, is as ambivalent as the picture of the father. On the one hand, "the infant experiences his greatest pleasure in his mother's gifts" (Piaget 1920/2: 38). On the other hand, in an autobiographical dream analysis, he described a quiet but "merciless hostility of the subject against his mother" and the "moral crises during which he attempted to free himself from his mother's upbringing" (Piaget 1920/2: 28). The 24-year-old, however, seemed to have failed in this emancipation:

> As soon as we go deep into ourselves we find our desires from long ago, still alive, and unconsciously we are still striving to fulfil them, while we believe that we had long given them up. Therefore it is true, and it is indeed so, that the mother's image pursues us all our lives. (Piaget 1920: 37)

The obvious reason why Piaget showed an interest in psychoanalysis and psychopathology at a relatively early age was to enable him to cope with his own conflicting feelings and desires. It was, however, not only Rebecca Piaget's mental problems that had an influence on her son: in contrast to his agnostic father, she was a staunch Protestant, who rated her children's religious education very highly and rigorously implemented it. In 1907, Piaget's parents decided to commit themselves to the cause of separation between Church and State. In 1912, she was the first socialist to be elected to the local school commission[1] and she made her pacifist convictions known. After the war broke out, she published a report in a local paper about a refugee camp on the French side of Lake Geneva, in which she called the Germans "invaders" and "barbarians" (in Vidal 1994a: 15). She also publicly supported Jules Humbert-Droz (1891–1971), a socialist clergyman, who had been incarcerated for being a conscientious objector to military service. Since Piaget remained a social democrat and pacifist all his life, his mother's influence could not have been as negative as his autobiography would suggest.

Primus inter Pares

From April 1904, Piaget was enrolled in the second year at a private primary school, although his father was a member of the school commission of the canton-run establishment. Jean was an excellent pupil: in his first exam, that had to be taken jointly with the pupils from the cantonal school, he achieved grade six (the top grade) in all subjects. At the end of the fourth class, he still attained an average of 5.4. In April 1907, Piaget entered the Latin School for Boys, and over the next five years studied a classical curriculum. From September 1912 to July 1915, he studied at the Latin-literary faculty of the grammar school. Piaget was the top student in every class throughout his grammar-school career, which he completed without ever having received a single unsatisfactory grade in his reports, and he was probably the only pupil in his year group to receive the award "very satisfying" in his baccalaureate (cf. Schaller-Jeanneret 1996). Despite this, he later distanced himself with obvious contempt from the "swots":

> In our class [...] like in all classes, there were some obvious lazybones, some who worked conscientiously, and a few pupils who with moderate scholastic achievements occupied themselves at home with 'interesting' specialities—chemistry, history, aeronautics, zoology, Hebrew—anything that was not part of the curriculum. Among the conscientious ones who did not consider school to be a game, some have become public officials, little teachers who really cannot today be considered examples of acting energy. The same goes for the lazy ones, if they have not disappeared from the scene altogether. (Piaget 1932: 414f.)

Although the aim of this remark was to highlight his own genius, the arrogance was not justified, considering the support he had received for his achievements. Piaget's teachers were all colleagues of his father, who later, in 1919, took over the presidency of the grammar school staff. "Studies in my home town were in fact organized so that several university lecturers taught us from grammar school onwards, which was a heavy workload for them, but a priceless privilege for us as pupils" (Piaget 1959/11: 44). At grammar school, Piaget was already in a privileged position. Some teachers encouraged and supported Piaget's career considerably, not only during lessons but also outside school hours and even after he completed his school education.

2

Piaget's Career as a Naturalist

Paul Godet and the Classification of Mollusks

At an early age, Piaget showed an interest in birds and fossils. In 1907, he sent a seven-line report on his observations of a part-albino sparrow to *Le Rameau de Sapin* (*The Fir Branch*), the associated journal of the local youth club.

> At the end of last June, to my great surprise, in the Faubourg de l'Hôpital at Neuchâtel, I saw a sparrow presenting all the visible signs of an albino. He had a whitish beak, several white feathers on the back and wings, and the tail was of the same colour. I came nearer, to have a closer look, but he flew away; I was able to follow him with my eyes for some minutes, then he disappeared through the Ruelle du port.
>
> I have just seen today in the *Rameau de Sapin* of 1868 that albino birds are mentioned; which gave me the idea to write down the preceding lines. (Piaget 1907/1)

The journal "published my lines and I was 'launched!'" (Piaget 1952/1: 107). The self-directed irony of the quotation marks must not detract from the fact that Piaget portrayed this report as the starting point of a brilliant career. This impression is underpinned by his preceding remark that he had decided to be more serious after his father had criticized his compilation on birds and he had entered Latin school. Almost all commentators adopted the interpretation that the schoolboy's report was the first manifestation of an innovative life's work.

After the publication of his report, Piaget wrote a letter to the director of the Museum of Natural History, Paul Godet (1836–1911) "and asked his permission to study his collections of birds, fossils, and shells after hours" (Piaget 1952/1: 107). Only five days after the publication, Godet agreed and allowed the pupil to assist him twice a week. "So he took me on as his assistant, made me stick on labels, taught me to collect my own specimens and introduced me to the system of land and fresh water snails" (Piaget 1959/3: 9). Piaget's account creates the impression that writing and publishing his report had been all his own work, which allowed him privileged access to the museum. The question arises, however, how an 11-year-old obtained an almost 40-year-old copy of the journal established in 1866. More plausible than Piaget's version would be to assume that young Piaget told Godet, a friend of his father, about having observed the sparrow, whereupon the biology teacher gave the boy this article of 1868 to read, suggested he write an account of his observation, and arranged for the article to be published in the Natural History Club's journal.

Godet taught his student an outmoded approach to natural history, no longer in line with the practical and theoretical discourses of contemporary international biology. His criterion for identification and morphological classification of a snail assumed the stability of morphological varieties; as variability is especially extensive among mollusks, he needed a large collection for the correct taxonomy. Over the following seven years, Piaget spent the greater part of his leisure time and holidays searching for mollusks, which made him a keen and useful apprentice who tried to help complete his master's work. Due to classification problems, however, Godet was unable to accomplish his life's project of putting together a mollusk catalog of Switzerland.[1] Piaget adopted not only his mentor's field of research but also his concept of science and the Lamarckist understanding of evolution. What counted was not the verification of theory-based hypotheses through experiments but the correct classification of phenomena. Later on, Piaget used to construct wide concept maps to classify the answers already implied in the questions.

Piaget's interest in the mollusk collection was also a result of the fact that he felt important and useful in the company of the 70-year-old natural scientist. Godet looked after his apprentice in a warm-hearted way and thus met the needs Piaget's parents failed to address.

My dear friend Jean

I am writing this short letter to you from the museum to tell you how much I am thinking of you, especially on Saturday afternoon, and that I hope to see you again, once you have overcome this nasty illness that you took so suddenly [. . .] I [. . .] pray to God that he will send you immediate relief and that he will preserve you for those who love you, of whom I am one, you may be sure of this [. . .] Get well soon to return to your place in the office of your very devoted Dr Paul Godet prof. (Godet 1909 ms)

Piaget's mentor was a believing and practicing Christian who understood nature as a book written by God that must be read as a revelation. Natural history education also meant moral and spiritual education:

> The study of nature is an inexhaustible source of enjoyment, and nothing is more useful to the soul, and sometimes to the body, than to devote one's spare time to it. This study develops the spirit of analysis and observation; it helps clarify ideas, and furnishes an admirable means of fighting ennui, often a bad adviser, and always hard to bear. (Godet, in Vidal 1994a: 19)

Godet supported young people in activities supposed to help them overcome the difficulties of puberty. With his regular contributions to *Le Rameau de Sapin* and as mentor of the Friends of Nature Club and the Jurassic Club, the natural science teacher encouraged and supported an entire generation's interest in science. Although Piaget was Godet's most important helper, he was not the only assistant in the museum.

The Friends of Nature[2]

Piaget joined the *Friends of Nature Club* in 1910, and, like many other nature lovers, published his first texts in *Le Rameau de Sapin*, the journal of the Jurassic Club. These two natural-science youth clubs formed part of a cultural network for the promotion of education, morality and patriotism. There were several associations in Neuchâtel that united interested amateurs and renowned scholars with the aim of exchanging knowledge from the fields of science and art. Founded after Napoleon's defeat of 1815, these learned societies with their journals reflected both the increasing importance of education and the attempt to promote political cohesion. The members formed a proper community, supporting and encouraging each other in their values, interests and ambitions. These networks of acquaintances and friends were superimposed over the institutions of classical education and their hierarchies. Piaget benefited from the integration into this social network that approved of his interests and projects and fostered him in a crucial way.

The most important of these societies, the Natural Sciences Society of Neuchâtel, was established in 1832 by the famous scientist Louis Agassiz (1807–1873). Around the turn of the century, this society was a center of serious debates, studies and publications. Piaget joined the youth section of this society in 1912. The members of the Jurassic Club were meant to show an interest in the flora and fauna of the Jura "during the often dangerous moment of transition when, having finished school, the adolescent has not yet taken his place in society, and is lured by frivolous pleasures and material enjoyments" (Favre *et al.* 1874). The Friends of Nature Club too, was intended to be a platform for the intellectual and social initiation of grammar-school pupils into experimental sciences, by observing nature directly on excursions, and for practicing Christian virtues. In contrast to other clubs, this club was managed directly by the young people and functioned largely independent of adults. It was founded in 1893 by Carl-Albert Loosli (1877–1959) and Pierre Bovet (1878–1965); the latter was to become Piaget's teacher of philosophy and the most important supporter of his career. Meetings took place every other Thursday afternoon when the boys exchanged their observations, organized botanic and zoological excursions or presented and discussed descriptions, biographies, theories and historical outlines (cf. Vidal 1996; 1999). The club awarded honorary membership to scholars who supported the young researchers: François-Alphonse Forel (1841–1912), physician, zoologist and politician, introduced the young friends of nature to limnology; Otto Fuhrmann (1871–1945), later one of Piaget's professors, taught them how to set up an aquarium and Piaget's art teacher Théodore Delachaux (1879–1949) helped them with scientific illustrations.

On 9 June 1910, Piaget was solemnly initiated into the Friends of Nature Club in the presence of the honorary members, Paul Godet, Pierre Bovet and Eugène Legrand Roy (1852–1926), another professor at the university, whose chair of astronomy was later taken over by Gustave Juvet (1896–1936). Juvet was one of Piaget's best friends and also a member of the Club. In humorous exaggeration, the candidate was already addressed as "professor of conchology"[3] and as the author "of a famous dictionary" and "of many articles." He therefore received the nickname Tardieu, the god of snails.[4] The topic for his initiation project, *A Special Mollusk in Our Lake*, had been decided by Godet who also furnished Piaget with the necessary specimens and information. Piaget's presentation was criticized for its dull encyclopaedia-like style, whereupon Godet came to his defense.

The subsequent projects of the new member also dealt with the classification of mollusks and were largely based on Godet's resources and approach. These researches, however, impressed the club members so much that after a few months they arrived at the sobering conclusion: "We all agreed that, apart from a very knowledgeable conchologist, the club members are rather mediocre Friends of Nature" (minutes, 13 July 1911, in Vidal 1999). Piaget was considered a stickler for detail who used too many Latin terms but his contributions to the discussions, his witty ideas and humorously written minutes significantly shaped the intellectual level and the good social atmosphere. In later years, when Piaget was a well-known scientist, he also often made humorous remarks during discussions. At one meeting, for example, the scientists who attended told of their earliest discoveries, made at the ages of 3 or 5. Piaget took the floor and said: "I am impressed with what I have just heard [. . .] I feel I must have been a retarded child. I was no less than 15 years old when I published my first scientific article" (in Zazzo 1988: 277).

During the next five years, the club was Piaget's intellectual and social home where he acquired significant qualifications for his scientific career. He was keen to join in club debates and presentations and took over organizational matters as club president. In the minutes, the members recorded many admiring remarks about Piaget's work and contributions, sometimes with ironic undertones:

> Look at Piaget, member of several scholars' societies, sitting at his laboratory desk, scientific disorder here, scientific disorder there, vials, testtubes, bottles, books, dust and tomes, all in a huge mess, those scientists know no order. In this chaos, the scholar is doubled-up over his microscope, bending over a non-classified specimen, spending his nights writing, catching cerebral anemia, working like a madman to spread his works among the learned, scientific, and conchologic journals of the globe. (minutes, 25 January 1912, in Vidal 1999)

This description exactly matches the famous portraits of Piaget that show him in his office, in the midst of disorderly piles of paper.

The Naturalist

Piaget's first printed article in a scientific journal appeared shortly after Godet's death in 1911. Godet's widow bequeathed a part of her husband's collections to the Friends of Nature, together with books, microscopes and utensils. Piaget had privileged access to the collections, so he presented himself publicly as Godet's successor. That Piaget understood himself to be in charge of completing his mentor's work was underpinned by the fact that Otto Fuhrmann, who took over Godet's Chair of Zoology, had a different research topic, focusing on the study of worms. But as an honorary club member, he supported Piaget by letting him have specimens for classification, helping him with difficult cases and putting him into contact with other specialists. Fuhrmann asked Piaget to write an article to accompany Godet's picture atlas, and to take over the cataloguing of Columbian mollusks (Piaget 1914/5) that Godet had planned. The central intention of Piaget's first works was to continue Godet's concern to reduce the number of species by interpreting them as varieties of a higher species, and he honored his teacher by calling a variety after him (Piaget 1913/6: 78). Fuhrmann presided over the meeting in which Piaget was initiated into the Neuchâtel Natural Sciences Society in 1912, and together with another professor of the University of Neuchâtel, he introduced Piaget to the Swiss Zoological Society in December 1913. In 1914, Piaget was also able to join the Swiss Natural Sciences Society. Therefore Piaget's autobiographic description of his work is not correct when he says: "When, in 1911, Mr. Godet died, I knew enough about this field to begin publishing without help (specialists in this branch are rare) a series of articles on the mollusks of Switzerland, of Savoy, of Brittany, and even of Colombia" (Piaget 1952/1: 108). It is true that he did work more independently but he owed his publications to the network of his new mentor.

Fuhrmann had been an assistant to one of the most well-known scientists of Switzerland, Emile Yung (1854–1918) at the University of Geneva. On Fuhrmann's initiative, Piaget contacted Yung, who agreed to supply him with mollusks from the deeper layers of Lake Geneva. As early as September 1912, Piaget received specimens for classification, and Yung offered to publish the results in the *Journal de Conchyliologie*. The recommendation for Fuhrmann's call to the University of Neuchâtel came from Maurice Bedot (1859–1927), professor and director of the Natural Science Museum of Geneva and founder of the *Revue Suisse de Zoologie*. Fuhrmann sent one of Piaget's papers on Alpine mollusks to Bedot, who in his reply recommended some changes. In addition, he suggested a possible assistant post for malacology for the unknown author and offered him to take over Godet's planned section on mollusks for a chart of invertebrates of Switzerland, which Bedot edited. Piaget had to decline the post of assistant: "The position of assistant in malacology you are so kind to mention would please me very much, but I cannot consider it before the end of my high school studies, that is, three years from now" (letter dated 10 May 1912, in the Archives Jean Piaget). Piaget gave the assurance that he would love to take the post, should it still be vacant, after he finished grammar school, as he intended to study medicine at Geneva. As there are no other indications that Piaget ever planned to study medicine, this statement of intent appears to be a strategic promise. In his autobiography, Piaget upgraded Bedot's offer to "position of curator of his mollusk collection" (Piaget 1952/1: 108). However, the grammar-school boy took over the offered contribution to the chart, noting that it would be easily manageable to complete this time-consuming task. Piaget corresponded extensively with Bedot, worked in the museum at Geneva and borrowed many books from its library.

Being only 16 years of age, Piaget showed a surprisingly confident attitude that proved ambition, focus and long-term planning. After four years of apprenticeship with Godet, Piaget mastered the complex rules of terminology of mollusk description. His relationships with Fuhrmann, Yung and Bedot offered him access to many challenges and resources, and provided benevolent support. This, combined with this outstanding ambition, would explain why Piaget managed to publish more than 20 articles on malacology in scientific journals and corresponded with more than 50 scholars who accepted him as a competent colleague, before he even left school.

The Philosophical Initiation

During the summer holidays of 1912, Piaget's godfather invited him to Annecy. Piaget felt close to Samuel Cornut (1861–1918), "a literary figure enamoured of general ideas" (Piaget 1959/3: 9), and they often had long discussions during their hikes through the woods:

> I still have a delightful memory of that visit: We walked and fished; I looked for mollusks and wrote a "Malacology of Lake Annecy," which I published shortly afterward in the *Revue savoisienne*. But my godfather had a purpose. He found me too specialized and wanted to teach me philosophy. Between the gatherings of mollusks he would teach me the "Creative Evolution" of Bergson. (Piaget 1952/1: 111)

Cornut was successful in his attempt to broaden Piaget's interest because, within a short time, Piaget assimilated the philosophy of Henri Bergson (1859–1941), the most widely discussed philosopher in France before World War I. Bergson presumed "that the theory of knowledge and the *theory of life* seem to be inseparable from one another" (Bergson 1907: IX), which was to form the basis of Piaget's thinking. According to Bergson, true reality is a stream of life and constant flux from the inside, because "existing consists in changing, changing in maturing, maturing in creating indefinitely oneself" (Bergson 1907: 7). The driving principle of this flow is what Bergson called *élan vital*, the creative force, which is also the cause of the diversity and variability of the different kinds and forms of life, which in itself escapes our grasp. Human intelligence serves the purpose of self-preservation, for which it formalizes and calculates matter, in order to use it for practical purposes. The analytical structure of intellect therefore remains necessarily fixed on rigid, mechanical and material things. Sensory perception is a sequence of static single impressions, put together like the pictures in a movie. Reality as such is therefore not accessible to the intellect and to science. When science claims to measure time, it will in fact only record a symbolic representation of "duration" which is the real continuity that has to be conceived intuitively. For Bergson, intuition is not something irrational, but a simple act of immediate thinking. "We do not *think* real time. But we live it because life surpasses intelligence" (Bergson 1907: 46). Life is not limited to the relation between cause and effect, because it is a creative flux that cannot be calculated like a mechanism. As there is no transition between one moment and the next, it is only memory that gives the world continuity. If time is of a psychological nature due to being rooted in memory, then the evolution of the universe too, shows spiritual characteristics. "Bergson wants to prove that [. . .] evolutionary processes, and especially the evolution of organic matter are the work of the spirit" (Kolakowski 1985: 11). In sum, Bergson combined a positivist scientific theory based on mechanistic laws of nature with a metaphysical vitalism that focused on introspective reality. From this point of view, Darwinism and Lamarckism seem one-sided theories, as neither causal nor teleological principles can explain the vast variation of living development. The *élan vital* is not a deterministic drive and pursues no goals but simply follows its tendency towards more freedom that culminates in the human consciousness. Intelligence proceeds with the help of categories and classification that allow scientific knowledge, while these artificial constructs prevent the true knowledge of life. Bergson (1907: 31) illustrated this nominalistic limitation of science with the example of the transitions between childhood, youth and adulthood: "life ages" are mere allocations, imaginary fixtures from external sources that cannot catch the subjectivity of life.

The application of nominalism to his problem of mollusk classification was the start of a philosophical expansion of Piaget's natural history interest. His reorientation can already be detected in the talk on *The Vanity of Nomenclature* he held at the Friends of Nature Club in September 1912. If the species constantly develop, it is "superficial to break up the flux of life, as Bergson says, and human analysis is only a procedure, a method, based on nothing" (Piaget 1912/5). However, Piaget was not at all sure whether the species were only intellectual categories. Thus, Bergson directed Piaget's interest to the subjects of adaptation and mutation in the evolutionary process.

All of Piaget's teachers and club friends as well as most French-speaking contemporary biologists held neo-Lamarckist positions. They accepted Darwin's explanation of adaptation through the selection of genetic variation only as a secondary principle. The primary cause for the development of new species remained, according to them, the organism's long-term adaptation to its environment and thus the ability to pass on the acquired qualities. Bergson differentiated between passive and mechanistic adaptation and active and psychological adaptation, whereby he identified the adaptive "effort" as instinct, and intelligence as "the psychological development principle" (Bergson 1907: 77). Piaget, too, believed that there was active and passive adaptation and this difference was to become one of the central topics of his work.

By 1913, Piaget was competently conversant in the vocabulary and ideas of Bergson, which led to heated discussions and an expansion of the fields of interest in the Friends of Nature Club. Apart from the honorary member Bovet, Piaget was the only person in the club who identified with Bergson's psychological vitalism, which Juvet rejected as scholastic: "What are the Advance of Vision, the Force of Life if not meaningless words?" (minutes, 9 October 1913, in Vidal 1999). From 1913 to 1915, intellectual life in the club was characterized by the controversy between the vitalist and the positivist philosophy. In November 1913, Etienne Rossetti, for example, held a talk on scientism and pragmatism, according to which contemporary philosophy oscillated between these two poles. He named the popular biologist Félix Le Dantec (1869–1917) as a representative of scientism, while the pragmatic doctrine was said to be represented by William James and Henri Bergson. Since Juvet and Rossetti identified with Le Dantec, a strong exchange of views ensued with Piaget, who criticized this materialistic approach. One climax of these debates took place after a talk by Juvet on transformism: "Piaget is seized by a furious torrent of words, Juvet too, Rossetti too, Romy too," which led to an "endless quartet of at least an hour" (minutes, 13 February 1913, in Vidal 1999). Rolin Wavre (1896–1949), a long-standing friend of Piaget, felt that "only the title 'philosopher' seemed enviable to us; the particular sciences, no matter how enthusiastic we might be about some of them, seemed a superfluous game if they did not lead towards the synthesis we longed for of our rational, religious, and moral aspirations" (Wavre 1937: 22). Issues of scientific theory and philosophy were discussed so often that, in 1915, the honorary club member Du Pasquier sounded a warning, because the aim of the club was not "to do metaphysics" (minutes, 29 April 1915). Piaget was offended by this criticism and retorted that "if he had been waffling, then only because he was just about to sit his baccalaureate, and the baccalaureate was the peak of waffling for a grammar school pupil" (minutes, 29 April 1915).

Piaget resigned in September 1915, because the Club of the Friends of Nature was reserved for grammar-school pupils. His parting letter shows how important the club had been to him as an intellectual and social home. "I have experienced five good years in this club, I have tasted its joys and got drenched in its faults, and now, when I think back, rest assured that only the hours of friendship and close and lasting camaraderie remain alive" (Piaget 1915 ms). Despite its catalytic function for Piaget's scientific career, the

Friends of Nature Club received no mention in his autobiographic writings, which fits the picture of Piaget as a lonely genius.

The Challenge of Darwinism

Late in 1912, Piaget entered into a debate with Waclaw Roszkowski (1886–1944), a Polish postgraduate under the zoologist Henri Blanc (1859–1930) at the University of Lausanne. Roszkowski had renounced the hitherto undisputed taxonomic value of the outer shells and concentrated instead on comparative anatomy. On the basis of the "rediscovered" laws of heredity of Gregor Johann Mendel (1822–1884) and the theory of mutation, Roszkowski classified two of Piaget's species as one and the same. Piaget defended his method of classification in several letters and articles, initially without paying attention to Roszkowski's experiments. The PhD student had bred deep-water mollusks in his aquarium and had arrived at the conclusion that shells were not a hereditary feature but a fluctuating feature. Quoting Moritz Wagner (1813–1887), Piaget postulated that the different shells were a hereditary result of geographical isolation. He found further ammunition in the interactionist theory of Etienne Rabaud (1868–1956), who argued that "the environment and the organism form a complex in which the components are in constant interaction so that through a series of variations the result is a true transformation" (Rabaud 1911: 265). Thus, the young naturalist was sufficiently sure of his position and continued to classify mollusks as before.

In May of the following year, however, he started repeating his opponent's experiments with specimens received from Fuhrmann. The fact that the aquarium-bred descendents of deep-water mollusks behaved like true shallow-water mollusks made Piaget more careful, and in his report with the apt title *First Study of Deep-Water Mollusks in Lake Neuchâtel* (Piaget 1913/5) he agreed with Roszkowski's classification. Yet he had misunderstood the internal origin of the inherited features and used Darwinist terminology without changing his frame of reference. Surprisingly, Piaget even named one of the varieties he had received from Young after his opponent (Piaget 1913/3: 618f.).[5] But this strategy of appeasement was in vain because Piaget's scientific knowledge was harshly criticized in the next issue of the *Zoologischer Anzeiger*:

> I recognize that it is rather comfortable for the collector to create arbitrary species that serve as frames for increasingly smaller frames, varieties, subvarieties, forms, and to do this without caring whether these divisions are based on features of equal value, or whether these features are hereditary

or not. But even if this notion of species often simplifies classification and terminology, it is no longer in accordance with the current ideas of biology. (Roszkowski 1913: 89)

Still, Piaget, carried by his mentors, was not one to give up. On 18 November 1913, Yung publicly supported Piaget by introducing his paper *Note on the Biology of Deep-Water Limnaea* at the Geneva National Institute and by publishing it. Piaget, following Bergson, now argued that a population's evolutionary tendency was the central criterion of classification. "A new species is not characterized by its properties, its acquired characteristics from the beginning, but by its *tendencies*" (Piaget 1914/4: 14). He tried to disprove his opponent by attacking Mendel's laws but he confused Mendel's factors with mechanist influences. In his last polemic, Piaget accepted the difference between hereditary and fluctuating features, but he doubted that hereditary features were exclusively the result of mutations and postulated "that isolation is a factor more important than heredity" (Piaget 1914/10: 330). Obviously, Piaget became aware of the fact that his argumentation was not stringent and not only stopped the debate with Roszkowski, but shortly afterwards gave up biology, too. The few articles that appeared after 1914 were works he had written earlier. Not one single natural science contribution appeared between 1917 and 1919, while Piaget was actually studying biology and working for his PhD. Not before 1928 did he give up his resistance and start to conduct experiments on the basis of Mendel's laws.

His defeat in this debate must have affected him badly. Fifteen years later, he sneered at the articles he had written between 1912 and 1914 and admitted that they "were totally lacking in biological culture!" (Piaget 1929/1: 489). As an old man, he confessed that he had given up biology at the age of 20 because he had been "very awkward" (Piaget and Bringuier 1977: 21). It must, however, be taken into account that Piaget had not been a single actor but was involved in a supporting network that believed in neo-Lamarckist theories of evolution. From this point of view, the young naturalist can be considered a victim of his environment, which treated him as a specialist too early and on the basis of superficial criteria. Yet Piaget personalized his achievements, as well as his errors and defeats, and he would have lifelong difficulties in handling criticism or lectures. Being lectured was not an enriching experience for him, but a humiliation, because "the most elementary psychological law is that no human being likes being given a lecture" (Piaget 1954/15: 28).

In his autobiographic writings, there is no mention of his debate with Roszkowski. Instead he wanted to present to the public an image of his intellectual career that led him in a straight line from "the snails' forms of adaptation to those of human beings" (Meili-Dworetzki 1978: 508):

> These studies, premature as they were, were nevertheless of great value for my scientific development; moreover, they functioned, if I may say so, as instruments of protection against the demon of philosophy. Thanks to them, I had the rare privilege of getting a glimpse of science and what it stands for, before undergoing the philosophical crisis of adolescence. (Piaget 1952/1: 109)

In fact, his defeat in the debate with the Polish PhD student was one of the reasons for Piaget's massive crisis of adolescence, which started in 1915. During the following five years, Piaget devoted himself almost exclusively to religious and philosophical issues.

3

Perturbations of Puberty

First Crisis

During his adolescence, Piaget lived through several phases, in which his identity and his convictions were severely shaken and his relationship with his social environment was upset.

> Between the ages of fifteen and twenty, I experienced a series of crises due both to family conditions and to the intellectual curiosity of that productive age [...] There was the problem of religion. When I was about fifteen, my mother, being a devout Protestant, insisted on my taking what is called at Neuchâtel "religious instruction," that is, a six-weeks' course on the fundamentals of Christian doctrine. (Piaget 1952/1: 109)

After attending Sunday school from age 7 to 12, youth service for at least two years, and religious instruction from age 14 to 16, Piaget followed the preparatory course for his confirmation between March and May 1912, every day for two hours (Vidal 1994a: 115f.). Pastor Charles-Daniel Junod (1865–1941) wanted the adolescents to examine their souls, because they were expected to have outgrown their childhood faiths and would now confirm their affiliation to the Church as mature and responsible believers:

> Two things struck me at that time: on the one hand the difficulty of reconciling a number of dogmas with biology, and on the other, the fragility of the "five" proofs of the existence of God. We were taught five, and I even passed my examination in them! Though I would not even have dreamed of denying the existence of God, the fact that anyone should reason by such weak arguments (I recall only the proof by the finality of nature and the ontological proof) seemed to me all the more extraordinary since my pastor was an intelligent man, who himself dabbled in the natural sciences! (Piaget 1952/1: 110)

The fact that Piaget became aware of the disparity between the theory of evolution and the doctrine of creation, as well as the doubtful proofs of God, was due to the pastor's antidogmatic teaching. Piaget's critical attitude towards Church doctrines did not mean, however, that he had doubts about Christianity. On the contrary, "according to the late Mme Burger, her brother, Jean, was very impressed by his religious education and, imbued with a deep Christian feeling, even thought of becoming a minister" (Vidal 1994a: 120). Piaget therefore was not experiencing a crisis of faith, but he simply could no longer accept its dogmatic foundation. The query of the dogmas also reflected the contrast between his critically thinking father and his devout mother. When Piaget talked about a crisis, he was more likely referring to the emerging conflict between him and his mother: the 15-year-old began to rebel against his mother's demands and the theological doctrines presented an excellent arena for debate. It is quite possible that the worried mother asked her son's godfather to exert his influence during the summer holidays, in order to strengthen the boy's faith. Yet before Samuel Cornut could pitch Bergson's metaphysics against the young zoologist's alleged one-sided scientific orientation, Piaget had already found argumentative ammunition to help him in his fight for intellectual independence. It was probably the parson Junod who had drawn his young charge's attention to Auguste Sabatier (1839–1901), whose work Piaget found in his father's library.[6]

Like Friedrich Schleiermacher (1768–1834), Sabatier based his theology on the factual existence of religious sentiments which should be psychologically, and thus scientifically, investigated. He strictly distinguished between the moral essence of Christianity, which manifests itself in the conscience, and dogmas, which he considered as symbolic manifestation. Dogmas are relative because they never correspond precisely to sentiments. The world has changed since Christianity was established; it is therefore necessary to align the symbols and terminology of faith with modern times. Following Auguste Comte (1798–1857), he identified three developmental stages of religious progress, according to which the mythological phase corresponds to paganism, the dogmatic phase to Catholicism and the psychological phase to liberal Protestantism. At the highest level, God reveals himself as an immanent encounter of the individual with the universe. Protestant theology, therefore, is an exercise in self-observation, for each individual must constantly compare his conscience with his thoughts, his actions and his faith. "I devoured that book with immense delight. Dogmas reduced to the function of 'symbols,' necessarily inadequate, and above all the notion of an 'evolution of dogmas'" (Piaget 1952/1: 110). This interpretation of dogmas and the negation of a conflict between science and religion allowed the rebellious adolescent to defend himself against his mother's orthodox notions while being able to believe in the existence of a personal God.

But such a concept of God was excluded in Bergson's metaphysics. In *Creative Evolution*, Bergson took up a peculiar middle position between a deist and an immanent concept. The universe is seen as the result of a pure, creative and infinite force, whose source Bergson identified with God. God as a spiritual force is immanent in the world but is not identical with the world. This force "has nothing of the already made; it is unceasing life, action, freedom. If creation is understood in this way, it is no mystery, we experience it in us as soon as we act freely" (Bergson 1907: 249). The godfather's teaching of this philosophy did not miss its mark:

> It was the first time that I heard philosophy discussed by anyone not a theologian; the shock was terrific, I must admit.
>
> First of all, it was an emotional shock. I recall one evening of profound revelation. The identification of God with life itself was an idea that stirred me almost to ecstasy because it now enabled me to see in biology the explanation of all things and of the mind itself.
>
> In second place, it was an intellectual shock. The problem of knowing (properly called the epistemological problem) suddenly appeared to me in an entirely new perspective and as an absorbing topic of study. It made me decide to consecrate my life to the biological explanation of knowledge. (Piaget 1952/1: 111)

The illuminating rhetoric of this beneficial shock linked two aspects of reorientation whose beginnings were at least 13 years apart. First of all, being confronted with Bergson made the young Piaget wonder how God was to be understood. In accordance with Cornut's wishes, Piaget occupied himself mainly with theological questions over the next few years. "This encounter with Bergson was true love at first sight [...] and reading Bergson was a revelation" (Piaget 1965: 15f.). Piaget's enthusiasm for the French metaphysician was due to his "desire for the absolute" (Piaget 1918: 95). This fascination was rooted in a genuine religious need for a final and therefore reliable orientation.

In his later autobiographical writings, Piaget stood back from his meta-physical stance and described his godfather's pedagogic action as a religious challenge by the "demon of philosophy" (Piaget 1952/1: 109). "I have experienced this speculation as a dangerous temptation. I found myself involuntarily drawn towards it!" (Piaget and Bringuier 1977: 37). In other places, the reader gains the impression that Bergson's influence had been a disappointing and ephemeral event. "Instead of finding science's last word therein, as my godfather had let me hope, I got the impression of an ingenious construction without an experimental basis" (Piaget 1952/1: 111). And after the beneficial reading of "Kant, Spencer, Auguste Comte, Fouillée and Guyau, Lachelier, Boutroux, Lalande, Durkheim, Tarde, Le Dantec; and in psychology: W. James, Th. Ribot, and Janet" (Piaget 1952/1: 112) and the writing of a *Sketch of a Neo-Pragmatism* and a paper on *Realism and Nominalism in the Sciences of Life*, he seemed to have definitively overcome his philosophical shock (cf. Piaget 1952/1: 113; 1959/3: 9; 1965: 17). But Piaget had, in fact, assimilated Bergson's philosophy with long-lasting effects, for the theory of the child's autonomous development is largely based on the underlying concept of the *élan vital*.

Piaget's problem was the concept of God. If God and life were identical, how could there be a personal God? In *Bergson and Sabatier*, he attempted to harmonize these concepts by identifying the parallels between the two thinkers. To do so, Piaget theologized Bergson and delivered an interpretation of the evolution of dogmas that was strongly influenced by Bergson:

> We feel strongly that a process is perpetually taking place, with or without external influence, which makes our conceptions vary constantly, evidently according to a certain plan, but in a continuous progression. External factors may intervene, but they are immediately transformed in our way, assimilated in a certain conscious synthesis, then repressed into the subconscious, where they germinate before they emerge vivified and rejuvenated. Such is the true evolution of dogma, and, in my view, Sabatier has not insisted enough on the striking parallelism that exists between this inner work of each individual and the collective work of humanity. (Piaget 1914/1: 199)

Thanks to this parallelism, Piaget could reconcile the development of dogmas with creation, and the religious experience with intuition and "duration." Sabatier's personal and moral idea of God and Bergson's "pantheistic" version were therefore not mutually exclusive.

The article was not only reconciliatory. Piaget was critical of the fact that Bergson's term *élan vital* "unfortunately remained in dense obscurity" (Piaget 1914: 195). This reproach was also in line with the thinking of Piaget's first mentor in philosophy, to whom he paid homage at the beginning of this article.

Instruction in Philosophy

In 1912, Arnold Reymond (1874–1958) was appointed professor in Neuchâtel, succeeding his friend Pierre Bovet, who became director of the Jean-Jacques Rousseau Institute in Geneva. Piaget, Juvet and Wavre attended Reymond's introduction to psychology, logic and epistemology from September 1913 to July 1915. This theologian and philosopher supported his ambitious pupils by reading and commenting on their sometimes voluminous manuscripts and by discussions outside of school. Piaget appreciated "the unforgettable experience of a small-group initiation to philosophy, with all the spontaneous questions and dialogues it involves" (Piaget 1959/11: 44). At the university, the three friends attended Reymond's three-year cycle on the history of philosophy, after which they continued their studies at Paris before returning to Romandy.

Piaget was one of the auditors at Reymond's inauguration lecture on *The Philosophy of Bergson and the Problem of Reason*, held on 18 April 1913. "My first reaction to his mainly mathematically determined reflection was negative" (Piaget 1965: 16). Like Bergson, Piaget was initially convinced that logic and mathematics could not be suitably applied to the processes of life, yet in time these fields became a fascinating and central issue for him due to Reymond's insistence in the use of a strong scientific approach to problems: "Here he excelled and was able to supply fascinating clarifications of questions arising from the existence of logic and mathematics. One could constantly feel that these questions reached the innermost core of his personal experience" (Piaget 1959/11: 46). These lectures had a strong influence on Piaget's later theories because a considerable part of Piaget's experiments in the cognitive development of children dealt with categories of logico-mathematical thinking.

Due to his mollusk classification problems, Piaget's initial interest focused on the realism–nominalism problem:

> I was particularly impressed by one remark of Bergson that seemed to me like a connecting thread for my first philosophico-biological work: his amazement about the disappearance of the problem of Universals in modern philosophy, which now was replaced by the problem of rules. (Piaget 1965: 16)

But, for Bergson, the problem of universals reappeared in modern psychology in the concept of "general ideas," and in biology in form of "genera" and "species." Reymond referred Piaget to the historical debates and the logical dimensions of classes. The support Piaget received from his mentor was not limited to mathematics and logic, but extended to moral philosophy and epistemology, history of philosophy, sociology, psychology and pedagogy. For example, Piaget wrote a draft intended for publication under the title of *Moral Conscience According to Cresson*. Reymond (1914) commented on the draft and encouraged Piaget to look for a better term to express the contrast between individual and collective morality. Therefore, Reymond "played a similar key role in Piaget's philosophical education as the director of the museum, P. Godet, had done in biology" (Kesselring 1999: 22). As a member of Reymond's Swiss-French Philosophical Society, Piaget stated that Reymond "has influenced us all deeply [. . .] regardless of whether we are theologians, historians or psychologists" (Piaget 1931/6: 379).

Reymond contradicted his teacher Théodore Flournoy (1854–1920), who claimed that faith and science were incompatible, and assigned an objective character to religion due to the permanency of religious phenomena. In 1913, Reymond delivered two talks to the assemblies of the Swiss Christian Students' Association on 'The notion of miracles and its meaning' and 'Scientific truth and religious truth'. Presumably Piaget attended these meetings, because he was already a member of this student association in 1914, before he even entered university.

Missionary Work in Universities[7]

The Swiss Christian Students' Association (ACSE) was established in 1897 as part of the Universal Federation of Christian Students' Association, founded in 1895 by the American John Mott (1865–1955) in order to carry out missionary work in universities. In 1911, under the auspices of Bovet and Flournoy, the revivalist preacher Mott embarked on a triumphant tour of Swiss universities.

Piaget portrayed the ACSE as a "fertile movement" (Piaget 1918: 38) distinguished by its openness, independence and need for harmony, therefore embodying true liberal religion. This association was indeed the most important network for the Protestant intellectuals of Romandy. From 1895 to 1922, the ACSE, together with the Young Men's Christian Association, organized annual meetings in Sainte-Croix that were attended not only by students but also by philosophers, theologians, clergymen, writers and other Christian academics (Vidal 1994a: 111f.). Against the backdrop of mystic mountain scenery, four days of speeches, religious services, discussions and Bible readings would unfold, which many participants considered to be a crucial religious experience.

> Nothing compared to the life and majesty of their common religious service, when they joined their forces and their researches around a Christ stripped of all dogma. Each could commune with this Incarnation of the eternal value of the divine, as no intellectual translation dimmed this living contact (Piaget 1918: 39).

At these meetings, the participants would form and confirm their identities as revived Christians. The main discussion topic was the inevitable crisis each adolescent undergoes as he outgrows his childhood belief. The association offered help and support by allowing the young men to discuss their problems. For most members, belief in a loving God was sorely tested when World War I broke out. Piaget too doubted the existence of the Christian God:

> Sébastien was in anguish. His faith and his reason were in turmoil. Since he could no longer believe in the God revealed he could no longer believe in the God almighty, since they are one. A God who leaves man in ignorance is a God who can do nothing against evil. (Piaget 1918: 29)

Piaget saved his faith by focusing on Jesus as the role model for a moral life and by assigning to God a supporting role as a compassionate comrade-in-arms. He found the comforting idea of a suffering God in the essay collection *To Believers and Atheists* by the theologian Wilfred Monod (1867–1943) and "experienced the instant relief this poem about a powerless God brought to the troubled minds of Protestantism" (Piaget 1918: 29). For him, this concept of God was in keeping with modern ideas of democracy, progress and science as well as with political and economical reforms.

The social issue was a frequently discussed topic in the ACSE. In one of his speeches of 1914, Monod considered Christianity and Socialism the two great moral forces to improve the world. A blend of liberal Christianity and social democratic politics was to be the solution for the problems of society and was to bring peace. The socialist Christians, with whom Piaget's godfather Samuel Cornut sympathized, were seeking the moral improvement of the existing society, whereas the Christian socialists were aiming for a different, new society. Most ACSE members understood themselves as predestined pioneers of a more moral Christianity. In their opinion only youth had the necessary energy, idealism and purity to save the world from disaster. This avant-garde consciousness was strengthened by the special position held by Switzerland, which, because of its neutrality, would have an important part to play in the postwar era. Piaget adopted this missionary idea as well as the issues, principles and terminology of this student group in a lasting way. Although the ACSE was Piaget's second field of social activity after the Friends of Nature Club, it again received no mention in his autobiographical writings. The student group, in which he was soon to play an active part, did, however, shape his self-concept as a Christian intellectual. In May 1915 he wrote the concluding paper on the annual colloquium for the *News of the ACSE*, titled 'What must tomorrow's generation be?'

> We are privileged in everything [...] privileged to be young, privileged to be able to meet among future intellectuals and to find outside the churches the strength that is lacking in official Christianity, privileged

above all to be living today. Heroism surges everywhere, and under an appearance of universal destruction, our times, in their burning mould, cast a new world, an unknown and unforeseeable world that we, young people, will have to uphold. For that purpose [...] we need Christ, we need a living faith, purity, moral energy. (Piaget 1915/3: 200)

The main obstacle as to why the ACSE might possibly fail in its mission lay, according to Piaget, in the liberal stance that manifested itself in a strong heterogeneity of convictions among the members. To gain political significance, the Christian youth movement would need a binding doctrine, "with which everyone could agree yet would leave enough freedom for everyone to keep his own symbols. Something like a pure but objective mould that everyone could fill according to his own temperament" (Piaget 1918: 40f.). Even though he was still at grammar school, Piaget started to draw up his own manifesto for the Christian youth movement. "What he wanted [...] was a human faith, accessible to all, and capable of nourishing by itself the postwar renewal [...] It is more important than ever that we save the social order, and a paralyzed faith will never be able to save the world" (Piaget 1918: 14, 21). A philosophy of pure values and purified of dogmas should form the common base for the unification of Christians from all nations. This mission helped Piaget to overcome his crisis of faith and filled him with the hope of gaining a leading position in the revivalist movement.

The Metaphysics of the Mission

By May 1915 at the latest, two months before his Baccalaureate exam, Piaget completed the manuscript *The Mission of the Idea*. The starting point as the *idées-forces* put forward by Alfred Fouillée (1838–1912), who interpreted Plato's ideas as immanent units of force that represent, move and transform the universe and its parts. Thus, "everything is idea, comes out of the idea, and goes back into the idea" (Piaget 1915/1: 4). Piaget's ontology distinguishes three hierarchic levels of ideas:

1. The Idea as an absolute, transcendent, and ineffable principle
2. ideas as collective singularities such as liberty, fatherland, or justice
3. ideas of individual expressions of these singularities.

All ideas are only weakened, fragmented and symbolic manifestations of the true Idea. "In the beginning was the Idea" (Piaget 1915/1: 14), from which history began and to which it will return. Progress towards Idea is led by the ideas themselves, and is not achieved through action but through wisdom: "The French Revolution was carried out in Rousseau's walks and not in meetings or street riots" (Piaget 1915/1: 11). Analogous to the *élan vital*, the idea is creative and emerges from the innermost depth of our being as an echo of the cosmic harmony.

Christ is the mediator between human ideas and the divine idea, because "Jesus is the idea made flesh" (Piaget 1915/1: 8). He was the only one to turn the idea into reality and "opened new directions for life" (Piaget 1915/1: 44). As a rebel, idealist and innovator, He is the model for man to fight for justice, equality, peace, self-discipline and faith. The implementation of the idea results in liberal achievements, such as freedom of speech or women's rights, while conservatism, nationalism, egoism, pride and inertia destroy the idea and lead to dogmatism. "The dogma is a dead idea" (Piaget 1915/1: 8). According to Piaget, the dogmas of individual redemption and of a punishing, vengeful God have destroyed true Christianity and therefore the Church was largely responsible for the misery of the world. "The Church has become the worst centre of conservatism, the wound that putrefies the whole organism" (Piaget 1915/1: 61). Dogmatic Churches and conservative politics had not only betrayed the people but had also betrayed Jesus, in whose name Piaget became incensed:

> Cursed be the mighty men of this world for they have been fighting against me for twenty centuries! Cursed be the conservatives, because for twenty centuries they have been shackling me! But you Christians be cursed seven times over because for twenty centuries you have been denying me! I came to bring battle to this earth but all you could think of was yourself and your salvation. (Piaget 1915/1: 31)

The renewal of Christianity, according to Piaget, must not be effected via the institution but must happen through free communion of the faithful since "the idea is not to be found in books" (Piaget 1915/1: 3). On two occasions (Piaget 1915/1: 42f, 57ff.) Piaget wrote about his conversion, where he discovered a merciful, compassionate but powerless God. This insight ought to be the foundation on which scientists, liberal believers and the people should unite to build a better world with a new morality.

Piaget considered the good not only identical with the idea but also with life itself. For this reason he opposed Darwin: "The evolution of life and the goal of morality coincide entirely. The struggle for life is not the essence of evolution [. . .] Everywhere, life brings harmony, solidarity" (Piaget 1915/1: 18). Development, Piaget feels, shows a tendency towards a moral absolute because it is from the instinct that moral conscience arises. Due to this moralization of the evolutionary concept that bore the hallmark of Bergson and Sabatier, he defined the bad as a result of insufficient development. Since every development contains some moral progress, Piaget necessarily had to look for the good in all changes. Although he spoke out against war, he arrived at the conclusion: "The war itself is [. . .] a sign of progress" (Piaget 1915/1: 25), because it serves as a catalyst for a higher consciousness, which in turn leads to a better society. Piaget's moral naturalization of history and his glorifying of idealism led him to ignore the political, social and economic causes of war: "The conservative spirit is the cause of war" (Piaget 1915/1: 16). Yet Piaget did not aim at a historical analysis, but wished to devise a program to coordinate his own ambitions as a scientist, Christian and philosopher: "The savant, who finds hypotheses, must place above them the grand edifice capable of enclosing them; the Christian, who has felt a life deep in his heart, must assimilate it by means of an interpretation provided by reason; the moral man, who wants a rule of life for his action, has to construct an idea to justify it" (Piaget 1915/1: 68).

Piaget wanted to reconcile science, Christianity and morality on a theoretical as well as on a practical level because "a stated ideal becomes a duty" (Piaget 1915/1: 63), and duty is the only moral foundation for making the world humane. Piaget's self-imposed task is contained in the epitaph of his text: "Lord, that our eyes may be opened" (Matthew 20.33). The 19-year-old missionary clearly described the role he wanted to play in history: "Genius means the crystallization of the idea within a person, heroism means this person's abandonment to the idea" (Piaget 1915/1: 8). Later, Piaget replaced the Christian content but did not abandon his faith in the world-saving function of his work or in the effectiveness of ideas. "It is sufficient to remember that a great idea contains within itself a force, and that our reality is largely what we want it to be" (Piaget 1934/1: 31).

After Piaget had deleted all anti-German references as requested by the editor, *The Mission of the Idea* was published in December 1915 and enthusiastically received by the student group, so that the author gained the reputation of an outstanding thinker. Some reviewers, for example YMCA-Leader Paul Pettavel (1861–1934), recommended the paper as an edifying work by a Christian youth for his fellow students. Wilfred Monod, a friend of Piaget's father, commented on the manuscript in a 14-page letter prior to publication. He praised Piaget's intention and courage but noted that many thoughts were obscure and some even dangerous. Piaget was told that although his work was more of a philosophical than a religious nature, his way of thinking lacked a clear insight into the substance of the matter. "You have written a *poem*, and I like it as such; but it's not a philosophical study" (in Vidal 1994a: 156). This assessment seems to have been painful for Piaget, as he never mentioned this first book in his autobiographical writings.

Later, Piaget assumed that all adolescents held messianic convictions: "The adolescent quasi makes a pact with his God, in which he promises Him his irrevocable service, but certainly expects, in return, to play an important role in the matter to which he has committed himself" (Piaget 1943/6: 255). Despite warning against metaphysics in his later life, he declared metaphysical rebellion as a sign of genius:

> Those who, between the ages of fifteen and seventeen, never devised systems to integrate their life plans into a great dream of reform [...] were not exactly the most productive ones. The adolescent's metaphysics as well as his passions and his delusions of grandeur are therefore true early stages of his personal achievements, and the example of genius shows that there has always been a continuity, starting from the personality-forming age of eleven or twelve, to this person's later work. (Piaget 1943/6: 257)

Suffering in Leysin

The writing of his manifesto and his Baccalaureate exams, in which he achieved the best grades of his year group, "affected my health; I had to spend more than a year in the mountains" (Piaget 1952/1: 112). Exhaustion, however, does not explain his long sojourns in the health resort of Leysin near Montreux, where he stayed from September 1915 to April 1916, from July 1916 till February 1917 and during the summer of 1917. Since he did not stay in the sanatorium but in private guest houses, he could not have suffered from tuberculosis as did most patients there. He did, however, receive medical treatment from Dr Louis Vauthier (1887–1963), who later married Piaget's sister Madeleine. In a letter of May 1916, Piaget mentioned measles that threatened his lungs, and in 1917 he claimed that his return to Leysin was due to serious influenza (in Vidal 1994a: 163). In his autobiographical novel, Piaget hinted at the third reason for his absence from the family: "I was hurt and retired to a nearby hill" (Piaget 1918: 147). Because he added that he had decided to stay up there, it is likely that his decision was based more on psychological reasons than on medical ones.

According to Marthe Piaget-Burger (in Vidal 1994a: 157) Arthur Piaget was proud of his son's rebellious work but his pious mother must have reacted with trepidation to her son's harsh criticism of the Church. One cannot exclude the possibility that Piaget's characterization of the Church as the source of all misery was explicitly directed against his mother: "Sometimes Sébastien let himself be carried off into revolt. He cursed mankind and blasphemed against God. He ranted against hypocrisy and desertion, but he forgot his pride. Because of his indignation [...] he entered a hidden and blinding passion, the passion to dominate" (Piaget 1918: 13).

Piaget justified the fight against the authorities as the brutal but necessary emancipation of the philosopher, for the sake of autonomous thinking:

"No more scruples and no more opportunism [...] This independence can only be gained at the price of a fight to the end, an open revolt [...] A revolt against his own people who try to beguile him, against orthodoxies that try to divert his thinking" (Piaget 1918: 117).

Piaget's obsessive desire to be right could have met his father's opposition as well: "The original desire for power is a desire for independence. The father, therefore, who is the authority, the obstacle on the road to independence and at the same time the model of what independence might be, is detested unconsciously. This hatred takes all forms" (Piaget 1920/2: 55).

Hatred, as a reaction to the refusal through which the parents attempt to stop the rebel's desire for independence, is the reverse of desolation. "And after the revolt, loneliness" (Piaget 1918: 117).

The atmosphere in Leysin, situated at an altitude of 1,450 m, must have been somewhat morbid: around half of the tuberculosis patients died and during the war around 6,000 injured and sick soldiers were taken to this health resort. Pain and impending death were omnipresent and created a depressing climate. Coming to terms with a fatal disease creates a paradoxical situation, in so far as self-acceptance would include accepting the disease, thereby accepting one's own destruction. In order to cope with this paradox and with the pain, many patients try to attribute some sense to their disease. They are searching for an explanation through meditation and introspection, and thus the disease is often glorified as a way to deeper self-knowledge. "The thinker [...] must know illness. Illness is holy like solitude, like sleep" (Piaget 1918: 115f.), for illness doubles the exchanges between the inmost depths and the consciousness. Piaget presupposed that the intensity of pain was proportional to the degree of inner imbalance. Suffering, in his opinion, would force the mind to examine one's own identity, thus leading to increased consciousness. In this way, Leysin was a place where Piaget was compelled to construct his own identity.

Divine Mysteries

Excluded from the active life in his social environment, Piaget fought against his unsatisfied craving for recognition, love and sexuality. "Suffering is doubled for a man who is alone" (Piaget 1918: 129). Through direct confrontation with war victims and through the suffering of the sick, the question of how to reconcile a kind creator with the misery of His creation arose anew and grew yet more urgent. "He started to read the *Mysteries of Jesus*, and the first lines with their abrupt and sublime incoherence made him burst into tears. But he could not get further than the second paragraph. He was crushed by this noble and divine truth" (Piaget 1918: 131). Piaget was on an emotional roller coaster of religious fervor and rage. Later he noticed a connection between the two:

> Hatred for the father readily provokes remorse [...]. There ensues over-compensation of respect which never finds a real object adequate to its needs. This leads to the gradual sublimation of the Imago of the father which links itself with the image of the heavenly Father, whose features have already been formed by religious education. [...] We see readily in the divine image, elements of paternal origin: respect full of love, but also fear, hidden hatred sometimes, from which springs the terrifying character which the child in his religious remorse can sometimes give to the face of his God. (Piaget 1920/2: 56f.)

Piaget experienced the fictitious compensation for lacking paternal attention in communion with a kind, suffering and equal God. On 22 December 1915, Piaget sent a "Prayer for the New Year" to Paul Pettavel, the editor of *L'Essor*. This friend of the Piaget family was delighted by *The Mysteries of Divine Suffering*, and published this text in the first brochure of the 'Youth Corner' in the February edition of 1916 (cf. Vidal 1993).

Piaget evoked mysticism by setting the scene at dusk, after a storm in the mountains. A sad, lonely man prays in the hope that the hidden God may reveal himself. After his plea "My God, my God, why hast thou forsaken me?" (Piaget 1916/3: 115) he hears God's voice amidst some distant music, telling him that He too is suffering deeply. "You will never know what pain I am suffering when I hear you sigh, when I hear my creatures suffer" (Piaget 1916/3: 115). Since He is neither omniscient nor almighty, He cannot save anybody. "Salvation lies in the independence of the soul from the body, and this independence can only come from virtue" (Piaget 1916/3: 116). God is not a completed being either but is developing as a part of the permanent creation of the universe. "My consciousness has followed degrees—the degrees of my creation—and it is only gradually that I understood my life [...] Life is a return to my being through the matter I thrust out of myself. This is the 'conversion' of my work, succeeding the initial 'procession'" (Piaget 1916/3: 116). Here Piaget resorts to Plotin's life cycle, which was understood as a step-by-step process. As with Bergson, everything is creation: "In the same way I create myself in creating the universe, you create yourself in your painful labours" (Piaget 1916/3: 116). God's full realization, however, is hindered by the thoughtless actions of man. Mankind does not act wrongly for evil motives but "the immense human cowardice stems only from ignorance" (Piaget 1916/3: 116). Despite His love for mankind, God, who is neither man's educator nor judge, has to watch helplessly as man acts. "The power is indeed only within yourself" (Piaget 1916/3: 116).

As man creates himself he becomes a "true image of deity" (Piaget 1916/3: 118).

With this decisive step in his theological development, Piaget reversed the relationship between creator and creature. "Continue the struggle, my son, it is not you alone, it is me you will create" (Piaget 1916/3: 117). It is only in recognizing the love for humanity and the suffering of God that constructive creativity becomes possible. Yet "this truth is not good for everyone. Only matured by his own suffering can man arrive at the acceptance of metaphysical suffering" (Piaget 1916/3: 117). The absolute is no longer a transcendental concept, but is an inner construction with the arising consciousness as its driving force. Following Pascal and Rousseau (Piaget 1918: 21, 24f.), truth is less a matter of rational than of intuitive knowledge: "What my reason understood is merely a symbol and a daring construction, but what my heart understood is eternally true" (Piaget 1916/3: 118).

Recognizing the truth is an esoteric matter, necessitating the prerequisites of suffering and abstaining from action. Action no longer destroys the idea (Piaget 1915/1: 10) but reality (Piaget 1916/3: 117). By "action" Piaget meant deeds controlled from the outside and directed toward the outside, as opposed to "activity," which arises from inside. The thinker will find truth and God only in himself. "If the truth is not the reality, it will not hover above but is an internal part thereof and guides it" (Piaget 1918: 117). Thinking creates itself and, at the same time, creates God, as the thinker becomes conscious of Him. This forms the base of Piaget's famous constructivism: "Intelligence [=mind] organizes the world by organizing itself" (Piaget 1937: 341).

Piaget could not maintain for long his theological mixture of God as creator and human mirror image, of a transcendent father and a suffering victim. Once he had published his creed, his belief in a transcendental God began to crumble. "Why did he now lose this faith? Because it was dead. [...] This work mechanically terminated itself and forbade him all religion" (Piaget 1918: 98). Yet Piaget did not become an atheist but developed an immanent concept of religion, as he wrote in his letters to Romain Rolland (1866–1944):

Everyone is a metaphysician at eighteen, and in addition a theologian, if one is Swiss-French. But I believe I have got rid of all that I have been searching for two years. I believe more than ever in Christ, but he teaches me to be a man, and all religious belief would prevent me from being so. Only faith is great, and faith is the decision to live in spite of the mystery that is at the bottom of everything. This is all my metaphysics, a metaphysics that is not at all intellectual, and that is merely the metaphysics implicit in all life. One cannot live without asserting an absolute value that gives sense to life. I assert it without proof: that is what faith is. (Piaget 1917)

When he was asked whether he had ever suffered a crisis of faith in adolescence, Piaget denied his fears, self-doubts and depressions: "No, I simply arrived at the philosophy of immanence right away ..." (Piaget and Bringuier 1977: 87). In *Recherche* (Piaget 1918: 70, 142), however, he described the painful conversion and compared himself to Jean-Christophe, the protagonist of the ten-volume educational novel by Rolland. This work deeply influenced the young Christians of west Switzerland. The words spoken by God to Jean-Christoph: "Suffer. Die. But be what you must be: A Man" (Rolland 1903–12, II: 231) had become catchwords for maintaining a stiff upper lip in the face of religious doubts. Thanks to his faith, Jean-Christoph Krafft successfully overcomes trends like individualism and nationalism. Inspired by Tolstoy, Rolland was committed to pacifism and a nondogmatic Christianity and decried the failure of governments, socialist parties and Churches at the outbreak of war. Piaget sent the writer a copy of his *Mission of the Idea* together with a dedication expressing his admiration for Rolland (cf. Vidal 1994a: 240). From September 1916 to January 1917, Piaget wrote his own autobiographical educational novel modeled on *Jean-Christophe*, *The Two Houses* written by Pierre Jeannet in 1914 and *The Testament of My Youths* (1903) by his godfather Samuel Cornut (Vidal 1994a: 184).

4

The Reconstruction of Identity

Biographical Reconstruction

The purpose of the first two chapters of *Recherche*[8] was not to produce an autobiography true in every detail, although Piaget called his description a "confession [. . .] There is nothing I have written that I did not experience" (Piaget, letter cited in Vidal 1994a: 185). The aim was to give a biographical access to the third part of the book where he outlined a research program intended as a scientific basis for the reconstruction of postwar society.

Ever since Aurelius Augustine (354–430), such accounts have been structured in such a way that the life story leads up to conversion. They deal with the protagonist's unfullfilled life and with his trials and tribulations, which preceded this turning point. This renders an autobiography a "medium to illustrate the difference from the vantage point of an ideal or goal attained, enabling the writer to look back from a critical distance" (Wagner-Egelhaaf 2000: 109). Piaget's trials were to be found in metaphysics, and he described, from a scientific point of view, how they were overcome.

The first part, "The preparation" describes Sébastien's personality and formative years, which were characterized by a series of disappointments. The name of Piaget's alter ego probably refers to Sébastien Castellion (1515–1563), a dissident collaborator with Jean Calvin. Castellion's condemnation of the execution of heretics at the stake, his advocating for tolerance, his autonomy and honesty made life very difficult for him. Piaget's protagonist also suffered from the brutality of the world, rebelled against the deplorable state of affairs and longed for peace and harmony. Sébastien therefore searched for a conciliatory doctrine enabling the end of dogmatism and coexistence between faith, science and morality. Analogous to Sabatier's historiography, he began his search for an absolute among the Catholics, discovering that Catholic mysticism had remained entrenched in a faulty symbolism. When searching among the Protestants and within a Christian student group, he was disappointed by their random and incoherent theology.

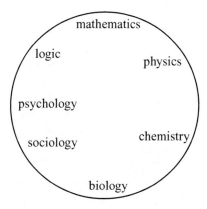

Figure 4.1 Piaget's circle of sciences. (cf. Piaget 1918: 59f. Vidal 1994b: 346)

In philosophy, metaphysicists such as Fouillée and Bergson had failed in reconciling faith and science, too. He also examined pragmatism and criticized its abandonment of the absolute as "bankruptcy of all knowledge" (Piaget 1918: 64). As the same failure was true for the sciences and literature he concluded that the entire culture was imbued with dogmatism and disorder, culminating in war. "That is where we are. Everywhere is disequilibrium; as in society, so in the minds, as in the thoughts, so in practice" (Piaget 1918: 87).

It is true that Sébastien followed Bergson in his "basic logic [...], only Bergson had not defined the genus. All the work, therefore, still remained to be done [...], and it was by means of biology that the construction must be built" (Piaget 1918: 53). In the field of biology, disequilibrium is manifest in the opposition between life as an empirical reality and life as a value. All sciences oscillate between the two poles of the real and the ideal. As one scientific discipline is constructed on the laws of another, the sciences form a circle: the most dogmatic scientists are the biologists, who deliver the basis for sociology and psychology, from which emerge logic and mathematics. These nondogmatic and idealistic sciences, in turn, form the basis for physics, from which follows chemistry, which is the foundation of biology (cf. Figure 4.1).

This circle allowed for a materialistic as well as an idealistic interpretation of the laws of biology. Piaget's program aimed at a synthetic theory of life that was able to combine the reasons behind values with a value-free reality. Through this, a new faith and a new morality should become possible. Since values and faith were founded on personal experience, Sébastien had to overcome his crisis in order to fulfil the conditions for proposing such a theory.

The second part of this autobiography "is based on a diary I kept in Leysin, without knowing I would use it later" (Piaget, letter cited in Vidal 1994a: 185). Many people of Romandy used diaries as a help to examine their conscience and to overcome personal crises. Since Protestants have no external place of recourse to gain absolution and assured guidance, they must resort to autodidactic methods. Educational novels were seen as an ideal means to portray self-analysis and self-therapy, whereby the publication of the successful conversion or catharsis achieved may not only be regarded as a pedagogic challenge to young people but also as an initiation into the "honorable society" of wise men.

The Crisis describes Sébastien's religious trials and depression, his struggle against sensual and egoistic passions, and his salvation through mystical experience. Doubts, fears and nightmares compelled him to examine himself and he noticed that thus far his life had been purely intellectual. This realization cast him into deep depression. While out walking, he experienced a revelation that helped him decide against his passions, because he saw that a moral decision already contains confirmation of the good. While science is able to supply knowledge of good and evil, one's personal faith is responsible for assigning value and thus meaning to life. Knowledge and faith do not exclude each other but necessarily complement each other. As he regained his faith, Sébastien's confidence increased in his mission to achieve a synthesis of life and science. His project was now no longer an abstract theory but a heartfelt experience. Since life and truth are the same, the thinker must live his theory in order to find the truth. "Truth is an ideal. Life contains two realities, [real] disequilibria and an ideal equilibrium to which the disequilibria tend. [...] The thinker must realize this ideal equilibrium, and [...] this means self-sacrifice" (Piaget 1918: 114f.). To counteract the passions and actions that destroy his intellectual equilibrium, he must live in loneliness and celibacy. But Sébastien became aware that he was prone to pride, egoism and a desire to dominate. Again, he entered a crisis and suffered from his own imperfection. "Sébastien now reached the peak of his moral distress. He doubted his mission" (Piaget 1918: 125). Even when he prayed, his heart remained empty and he felt abandoned. Rescue from his depression came in the form of a night-time encounter with God, providing him with the crucial insight that "the equilibrium can only be found by means of disequilibrium, such is the great law of real life" (Piaget 1918: 135). Equilibrium and disequilibrium, the ideal and the real, faith and knowledge do not contradict but presuppose each other. Gaining a personal equilibrium requires the grasp of consciousness of one's own disequilibrium, since truth is to be found within oneself. The absolute is no longer a transcendental entity but a process towards the ideal, for which Jesus serves as a role model. Sébastien revived his mission:

> You will found a morality based on science and you will shock mankind by showing them that in the good is a biological equilibrium, a mechanical law of material evolution [...] You will deliver a totally experimental religious psychology. You will demonstrate another equilibrium in faith [...] You will, above all, fight against metaphysics and show that the Christian faith in all its beauty is comprised in a simple decision of will. (Piaget 1918: 137f.)

Piaget was surprisingly confident that his second mission would be successful: "I know that I shall be doing something great, and I don't care any more whether it is God or me who does it" (Piaget 1918: 143).

Philosophical Revisions

In the third part of *Recherche*, Piaget explained the basic principles of his future philosophy and presented a program for the reconstruction of postwar society. He suggested a change of paradigm: the sciences should progress from the study of quantity, to which they had been limited since Descartes, to the study of quality. A "positive theory of the quality concerned exclusively with the relations of equilibrium and disequilibrium among qualities" (Piaget 1918: 150) would allow a "science of genera" to be constructed upon the ruins of metaphysics. Piaget now conceived "genera" as the basic forms of organization of life. Thus, he transformed the problem of universals into a program of scientific research, which could be investigated psychologically as forms of knowing and biologically as forms of life. To do so, Piaget expanded the theories of equilibrium of Herbert Spencer (1820–1903) and Le Dantec by incorporating a Bergsonian theory of states of consciousness. Mechanical forces stop being noticeable when they combine with other forces, and their equilibrium is subject to "inductive laws." In contrast, the combined individual qualities of the deductive "science of genera" remain as they are, and at the same time, form an additional quality. This kind of "psychological" equilibrium is an "equilibrium *sui generis*" (Piaget 1918: 153) and can only be understood as a probability in relation to a whole. In order to maintain the connection between the mechanical and the psychological equilibrium, Piaget had to assume a "parallelism between the equilibrium of qualities, presupposed by consciousness and the reactions of the organism itself" (Piaget 1918: 156).

Piaget distinguished four forms of equilibrium (the equilibrium of the whole, the equilibrium between the parts and the whole, the equilibrium among the parts, and the equilibrium between the whole and the environment) and four laws: if the qualities of the parts are compatible with the whole, reciprocal action and maintenance take place. "My personality, for example, tends to conserve its partial qualities (the believer, the philosopher, and so on) in the same way that these qualities tend to conserve the personality" (Piaget 1918: 154). If the parts are incompatible with the whole, "they tend to exclude each other" (Piaget 1918: 156). The second law states that the second type of equilibrium is a compromise between the first type and external disturbances. According to the third law, all further equilibria are combinations of the ideal equilibrium and the real disequilibrium. According to the fourth law, all organisms aim for the ideal equilibrium. Life is nothing else than "an organization in unstable equilibrium, but its law is a stable equilibrium towards which it tends" (Piaget 1918: 158). To understand "genera" as relational totalities with an organizing tendency included the rejection of his earlier nominalist position. Later on, this notion was to become the concept of "structures d'ensemble" (structures-of-the-whole).

In a further step, Piaget expanded the concepts of functional assimilation and imitation, which Le Dantec employed to describe the interactions of organisms with their environment in order to achieve equilibrium. The term assimilation originates from the science of nutrition and was applied to mental processes by Spencer in 1863. Le Dantec expanded this concept into the field of functional assimilation and defined life as "adaptive assimilation" (Le Dantec 1897: 142). Piaget criticized his "naïve doctrine" (Piaget 1918: 160) of the one-sided opposition of the whole and its parts, and argued that, on a psychological level, assimilation and imitation were not opposing, but complementary processes. Piaget claimed that Le Dantec was completely ignorant regarding philosophy:

> His philosophy can be summarized in few words: the human being is a stomach that suffers from two parasites, a genital system and a brain. All of this is enclosed in "a leather bag, which is the skin." To be fair, we must add that the first of these parasites dominates the second. (Piaget 1918: 60)

His aggressive stance was perhaps a result of Le Dantec's atheist theory that life was an egoistical struggle, whereas Piaget's major problem with his own biological foundation of morality consisted in proving that the principle of self-preservation did not imply egoism.

Following Jean-Marie Guyau (1854–1888), Piaget believed that life must involve a kind of altruism, since "evolutionary moralities have proved that the good is life itself" (Piaget 1918: 173f.). Egoism is not only damaging to the relations between individuals, but also to equilibrium of the individual itself.

> Every being, to which we relate, causes in us an increasingly infinite complex and multi-shaded image, the longer this relation lasts; and this image exists on its own account in our own inner selves and becomes an inherent part of our own substance. Therefore, it is easy to see that every egoistic action, no matter what kind, favours one part of ourselves to the detriment of others. (Piaget 1918: 178)

This kind of disequilibrium becomes most obvious in sexual passion, as this is "a deviation fixed through heredity" (Piaget 1918: 182). It is not sexuality that is the normal human condition, as claimed by Sigmund Freud (1856–1939), but mysticism. "Mysticism is practically the normal state" (Piaget 1918: 122), because moral and psychological equilibrium originate in mystical experience. Morality, therefore, is not a question of reason, and "knowledge must be replaced by one's individual decision-making" (Piaget 1918: 184). Analogous to Kant, Piaget's categorical imperative was purely formal: "Act in such a way as to realize the absolute equilibrium of the organization of life, both collective and individual" (Piaget 1918: 177). For Piaget, this meant pursuing the Protestant ethics that focus on duty and on individual responsibility, since "the problem of liberty is irrelevant to morality [...] Let me be indifferent to freedom and its implied subtleties, as long as it comes from my heart" (Piaget 1918: 183). Neither reflection of motives nor analysis of situations but the ideal of an absolute value is the condition for right decisions. Since it is impossible to obtain objective reasons for values, this leaves only one possible decision: the decision for life as the highest value: "One must believe or not believe, that is to say, live or not live. There is nothing to say or to understand, there is only one decision to be made" (Piaget 1918: 166).

Voluntary morality, however, is just one of three ways in which the individual and society relate to each other. The second way is feeling, which forms the basis for aesthetics. The beautiful is the individual's love for the ideal, leading to sympathy. Since the real strives for the ideal but cannot reach it, suffering is inevitable. "Only the greatest artist would be able to take beauty so far that it becomes religion and becomes identical with the good and the sacrifice" (Piaget 1918: 187). Piaget had artistic ambitions himself and knew the "divine joy of creating, which scholars and philosophers, as well as poets and musicians, experience" (Piaget 1918: 97). He published a romantic nature poem, entitled *First Snow*, and the love poem *I Would Like*, in the magazine *L'Aube* (Piaget 1918/3).

Religion as a combination of morality and art is the third relationship between the individual and society. Piaget claimed that the connection between the will and feeling, between the ideal and the real, supplied "the experimental basis for a psychology of religion" (Piaget 1918: 173). Piaget's interest in a psychological explanation of religion was kindled through a talk by Théodore Flournoy on *Religion and Psychoanalysis*, held at the ACSE annual meeting in Sainte-Croix in 1916 (Piaget 1945/1: 171). This professor from Geneva was a pioneer researching the unconscious and introduced psychoanalysis into West-Switzerland. He postulated the exclusion of transcendence from the sciences for the sake of a biological interpretation of religious phenomena. "Religion is thereby treated and examined like a vital function" (Flournoy 1903: 45). As a positive science, religious philosophy must 'de-theologize' and psychologize the dogmas and symbols, but faith should not be queried since the inner experiences "remain incommunicable in their concrete reality" (Piaget 1918: 46). For Piaget too, the symbols believers had to create for themselves were external manifestations of the values that formed the core of faith. God is the absolute value who produces all possible values, and Jesus was the only one to reach the ideal equilibrium and to confirm the absolute value for man through his death on the cross. By justifying Christian ideals with the theory of equilibrium, Piaget solved his central dilemma: "Hence the great problem is to base morality on science, since faith is independent of metaphysics, and metaphysics is vain; and that is the problem that makes up my life" (Piaget 1917).

Piaget felt that the most important contribution science could make to social reconstruction was to elaborate the interdependence of ethics, aesthetics, religion and education. The pedagogic program, however, "is simple: back to nature [...] Rousseau had seen it, nature is moral, it mechanically gives life its highest ideal" (Piaget 1918: 202). A natural education that does not establish any opposition between individual and society would lead to social reforms aiming for equilibrium between the individual and society and between the societies. Since Piaget understood society as a "moral personality" (Piaget 1918: 210), he needed to draw a third parallel between the individual and society: "Any moral equilibrium or disequilibrium that is seen as an objective and sociological phenomenon is [...] represented by a symmetrical equilibrium or disequilibrium which is also moral, but subjective and psychological" (Piaget 1918: 178). Thus, Piaget believed in reconciling the socio-psychological perspective of Gabriel Tarde (1843–1904) with the sociological viewpoint of Emile Durkheim (1858–1917) and hoped that this would neither lead to a depreciation of the individual (as happens in "primitive" cultures) nor to a dominance of individualism (as with liberalism). On a national level, equilibrium would establish itself in the form of a cooperative and federative socialism, which would demand respect, equality, freedom and fraternity; on an international level this equilibrium would correspond to the idea of humanity. "For it is in Humanity alone that we can commune with each other in our various undertakings: It alone will reconcile science and faith" (Piaget 1918: 210).

The Political Identity[9]

Inspired by his mother's political convictions, Piaget became interested in socialist and pacifist movements. The outbreak of war made his anti-bourgeois stance more radical, and he was seeking role models for his fight against authoritarian tradition. For instance, he characterized the murdered socialist and antiwar activist Jean Jaurès (1859–1914) as "a saint, a prophet who incarnated an ideal of humanity that could have saved the world" (Piaget 1916/3: 114). Piaget understood socialism not mainly as a political-economic theory, but as a belief that had to be a combination of science, art and morality, in order to unite the social and individual forces. In an outline of history (Piaget 1918: 83f.) he identified states of equilibrium among the Greeks, in French Classicism and in the Romanesque period, while disequilibrium was due to positivism and metaphysics, and it was up to the socialists to surmount the contemporary chaos.

The European socialists, however, were no longer a unified movement, after their split at the secret meeting in Zimmerwald in September 1915. The reformist majority had hoped to end the war through peace treaties, while the "Zimmerwald's left," led by Lenin, hoped that the war would escalate into civil war, which would then lead to revolution. As a result of this split, the Swiss-French Federation of Christian Socialists, of which Piaget was an active member, took up a more radical stance. As this group judged Pettavel's Christian-socialist publication organ *L'Essor* as being too bourgeois, they founded their own journal in 1918. Piaget was listed as a correspondent for the *Voies nouvelles*, but no article appeared under his name. He obviously chose to steer a middle course between the reform-oriented Christian Socialists and the revolution-oriented Christian socialists, since he was also on the editorial staff of *L'Essor*, which he had joined on 17 May 1916. The social-democratic faction, which had approved of all war loans, was too nationalist for his liking and the communist faction was too actionist. Consequently, he suggested a research program for a third course "between a reactionary right and a left without culture" (Piaget

1918: 148). Not collectivism but "socialist co-operation," which respected individual autonomy, would lead to a just distribution of wealth. For the ASCE members, who were primarily middle class, the core problem was the lack of solidarity in society, and not exploitation, poverty, or the workers' lack of power. As the aim was to rechristianize society, they avoided arguing in political or economic terms and used a moral and biological approach.

Piaget's political anthropology was influenced by the anarchists Leon Tolstoy (1828–1910) and Peter Kropotkin (1842–1921). "Kropotkin also looked at the facts, but with very different eyes than Darwin's. He saw mutual aid in nature and by virtue of this, thought himself justified in condemning war" (Piaget 1918/1: 375f.). Piaget believed that Darwin had legitimated the war, although "love and altruism—that is, the negation of war, are inherent in the nature of living beings. Only later complications, due to environmental inertia [...], force living creatures to a restricted assimilation, that is egoism, stupidity, and, in the human species, war" (Piaget 1918/1: 380). This biological concept of human nature formed the basis for Piaget's moral education and social theories. But despite his claims for a biological foundation to his philosophy, he had barely discussed biological aspects.

Piaget's vision of an ideal political system was modeled on the Swiss federative democracy (Piaget 1918/1: 209). Because of his patriotism, he rejected the idea of a general objection to military service, which he found would weaken the nation. Instead he advocated the reconciliation of "the two potentialities of life, fatherland and humanity" (Piaget 1918/2: 122), since patriotism helped to improve humanity and to avoid any loss of culture during the war (Piaget 1918: 170). Nationalism, on the other hand, was an expression of orthodoxy, and thus the source of war. This naïve assessment of good patriotism and bad nationalism is reflected in Piaget's great hope regarding the saving grace of post war times, while remaining passive. His sojourns in Leysin certainly contributed to the fact that his contacts with political groups remained marginal and that religious and moral issues were more important to him than political questions. The image of a political outsider, which Romain Rolland idealized and Piaget strove for, did, however, fit the image of the intellectual who, thanks to his free consciousness, rose above conflicts and thus exerted a harmonizing effect. Like most systematic thinkers, Piaget believed that theory ruled the world: "Once a conflict has been eliminated theoretically, it will also dissolve in practice. As soon as the individual personalities become conscious of the meaning of their efforts, conflicts of consciousness[10] will disappear" (Piaget 1918: 180). Even though Piaget no longer aimed for a metaphysical system but rather for a positive one, his resolve to enter history as the savior of the world remained unchanged.

Criticism and Crisis

Immediately after the publication of *Recherche*, Piaget asked his philosophy teacher to write a review in one of the leading journals. Reymond agreed, but his critique was not what Piaget had expected. Raymond said that he only commented on this "curious mixture of passion and reason" (Reymond 1918: 550) because the book showed the dangerous aspirations of some of the youths in Romandy. "Sébastien keeps plagiarizing authors whom he had ironically just condemned" (Reymond 1918: 550). He deemed Piaget's critique to be superficial and unoriginal, his religious stance to be incoherent, and the character Sébastien not to have been politically embedded. Other reviewers (in Vidal 1994a: 220ff.) were slightly more diplomatic, but they too disliked the arrogance of Piaget's comments and found fault with the theory of equilibrium, as well as with Piaget's literary and political knowledge. The only positive review was written by Bovet's friend and Pettavel's successor Adolphe Ferrière (1879–1960), who praised the book as a sign that a philosopher was born. As Piaget despised the effusive manner of this visionary, this edifying appreciation meant little to him.

This accusation of remoteness from reality and the devastating criticism of his theory destroyed Piaget's career plans and his self-image as philosopher. In a dream analysis, he described "a complete moral crisis" (Piaget 1920/2: 28). The criticism of arrogance "raises his doubts about the purity of his motives and he is afraid that at the bottom of his current negativism, he may discover disreputable instincts" (Piaget 1920/2: 28). Piaget's comments bear witness to the humiliation he felt. Even though he denied ever having read *Recherche* again (Piaget and Bringuier 1977: 32), he quoted, in his autobiography, several sentences from his theory of equilibrium in order to prove the continuity of his work (Piaget 1952/1: 116f.). At the same time, he reduced his educational novel to a philosophical draft for lay people: "I was haunted by the desire to create [...]—for the general public, and not for the specialists—a kind of philosophical novel, the last part of which contained my ideas [...]. My strategy proved to be correct: No one spoke of it except one or two indignant philosophers" (Piaget 1952/1: 116). Piaget claimed therefore that he had written a book that should not be read. In fact, however, he was neither seeking to live out his creative drive, nor did he try to invent the genre of "science fiction", but he wanted to give an insight into the personal and theoretical history of the development of his theory and to supply a research program to launch his career as a professional philosopher. "It is a study of the self. I need it to make the philosopher understood when he speaks (which will be, for the first time, in my dissertation)" (Piaget, letter cited in Vidal 1994a: 186). The reviews discouraged

Piaget from writing his second dissertation in philosophy with Reymond, planned long ago. He made several attempts but, as far as his philosophical projects were concerned, he suffered as acutely from writer's block as he had done with his biology projects after the debate with Roszkowski.

Studium Intermissum

Because of his repeated stays in Leysin and the writing of *Recherche*, Piaget hardly attended to his studies during the first half of his university course. During the winter terms of 1915/16 and 1916/17, he did not attend the minimum of seven lessons per week, and in the summer term of 1916 he did not even matriculate. "Arrangements made locally, probably with his father's assistance" (Schaer 1996: 67), however, made it possible for him to complete his studies within the normal timescale. During the summer term of 1917, he took 18 lessons per week and in July he passed the first part of his degree with outstanding grades (six grades at level 6, the highest grade possible, and one grade at level 5). During his last year at university, he attended additional lectures in mathematics and philosophy lectures where Reymond taught about the unconscious, about school and the child, and about Edouard Claparède's *Psychology of the Child*.

Piaget's zoological work was "essentially compiled from papers he had published while he was still at grammar school" (Schaer 1996: 77). Nevertheless, in the academic year of 1917/18, Piaget was awarded the much coveted Léon-DuPasquier prize for his Swiss Malacologic Minglings. The exam board, chaired by his mentor Otto Fuhrmann, was generous and paid Piaget the maximum sum of Fr. 500[11] for his 679 handwritten pages, now lost. In addition, in 1917, he received the prize sponsored by the private Academic Society for his 320 pages on *Realism and Nominalism in the Sciences of Life*. The board, of which Arnold Reymond was a member, again awarded Piaget the maximum sum of Fr. 100, despite the assessment that Reymond had submitted to the board, which criticized three main areas: the absence of a bibliography, Piaget's ambivalent concept of God and his unclear distinction between the metaphysical and psychological fields (Liengme Bessire and Béguelin 1996: 85). Some of Reymond's points actually anticipated the reservations he would later put forward with regard to *Recherche*.

In July 1918, Piaget passed his final examinations with a grade 6 in zoology and geology and a grade 5 in botany, thus achieving a grade average of 5.85, coupled with the assessment of "very satisfactory." In the same year, Piaget submitted his PhD thesis, although he had not continued as a matriculated student and thus had broken the formal rules. The contents of his thesis largely reflected the work for which he had received the Léon-DuPasquier prize (Schaer 1996: 78). The 130-page-long catalogue regarding the distribution of mollusks throughout the Valais canton was

> compared to the total of works published during his youth, a small, minor paper, which was admitted on a simple written request, but was never supported, as if the university authorities had tacitly assumed that Piaget's scientific interests placed him above the usual academic sphere. (Barrelet 1996: 17)

These privileges were more likely due to the tightly woven network of the corporate élite than to Piaget's scientific interests. The university of Neuchâtel, where Arthur Piaget had been rector until 1911, was characterized by strong personal and family ties that resulted in a culture of intellectual incest (cf. Liengme Bessire and Béguelin 1996: 93). Otto Fuhrmann presided over the PhD commission and in 1919 assessed Piaget's dissertation with grade 6, although the PhD student had written in his introduction that he did not really understand his subject matter any more:

> The more frequently I return to Valais, the less I understand. One drifts among the uncertainty of the subjective definitions of the species or among the subjective assessment of the natural forms [...] This catalogue is a summary of prior research, done by someone who cannot go any further without changing methods and who needs to take stock before he sets out to work [...]. Admittedly, it is merely a catalogue of species and places. It does, however, raise some questions, which is nevertheless an estimable result. (Piaget 1921/2: 1ff.)

The catalogue which was, in fact, the completion of Godet's life project, contained no theoretical developments. In spite of employed neo-Darwinist terminology such as "competition between species" and "phenotype" (Piaget 1921/2: 61), he did not define these terms and lacked detailed knowledge of the connection between adaptation, heredity and species. This is why he mentioned the need for re-orientation of biological research "in a distinctly biological direction, with the help of biometrics and in close relationship with the work of botanists and psychologists [...] towards a sort of indirect genetics" (Piaget 1921/2: 1ff.).

His first biometric-statistical work was, however, rejected by Maurice Bedot, a rejection that Piaget accepted as being justified: "You were right to reject my statistical study [...] This work is indeed superficial, and since it seems impossible for me, at present, to improve on it, it would be better to let the question rest" (Piaget, letter cited in Vidal 1994a: 237). One month later, however, Piaget returned to his contribution to the *Catalogue of the Invertebrates of Switzerland* that he had promised in 1912: "At the moment I am in Zurich to study the statistical and biometrical methods applicable to mollusks. I am telling you this in order to show you that, with the passing of time, my meagre knowledge can only be improved, so that I can work better afterwards" (Piaget, letter cited in Vidal 1999). The goals of Piaget's studies, however, had very little connection with statistics, but with psychoanalysis.

Autistic Confusion in Zurich

In the autumn of 1918, the graduated scientist traveled to Zurich with the aim of working in a psychology laboratory. Although he "felt at once that there lay my path" (Piaget 1952/1: 117), he was disappointed by the experiments and lectures of Gotthold Friedrich Lipps (1865–1931) and Arthur Wreschner (1866–1931) on philosophy, pedagogy and mental development, because they "seemed to me to have little bearing on fundamental problems" (Piaget 1952/1: 117). This would have been religious psychology, since he had already announced in *Recherche* that he wished to examine more closely the origin of religious manifestations in the unconscious (Piaget 1918: 190).

For Flournoy (1916), the Vienna School was too Judaic, materialistic and positivist, whereas Zurich was the Protestant centre of psychoanalysis and receptive to moral, religious, social and pedagogical issues. Eugen Bleuler (1857–1939), head of the psychiatric clinic Burghölzli, and his assistant Carl Gustav Jung (1875–1961) were among the first to dispense and to apply psychoanalysis at a clinical level (Moser 1992). In 1907, the *Society for Freudian Research* was founded and chaired by Bleuler. "The Zurich analysts therefore became the core of the small squad fighting for the appreciation of analysis. They alone offered the opportunity to learn this new art and work within it. Most of my present supporters and co-workers came to me via Zurich" (Freud 1914: 66). Psychoanalysis became de-sexualized and imbued with pedagogy after liberal Protestants such as Oskar Pfister (1873–1956) had adopted it (cf. Vidal 1989). This is why Piaget did not continue his studies in Vienna but in Zurich.

We learn from a dream analysis that the 22-year-old felt lost as he arrived in this German-speaking town: "I feverishly ran through the streets, searching unsuccessfully for a room to live in [. . .] In fact, the choice of a room had recently been mingled with a secret conflict he had with his mother" (Piaget 1920/2: 26, 28). Since Piaget put this conflict in the context of his emancipation from his mother, we can assume that he wanted to find his own place to live, although his mother would have preferred her son to find lodgings with pastor Pfister.[12] This close friend of Bovet held regular seminars on psychoanalysis at the Rousseau Institute in Geneva. Piaget attended some of his seminars and felt close enough to him to discuss his mother's psychotic illness with him. Pfister could have thought of Piaget when he described juvenile narcissism:

> Some boys are positively in love with their thinking and attribute to it some immense importance. With anxious piety they hold on to every scrap of paper on which they have noted a thought, to preserve it for posterity, or at least as a memento of their own mental development in order to use it for a future biography; finding their brainwaves little appreciated, they draw consolation from the idea of unappreciated genius. (Pfister 1922: 157)

Piaget also attended Jung's lectures. Since both were strongly influenced by Flournoy, they used terms like "complex" in a similar way. For Piaget, a complex refers to an ensemble of past ideas, emotions and "images of others," that become an "inherent part of our own substance" (Piaget 1918: 178). The personality is the whole, which is composed of "complexes," i.e. autonomous partial qualities. Piaget emphasized that his term of autonomous inner "figures" was not metaphorically used because "each of these images is a true living being whose roots reach into the deepest areas of the self" (Piaget 1917 ms). The great challenge for man is to prevent these complexes from becoming one's tyrants. Ten times, he wrote to Rolland, he had suppressed the desire to visit the author because of his own disgusting pride and egoism.

There are only few opportunities to find access to the unconscious self. "In a moment of freedom, one manages to discern the 'selves' who are in oneself, and to transform them from masters to friends" (ibid). This was the harmony Sébastien experienced after his communion with God: "He felt within himself his friends who shared his personality so that each could occupy a special part. And this beautiful and great assembly existed independent of him" (Piaget 1918: 141). Such a mystery was not opposed to scientific thinking: "On the contrary, our scientific position compels us to recognize the mystery" (Piaget 1918: 198). Piaget identified mysticism as a form of autistic thinking. Reason is a mental synthesis of rational thinking in terms of quantity, and autistic thinking in terms of quality. Since pure quality is not recognizable, symbols are needed. Different qualities can coincide in one symbol through "concentration," and "displacement" can link the affective content of the qualities to new objects. These two mechanisms enable symbolism in dreams, art, mysticism, metaphysics and religion. Any contradiction between the symbols and one's reason, as would be the case with dogmatism or pride, represents disequilibrium. Equilibrium, however, can only be achieved if action is renounced, since action will always pursue one's own interest. The thinker, therefore is always "a madman" (Piaget 1918: 117) who has to struggle against his passionate and egoistical parts. Equilibrium cannot be achieved unless there is a permanent "struggle between the divine and the diabolical in man" (Piaget 1918: 181).

This construction became shaky when Piaget attended a clinical course and lectures on diagnostics, psychopathology among children and adults and on psychoanalytical therapy. "My teacher Bleuler [. . .] made me sense the danger of solitary meditation; I decided to forget my system lest I should fall a victim to 'autism'" (Piaget 1952/1: 246, 117). In 1911, Bleuler had coined the expression schizophrenia and had identified autism as one of its fundamental symptoms. Autistic thinking "has its own special law that deviates from (realistic) logic; it does not seek truth but satisfaction of its desires" (Bleuler 1919: 1). With a sane person, autistic thinking decreases as knowledge increases, through which thinking becomes disciplined; and the combining of complexes would lead to a relatively homogenous person-ality. With schizophrenic patients, the complexes behave like autonomous beings, dominating the patient's personality and causing delusions. Piaget described precisely this splitting of the self into autonomous figures, when Sébastien felt an inner society of individuals emerge from his unconscious. They were "his friends, sharing his personality, each one occupying a par-ticular area" (Piaget 1918: 133).

It was not the fear of becoming autistic that made Piaget give up his system, but he became aware that he already was the victim of "solitary meditation" (cf. Harris 1997). Later on, Piaget suspected "the Bergsonian intuition [. . .] of leading a bit too much to a kind of 'autism'" (Piaget 1929/5: 118). And he warned that "if there were not other people, the disappointments of expe-rience would lead to overcompensation and dementia. We are constantly hatching an enormous number of false ideas, conceits, utopias, mystical explanations, suspicions, and megalomaniac fantasies" (Piaget 1924: 204). Considering the dangerous dimensions of these inner phenomena, Piaget's theory of equilibrium may be understood as an attempt to overcome his own autism, "of which he had been afraid since his adolescence" (Kessel-ring 1999: 48). In his conference of 1919 on psychoanalysis, Piaget agreed with the compensation theory by Alfred Adler (1870–1936): "The stronger the inadequacy, the stronger the overcompensation, resulting in a discharge of autistic imaginings to create an ideal world in which one plays the role one desires" (Piaget 1920/2: 53). According to Adler (1912: 44ff.), this overcompensation in order to escape the torturing feelings of inferiority manifested in a tendency towards security, striving for higher self-esteem, power and recognition, or male protest. Piaget matched every symptom of this diagnosis: his need for a mission, his identity as a genius and restorer, his role of martyr in his rebellion, his striving for dominance, his detestation of weakness, fear and cowardice and his praise for will power, determination and toughness (Piaget 1918: 13, 55, 124, 129).

Probably, Bleuler's teaching was not the only reason for quitting his studies in Zurich after only one semester. Another motive might have been his therapy experience gained, since he had "become familiar with practical and theoretical psychoanalysis, to which he applied the utmost energy" (Pfister 1920: 294f.). Still in the same year, Piaget recounted that he already had at least five analysis patients (Piaget 1920/2: 39), one of whom was "a young autistic person whose case I did not make any worse, I think" (Piaget 1977/14). We may assume that Piaget did not only analyze patients but that he had himself been analyzed in Zurich. Piaget said in an interview in 1979 that he was analyzed by a direct student of Freud, a lady called De La Fuente[13] (Carotenuto 1986: 366). However the details of the confrontation with autism might have been, Piaget fled from Zurich. "In the spring of 1919 I became restless and left for le Valais; there I applied Lipp's statistical method to a biometric study of the variability of land mollusks as a function of altitude! I needed to get back to concrete problems to avoid grave errors" (Piaget 1952/1: 118).

During this summer, Piaget undertook one of the few studies in which he applied statistical methods. He used a new method of Charles Edward Spearman (1863–1945) to demonstrate a connection between the habitat of mollusks and their morphological variations. This work was considered to be the start of a "long-term research" (Piaget 1920/1: 125) on mechanisms of adaptation, heredity of acquired characteristics and the relationship between genotype and phenotype. Since he did not differentiate between an individual specimen's adaptation and its genus, he again arrived at the conclusion that there must be two different types of influence: "1st Environmental factors (drought, lack of food) acting on the phenotypes; 2nd hereditary factors acting on the genotypes" (Piaget 1920/1: 132). His interest in the "psychological" aspect of animal behavior may have been one of the reasons for his decision to continue psychological studies in Paris. A further reason was his ambition to make psychological history: "Psychology is still such an unexplored field that new things can be discovered very quickly and at any time [...]. Biology, on the other hand, had a head start of one century, and much more work is necessary to make new discoveries!" (Piaget and Bringuier 1977: 29).

Psychoanalytical Traps in Paris

Study visits to Paris were part of the tradition for anyone wishing to pursue an academic career in west Switzerland. For Piaget's career, too, the two years he spent in the French capital were crucial. As a guest student, he attended lectures in psychology, psychopathology, logic and scientific philosophy; he participated in tutorials and gained laboratory experience, working with children. Unlike Zurich, he knew Paris well, since he had often visited relatives in this town. Moreover, together with some of his friends from the Friends of Nature Club he "eagerly attended the courses of Pierre Janet in Paris" (Piaget 1937/3: 39).

The philosopher and physician Janet (1859–1947) taught experimental and comparative psychology at the Collège de France, and from 1919 to 1921 he covered the topic of "evolution of personality." At the university's Institute of Pedagogy, Théodore Simon (1873–1961) conducted practical tutorials in experimental pedagogy and conducted intelligence research, using the test he had created with Alfred Binet (1857–1911). Piaget owed his interest in intelligence research to his next mentor. "I was recommended to Dr Simon who was then living in Rouen, but who had Binet's laboratory at his disposal" (Piaget 1952/1: 118). The recommendation came from Bovet (Piaget 1975/1: 107) and in response Simon cared for Piaget's formation, allowed him to work in the laboratory, and he even conferred upon him the prestigious task of giving the main speech at the General Assembly of the Alfred Binet Society. "'Psychoanalysis', he told me, 'is little known in France. It is only studied by our psychiatrists. A sketch of psychoanalytic trends in pedagogy would be interesting'" (Piaget 1920/2: 23).

On 15 December 1919, Piaget was one of the first to present the fundamental theories from Vienna and Zurich to a French audience (Cifali 1982). The 23-year-old demonstrated extensive knowledge about psychoanalysis and praised Freud's genetic approach, according to which the problems in adulthood could be accessed by examining the patient's childhood. He explained and accepted the mechanisms of the unconscious (repression, sublimation and transfer) and the Oedipus and Electra complexes. Like Flournoy, Piaget criticized the sexual basis of Freud's theory: "There is something obsessive in wanting at any cost to reduce to the sexual instinct certain tendencies which seem even more primitive, such as the revolt of the son against his father, often a simple outcome of the instinct of self-preservation" (Piaget 1920/2: 50f.). He agreed with Adler, who considered children fundamentally innocent and held that parents were responsible for their children's psychological difficulties (Piaget 1920/2: 45). Freud, Piaget considered, went deeper with respect to the parent–child conflict, "but as far as childhood is concerned, Adler's psychology seems to be indisputable" (Piaget 1920/2: 53). For Piaget, Bovet's theory of the fighting instinct confirmed Adler's concept of desire for power. Aggression and sexuality ought to be sublimated through a process of intellectualization and socialization into activities that do not harm others. Despite his criticism of

Jung's adventurous theory of the collective unconscious, Piaget hoped that Jung might reconcile Freud and Adler (Piaget 1920/2: 60). Yet even in later years, Piaget still had his reservations about Jung's personality and theories: "One could see that he was the son of a country pastor. He wanted to appear close to people but he did this very naïvely, in a truly unpleasant manner" (in Altwegg 1983: 258).

Piaget found that psychoanalysis could be successfully applied to pedagogy and could help with the examination and treatment of many problems. He identified as the main educational problem that adults blame children. "Up till now we have been looking at punishing or rewarding our children from an extremely one-sided viewpoint, of such a brutality that future generations will be amazed"(Piaget 1920/2: 66). Teachers ought to know about the unconscious complexes and processes such as projection:

> With children, transfer lies at the base of all their feelings. Transfer explains the most banal actions. Thus a teacher often becomes a father symbol and the pupil uses him as a target for all his unsatisfied desires to revolt. Being thus aware and combining it with our knowledge regarding the development of complexes this must in turn transform pedagogy. It will no longer be a matter of punishing but of understanding. (Piaget 1920/2: 67)

Piaget herewith expressed the core of this pedagogic theory to which he would adhere: moral judgments by unprofessional adults cause feelings of guilt, thus preventing true morality. Young people therefore have to emancipate themselves from coercion, a process that involves conflicts and crises.

According to Piaget, psychoanalysts dealt with our emotional side and neglected to examine our intelligence. The reason for this was "too strong a contrast between their concepts of the conscious and unconscious" (Piaget 1920: 71). Psychoanalysis was therefore a simplifying theory, unable to explain the mechanism of sublimation or moral consciousness. Piaget referred to Janet and concluded that there existed a continuous relationship between the unconscious and the conscious, and between autistic and logic thinking. "In the child, autism is everything. Later, reason develops at its expense" (Piaget 1920: 80). Repression leads to sublimation which "takes for its object a product of autistic thought itself, a poetic or mystical product" (Piaget 1920: 49f.). As before, Piaget identified autistic thinking with values, but he now replaced the division of self into several persons, who were to be harmonized by the mechanisms of repression, sublimation and emerging consciousness.

Pfister praised Piaget's portrayal, except for overlooking Freud's distinction "between the unconscious in its stricter sense [. . .] and the unconscious in its wider sense, which comprises also the pre-conscious and things we have forgotten in the normal way, as well as other unrepressed dispositions of consciousness" (Pfister 1920: 295). This aside, he reckoned that the psychological movement could surely look forward to important contributions from this young scientist. On 8 October 1920, Piaget joined the Swiss section of the International Psychoanalytic Society, which Pfister presided over and of which Bovet was a member.

In contrast with Pfister, the audience did not seem enthusiastic about Piaget's presentation, since it provoked an awful scandal. "Everything I said provoked 'boos' in the auditorium. Simon, sitting beside me, maintained a fixed and imperturbable smile. Had the audience been in possession of rotten eggs and tomatoes, I do not know how I would ever have extricated myself" (Piaget 1975/1: 109).

On the one hand, Piaget explained this hostility by the fact that psychoanalysis was completely new among pedagogues and would therefore cause outrage. But the expanded transcript, which appeared in two parts in the *Bulletin Mensuel de la Société Alfred Binet*, gives no insight into what may have caused the audience's displeasure. On the other hand, Piaget described himself as a victim in a trap, because he did not fulfill his agreement with Simon to adapt the intelligence test of Cyril Burt (1883–1971) as the objective of his laboratory work:

> Now, two years later, I finally wrote long articles on the logic of these tests without having tackled standardization. Simon, however, was very smart; he read my articles and found that the results were valuable and standardization was unimportant. Yet he took revenge for my independence by asking me to hold a conference on psychoanalysis. (Piaget 1975/1: 109)

Since Piaget undertook this talk three months after his arrival in Paris and Simon approved of his quite independent work, we may assume that the aim of this portrayal must have been to obscure Simon's function as his mentor. Piaget, who later became famous for the examination of intelligence by way of a "clinical" survey of children in a scientific "laboratory," owed his work mainly to his Parisian patron. Simon's devaluation as being vengeful because of Piaget's independence would therefore preserve the appearance of Piaget's originality.

Notes

1. Switzerland, like the USA, has a public school system that is regulated by elected local authorities and the cantons. School commissions consist

of citizens, who usually are proposed by political parties. After being elected, they control and manage the schools in their spare time (cf. Criblez *et al.* 1999).

2. See the extensive studies of Vidal 1994a, 1996, 1999.

3. Conchology is a subdivision of malacology, the science of mollusks, and deals with the structure of their shells.

4. 'Tardieu' is a composition of 'Tardy the snail' from the medieval *Roman de Renart* and 'dieu' (God).

5. Piaget's species nomenclature definitively disappeared with the systematization of Bengt Hubendick who reduced the round 1,000 species down to 40 in 1951.

6. Piaget made contradictory statements about his reference material. Presumably, the first work he read was "*L'évolution des dogmes*" (1965: 16), by which he probably meant the roughly fifty pages long booklet *The Vitality of Christian Dogmas and their Power of Evolution* of 1890. Presumably Piaget did not read the much larger work *Outlines of a Philosophy of Religion Based on Psychology and History* of 1897, which he mentioned in his autobiography (1952/1: 110), until he wrote his comparison *Bergson et Sabatier* (1914/1).

7. I follow the detailed study of Vidal (1994a: 92ff.).

8. The French word means search as well as research. Vidal (1994a: 162ff.) brought out the personal and theoretical dimensions of Piaget's reorientation.

9. This and the next section are based essentially on Vidal (1994a: 175ff.).

10. The French "conscience" can mean both consciousness and conscience.

11. At the time, an annual scholarship would amount to Fr. 400 and the annual salary of a university laboratory chemist to Fr. 600.

12. Piaget lived in lodgings with Henriette Plojoux, who regularly let rooms to students. Her son William was born in 1896, the same year as Piaget, and he too studied at the university.

13. Despite my researches in Zurich, Neuchâtel, Paris, Geneva, Vienna, Frankfurt and the cantons of Valais and Vaud, I have been unable to retrieve any information on Ms. De La Fuente. Thanks to all archivists, librarians and government officers who helped me.

Part 2

Critical Exposition of Piaget's Work

5

Early Psychological Work

Discovery of Clinical Child Psychology

Every afternoon, Piaget conducted experimental studies regarding logical classes and relations, causality and the numerical concept with some boys from the school next to the laboratory. After Binet's death, the Parisian psychologists lost interest in intelligence tests; thus Piaget also showed little enthusiasm about the standardization of Burt's tests. In the mornings, Piaget was studying the book *Algebra of Logic* by Louis Couturat (1868–1914) in the National Library. "It turned out that the elementary logical operations, the symbolism of which I studied with great effort in Couturat, offered me the very model I needed in order to understand the difficulties my youngsters had in trying to solve Burt's problems" (Piaget 1959/3: 10). Suddenly, he was fascinated by the errors that the surveyed children displayed. "Thus I engaged my subjects in conversations designed in accordance with psychiatric questioning, with the aim of discovering something about the reasoning process underlying their right, but especially their wrong answers" (Piaget 1952/1: 119). Evidently, he was sure that there had to be an underlying logical structure to the pupils' difficulties.

Piaget regarded it as a key experience when he observed a 10-month-old baby, who had been brought on a visit to Piaget's grandmother:

> I watched him as he was enjoying himself playing with a ball [. . .] The ball rolled under an armchair. He went looking for it, found it, and pushed it away again. This time it disappeared under a large sofa with a fringe . . . he could not see it any more. So he turned back to the armchair, where he had found the ball earlier". (Piaget and Bringuier 1977: 56, cf. Piaget 1937: 64, observation 52)

Piaget concluded from this that the child was feeble-minded. When he observed epileptic children at the Salpêtrière Hospital, he again believed to have "discovered a method to distinguish normal from abnormal children"

(Piaget 1970/9: 29) because they could not see that two strings of pearls contained the same number of pearls, if the strings were of different lengths. Piaget had studied the "clinical method" under Bleuler and George Dumas (1866–1946) in the Sainte-Anne Clinic, where patients were surveyed each Sunday at 11 o'clock. In the course of his own interviews, Piaget noticed that "a child systematically fails to understand the expressions: 'a part of' or 'some of'" (Piaget 1921/1: 449). He therefore simplified Burt's questions and presented them to the children in writing:

> Jean tells his sisters: "A part of my flower bouquet is yellow." Then he asks his sisters what colour his bouquet is. Marie says: "All your flowers are yellow." Simone says: "Some of your flowers are yellow," and Rose says: "None of your flowers are yellow." Which sister is right? (Piaget 1921/1: 450)

Piaget classified the answers according to three hierarchical stages of development, as he would do with much of his future work. In the implicit stage, the test pupils did not understand the expression "a part of." In the intermediate stage he noted confusion between a collection and parts. In the explicit or reflective stage, starting from about 10 years of age, correct classes could be formed. Piaget's first article on child psychology was dedicated to Simon, corrected by Lalande and published in the journal of his friend Ignace Meyerson (1888–1983). Piaget mentioned that studies undertaken at the Rousseau Institute had reached similar conclusions (Piaget 1921/1: 478) and referred the readers to his next article in the journal *Archives de Psychologie*.

In this study, the pupils were given the following problem to solve: "Edith is fairer than Suzanne. Edith is darker than Lili. Who is the darkest, Edith, Suzanne or Lili?" (Piaget 1921/4: 144). In his analysis of the answers, Piaget divided the implicit stage into two levels: one at which the children could not give reasons for their answers, and the other, where justification for the relationship between the colors had been sought. Following Ribot and Janet, Piaget considered "the field of attention and the form of judgement" (Piaget 1921/4: 167) as the two crucial factors for understanding comparisons. Without further explanation, Piaget described the explicit stage of correct comparisons as the "stage of equilibrium" (Piaget 1921/4: 161). Piaget sent this study to Edouard Claparède (1873–1940), the founder of the Rousseau Institute and editor of the *Archives de Psychologie*, to whom he dedicated the first and the last quote in this contribution. "In addition to accepting my article, he made a proposal which changed the course of my life. He offered me the job of 'Director of Studies' at the Institut J. J. Rousseau in Geneva. Since he barely knew me he asked me to come to Geneva for a month's trial" (Piaget 1952/1: 121). In his autobiography, Piaget twice made reference to the fact that he hardly knew Claparède. Yet he never mentioned his longstanding mentor Pierre Bovet, who, as the Director of the Institute, was the one responsible for this appointment. This creates the impression that the quality of Piaget's article had been the decisive reason for his appointment, whereas this might have been planned much earlier. Piaget finished his trial month at Geneva in the summer semester of 1921. For obvious reasons, his autobiography fails to mention that the University of Geneva recognized Piaget's 31-page article as his habilitation, the postdoctoral qualification that allowed him to start as a private lecturer at 25 years of age. "I noticed immediately that Claparède and Bovet were ideal *patrons* who would let me work according to my desires" (Piaget 1952/1: 121). These two men were indeed the most significant patrons of Piaget's university career and the title *patron* would later be elected by Piaget himself whenever his colleagues addressed him.

The Jean-Jacques Rousseau Institute (JJRI)

The conditions of research as a "chief of studies" were exceptionally favorable (cf. Grunder 1992; Hameline 1995; Oelkers 1996a). In 1889, the University of Geneva had established its first chair of Experimental Psychology at the Faculty of Science, whereby psychology was granted autonomy of philosophy. Once Claparède had succeeded his cousin and teacher Flournoy as director of the psychology laboratory in 1904, he proposed to establish an independent institute for the research of child development and teacher training. After several failed attempts to convince the university authorities of the usefulness of such an institute (Helmchen 1995: 2), Claparède decided to establish a private institute in 1912, with the support of Théodore Flournoy, and in cooperation with Pierre Bovet and Adolphe Ferrière. It was modeled on G. Stanley Hall's Children's Institute of Clark University in California. The occasion for this foundation was the bicentenary of Rousseau's birthday, whom Claparède considered the Copernicus of pedagogy and pioneer of all modern ideas. As a centre for training, research, services and information, the Jean-Jacques Rousseau Institute was responsible for substantiating and propagating the ideas of the New Education (cf. Oelkers 1995; 1996a: 166f.), in order to accelerate social progress. Around this time, many pedagogic-psychological institutes sprang up all over Europe and the USA (Oelkers 1996b; Hofstetter and Schneuwly 2004: 582f.). Unlike most other training establishments for primary school teachers, the JJRI had to rely upon donations and tuition fees from student teachers. Claparède considered this private funding a temporary solution because, from the very start, the JJRI had been so closely connected with the university that several academic courses were offered as part of the institute's program.

About 20 students signed up for the first course but, by 1932, 816 students (555 women and 261 men) from 49 countries attended the JJRI. With 435 non-Swiss students, the institute's international reputation spread rapidly. The three-year teacher-training course comprised practical placements in annexed schools where new teaching methods were tried. In addition, the candidates were instructed in psychological technique (observation and measuring tasks according to the examples of Binet/Simon and Ovide Decroly). According to the motto *Discat a puero magister* (the teacher should learn from the child), a change of paradigm was to be effected within schools, which would comprise the viewpoint of the child as an active subject, of individualized didactics, improved methodology for teachers and the practicing of democratic forms of school life. In 1913, Mina Audemars (1883–1971) and Louise Lafendel (1872–1971), both coming from the Fröbel movement, opened the Maison des Petits (following Maria Montessori's Casa dei Bambini). In 1917, the secondary school Maison des Grands, which led to the Baccalaureate, was established and was directed by Paul Meyhoffer until 1921, when it had to close due to financial problems. For the same reason, the Toepffer-School with a roll of 200 students, annexed in 1918, had to be abandoned two years later. The Maison des Petits escaped this fate, because the parents granted the school additional subsidies, and in 1922 the Geneva Canton integrated the school into the state education system.

Claparède expected scientific support for school reforms to result from experimental studies. The heart of the JJRI was his child psychology laboratory where tests on developmental psychology were conducted. In 1905, he published a small book entitled *Psychologie de l'enfant et pédagogie expérimentale*, which he constantly updated and expanded until it became an extensive and influential synthesis of child psychology. In 1913, he set up a medico-pedagogical consultation centre, where children with learning difficulties were treated. In 1917 the Patronage Society of Former Remedial Pupils was established together with several initiatives in support of so-called retarded children. The opening of a careers guidance office in 1918 placed the Genevans among the pioneers of applied psychology. They also introduced studies regarding job suitability, work organizations and the connection between work and socio-economic backgrounds.

Geneva was much more of a centre for documentation and propaganda for New Education than the other institutes. The International Bureau of New Education, founded in 1899 and led by Ferrière, had contacts with almost all reform schools, whose work he documented. The JJRI organized many exhibitions, congresses and conferences, and important guests such as Ovide Decroly, Célestin Freinet, Wilhelm Paulsen, Elisabeth Rotten, Rabindranath Tagore, or Karl Wilker would hold colloquiums and talks for lecturers and students. On their numerous trips, the JJRI employees established contacts with other reform-pedagogical institutions and their representatives. In 1906, Bovet instigated a series of books, the *Collection d'actualités pédagogiques*, publishing 58 books between 1912 and 1948. In 1912, the Geneva journal *Intermédiairs des éducateurs* was founded with the purpose of giving educators a new, scientifically based perspective on their children. As the JJRI gained the support of the teachers' union, this journal was added as a special supplement to *L'Educateur* and thus appeared since 1924 every two months with an edition of 2,000 copies. The *Archives de psychologie*, founded in 1901 by Flournoy und Claparède, was one of the most influential journals and a very important vehicle in the exchange between American and European psychologists. After Flournoy's death in 1920, Piaget replaced him on the editorial staff.

When the JJRI experienced financial trouble after World War I, State Councilor Jules Mussard, who presided over the Department of Education, created a chair of Experimental Psychology at the University of Geneva for director Bovet in 1920. This financial relief permitted the employment of Piaget, who was only the second employee paid primarily for research after Aline Giroud. She had worked with Binet and Simon before she conducted experimental studies about attention, memory, imagination and mental levels, and transferred to the Ecole de Service Sociale in Paris in 1915. During the six intervening years, it was primarily Alice Descoeudres (1877–1963) who was responsible for research. Like Decroly and Julia Degand, she examined the development of concepts such as color, shape, number and the development of language and manual dexterity. For her book of 1921 titled *Child Development between Age Two and Seven*, she interviewed 500 children. Piaget, who praised her test methods and used some of them himself, continued his research in her way, with the help of a large team of mostly female students and assistants. Thus, Bovet and Claparède handed to the young researcher at the JJRI a well-established research place with international connections.

> For four years we applied our policy to expect only one thing from our young co-worker: to lead the research, for which we had appointed him. Together with one or two students, he went every afternoon from 2 pm to 4 pm to the primary school in order to interview pupils. In the mornings, he worked in his small room (rather dark and cluttered, in the Taconnerie street), where he classified observations he had collected or which the pupils brought him from the Maison des Petits or from elsewhere. No correspondence, no administration, no lecturing trips. (Bovet 1932: 77)

Piaget's study of child thought was strongly interwoven with his unsolved problem regarding the scientific justification of morality and religion. And he continued to occupy himself with psychoanalysis, theoretically and practically, both as an analyst and as one being analyzed.

Psychoanalytical Confrontations

In 1920, Claparède founded the Geneva Psychoanalytic Association and the International Society for Psychotechnics, whose weekly meetings Piaget attended from 1921 onward. Flournoy, Bovet, Pfister, Charles Baudouin (1893–1963), Ernst Schneider (1878–1957) and Sabina Spielrein (1885–1941) had already held talks and courses on psychoanalysis at the JJRI. Between 1915 and 1920, Spielrein lived in Lausanne, from where she commuted during the winter semester of 1920/21 to attend a laboratory course at the JJRI. In 1921, this former patient, student and lover of Jung moved to Geneva to work with Claparède. She was a Jewish Russian, had gained her PhD under Bleuler with a work on schizophrenia, and was subsequently one of the first women to be admitted into the Psychoanalytic Organization of Vienna. After the birth of her daughter Renata in 1913 she focused increasingly upon child psychology: She conducted interviews with children, used recorded observations about her daughter for study purposes and wrote the first psychoanalytical paper on child psychology. In September 1920, she presented her investigation into the Development of Speech at the VI International Psychoanalytical Congress in The Hague, whereby she distinguished between an autistic, a magical and a social stage.

In the winter semester of 1921/22, Spielrein taught a course on psychoanalysis and pedagogy and attended Piaget's lecture on "autistic thinking" at the university. In addition, Piaget, whom Spielrein termed a "psychoanalyst," lectured on "the child's intelligence" at the JJRI and offered a practical course on research methods. "From then on, we were working mostly in the same field, but independently" (Spielrein 1923: 301). Piaget went to be analyzed by this colleague in sessions that took place every morning at 8 am in the JJRI, where they are said to have laughed a lot (Richebächer 2005: 230). Reportedly, one day Piaget suddenly became aware of his strong mother projection onto Spielrein, whereupon he got up and left the room, saying: "I understood!" (Richebächer 2005: 346). Eight months later, however, she broke off the therapy because Piaget had criticized the psychoanalytical theory. "I did not see the need to interpret the facts that the analysis revealed to me, in the way of Freud's theory" (Piaget and Bringuier 1977: 183) Piaget's comments on this analysis are contradictory: Sometimes he stated that she had stopped his therapy (Piaget and Bringuier 1977: 183);

on other occasions he claimed that the therapy had been successful and that he had ended it (Piaget 1977/13; 1977/14). Other times he talked about didactic analysis (Piaget 1945: 236; 1965: 247; 1977/14; Piaget and Bringuier 1977: 182), then again he claimed that it had not been an analysis at all but had simply been propaganda to spread the Freudian theory further (Piaget and Bringuier 1977: 183; Piaget 1979/10). At the same time he confirms his enthusiasm in his therapy: "Well, everything I saw in it was interesting. It was marvellous to discover all one's complexes" (Piaget and Bringuier 1977: 182). It is probable that the various statements refer to two different therapies. One was with Ms De La Fuente, in which the treatment of his complexes was the main concern and which was cut short by Piaget. The other would have been a study analysis started with Spielrein, which she broke off when a controversy occurred because of a question of interpretation.

Piaget was not the only member of the JJRI to be analyzed by Spielrein. Henri Flournoy, Bovet and Claparède also found themselves upon her couch (Schepeler 1993: 257; Richebächer 2005: 230). The Geneva psychoanalytic group "took a new upswing because she analysed us, that is, some of us, regularly, according to Freud's rules" (Bovet 1932: 101). Spielrein, however, did not only dispense therapy. In fact, Freud expected her to convince the mutinous Genevans of his teaching. On 12 June 1922, he wrote to her:

> The people of Geneva are each and every one of them dilettantes to whom you must gradually transmit something of your analytical training. Claparède himself is no exception [...] The same people are also so exclusively jealous of their independence, and so insusceptible to advice from afar, that to this day they have not even joined the Psychoanalytic Organisation.[1] (Cited in Schepeler 1993: 260)

With respect to her mission, Bovet described Spielrein after her arrival in Geneva "like a newly appointed governor in his province, like a newly nominated bishop in his diocese" (Bovet 1932: 101). For the same reason, Piaget claimed that her analysis was only a matter of propaganda. Still in the same year, Spielrein got into an argument with the Genevans and turned to Freud for support. He agreed with her interpretation of theoretical questions but was not prepared to travel to Geneva to discuss these matters (Vidal 2001).

As representatives from Geneva, Piaget and Spielrein attended the VII International Psychoanalytical Congress in Berlin from 25 to 27 September 1922, where each delivered a lecture. "I knew Freud at the 1922 Congress of Psychoanalysis in Berlin. I gave a lecture at this Congress and I remember the anxiety I felt as a lecturer in front of a large audience" (Piaget 1973: 3). Piaget's fear was more likely due to the fact that he diverged from the Freudian theory and expected contention. With his lecture *Symbolic or Visualized Thinking and the Child's Thinking*,[2] Piaget wanted to increase the scope of psychoanalysis by incorporating Claparède's functional psychology and Janet's constructivist psychology, by demonstrating their parallels. Piaget criticized the fact that Freud understood symbolic thinking and logical thinking as opposites, whereas he believed that symbolic thinking was an early stage of logical thinking because the phenomena of displacement and condensation showed the first indications of generalization and abstraction. "Symbolic thinking is a more primitive, or at least a more economical, way of thinking. Before we think in words and concepts, we think in images" (Piaget 1923/2: 86). He related the economy of preconceptual thinking to the relaxed state of consciousness during dream or play. Because of its nondirectedness and weak awareness, autistic-symbolic thinking and a child's way of thinking were analogous. Until the age of 7–8, the child follows the logic of symbolism that is "individual, independent of social life and cannot be communicated" (Piaget 1923/2: 104). This intellectual narcissism will dissolve once thinking is socialized. "This type of thinking, this intermediate stage between integral autism of non-communicative dreaming and the social type of adult intelligence, could be termed 'egocentrism'" (Piaget 1923/2: 105). Spontaneity, fancifulness, magic, visualization, a lack of self-awareness, accompanied by total self-centeredness and a lack of causality are the characteristics of a child's way of thinking. "Before the child adjusts to things, he will adjust things to himself and to his desires [and this] is the most spontaneous way of thinking" (Piaget 1923/2: 142). With his reference to the energetic model, Piaget adhered much more closely to Janet than to Freud, who had no intention of surrendering his monopoly of interpretation to the young Swiss.

> Freud was seated to my right in an armchair smoking his cigars, and I was addressing the public, but the public never glanced at their lecturer. They looked only at Freud, to find out whether or not he was happy with what was being said. When Freud smiled, everybody in the room smiled, when Freud looked serious, everybody in the room looked serious. (Piaget 1973: 3)

After Piaget's lecture, a number of talks on important theoretical topics followed and, as a result, his contribution waned in significance.

In addition to the financial constrictions, the ongoing theoretical differences between Vienna and Geneva contributed to Spielrein's resignation in the early summer of 1923, when she complained about the hostility towards her (in Richebächer 2005: 236), although Piaget maintained: "There have never been any conflicts here between psychoanalysis and the 'official psychology" (Piaget 1944/3: 100). Their planned joint book (cf. Piaget 1923/2: 110) on the origin of symbolic thinking was never written, because Spielrein returned to Russia.[3]

After this, Piaget occupied himself rather less with psychoanalysis. Robert Jéquier, a young theologian who wrote the dissertation for his PhD at the JJRI, was analyzed by Piaget on a daily basis for two months during 1924. In accordance with the Freudian idea of the therapist's role (cf. Piaget 1923/3: 73), Piaget never gave a single interpretation and Jéquier commented: "He was not born a psychoanalyst, he was doing this out of interest" (in Vidal 1986: 186). Piaget also tried to analyze his mother. His sister Marthe, who was married to Daniel Burger, Piaget's friend from boyhood days, was analyzed by Piaget's colleague Raymond de Saussure and became a psychoanalyst, too. She reported that this attempt ended abruptly because their mother did not accept Piaget's interpretation. Her brother, who in this case had obviously not adhered to the rule of passivity, "was strongly affected by this failure" (in Vidal 1986: 189). In 1927 he asked the friend of the family Paul Pettavel to convince his mother of her need for psychiatric hospital care (Thomann 1996: 119).

On 25 February 1924 Piaget lectured on symbolic thinking at the JJRI and sounded a strong warning against carelessly undertaken psychoanalysis. He felt that one needed to be almost a

Superman [...] to practise psychoanalysis. One has to be very careful in the choice of one's analyst, because analysis can, in certain cases, be very dangerous. Sometimes, the deepest roots of our selves must stay in darkness, since bringing the subconscious into the open can have disastrous consequences if the subconscious did not have enough time to work through one's indispensable experiences, which are nourishment for the soul. Useful sowing can only be done with a well-equipped subconscious. (Piaget 1924/9)

In a letter to Bovet, Spielrein remarked that psychoanalysis did not deprive one of one's personality, as shown by the example of Piaget, who remained mystical, despite his analysis (in Richebächer 2005: 233).

In his autobiography, Piaget reduced his involvement with psychoanalysis to a matter of interest on account of his mother's problems. "I have never since felt any desire to involve myself deeper in that particular direction, always preferring the study of normalcy and of the working of the intellect to that of the tricks of the unconscious" (Piaget 1952/1: 107). And "I am interested in the general features of the development of intelligence and knowledge" (Piaget and Bringuier 1977: 133f.). His fear of getting in touch with the unconscious, as well as his interest in general features, would offer an insufficient explanation for the end of his career as a psychoanalyst and would gloss over Piaget's failure in psychoanalytical practice. Yet, as far as the theory was concerned, Piaget displayed a continued interest in psychoanalysis. "Freud's work contains a number of other valuable discoveries [. . .] I even think that we shall have to retain the main points of the Freudian descriptions" (Piaget 1954/12: 56). At a later date he even felt "convinced that the psychology of cognitive functions and psychoanalysis will one day be compelled to fuse into one general theory" (Piaget 1971/8: 31).

Religious Psychology

In August 1921, Piaget published a paper in which he demonstrated his loyalty to the Protestant tradition of Romandy and his approval of Pierre Bovet's religious-psychological work. Piaget's most important mentor was a neo-Kantian whose psychological research focused mainly upon the emergence of moral obligation and religious sentiments. Bovet (1920) saw the origin of religious sentiments in a child's love, first for his mother and then his father. At the same time, he presupposed that children, in order to overcome their fears, explain the mysterious world in animist concepts, whereby they attribute infallible qualities, such as omnipotence and omniscience, to their parents. Educators, he felt, should foster the existent core of religious sentiments by supporting the child's spontaneous reality. At the age of five or six, the child discovers the truth about parental power, which causes an intellectual and moral crisis. The child therefore transfers his feelings, his experiences and his need for an absolute onto the Heavenly Father. With education and increasing reason, the search for a moral and spiritual life brings the child from loving his parents to loving Christ. For Bovet, only a religious person could be a good educator.

"What is the secret motive of Geneva's effort to apply psychological methods to education [. . .] if not the moral and consequently religious motive?" Piaget asked (1921/3: 410). The specific aspect to liberal Protestantism, to Piaget, was the convergence of a psychological and a philosophical outlook. The psychological tradition was represented by Flournoy and Bovet and the logical tradition by Reymond. The former confirmed the subjective and concrete values of faith, and the latter demonstrated the objective characteristics of Protestantism, which were contained in the recognition of moral values and in the believer's decision for these values. With his statement that this insight of Reymond "should be our moral and intellectual catechism" (Piaget 1921/3: 412), Piaget obviously tried to appease him. To Piaget, the history of ideas was a process of objectification whereby "individual thought subjects itself to a simultaneously logical and moral norm that transcends it, and which is for the logician the true object of religious experience" (Piaget 1921/3: 412). Because the "subjective factors [...] depend on the laws of objective thinking" (Piaget 1921/3: 412), the gap between science and religion could be bridged by reconciling Reymond's logical and historical-critical method with Bovet's and Claparède's functional and genetic method. The fusing of logical and psychological analyses would have remarkable religious consequences: "The act of faith remains, but it becomes rational, it invokes a God who becomes more and more identical with the world itself, that is to say identical with reason and its categories, within one's experience" (Piaget 1921/3: 410).

This argumentation followed closely his teacher Léon Brunschvicg who described the history of thinking as the gradual development towards immanence. Thinking takes place in acts of judgment that synthesize the forms and contents of one's thinking with one's experience. As judgments are fundamentally relative, philosophy, as a reflection of the sciences, is unable to recognize any higher truth. But in the same degree as one's judgments are purged from egocentrism, the human subject becomes universal and his spirit approaches closer to religious truth, because God is the universal reason. Bergson had effected Piaget's detachment from a transcendent concept of God and had led him towards a quasi-immanent one: God as a superior external force, yet immanent within life. Now Bergson's pupil Brunschvicg placed God definitively deep inside human thinking. "God is within the judgment, or better still, He is the inwardness to which each reasonable judgment bears witness" (Brunschvicg 1897: 238). Scientific research, philosophical justification, moral judgment and religious thinking were therefore inseparable.

Shortly after he started working at the JJRI, Piaget got together a group of ACSE members in order to investigate the question of whether certain religious experiences were superior to others and what criteria might justify faith. Bovet, as a former director of the ACSE, encouraged Piaget's religious-psychological research projects. On 12 October 1922, Piaget held a talk on "psychology and religious values" at the ACSE meeting in Sainte-Croix and proclaimed: "Broadly speaking, the problem of science and religion can be considered solved" (Piaget 1923/3: 38). Like Flournoy, he made a strict distinction between judgments based on science and judgments based on values. Faith as a value judgment "allows us to speak of a God as an absolute value and to live religiously" (Piaget 1923/3: 39f.). For science, different concepts of God are equally true "as individual symbols of a unique ineffable reality" (Piaget 1923/3: 48), because science cannot legitimize the values. Yet he felt that it was possible to identify the superiority of certain values over others: "From an empirical point of view, and only relative to individual psychological development, one religious type is more evolved than another, and therefore superior" (Piaget 1923/3: 49). The criterion of superiority was consistency, which Goblot (1918: 141) defined as the reversibility of the act of thinking. Piaget termed this reversibility as "logical experience" (Piaget 1923/3: 60) and drew a parallel with the term of "moral experience" coined by Frédéric Rauh (1861–1909). Moral consistency means "faithfulness [...] towards oneself [...], the condition of having a good intellectual consciousness by being and remaining coherent" (Piaget 1923/3: 61). This "law of psychological equilibrium" (Piaget 1923/3: 78) causes the value rating: As an affective value's potential to create other values increases, so does the value increase; love, therefore, is the highest value.

In his papers on developmental psychology, Piaget identified the principle of consistency as a necessary immanent and biological function. He explained development as a process of "purging: The child arrives at adult logic through the long and painstaking acquisition of consistent thinking" (Piaget 1923/3: 77). With this, Piaget reversed Kant: While Kant with his *Critique of Pure Reason* (1781) attempted to investigate the yet unsoiled reason, in its virgin state, Piaget, with his developmental psychology, showed reason a way out of its original sin, of autism and egocentrism, towards pure objectivity.

The Heritage of Child Psychology

Piaget's third article on child psychology bore witness to the change in his theoretical understanding. After having read Théodore Ruyssen (1868–1967), who stressed the continuity of action and judgment, Piaget's psychology of the stages of consciousness gave way to a dynamic theory of acts of thinking. "As Ruyssen clearly demonstrated, a judgment, seen from a genetic view, is an adaptation" (Piaget 1922/1: 260). Piaget replaced the implicit stage of the cognitive development by the "nonreflected stage," in which the child keeps confusing fantasy and reality. In the explicit stage of "formal reflection," the young adolescent, on the other hand, can distinguish between "at least three distinct levels: the level of formal necessity, the level of pure possibility [...] and the level of reality" (Piaget 1922/1: 252).

In his first four years at the JJRI, Piaget, together with his assistants and students, examined the way children expressed and explained themselves. "Despite himself, and without realizing it, Piaget becomes a young street urchin: he is his test pupil's mate, his questions seem like an exchange of confidences, as if two school boys were chatting to each other as equals" (Bovet 1932: 76f.). This method of interviewing children was not new but Piaget dispensed with the measuring techniques hitherto employed and used a rather open interview technique instead. The founders of the psychology of thinking, Oskar Külpe (1862–1915) and Narziss Ach (1871–1946), had already recognized the limitations of laboratory examinations, where people could only be observed in isolation instead of in their interaction with others. Piaget radicalized child-psychological research by concentrating on the logical errors in the explanations the children gave and by treating them like intellectuals.

> Piaget became famous because of his surprising explanation of something most people had noticed but had treated as of no particular interest. Countless generations before him had observed that young children commonly held peculiar false beliefs. Piaget's genius was in pointing out that these false beliefs were not things children learn from nature, [...] nor from their parents or other adults [...], nor were these false beliefs random, [but] a key that allowed Piaget to unlock the door to the underlying process of the mind's development. (Egan 2002: 101)

But the fundamental logic of the child's mental development had been investigated, and Piaget examined prior research.

A demand for scientific knowledge about children's perceptions and thinking had arisen due to the expansion of the state school systems in the nineteenth century. Research into the development of the "normal" child became a scientific domain around 1870 (Ottavi 2001). Franz Brentano (1838–1917), Hippolyte Taine (1828–1893), George John Romanes (1848–1894), Bernard Pérez (1836–1903), Wilhelm Thierry Preyer (1841–1897), James Sully (1842–1923) and Théodule Ribot (1839–1916) were the most important pioneers and representatives of this kind of research to have an influence upon Piaget. Brentano coined the expression "intentional inexistence," which meant that an object serves as an external reference to an actively formed representation. A sound, for example, is both an external noise and an internal experience. Taine, in his research into the origin of language, came to the conclusion that intelligence develops autonomously through spontaneous changes. Romanes postulated the existence of prelanguage thinking, which consists of "percepts" (singular ideas derived from perception) and "recepts" (ideas derived from repeated experience). Consciousness develops through experiences in action because the child experiences himself as an active being. Pérez demonstrated the way in which the different skills are the results of previous and continual development processes. Preyer described the transition from seeing an object to watching it as a process of accommodation. The child coordinates the data received from different senses, thus developing self-confidence, since motor and intellectual development run parallel. Having observed his own son, Preyer concluded that logic, not language, was the key to man's intellectual superiority.

The child learns in playful confrontation with the world, according to a form of dialectic of spontaneity and experience. Karl Groos (1861–1946) wrote a theory on the biological and psychological significance of play involving hunting, fighting, imitation and eroticism as training for the mastering of one's environment. According to this, man is simply a further developed animal, largely freed from instincts, which is why human childhood lasts longer. Sully was interested in the processes of the *self-taught* and in spontaneous child development, which, in his view, reflected earlier stages of evolution. Since thinking in images preceded thinking in language, games and art expressed the original imaginative thinking. Georges-Henri Luquet (1876–1965) took these analyses further: when children draw objects, they draw less of what they see and more of what they know, which he termed "intellectual realism." Ribot understood concepts such as numbers as abstract creations of an active mind, which developed in different stages. He considered reflexes, instincts, memory, imagination, feelings and intelligence as a combined unit of psychological life.

According to James Mark Baldwin (1861–1934), the child is the producer of his own progress. The core of his work, to which Piaget was introduced by Janet, deals with the issue of the connection between the evolution of mental skills and the progress of civilization. An individual's survival chances are determined by how well this individual adapts to his environment and not by hereditary features. Baldwin, by observing his daughter Elisabeth, found that ontogenetic adaptation occurs largely through learning the knowledge of the parents' generation. Thinking does not mirror reality but results from action. To Piaget, Baldwin's theory of genetic logic was an "ingenious train of thought" (Piaget 1926: 44) and he understood the genetic method as an alternative to the causality explanation (Piaget 1924: 201). Granville Stanley Hall (1846–1924) used questioning methods for his child studies in order to research child development and he believed that detailed knowledge about this development was a prerequisite of effective education. Although he rejected the recapitulation theory, according to which the child repeats genetic-historic experiences, he described many parallels between the child's behavior and a presumed primeval behavior, such as children enjoying climbing, which he considered an inheritance from apes. Since adults had no such needs, this evolution-psychological perspective supported his thesis that children were fundamentally different. American, as well as British and German experimental pedagogy, constructed an entire network of child psychology laboratories in accordance with Hall's model (Depaepe 1993). Numerous scientific associations and research centers, congresses and journals were established but gradually lost ground in Europe during World War I. Piaget was further influenced by Clara Stern's (1878–1945) work *Children's Language* (1907) and the much-noted standard work *Psychology of Early Childhood* (1914), which she wrote together with her husband, William Stern (1871–1938) and which was based on observations of their three children, Hilde, Eva, and Günther (Anders 1902–1992). Further stimulation came from the works of Charlotte Bühler (1893–1974) and her husband, Karl Bühler (1879–1963), for instance through their book *The Mental Development of the Child* (1918).

The main part of the findings that Piaget studied was the research done at the JJRI. Bovet, for example, had interviewed 8- to 12-year-olds about their fights as part of his research into the fighting instinct. He classified the answers into two groups, which "marked two very different stages in the development of aggression: single combat is primitive, but this is not the case for a battle fought by a legal and organised army [. . .] There is a transition from single combat to military battles" (Bovet 1917: 15). Piaget adopted this type of research as well as many fundamental concepts from other researchers at the institute. "He fitted in from the first day, and [. . .] his arrival had caused no revolution but simply caused everything we ever wanted or had already achieved, to flourish" (Bovet 1932: 76).

The Egocentric Child

In his first child-psychological monographs, Piaget saw egocentrism as the central characteristic of a child's thinking. Karl Bühler was the first to use this term in child psychology and observed "that the child considers all events to be directed at, and meant for, himself and his needs" (Bühler 1918: 307). Piaget described a child's activities as "doubtlessly egocentric and egotistic. Clear forms of social instinct will develop quite late" (Piaget 1924: 209). Piaget adopted this idea from André Lalande, who thought of man as a dual being: biologically, man is subject to the differentiating principle of evolution; mentally he follows the homogenizing principle of involution. Mental development veers towards identity and follows a tendency "towards assimilation and dissolution of one's egocentrism" (Lalande 1899: 364). Adaptation is effected through mutual assimilation on the part of the subject and the objects, whereby the individual suppresses his desires against the "egotism to which his biological nature drives him" (Lalande 1899: 142).

As for Piaget too, the egocentric character is rooted in the child's nature, "there is no sustained social life among children of less than 7 or 8" (Piaget 1923: 58). Unlike Bleuler (1912: 28), who considered it realistic that an infant would want to satisfy his needs, Piaget (1924/2: 50f.) subscribed to Freud's theory of early childhood narcissism, according to which the principle of enjoyment was the ontogenetic primary issue and the reality principle was the secondary issue. Piaget saw the proof for a young infant's lack of sociality in his inability to communicate and to adapt: "Autistic thinking [...] remains strictly individual and cannot be communicated through language. This kind of thinking usually proceeds in images" (Piaget 1923: 50). Until the age of 2 or 3, thinking is magical and closely related to dreams. "For each desire, there is a directly corresponding image or illusion, which transforms the desire into reality, thanks to a kind of pseudo-hallucination or game" (Piaget 1927: 329). When the child learns to speak, his verbal expressions demonstrate the egocentric limitation to his needs. The development of egocentric language starts with an echolalia of sounds heard and the repetition of sounds the child creates for the sheer joy of speaking. Then "the child talks to himself as though he were thinking aloud. He does not address to anyone" (Piaget 1923: 19). While language among adults has the function of communicating observations and aspects of thought, of arousing feelings or instigating action, a child's language lacks this communicative function, because "he does not bother to know to whom he is speaking, nor whether he is being listened to. He talks either for his own sake or for the pleasure of associating anyone who happens to be present in the activity of the moment" (Piaget 1923: 18f.). In the paradoxically termed "collective monologue," the child formally talks to others without, however, wishing to communicate anything. This feature dominates the child's utterances until around the age of five (Piaget 1923: 81). Piaget's empirical studies demonstrated that "between the ages of 5 and 7, 44–47 per cent of a child's spontaneous utterances are egocentric, although these children are perfectly able to work, play and speak, according to their own desires. Between ages 3 and 5, we calculated a percentage of 54–60 per cent" (Piaget 1924: 206).

When children relate stories they have heard, they act as if the listener possessed the same information as they themselves possess. Piaget therefore understood egocentrism "in an intellectual, not in an ethical sense" (Piaget 1923: 20) and felt that "throughout the time he is learning to speak, the child is constantly the victim of confusion between his own point of view and that of other people" (Piaget 1923: 28). Piaget concluded that the child's way of thinking occupies a place situated between the autistic and the social, which are "two fundamentally different ways of thinking" (Piaget 1923: 61). Since the two have different origins, he postulated a dualistic concept: The child "according to his stage of egocentrism or socialization, finds himself facing two equally real worlds, and none of these worlds manages to supplant the other" (Piaget 1924: 240). Egocentrism is strongly imbued with autism, because "when we think egocentrically, we let our fantasy flow freely. When we think socially, we are much more inclined to subject ourselves to the 'imperative of truth'" (Piaget 1923: 166).

For Piaget, egocentrism manifests in syncretistic, subjective, transductive, realistic, animist, artificialist and finalist thinking, thus hindering an adequate reality-orientation. "Until the age of around $7\frac{1}{2}$, the entire thinking of the child is shaped by the consequences of egocentrism, and, in particular, of syncretism" (Piaget 1923: 160f). Claparède had noticed that his son perceived images and shapes in a confused and global way, what he called syncretism. The religious scientist Ernest Renan (1823–1892) had used this term to characterize the nonreflected level of spiritual development, where several phenomena are mixed up. Syncretism is based on inappropriate implication, whereby several different meanings melt into one concept, which would correspond to Janet's "lack of synthesis." Piaget examined syncretism by asking children to link sayings to their respective meanings. Mat (10 years old) matched the saying "He went to the well once too often" to "*As we get older we get wiser*" (Piaget 1923: 184). He only focused on one random element (long period of time) and made it the common reference, disregarding the overall meaning of these sentences. Roger Cousinet (1881–1973) termed this phenomenon "immediate analogy," and William Stern denoted such erroneous logical coordination as "transduction." Thus To $(7;6)$[4] stated that small ships floated because they were light, and big ships floated because they were heavy (Piaget 1924: 173f.). Children do not generalize their experiences in a systematic way (induction) and do not explain them through rules (deduction). Instead, they draw transductive conclusions from one individual case and apply it to the next. "Given situations, therefore, are not enough to lead the mind to their verification, since these situations themselves are shaped by the mind. Moreover, a child never really establishes a connection with these situations, because a child does not do any work" (Piaget 1924: 204). The child is incapable of synthesis, because the parts or elements are left without connection (parataxis), as in a drawing of a bicycle, where the chain is not connected to the wheels.

Brunschvicg (1900: I) had observed that children regularly forget to count themselves when they are asked to divide a cake equally, to share with a group. Many children cannot grasp the idea that they are brother or sister to their siblings (Piaget 1924: 87ff., 113ff.). They find it difficult to determine left and right for a person who is facing them (Piaget 1924: 116ff.) or they deny that one can be Swiss and Genevan at the same time (Piaget 1924: 127ff.). The child

does not realize that a brother must necessarily be the brother of somebody, that an object must necessarily be to the right or left of somebody, or that a part must necessarily belong to a whole, but thinks of all these notions as existing by themselves, absolutely [. . .] because he fails to grasp the *reciprocity* existing between different points of view. (Piaget 1924: 138, 141)

Piaget saw the main reason for this in a lack of differentiation between subject and object, a phenomenon which Baldwin termed "adualism." This mixing of subjective and objective, as well as material and immaterial (Piaget 1926: 44ff), is "simply due to the child's inability to conceive the dualism of inner and outer" (Piaget 1931/1: 379). The differentiation starts when the baby realizes that his body obeys him, in opposition to the things that can only be manipulated indirectly. For a child, as Sully and Gabriel Compayré (1843–1913) had discovered, not only the things of nature but also dreams, mental images, thoughts, feelings and names have objective reality. Fert (7;0), for example, thought that names were a natural part of the objects by this name: "Where is the sun's name?—In it.—In what?—Inside, in the sun" (Piaget 1926: 77). The child does not yet realize that names are the result of an arbitrary act. "Zwa (9;6).—What was there first, things or the names of things?—The things.—Did the sun exist before it had a name?—No. Why not?—Because one would not have known what to call it.—Did the sun exist before God gave it a name?—No, because the sun would not have known what it should come from" (Piaget 1926: 71). Furthermore, children do not realize that dreams or feelings are something they produce themselves. They think, for example, that dreams come "from the blanket", "from the night" or "from the room" (Piaget 1926: 93ff.). A child's "realism" means a lack of differentiation between sign and thing and between matter and thought. After the age of 2–3, in which the principle of enjoyment dominates, the child begins to live in a dual reality: the world of games and the observed world are equally real. From 7–8 years of age, a hierarchy of these two worlds begins to form, with the categories of the possible and the necessary, which will be finalized by the age of formal thinking, at around 11–12. The degree of the dominance of the reality principle corresponds to the degree of objectivity, which is dependent on the socialization of thinking.

Several researchers, such as Stanley Hall, Sully or Vilhelm Rasmussen (1869–1939), observed that children attribute consciousness and willpower not only to human beings but also to animals, things and natural phenomena. This animism initially includes each object that appears to be active in some way. Later it includes only those objects that move on their own. Water, for example, can feel something, because "when the wind blows there will be waves" (Piaget 1926: 167). In addition, children believe that things have moral obligations: "Ros (9;9): Does the sun do what it wants?—*Yes.*—Can it move faster if it wants?—*Yes.*—Can it stand still?—*No.*—Why not?—*Because then it would have to shine for quite a long time.*—Why?—*To keep us warm*" (Piaget 1926: 203). This finalism is typical because children equate physical causality with psychological intention. If the child explains the movement of the sun with reference to his own behavior, then we are dealing with participation, as the ethnologist Lucien Lévy-Bruhl (1857–1939) described the erroneous connection between two phenomena or actors. In primitive thinking, "objects, beings, phenomena, [...] emit and receive forces [...], which make themselves felt at a distance without having to change location" (Lévy-Bruhl 1910: 77). For Nain (4;6), the moon "goes with me, it follows us" (Piaget 1926: 138). Magical practices may result from this belief in a relationship between two phenomena: A child who dearly wishes for something to happen, would, for instance, step only on every alternate slab on a path. If he succeeds in doing this until he reaches the end of the path, then this will be a sign that his wish will come true. Piaget described his own logic of participation in his search for mollusks:

> When he was looking for a specific rare species and happened to find a different interesting species, he concluded from this that he would also find the desired species, or vice versa, as may be the case. This was in no way based on similar habitats for the two species, but was based purely on an occult connection: A certain unexpected discovery must be followed by another in the course of the day. (Piaget 1926: 135)

Such connections even contained moral aspects because "on a day when he reproached himself for something, he felt that the poor results of his search were due to his prior mistakes" (Piaget 1932: 295).

Brunschvicg termed "artificialist" the children's belief that everything in the world was made by beings or forces, according to human ways of production: "How did the sun start?—*With fire.*—Where did the fire come from?—*From a match* [...] *God threw the match away*" (Piaget 1926: 231). For Piaget, artificialism was proof of a child's spontaneous transcendence in his thinking, which "is totally shaped by the relationship the child had with his parents beforehand" (Piaget 1929/4: 149). A child's natural development progresses, like religious history, from transcendence to immanence, unless religious education disturbs this development through dogmatic ideas. Piaget therefore felt that agnosticism was not an insight into the borders of knowledge, but a pathological phenomenon of sublimation, which "temporarily takes the place of overly daring cosmologies" (Piaget 1926: 248). Death plays a decisive role in the course of the development of any reasonably sensible cosmology.

> Because a 6–7 year old child has not yet integrated any theological concept into his mentality, death appears to him as the most arbitrary and secretive phenomenon of all. Among all the questions about plants, animals and the human body, those questions which concern death are therefore the ones which will lead the child beyond the stage of pure finalism and will help him to acquire the concept of static causality or coincidence. (Piaget 1923: 205)

The main mechanism in overcoming childlike logic is the grasp of consciousness (in this case becoming conscious of the fact that death is coincidental). Following Claparède, Piaget understood consciousness as a biological function within the process of adaptation. At the same time, he recognized a social compulsion to correct one's wrong interpretation of the world:

> What then gives rise to the need for verification? Surely it must be the shock of our thought coming into contact with that of others, which produces doubt and the desire to prove [...] Proof is the outcome of argument [...] Logical reasoning is an argument which we have with ourselves and which internally reproduces the features of a real argument. (Piaget 1924: 204)

Thus joining Janet and Charles Blondel (1867–1939), Piaget paralleled the disappearance of egocentrism with an increase of social and reflective skills. In this process of decentration, the child acquires distance from his immediate action, experience and knowledge and becomes aware of other points of view. After the age of 7–8, perception and logic become more analytical and objective. "But on the verbal plane [...] the old difficulties survive and even reappear in new form" (Piaget 1924: 228).

For the first time, Piaget separated the logic of action from the logic of thought, stating that a young child possessed "logic of action but as yet no logic of thought" (Piaget 1924: 212). Children often manage to solve a problem but are unable to explain the method by which they solved it: "Weng (7;0): This table is 4 metres long. This one is three times as long. How many metres is it?—*12 metres.*—How did you do that?—*I added 2 and 2 and 2 and 2 and 2 and 2, always 2.*—Why 2?—*So as to make 12*" (Piaget 1924: 146). The logical justification of a judgment takes place at a higher level than the actual judgment. In order to justify one's judgment, "introspection" is required, in which one has to reflect on one's own operations. Until the age of 7–8, the transfer of an action to the plane of language is impossible. Piaget saw these two levels connected through an analogous rhythm, as he found that intelligence did not develop steadily, but in stages.

Piaget regarded egocentric thinking as a psychological disequilibrium because of its contradictions. Coherent acts of thinking need fixed points to oppose the irreversible stream of consciousness. These points are concepts and relationships that are independent of time and fit together. Operations based on such points are reversible, like division is the reverse of multiplication. They become possible due to two mechanisms "whose interaction regulates precisely this reversibility; these are *imitation* of the real through the organism or through thought, and *assimilation* of the real to the organism or to thought" (Piaget 1924: 177). Imitation, in the form of physical or mental repetition, results in adaptation to the environment. "Biologically and psychologically, assimilation means to reproduce oneself with the help of the outside world, it means to change one's perception until it becomes identical with one's thinking, i.e. with previous schemata" (Piaget 1924: 178).

Schemata are the patterns according to which cognitive processes occur. Kant introduced the concept of schemata as a link between the sensuousness and reason. "In fact, our purely sensory concepts are not based upon images of objects, but upon schemata" (Kant 1781/87: B 180). Piaget's teacher, Lalande, identified such general concepts, which are neither words nor images, as "operative schemata of understanding" (Lalande 1893: 27). They simplify objects of a different kind into objects of the same kind (e.g. those things you can throw, those you can hammer with, or those you can multiply, etc.). Schemata transform the perceived objects and are transformed by adaptation to them. These two processes of assimilation and imitation cannot be identical, since one would get caught in the vicious circle of having to explain the consistency through itself (Piaget 1924: 182). In the primitive stages, before these two complementary mechanisms are coordinated, reversibility of logical thinking is not possible, because confusion occurs instead of synthesis.

Piaget distinguished two forms of experience: Mental experience is "the construction of reality and the awareness of this reality" (Piaget 1924: 233), and logical experience means "awareness and ordering of the actual mechanism of the construction" (Piaget 1924: 233). This latter experience queries the first one, and thereby queries itself. "The necessity resulting from mental experience is a necessity of facts; that which results from logical experience is due to the implications existing between the various operations; it is a moral necessity due to the obligation of remaining true to oneself" (Piaget 1924: 233). Once the mechanisms of imitation and assimilation are coordinated in equilibrium, they will manifest themselves in precise and conscious value judgments and in a rational interpretation of the world.

But the socialization of thinking that enables relativity, reciprocity and objectivity, depends upon language, which supports egocentric thinking.

It is on a verbal level where the child makes his principal effort in adapting to adult thinking and in learning logical thinking. Because the child partially perceives the world through his verbal thinking and not directly through his senses, the verbal level permeates his entire idea of things. (Piaget 1924/2: 56)

The language we teach a child is certainly not only a system of signs. It is above all a system of concepts, of implicit judgements. It represents a kind of crystallized thinking and impersonal thinking that has been transmitted from previous generations. An infinitely tyrannical thinking, weighing heavily on every state of individual consciousness, no matter how intimate this may be. (Piaget 1925/5: 204f.)

If language is mainly a system of constraints and if children's conversations are "hardly more than an egocentric soliloquy" (Piaget 1923/2: 106), then socialization is a delicate process. Not everyone, therefore, will reach the level of objectivity and reciprocity: "There are adults whose way of thinking has remained egocentric. These are people who build an imaginary or mysterious world between themselves and the reality, and who relate everything to their individual point of view" (Piaget 1924/2: 57). Further complications occur if children dwell in cities: "In the country, artificialist explanations disappear much earlier, of course" (Piaget 1926: 270). Nonetheless, Piaget was certain that a child's way of thinking was completely different from adult's logic:

Rousseau had already repeatedly maintained that a child was not a small adult but had his own needs and a mentality that befitted his needs [...] The child has a coherent way of thinking *sui generis*. Otherwise a child's logic could simply be regarded as being stained with sophisms, caused by random incidences of non-adaptation. (Piaget 1924/2: 48f)

Causality as a Construct and as Reality

Piaget was confronted with the question whether mental development is a contingent process or not, when he studied Brunschvicg's *Human Experience and Physical Causality*. This Neo-Kantian philosopher based his epistemology on "the necessary connection, the reciprocity, between reason and experience" (Brunschvicg 1922: 309). Reason guides experience, which in turn adjusts reason to reality. There is no direct access to reality because experience is not a copy of reality but a construction. "True reality, therefore, is the interaction of reason which puts things in order, and of a reality which adapts to reason" (Piaget 1924/3: 88). This adaptation is never final and requires constant correction, so that we end up constructing a system of causal relations. Suddenly, Piaget saw a new option to make his wish come true for a unifying theory of human behavior, which would embrace man's intelligence, affectivity, morality and sociability. Brunschvicg's book "compels you to revise your values and to re-adapt your principles" (Piaget

1924/1: 587). His concepts of perception, numbers, time, as well as his theory of reflecting abstractions were indeed deeply influenced by this work.

Piaget did, however, struggle to combine Brunschvicg's theory of reason as the organizer of reality with his other favorites. Baldwin understood his genetic psychology as a positive science and therefore considered reason as subject to environmental influences. In order to reconcile these two approaches, Piaget settled for "openly accepting a circle. [Scientific] laws become, in one sense, constitutive for the real, but in another sense, they are contained in the real" (Piaget 1924/1: 605f.). If we start from the premise that "the laws of thinking derive from the laws of organic life itself" (Piaget 1924/1: 606), therefore from the laws of reality we will find continuity in the development of the different levels. "Thus, there is no circle but a spiral development" (Piaget 1924/1: 607). Although Piaget "believed to accept completely" (Piaget 1924/1: 594) Brunschvicg's relativist position, he never abandoned his realist base. He tried to link constructivist idealism to a positivist epistemology by claiming that "relativity has not abolished objectivity in physics" (Piaget 1932/1: 66). Because of the parallel of the real world and its cognitive construction, Piaget postulated "two kinds of egocentricity, a logical and an ontological egocentricity. In the same way as the child creates his truth, he also creates his reality" (Piaget 1926: 21).

In order to avoid the contingency of mental development, Piaget suggested the concept of "orthogenesis." Baldwin named the hypotheses and theories organisms construct with regard to the world "orthoplasia": "All the influences, which support animal adaptations and accommodations, are combined in one resulting effect to give a determined orientation to the course of evolution. We call this *orienting* influence *orthoplasia*" (Baldwin 1894: 41). Piaget combined this idea with Lalande's distinction between two kinds of reason. While the "constituted reason" is variable and historically distinguishable, there is an evolutionary principle behind it, the "constituting reason," which manifests itself in "characteristic value judgements of certain psychological equilibria" (Piaget 1924/1: 605). According to Piaget, the ontogenesis of the openly visible reason can be proved in experiments but the orthogenesis of the concealed reason can only be deducted through logic. Piaget always tried to trace the cognitive development back to a determinated substructure.

After his intensive study of Brunschvicg, Piaget formulated the features of a child's thinking anew within the categories of causality, which had already been an important topic in his first two monographs. In *The Child's Conception of Physical Causality* Piaget and his co-workers differentiated between 17 forms of causality. After the autistic phase (up to age 2–3), children's explanations are of a psychological, phenomenological, finalist, participialist, magical or moral nature. The psychological causality refers to motivation and is "the most primitive, but [...] also the one that survives the longest" (Piaget 1927: 292). The phenomenalist explanation designates a relation of contiguity and is "essentially unstable" (Piaget 1927: 193). In the second phase, the egocentric phase, animist, artificialist and dynamical explanations are added. In the dynamical concept of force, for example, "we attribute forces to things via a transfer" (Piaget 1927: 146). In the third phase, from age 7–8, these precausal explanations gradually disappear in favour of more realistic reasoning. "The explanation of the surrounding medium" is an extension of dynamism, for instance when air is said to support the movement of clouds (Piaget 1927: 75). The elimination of dynamism begins with mechanical explanations and continues with "causality by generation." This explanation supposes a transformation of substances. Piaget also includes "substantial identification," "condensation and rarefaction," "atomistic composition" and "spatial explanation" among causal explanations. The last type of "objective causality" is an adequate explanation in the form of a logical deduction, a stage that will be reached by the age of 11–12.

This development follows a course from transcendental physics to mechanist laws immanent in the cosmos. The better a child understands the laws of nature, the weaker his moral explanations of natural phenomena will become. The concept of natural law, however, remains dominated by social connotations for a long time, which is "perhaps the outcome of the social surrounding" (Piaget 1927: 315). Considering Bovet's study, one would have to conclude that children's explanations have a social origin. "It would therefore be in the relation of the child to its parents that we should have to look for the origins of law" (Piaget 1927: 316). This, however, would bring about the collapse of Piaget's thesis of solipsistic early childhood. He therefore shifted his argument onto a biological level and explained the "paradox" of the confusion between the social and the physical as a consequence of the insufficient coordination of assimilation and imitation. If assimilation dominates, objectivity is lacking, and vice versa. Because Piaget understood assimilation as a biological mechanism (Piaget 1927: 325), the difference between the biological and the social development factors could no longer be identified. This resulted in two adventurous statements: With regard to a child's convictions, we have to "distinguish between two entirely different types. There are those which originate [...] from adults, but are not dictated, whereas the others have simply been forced onto the child, be it by the school, by his family, through conversations between adults that the child had overheard etc" (Piaget 1926: 38).

His difficulty in determining the origin of thought caused him to reform the relationship between acting and thinking. Following Alexander Bain (1818–1903), he defined thinking as "a shortcut to acting [...] one supposes schemata, preformed by action, which merge with the insights of the educational process" (Piaget 1927: 321f.). Piaget claimed that Brunschvicg had demonstrated, with the help of the history of science, that "the schema of assimilation is malleable" (Piaget 1927: 323). With acting experience and adaptive assimilation, Piaget could substantiate his epistemological position: "Experience fashions reason, and reason fashions experience" (Piaget 1927: 337). This dual base required, however, that one assumed a correspondence between logic and the real categories. Following Brunschvicg's postulation of the inseparability of matter and content, Piaget therefore defined matter as content (Piaget 1927: 318) and the schemata as the form (ibid: 319). Accordingly, he stated that there were basically

> two groups of operations: on the one hand, the operations of formal logic, which condition the very structure of reasoning, and on the other hand, what Høffding calls the "real categories" [...], notions such as causality, reality, etc [...] We hope to be able to show that there exists a parallelism between these two kinds of evolution from logical and ontological egocentrism to formal and empirical truth (Piaget 1927: 338).

This hope remained unfulfilled, although Piaget intended, for a long time, to elaborate a genetic ontology (cf. Fetz 1999: 162).

Critique and Adjustment

It was not only teachers and friends such as Delacroix, Piéron, Claparède and Meyerson, but also independent critics in France (Parrat-Dayan 1993a, 1993b), in Germany (Tryphon, Parrat-Dayan and Volkmann-Raue 1996), or in the USA (Beatty 2004) who praised the originality and accuracy of Piaget's analysis and his method of studying children "in their spontaneous activities instead of the artificially controlled set-up of a laboratory" (Mitchell 1927: 136). His research met with great interest, and he was invited to give lectures in France, Belgium, England, Holland, Scotland, the USA, Spain and Poland. Some researchers, such as the Russian pediologist Pavel Blonsky (1881–1941), repeated Piaget's experiments or adopted the clinical method. Blonsky (cited in Van der Veer 1996: 223ff.) achieved similar results with his research. He concluded, however, that the child's development was crucially influenced by the way in which he was taught at school and by his social interactions with persons to whom he relates most closely. Other reviewers, such as Murray (1931: 55), were of the opinion that Piaget had simply repeated what other researchers, such as Sully, James, Hall and Binet, had already discovered.

Most critics rejected Piaget's radical distinction between a child's and an adult's thinking and would only accept a gradual difference. Delacroix believed that "a child's way of thinking often just highlights, in an exaggerated way, certain errors in the way adults think" (Delacroix 1924: 259), an argument which Piaget accepted (Piaget 1932: x).[5] Besseige (1926) called Piaget's child a logically disabled person, which would put him beyond the reach of adults and pedagogic influence. Jean Bourjade (1927) criticized Piaget's strong emphasis on illogical elements and his neglect of the rational aspects of child thought. Blondel (1924) found that Piaget had, on the one hand, identified a continuity in the function of a child's thinking, but, on the other hand, had identified a break between child thought and adult thought, whereby it remained unclear how a child overcomes his autism and to what extent adults could influence this process.

Piaget defended himself by expanding upon the difference between function and structure: the break between child and adult occurred only on the structural level but not on the functional level. "Between the infinitely flexible content and the fixed function we can distinguish a structure, i.e. successive forms [...], which depend on both the *a priori* function of the explanation and the flexible content of the explanation" (Piaget 1928/3: 39). Thus he softened the difference: "Everything we find in a child we find again in the adult, and everything we find in an adult existed already in the child [...], we can therefore neither identify the child and the adult, nor can we radically oppose them against one another" (Piaget 1931/2: 160). Adults, too, are egocentric in certain situations, especially "in all situations where their spontaneous, naïve attitudes and thus, their child-like thinking, dominates" (Piaget 1933/6: 279). Only for a minority of adults has egocentrism disappeared: "One only needs to listen to how the man in the street talks about astronomy, biology or politics to see that the artificialist mentality never really disappears, except for the elite" (Piaget 1928/3: 46). In both the child and the adult, there is egocentrism, social constraint and cooperation but at a different ratio.

Henri Wallon (1879–1962) criticized the ambivalence of the egocentrism thesis, which tied the development of intelligence to that of sociability (in Piaget 1928/5: 134). He argued against the inevitable link between cognition and cooperation and advised Piaget to explain the mental structuring on the basis of organic development. The child "is a social being from the first moment of his existence, and at each age, his required sociability is expressed in the active functions" (Wallon 1927: 400). Clara and William Stern were of the opinion "that Piaget had not taken into account sufficiently the *importance of the social situation*. Whether a child expresses himself more in an 'egocentric' or more in a 'social' fashion does not only depend on his age but also on his environment" (Stern and Stern 1928: 148). Piaget's research took place in a children's home, but within a family setting different results would have been produced. The research of Martha Muchow (1929) demonstrated that the "egocentrism coefficient" was influenced by the way nurseries or children's homes are run. Piaget accepted that the school environment (Piaget and Leuzinger-Schuler 1947/9: 55) and the type of social interaction (Piaget and Leuzinger-Schuler 1947/4: 74) influenced children's egocentricity.

Abraham Grünbaum (1927: 447ff.) did not interpret the illusion of understanding in children's "collective monologues" as a symptom of egocentricity, but saw it, on the contrary, as a sign of their social integration. This view was supported by Charlotte Bühler: "Infants are not incapable of social relations per se; on the contrary, their earliest relationships are of the most affective and most intensive kind" (Bühler 1928: 180f.). David and Rosa Katz studied their sons Theodor and Julius and arrived at the conclusion that they rarely behaved in an egocentric way towards each other and hardly ever towards their parents. In their behavior towards strangers, whether they were children or adults, the parents observed more frequently utterances that would indicate stronger egocentricity. They explained Piaget's results by suggesting that Piaget's dialogues with his pupils had "the character of exam situations" (Katz and Katz 1928: 2), whereas their own children could "speak freely." Piaget doubted these results: "One would find it hard to believe that among 500 or 1000 random utterances recorded, there should not be at least some 'egocentric' sentences" (Piaget and Leuzinger-Schuler 1947/9: 56). Piaget's co-worker Leuzinger-Schuler subsequently observed her own son, Hans, and noted that he used a more socialized language towards other children than he did towards adults. Piaget concluded that communication between children was characterized by cooperation, whereas communication between children and adults was characterized by intellectual subordination. He therefore distinguished sharply between minimal interference education, as in the Maison des Petits, and authoritarian education, which, he suggested, was applied by Mr and Mrs Katz. The latter kind constantly interfered in children's self-talks and eliminated symbolic play, replacing them by intellectual activity.

With this thesis, Piaget also replied to Susan Isaacs, who in 1929 had criticized Piaget's neglect of the children's social environment and experiences and the influence of the test situation. Isaacs (1930: 49–111; 1931) considered the stages Piaget had devised, with regard to age and the respective implicit logic, as a sequence of pseudo-biological metamorphoses. According to her, his concept was a hybrid composition of biology (maturation theory) and Kant's epistemology, which had yielded a structure that lay somewhere between a categorical and a digestive system. Furthermore, Piaget had not explained why it so happens that the intellectual shock, caused through acquiring different perspectives, occurred at age 7. Piaget (1931/2) replied that he was less interested in actual experiences than in the ability of scientific experience. This ability organizes reality, and the resulting organization is what he called "the structure" with the two poles of maturation and experience. Franziska Baumgarten (1927) criticized Piaget's talk of external experiences without specifying them. Max von Kuenburg (1926) pointed out that Piaget had neglected to mention the type of school of the children surveyed, or the educational background of their parents. Boris Kleint (1928) noted that the surveys had only been carried out in urban areas, which could have influenced the results. Therefore Piaget's image of the universal child was abstract, as several critics had noted. Wallon (1927) and Delacroix (1927) found that Piaget had stylized the child in such a way as to fit his system of stages. According to Joseph Peterson (1929), Piaget's theory of stages showed a positivist scientific approach, because he had evaluated the children's explanations at the various stages according to current scientific theories.

Delacroix (1927) queried the parallel between children's and mankind's mental development. Although Piaget had warned against "drawing dangerous parallels here" (Piaget 1924: 251), he repeatedly compared a child's logic to the Greek thinkers. He put Aristotle on a level with an egocentric child on the grounds of his trajectory theory (Piaget 1925/5: 199; 1931/1: 384), his concept of nature (Piaget 1926: 201), his substantialism (Piaget 1926: 227), his missing concept of coincidence (Piaget 1927: 131) and his absolute classification (Piaget 1927: 334). Piaget had also related Empedocles to child thought because of his visual perception (Piaget 1926: 56), likewise Plato, because of his innate ideas (Piaget 1926: 60), and Pythagoras, because of his participation (1927: 66). Bourjade therefore believed that Piaget had a tendency to "contemplate a functional conception of childhood in the form of a rigorous law of recapitulation" (Bourjade 1927: 5), from which Piaget expressly distanced himself (Piaget 1925/5: 206; 1928/3: 37). In fact, Piaget never advocated a theory of recapitulation, but he was convinced that there is an analogy of the intellectual ontogenesis and the history of science.

Peterson (1929) regarded Piaget's reports as literary, because he had failed to mention important information, such as the children's ages and the number of children interviewed, which, for Muchow (1926), was too small. In his defense, Piaget claimed that only 5 per cent of his investigation had been published in books and that he had personally interviewed 600 children (Piaget 1928/3: 49). Isaacs (1929a) also criticized that Piaget's procedure did not allow for control tests. The clinical method is indeed an esoteric procedure since it "can only be learned through long practice" (Piaget 1926: 21). Piaget claimed to have conducted his investigation "without following scientific test procedures in a petty way. By allowing the child to take the lead with his answers and by following his lead and allowing the child to speak more and more freely, we finally obtain a clinical investigation record for each area of intelligence (logic, causal explanations, function of the real, etc.), which is analogous to the records psychiatrists use for diagnostic purposes" (Piaget 1923/2: 89f.). Therefore, Baumgarten (1927) concluded that this method suggested a general pathology of children. Competence in logic, which must be distinguished from the ability to supply explanations, develops at a much earlier stage than Piaget assumed. Adolph Ferrière (1928) objected to the verbal approach of the experiments and to the fact that the children had not been given the opportunity to think about the questions beforehand. Victoria Hazlitt (1930) criticized the fact that thinking was equated with the ability to verbalize. And she held that even children under the age of five could reason formally as they were able to give correct answers to problems involving generalization. For Isaacs (1929b: 607), the "most serious methodological error in Piaget's work" was his tendency to "take the child at a disadvantage—in verbal intercourse with adults on relatively formal occasions." She thought that the questions asked were too abstract and that children should instead be confronted with real, attractive and meaningful problems because in real situations, the children's reactions would be different from the way Piaget's laboratory children behaved. Bühler (1928) also criticized the intellectuality of the contact Piaget and his colleagues had with the children. She found that the interviewers' questions were interlaced with the children's questions and were often suggestive. They were "so highly selected as to be wholly inadequate to support general conclusions concerning the evolution of the child's reaction to the external world" (Warden 1931: 298). Although Piaget was aware of the danger of suggestion and of exaggerated demands on the children's logic, his questions to 5–7-year-olds were nevertheless quite astonishing at times: "Who makes the lake flow? (Piaget 1923: 294); "Do you know what this is: thinking?" (Piaget 1924: 171); "The brain, what is this?" (Piaget 1923: 294); "Has a word got any power?" (Piaget 1926: 63); "How did names start?" (Piaget 1926: 69); "Where is the sun's name?" (Piaget 1926: 77); "Who sends us our dreams?" (Piaget 1926: 105); "Can clouds go faster if they want to?" (Piaget 1926: 203); "Why are there mountains?" (Piaget 1926: 305); "Has the moon got any force?" (Piaget 1927: 136); "What is force?" (Piaget 1927: 260). These anthropomorphisms, hypostases and metaphors provoked, on a verbal level, the very symptoms Piaget had hoped to discover. "We must look behind the answers [...] in order to find the most spontaneous tendency possible" (Piaget 1926: 307). But Piaget confused spontaneity with ignorance: "I have met many children who could no longer be usefully inter-viewed, since their minds had been filled with so-called exact knowledge" (Piaget 1928/2: 71).

Vygotsky and Piaget

The most thorough analysis of Piaget's theory was delivered by Lev Vygotsky (1896–1934). Piaget had met Vygotsky's colleague, Alexander Luria (1902–1977), at the ninth International Congress for Psychology in New Haven in September 1929 and had subsequently written to his friend Meyerson regarding the search for potential collaborators for a new journal: "For Russia, I have found a splendid fellow in the person of Luria, 28 years of age, who has written numerous first-class articles. He works with Vygotsky, and we should hire these two" (in Vidal and Parot 1996: 66). These two members of the Russian Psychoanalytical Association worked together with Alexej Leontjev (1903–1979), mainly in the field of psychology and support of children with special needs.

Vygotsky took charge of the translations of Piaget's first two monographs and organized a series of control experiments. He praised his clinical method and stated that this "most astute researcher" (Vygotsky 1934: 261) "revolutionized the study of child language and thought" (Vygotsky 1932: 1). He was, however, of the opinion that one could not draw the conclusion of egocentric thinking from egocentric speech. In his own research, he found that "the structural peculiarities of egocentric speech will not decrease with age, but will grow stronger. At age 3, they are at their minimum, at age 7, they are at their maximum" (Vygotsky 1934: 419). According to Vygotsky, Piaget's concept of egocentric speech lacked function, because Piaget had not understood the child's self-talk as a strategy to overcome problems. Piaget's concepts of the unconscious and of the grasp of consciousness were of little value because the egocentric child is said to experience his nonadapted state constantly. It is not egocentrism that is responsible for the children's lack of awareness, but the fact that their "concepts are not organized into a system" (Vygotsky 1934: 298).

Vygotsky noted that Piaget stressed the traits that egocentric thought has in common with autism, rather than with logical thought. Along with Bleuler, he argued that, "from the view of biological evolution, the assumption that autistic thinking was the primary form in the course of psychological development, is not sustainable" (Vygotsky 1934: 97). The child's realism would, on its own, contradict such a thesis, because "the nature of consciousness itself compels the child from the start to reflect

objective reality" (Vygotsky 1934: 115). Since Piaget linked mental development with socialization, he neglected the importance of mastering the
objective world, something that children, as well as "primitive tribes," would
constantly have to deal with, and that would compel them to face reality.
Along with Freud's pleasure principle, Piaget had "also taken on board
the metaphysical approach of a pleasure principle" (Vygotsky 1934: 99).
This had resulted in a dualism between autistic thinking, which knows no
adaptation to reality, and realistic thinking, "as standing apart from concrete needs, interests, and wishes, as *pure* thought" (Vygotsky 1934). This
dichotomy caused Piaget's child to live in a dual reality, whereby logical
thinking systematically deformed the spontaneous, egocentric and unconscious interpretation of the world. This antagonism between spontaneous
and nonspontaneous concepts was reflected in Piaget's disjointed ideas of
development and learning and was the result of his assumption that knowledge "was not acquired through a process of practical acquisition of reality, but through a process of adaptation" (Vygotsky 1934: 117). As nature,
instead of culture, plays a crucial role in development, Vygotsky claimed
that "Piaget kept as his main dogma the thesis that the child is blind to
experience" (Vygotsky 1934: 120). The gauge for measuring a child's developmental level is "not designed to find out what knowledge the child is able
to acquire, but is designed to find out how the child thinks in a field in
which he has no knowledge [. . .] Consequently, Piaget makes sure that he
asks questions from topic areas the child knows nothing about" (Vygotsky
1934: 302). Furthermore, Piaget had basically dispensed with an explanation regarding cognitive development, because he "attempts to replace a
causal understanding of development by a functional one and thus, without realizing it, strips the concept of development of all content [. . .]. As a
result, the author omits to ask questions as to the causes, the development
factors" (Vygotsky 1934: 105f.).

This 'Mozart of Psychology' died in 1934, before his main work was published and was banned shortly thereafter in the Soviet Union. Thus Piaget
did not have to respond to Vygotsky's criticism until 1962, when he was
called upon to do so, which caused him some degree of "embarrassment":

> It is not without sadness that an author discovers, 25 years after its publi-
> cation, the work of a fellow author who has died in the meantime, when
> that work contains so many points of immediate interest to him which
> should have been discussed personally and in detail. Although my friend,
> A. Luria, kept me up to date concerning Vygotsky's sympathetic and yet
> critical position, with respect to my own work, I was neither able to read
> his writings nor to meet him, and in reading his work today, I regret this
> profoundly. (Piaget 1962/1: 243)

Yet Piaget had known the most important points of contention (cf. Piaget 1933/6: 285) at least since 1932, when the Russian translation of Piaget's monographs appeared, containing Vygotsky's 50-page critique. In his introduction, Piaget therefore played down the importance of his work: "I am well aware that my results are only fragmentary and questionable [...] This is just an outline. In real life, social influences and individual organic aptitudes of thought are interwoven in a most subtle fashion" (Piaget 1932/4: 56). He pointed out that it was a difficult problem to define the relationship between the two factors. Given that he only worked within one single social environment, "as I was forced to do, this determination is impossible" (Piaget 1932/4: 56).

In a later comment, Piaget conceded "that I have over-emphasized the similarities between egocentrism and autism, without adequately highlighting the differences" (Piaget 1962/1: 246). He admitted having taken over the Freudian model of the "pleasure principle" uncritically. Apart from these statements, he did not respond to any of the points under criticism, but limited himself "to ascertaining whether what I have done since then confirms or invalidates Vygotsky's criticisms" (Piaget 1962/1: 246). Except for the problem of spontaneity, he portrayed all other differences as misunderstandings and concluded: "I would have been better understood had I begun with The Child's Conception of the World" (Piaget 1962/1: 247). In fact, Piaget obviously had not understood the criticism regarding his dichotomy of spontaneous and taught concepts, as his response ended with the statement "that operational structures which are spontaneously constructed in the course of mental development, are in essence the structures of action co-ordination" (Piaget 1962/1: 253).

Piaget always tended to brush aside criticism as misunderstandings or unclear descriptions (cf. Piaget 1933/6: 284; Piaget and Leuzinger-Schuler 1947/9: 55; Piaget 1952/1: 125). Sometimes he gave strange excuses like having published his first books "without taking sufficient precautions concerning the presentation of my conclusions, thinking they would be little read and would serve me mainly as documentation for a later synthesis to be addressed to a wider audience" (Piaget 1952/1: 122f.). This inability to take criticism contains its own egocentrism:

> *J. P.*: It is true that it is generally useful to hear contradiction and criticism from others, but if one is honest, one realizes this all on one's own [...] I notice myself, what could be said against my claims, but I keep this to myself.
> *J.-Cl. B.*: You are keeping it for later ...
> *J. P.*: Oh, I make use of it ... (he laughs) (Piaget and Bringuier 1977: 171)

It is typical for those who cannot take criticism to see themselves as victims: "I have doubtlessly been one of those psychologists of this century who had to endure a *maximum* of criticism" (Piaget 1976: 26). Yet, in the same breath, he invalidates this 'fate': "Since such criticism bears witness to a more or less complete incomprehension of the problem itself, I paid little attention to it" (ibid).

This does not mean that such criticism remained without consequences, because Piaget did reformulate certain aspects of his theory. He reduced his concept of egocentrism to a purely intellectual aspect and "almost an epistemic phenomenon" (Piaget 1933/6: 279). He inserted a new chapter (Piaget and Leuzinger-Schuler 1947/9) into the third edition of his first monograph, in order to safeguard this interpretation.

On the whole, Piaget spoke highly self-critically about his early work: "It was really bad! I was too young" (Piaget and Bringuier 1977: 101). This self-criticism is justified considering that, despite several attempts, he did not succeed in making the children's artificialist, animist and finalist explanations understood. Piaget correctly assumed a pattern of interpretation, in which the psychological and logical explanations are not yet properly differentiated, and where some motivation or intention "drives actions or events" (Piaget 1923: 267). Based on Ignace Meyerson's approach, he declared that participation was, to a certain extent, the result of a command habit, formed because of the mother's response to the child's needs. With his statement that "the entire universe could be understood to function according to this basic principle" (Piaget 1926: 144), Piaget hinted at a potential socio-psychological theory, which he, however, rejected, although he accepted Grünbaum's reservation that the child projected his own qualities into things (Piaget and Leuzinger-Schuler 1947/9: 86). Piaget was unable to draw consequences from his insights because of his fixation on the criterion of scientific theory that demanded objective logic. Not once did he overstep the limits regarding the subject–object relation, which is the core of the traditional Western epistemology. Perhaps due to biographical reasons as well, it had not occurred to Piaget that the child's first relationships are not with objects but with people. Mother, father and other individuals, to whom the child closely relates, act intentionally, react emotionally and deliberately link their own behavior to the child's. The first frameworks for interpretation which infants will construct are therefore "subjective schemata" (Dux 1982: 97) and objective schemata are secondary. This is not contradicted by the fact that infants who are just a few weeks old can already distinguish between subjects and objects (Trevarthern 1979). Because of the child's logic of his own actions and the grammatical structure and abstractness of language, the subjective schemata remain dominant for a long time when dealing with moving objects or with objects that resemble living creatures. The "egocentric" interpretation patterns of children, and also of most adults, do not follow a spontaneous tendency, but are the result of insufficient differentiation between subject logic and object logic.

At Home in Exile

In 1924 Piaget married his colleague from the JJRI, Valentine Châteney (1899–1983). Her father, Gaston Châteney, was a physician but did not practice, because of his great wealth, which he spent liberally. Her mother, Blanche, was socially active and founded a charity for poor elderly people in Lausanne. Valentine attended the Ecole Nouvelle of Alexandre Vinet in Lausanne and, because of her passion for pedagogy, studied at the JJRI. Her father, convinced that a student needed her own transport, bought her a car, which was a fantastic luxury in those days. "Val," as Piaget called her, taught him to drive. During his driving test, which took place in winter, he drove into a tree, causing ice and snow to fall on top of the car, so he had to resit (Laurent Piaget, unrecorded interview by R. Kohler, 2006). After the war they no longer possessed a car and Piaget, smoking his pipe and wearing his beret while cycling to the university or to the nearby French border, used to be a familiar sight in Geneva. The young couple moved into a villa in Pinchat and retained this residence, even though their many duties frequently took them's thought.

If the report of Piaget's speech on psychoanalysis is anything to go by, Piaget, regarding sexuality, must have felt inferior to his wife: "The original sexual act is a purely physical expression, up to the point where the desire, through voluntary projection onto the higher centers (willpower, reflection) turns into a very psychological act. This is where the woman's influence becomes significant, because she alone can accelerate the arrival of the superman" (Piaget 1924/9). Whatever their sexual relationship, Jean and Valentine lived together in harmony and rarely disagreed in their views on lifestyle, education or politics. After the birth of their first daughter Jacqueline, on 9 January 1925, Valentine dedicated herself fully to the role of mother and stopped working. She supported Piaget's career significantly by documenting their children's development, rather than simply looking after the house and bringing up the children. The Piagets continued this precise documentation on their children's behavior after the births of Lucienne (3 June 1927) and Laurent (29 May 1931). These observations formed the basis for Piaget's books on the development of morality and infant's thought.

In 1924 the Canton representative André Chamay raised questions concerning the JJRI's financial support from state funds. Despite continuing subsidies, following a parliamentary debate, the JJRI's financial situation remained so strained that Piaget was forced to accept redundancy in 1925. Shortly afterwards, the Rockefeller Foundation started to subsidize the institute.[6] "The announcement regarding the American subsidy arrived too late to allow us to retain Mr Piaget" (Bovet 1932: 78) but it allowed the continuation of their projects through Richard Meili (1900–1998) and Hélène Antipoff (1892–1974). Meili's research concerned syncretism within children's perceptions, as well as different forms of intelligence. Antipoff founded the *Archives Pédologiques* and worked in the psychology laboratory until 1929.

After Reymond had criticized Piaget's philosophical novel, Piaget had made several attempts to write a doctoral thesis in philosophy. In 1924 he renewed his efforts regarding his doctorate, but in February 1925, Reymond obtained an appointment in Lausanne and resigned from Neuchâtel, whereupon Piaget, Jean de la Harpe (1892–1947) and Pierre Godet, among others, applied for the vacant position. De la Harpe, like Piaget, had been a member of the ACSE and, taught by Reymond and Bovet, had studied under Lalande, Meyerson and Brunschvicg and had worked on the same topics. Godet, however, was the son of a university professor, like Piaget, thus the chair was divided between them, "evidently in order to avoid hurting the dynastic susceptibilities" (Liengme Bessire and Béguelin 1996: 90). Piaget portrayed this in a different light: "I was appointed on the grounds of my work, although I regret not having been able to underpin my appointment to the chair of philosophy by having a PhD in this field" (Piaget 1965: 22). Despite his appointment, Piaget could not identify with this subject and passed on to Godet the subject of history of philosophy.

My duties at this time were heavy: They included (in the Faculty of Arts) the teaching of psychology, of philosophy of science, of a philosophy seminar, and also of two hours of sociology at the Institute of Social Sciences. In addition, I continued to teach child psychology at the Rousseau Institute. (Piaget 1952/1: 127)

Piaget was much more interested in child psychology and sociology than in philosophy. When he was called back to Geneva, after eight semesters in Neuchâtel, and became a full member of the Faculty of Sciences, he felt as if he had been "freed from the hold of philosophy" (Piaget 1965: 35).

Later, Piaget quoted his colleague, who had freed him from the burden of philosophy, as an example of conformism within science: Godet had declared that he was "intrigued by my psychogenetic viewpoint in the field of epistemology" (Piaget 1965: 26) but he would not represent it in public for political reasons. In contrast to Godet, Piaget appeared to be a brave pioneer of an unorthodox theory, because it took "extra-ordinary courage to clarify the epistemological conditions of philosophical reflection in relation to the conditions of positive knowledge; to surren-der to the illusion created by the absolute starting points of speculation, is really easy in comparison" (Piaget 1965: 114). Piaget did, indeed, wish to replace philosophy by scientific psychology: "[Psychology], together with sociology, dreams of annexing all that belongs or will belong to the study of philosophy: the analysis of thought, of knowledge, of people's customs in all aspects" (Piaget 1928/12: 261). In his inaugural lecture in Neuchâtel, Piaget provided an outline for his concept of genetic psychology on the basis of "a kind of ideal notion, which guides reason, an ideal, which is at once active and unrealized" (Piaget 1925/5: 210). He adhered to Kant's opposi-tion of philosophical and scientific research, even though he was critical of the invariance of its perspectives and categories. In contrast to "hypercriti-cal" but "superficial" pragmatism, genetic psychology as "a natural science [...] will precisely define the deep rapport, which unites action and reason" (Piaget 1925/5: 197, 209). Only the genetic method would make it possible to treat philosophical and historical problems as facts.

Over the next 10 years Piaget worked on several very different subjects simultaneously. He processed the observations of his children, made by himself and his wife, into a theory of early childhood development. He also resumed his experimental studies of mollusks in order to found a new theory of evolution. At the same time, he studied and taught the theory and the history of science and worked on sociological, pedagogical and religio-psychological theories and on morality development. Rather than giving a chronological description, which might be confusing, Piaget's work will be summarized along broad thematic outlines.

6

Theological Foundations

The Theory of Immanence

His disaffection with metaphysics was no obstacle for Piaget to continue to deal with the question of how religion and science could be reconciled and to pursue his goal of finding a scientific foundation for morality. In March 1928, the ACSE invited its two former members, Piaget and de La Harpe, to discuss the religious approaches of immanence and transcendence. With this invitation, the liberal representatives of the student association hoped to attack and demolish "the violent movement in support of the dogmatism of transcendence" (in Piaget 1928/1: 4). After World War I, there had been a renaissance of orthodox belief, led by the Protestant theologian Karl Barth (1886–1968) from Basle. Thus, Piaget and de La Harpe spoke in front of "an audience that was deeply influenced by the reactionaries" (Piaget 1928/1: 4).

The previous year, Piaget had radicalized his religious conviction, when he was reading Brunschvicg's work *The Progress of Consciousness within Occidental Philosophy*. He felt that Brunschvicg had caused a "Copernican revolution" (Piaget 1928/1: 30) within the philosophy of the science by proposing a new definition of reason. "Reason is neither a system of ideas or categories, nor a system of laws, but it is constructive activity" (Piaget 1928/1: 32). What we assume to be the laws of the outside world corresponds to the laws of thinking. Because reality can only be recognized through experience, "the real is [...] always partially constructed by the mind" (Piaget 1928/1: 30). In spite of his conclusion that "the perceptible world is less real than thought" (Piaget 1928/1: 33), he did not abandon his understanding of positive science, which he hoped to combine with constructivism: "One could conceive of a complete science of the universe and of a complete knowledge of thought, and these two realities would be one and the same. The classical alternative 'realism or idealism' would then appear as a parallelism" (Piaget 1928/1: 39). Until such day, one would have to be content with the circle of the sciences. Amazingly missing in this circle were sociology and psychology, upon which Piaget based his analysis of immanence and transcendence.

In agreement with Durkheim, Piaget saw a "close correlation between the structure of social groups and the structure of religious beliefs" (Piaget 1928/1: 9) and considered religion to be a social product. Ethnological studies convinced him that human beings created their gods not only after their own image, but also after their own type of society. Primitive societies, where social constraints compel the individual to hold convictions and duties as sacrosanct, would favor transcendental belief. On the other hand, there are the "*differentiated societies*, where the individual acquires the right to examine, and the freedom of conscience, and where solidarity is based on co-operation rather than compulsion" (Piaget 1928/1: 13). Social differentiation, according to Piaget, necessarily entails a loss of faith in the supernatural, but not in religion. Since Piaget presupposed that "all morality is religious" (Piaget 1928/1: 12), he equated conscience with obeying social rules. In modern societies, these rules can no longer be derived from a transcendental God, but the individuals have to make up their own rules. Religion thus becomes a private matter, and consequently God "becomes part of our conscience" (Piaget 1928/1: 14). This does not mean that a "religion of the self" would emerge: "Immanentism means the identification of God, not with the psychological self, but with the norms of thought" (Piaget 1928/1: 36), which are universal and impersonal. Logic therefore is the highest value; and because religious sentiments form the core of social behavior, love for one's neighbor is the affective counterpart to the absolute value.

As for the psychological component, Piaget referred to Bovet's theory that children develop respect for their parents. Because of the parents' prestige and because of the child's love for, as well as his fear of, his parents, parental orders and bans are accepted. The sum of these internalized commands forms the child's conscience, and the reverence, which the child has for his parents, is transferred onto God. "Thus, the religious sentiment finds its psychological explanation in the child's feeling, in the 'pity' he feels for his parents" (Piaget 1928: 18). Piaget differentiated between the child's unilateral respect for adults and the mutual respect between peers. According to his thesis, the type of respect was the psychological source of one's religious attitude. "Individuals, in whom the unilateral respect predominates, are predisposed to transcendence and to a morality of obedience, and [...] individuals, in whom the mutual respect predominates, are predisposed to immanence and to a morality of autonomy" (Piaget 1928: 21). The transition from heterogeneous to autonomous morality in modern societies takes place during the inevitable "moral and religious crisis" (Piaget 1928: 22) one must undergo during puberty. When the adolescent becomes conscious of his dependence on adults, he revolts against his parents' authority, which leads to guilt feelings that are unjustified, since "revolt is a product of excessive constraint imposed by adults" (Piaget 1928: 22).

For Piaget, the transcendental God was merely "a symbol, which stems from a child-like mythological imagination, and has nothing to do with the spiritual and true God, whom our conscience postulates. On the other side, and this is graver, I believe that the theological morality of sin and expiatory sacrifice is a product of social and educational constraint" (Piaget 1928: 27f.).

The Christian theology of an almighty God, who created a world of misery because of original sin, and who then sacrificed his own son, appeared to Piaget as some blood-drenched Pauline legacy. "This somber mythology appears to be the most obvious proof of the inhuman nature of the moral and religious attitude of transcendence" (Piaget 1928: 29). The morality of Jesus, in contrast, was love, and was therefore the opposite of Christian dogmatism, with its unfounded claim of knowing God's will. "God cannot be grasped by reason or consciousness. Only when the thinking reflects on itself and scrutinizes the conditions of its activities, it shall find God" (Piaget 1928: 30f.). Nicolas de Malebranche (1638–1715) had already identified human reason with the divine Logos, and Piaget stated explicitly: "God is thought. He is not a being, but the condition of existence, and the condition of existence is thought [...] To consider God as a being means to compromise the divine reality" (Piaget 1928: 34).

Piaget agreed with Brunschvicg that the philosophy of immanentism is not subjectivist, but the most objective one.

From the aspect of intellectuality, the self is subjected to norms of reason [...]. They impose themselves onto the self as soon as the individual stops seeking personal affirmation and bows to objectivity. From the aspect of morality, the self is also subjected to norms, such as reciprocity or justice. These are the very norms of reason, which apply to action as much as to thought. Morality is a logic of action, as logic is a morality of thought. The activity of reason is logical as well as moral. (Piaget 1928: 36f.)

Religion, morality and science converge when one becomes conscious of the norms of thinking, which embody God, justice and truth. "Reflection upon oneself gradually purifies and changes one's thoughts" (Piaget 1928: 33).

With his religious analyses, Piaget followed the intellectualizing trend of Christian theology. Christian exegesis had always been directed towards reflectivity and subjectivity because it had to find the answers to the delicate question of how the limited human reason could grasp the divine order, or to sophisticated problems, such as original sin, the holy trinity, Jesus' dual status of being human as well as divine, or free will. Protestantism, which initiated the "subjective turn" (Ohlig 2001: 17) at the beginning of modern times, Puritanism and pietism were radicalizations of this inherent compulsion to individualization. Piaget believed that he had discovered the inherent tendency of mental evolution, which proved the intellectual and moral superiority of immanentism over primitive transcendental belief.

Piaget's thesis caused lively debates. The young theology student, Jean-Daniel Burger, discovered numerous questionable statements[7] and criticized Piaget's understanding of science and of philosophy. Piaget's characterization of philosophy and religion is indeed surprising: "Philosophy is talk, but religion is life" (Piaget 1928/1: 38). According to Burger, Piaget had exaggerated Brunschvicg's theses, since the French philosopher had never negated reality. The differentiation between the two types of society "seems at best immature" (Burger 1929: 38), because the savages were no isolated mavericks. Piaget felt personally offended by "this polemic tone" (Piaget 1929/4: 146), which, in his view attacked the person and not just the doctrine itself. He then used equally strong language and insinuated that Burger had not understood Durkheim. He declared the criticism leveled against the two types of society to be a problem of definition and not a factual problem (Piaget 1929/4: 149f.). On the whole, he confirmed his negation of reality with statements such as "the material nature exists only thanks to the mind" (Piaget 1929/4: 151), or the idealistic, circular argument: "The thought is, at once, the condition of a fact and a fact" (Piaget 1929/4: 150). Arnold Reymond (1929: 165; 1942 II: 343) remarked, therefore, that Piaget lived in Berkeley's world of *esse est percipi* (to be is to be perceived). As a result of this idealism, Piaget would reduce God "to a simple symbol of the unifying tendencies of human thought" (Reymond 1929: 169). Piaget answered that immanentism was no subjectivist position because there was an "inner demand which pushes us to consider the life of the spirit as corresponding to an absolute value" (Piaget 1929/6: 330). Nevertheless, Reymond saw a considerable danger in the theory of immanence for the hitherto exemplary unity of political, religious, moral, philosophical and pedagogical thinking in west Switzerland: "If immanentism must eventually lead to the rejection of any ontological finalism [...], the divorce between philosophical thinking and theological thinking will be completed in West-Switzerland" (Reymond 1931: 376f.).

Piaget did not share this fear, because "no perception, no idea, no judgment is possible for any of us, unless a supreme ideal is involved in these acts, a norm which is simultaneously intellectual and moral, and which will enlighten our consciousness!" (Piaget 1929/4: 151f.). He believed that, in the end, faith in immanence came down to the ethics of action. "Reflected action that is both a scientific experiment and social practice [...]. Each unselfish step of reason and each act of love make man a collaborator with God" (Piaget 1929/4: 152).By combining morality, religion and science as parallel phenomena of development, Piaget set himself apart from Kant: "We believe that it is absurd—and in some aspects even scandalous—to base one's attempt to prove God's existence on considering the limitations of science" (Piaget 1930/3: 21). For him, the "progress in the realm of intelligence corresponds to a moral and social progress, which is, ultimately, an emancipation of the inner life" (Piaget 1930/3: 54). Emancipation means, in fact, the substitution of the imposed values through the universal, divine norms.

These norms form an inner, psychological transcendence, otherwise religion would be superfluous: "A God, immanent within thought, remains [...] transcendent with regard to the self. The values and norms of thought produce within us a feeling of inner transcendence, which in no way contradicts immanentism" (Piaget 1930/3: 45). Because of this differentiation, "an inner communion of the self with the absolute of thought" (Ibid), and prayer as a subjection of the self to the absolute (Piaget 1930/3: 49) become possible. "Who would not feel the joy of such communion between the human and the divine and enjoy the beauty of the ascension that leads from a feeling of agreement and equilibrium, which is the usual result of this communion, to the fullness of a feeling of presence?" (Piaget 1930/3: 48). This ecstasy corresponds to the God-experience of Brunschvicg, who understood God to be "a principle, the existence of which is attested by a unique intellectual feeling of *presence*" (Brunschvicg 1921: 151). If this feeling is not to remain a mere illusion, then there must be several levels of reality within and outside the organism, of which Piaget named the "social and psychological realities, the mechanical and chemical realities, and the most intimate mystical experiences, as well as the external, measurable experiences" (Piaget 1930/3: 12). For Piaget, mysticism was still a creative experience (cf. 1928/1: 38f.): "In childhood memories, there is nothing more characteristic than this complex impression that you approach your innermost self while you are dominated by something higher, which appears to be a source of inspiration" (Piaget 1932: 101). Mystical experience is not in conflict with immanentism, because God is active within one's thought, as a value of the relationship between the mind and the universe (Piaget 1930/3: 32).

For Piaget, the theory of immanence formed the core of all of his psychological, social, political, pedagogical and moral topics, as well as being the core of topics concerning cognitive theories and biological issues. The investigation of the impersonal norms and their origins became Piaget's general program of research. Thus, Piaget's psychology of cognition was originally of a theological nature, because the norms of thinking "are the true and sole expression of the divine" (Piaget 1928/1: 37). He retained his internalized metaphysics as a guideline for psychological research: "Before one takes recourse to a transcendental organization, it is advisable to exhaust the resources of an immanent organization. [When searching] the secret of the rational organization in the vital organization, *its excesses included*, the method consists in trying to understand knowledge through its own construction, which is not absurd, because it is *essentially construction*" (Piaget 1967: 414). The terminology of his system is linked to the idea of an inner absolute, as can be seen in expressions such as equilibrium, intelligence, logic, or autonomy. Genetic psychology, which combines development with an unalterable goal, tallies well with the Calvinist doctrine of predestination. "From an intellectual and from a moral point of view, the child is born neither good nor bad, but as the master of his fate" (Piaget 1932: 107). Although it remains unclear what could have been meant by the "intellectual good," the role of development is unambiguous: the individual must free himself from his primitive, antisocial condition of autism and must, by way of undergoing three revolutions, develop into a human being who thinks socially and scientifically.

The Personality Theory

The inner split of the human psyche into the self and an inner transcendence can also be found in Piaget's personality theory.

> Man is dual, indeed. At every moment, and in all areas of his mental development, whether this regards reason or morality, man is torn between two equally strong tendencies. The first consists of accepting the world as it appears at first glance, whereby it always, and in all situations, seems to form a system with oneself at the centre. The second consists of correcting this point of view spontaneously, and overcoming it, then recording it within a general system that is able to co-ordinate this special perspective with a growing number of different views. (Piaget 1931/4: 106)

The first tendency corresponds to the child's realism, which reduces the world to the child's self. The second tendency corresponds to the awareness that our own view is relative, which allows us to observe the world objectively. There is a constant struggle between egocentrism and logic, between the self and the personality. "The individual could either be the *self*, which concentrates on itself, or it could be the *personality*, which itself submits to forms of reciprocity and universality" (Piaget 1933/2: 84).

The self is a purely individual entity and not only different from other selves, but opposed to them, as it "precedes socialization and revolts against it" (Piaget 1933/2: 85). Nevertheless, social contact is essential for overcoming egocentricity. Socialization starts with imitation, because the "internalisation of 'outside' society effectively leads to the suppression of the (self-centered) self" (Piaget 1933/2: 116). Another prerequisite for freeing oneself from egocentrism is the development of self-awareness which "is a social product: the more we compare ourselves to others, the better we shall be able to know ourselves" (Piaget 1930/9: 227). The grasp of consciousness corrects the distortion of perception that prevents adapted behavior. Only one essential thing is missing from the child's thinking:

> a *normative* structure, that is to say, a set of rules of truth, which allow the distinction between subjective attachments and objective connections. For these norms to develop to the point where they can overcome the self, one condition is necessary: the self must socialize [...]. Between the organism and society, there is the self. (Piaget 1928/3: 42f.)

The self would, however, stay closely connected to the organism: "The self is the reason why one's thinking, limited by the organism and thus subject to the illusions of individuality, is different from that of others: the self, therefore, is the source of intellectual and moral anarchy" (Piaget 1930/3: 48).

Later Piaget doubted the idea of a factual self: "There is no direct inner experience, and there is no direct outer experience. The self only recognizes, or rather works itself out, with the help of schemata, which are constructed in function to outer objects" (Piaget 1950 III: 264). Influenced by Janet, Piaget here equated the self with the personality. Piaget's teacher understood personality to be the "total of operations, of actions great and small, which help the individual to construct, to maintain and to perfect his unity with, and his distinction from, the rest of the world" (Janet 1929: 9). Personality therefore is not a condition, but "an activity of permanent construction" (Janet 1929: 42) and it develops by way of forming "schemata of action" (Janet 1929: 74). Basically, however, Piaget did not consider the self to be a dynamic entity, which would have made the duality between self and personality superfluous. Instead, he retained egocentrism as "being centred upon a self, which does not know itself" (Piaget 1965: 147).

In contrast, "personality is the opposite of individuality and of the self" (Piaget 1930/3: 48). The individual gradually grows into a personality, as the self renounces itself more and more by embedding its own point of view among the others, and by bowing to the rules of reciprocity" (Piaget 1933/2: 85). Step by step, the self becomes decentered through extending and adopting the perspectives of one's family, school friends, neighborhood, town, country and finally of mankind and the universe. Socialization is achieved when the self is disciplined and obeys the rules of reason. The essential point of socialization is the experience of equivalence in the course of cooperation that allows true respect between two personalities. But social adaptation is motivated as well by "the moral fear of losing face in the eyes of the respected individual" (Piaget 1932: 434). Adults who think and act in an egocentric way, have been failed by their educators, whereas a child's egocentrism is a natural state. "It is the most normal of all starting points, provided one succeeds in overcoming it" (Piaget 1932/1: 67). Thus, everybody must fight a battle against himself, in accordance with Christian tradition. According to Piaget, the "unconscious self of a child's egocentrism [...], the anarchic self of egoism" (Piaget 1932: 103) never quite disappears. It all depends on the ratio: "The more powerful it is, the more hateful the self is [...], whereas a strong personality is that which can discipline itself. Personality [...] is the submission of the self to an ideal which it embodies, but which surpasses and dominates it" (Piaget and Inhelder 1955: 311).

Personality was now no longer considered to be a unit composed of various persons, but it was "a synthesis *sui generis* of that which has always been in each of us, together with the norms of co-operation" (Piaget 1933/2: 86). Yet Piaget did not give up his idea of transformation, since the personality "demands a conversion of the self and thus condemns its egocentrism" (Piaget 1933/2: 86). Successful socialization results in "an agreement between the original characteristics of the self and the discipline of the rule" (Piaget 1933/2: 117), although this remains a fragile harmony. "We cannot hope that an achieved status will remain stable and be final [...] Conflict will re-emerge in every area [...] and at every mental level, whatever we do and whatever our age" (Piaget 1931/4: 107, 109). Life is a battlefield, in which reason fights for its true destiny. It is under constant attack from "the lawlessness of egocentrism" (Piaget 1949/6: 36f.) and is in constant danger of succumbing to fantasy and subjectivity, to instincts and feelings.

Piaget saw the destiny of reason as predetermined through the logic of development. There were "certain functional invariants, certain 'norms', which reappear in new forms at each new stage, and whose relative character thus remains constant. These norms of thinking constitute the most profound reality, and it is the task of the human mind to strive towards this reality" (Piaget 1930/3: 39). Development is driven by an *élan spirituel* (Piaget 1930/3: 40), and its progress is gradual and directed towards consistency as the uppermost value of perfect reason. "Reason is an ideal, and the deeper it reflects, the more it will gradually become conscious" (Piaget 1933/2: 82). Piaget believed in catharsis, in which the mind reaches the norms "by building structures as the relevant consciousness is raised"

(Piaget 1932: 455). Construction and reflection are the two inseparable mechanisms in the development of reason, which will comprise the logical, and also the affective and social realm.

> The normative activity of the mind imposes itself on all of us. From the affective point of view, this means that in any act of love, in any beautiful emotion, in any everyday fervor, as in any decisive and passionate moment, the human being will no longer feel enclosed within the self but will blend into the principle of all reality. From the intellectual point of view, this means that, with each true statement in the conquest of knowledge and in the daily battle against lies and error, the consciousness will feel solidarity with the eternal values. From the social point of view, this means that, in each unselfish act in the fight for good and for justice, individuals and groups will be filled with a strength, whose victorious momentum seems to come from the profoundest depths of being. Thus, each manifestation of faith involves values that more and more refer to an inner absolute. It is this absolute that man has always equated with his idea of the divine. It is this absolute that caused the greatness of the transcendent gods. It is this absolute that defines the immanent God (Piaget 1930/3: 41).

For Piaget, therefore, anthropology and theology have been the same thing and merged into his cognitive psychology. Consequently, the mental development must be a process of perfecting and of cleansing.

> Once reason is cleansed from the things that, in human beings, stem from sensitivity and from discursive demands, it will reduce itself to rational norms. Resolve, which stems from decisions and conflicts, will reduce itself to the norm of the good. Love, freed from its organic components, will reduce itself to the value of the ideal. Thus, the divine will merges with moral obligation, divine reason merges with intellectual obligation and divine love merges with the infinite value that renders existence valuable (Piaget 1930/3: 48).

Human personality depends on divine personality, which is encountered in mystical experiences. The term "personality" was developed in Protestant theology and described the moral approach to God's perfection by following the model of Christ. In the second half of the nineteenth century, a "culture of personality" (Sennett 1977: 262) developed alongside the dissolution of the transcendence belief. "Personality" contained the idea of self-creation and the realization of God within one's own self. This answered the question of the meaning of life, in a world that became more and more secular, by transposing the otherworldly paradise into one's own psyche. "To have a personality means [...] to succeed in incorporating all parts of oneself into the impersonal frames of theoretical and practical reason [...]. It is therefore important to reserve for God the characteristics of personality and to dissociate them from those of individuality" (Piaget 1930/3: 48).

Even though Piaget disengaged his terminology from religious contexts and applied it to logical, moral and social issues, his basic convictions remained unchanged: "We can be sure of this much at least, that personality is not simply a result of the self, and that personality, to some extent, orients itself in the opposite direction: personality requires decentration of the self, which subjects itself to certain functions or to a hierarchy of social values. (Piaget 1960/8: 192).

7

The Social-psychological Work

On Reymond's recommendation, Piaget could teach sociology at the Institute of Social Sciences when he was appointed Professor of Philosophy and Psychology at Neuchâtel in 1925. Later, he taught experimental psychology and sociology at the University of Lausanne from 1936 to 1951. From 1939 to 1951 he was also Professor of Sociology in Geneva. The description of how Piaget secured this chair is revealing: "When the professor of sociology at the University of Geneva gave up his position in 1939, I was, without my knowledge, nominated to that post; I accepted the call" (Piaget 1952/1: 134f.). Piaget's description suggests that, on the grounds of his qualifications, the usual procedure was dispensed with, although he had never studied sociology.

The Theory of Society and Social Change

The early stages of Piaget's involvement with sociology were dominated by the question of the reality of society, in connection with the general problems of realism and nominalism. "The dispute of Durkheim and Tarde on reality or non-reality of society, as an organized whole, plunged me into a [...] state of uncertainty" (Piaget 1952/1: 113). According to Piaget, Tarde had underestimated the influence of social constraint, whereas Durkheim had rejected psychological explanations, because he regarded society as a totality. Piaget correctly reproached Durkheim for having reified "society" and the "collective consciousness" into metaphysical units. "In the world of experience, I know only *one* subject which has a richer, more complex reality than we have: and this is collectivity. But there is yet one other subject that could fulfil this role: and that is divinity. We have to choose between God and the society" (Durkheim 1924: 105). Piaget responded: "There is no society. There are social constraints, some of which engender rationality, and some of which are sources of errors [...] There are no individuals. There are individual mechanisms of thinking, some of which engender logic, and some of which engender anarchy" (Piaget 1928/2: 65f.). What Piaget meant was that societies do not exist as beings, nor do individuals exist in isolation. "Society is the totality of all social relationships" (Piaget 1932: 450). The task of psychology was to examine these relationships from the inside, and sociology must examine these relationships from the outside. Thanks to this parallelism, conflicts between these two sciences were ruled out (ibid: 409, 422). It is true that sociology has to rely on describing society as a whole and as something that is present. "It is, however, important to remember the static character of the sociological concepts, otherwise one's words will take on a mythological sense" (Piaget 1947: 177).

Piaget adopted an action-theoretical foundation for his sociology (cf. Lidz and Lidz 1976): Society is "a system of interactions that modify individuals in their interactions" (Piaget 1950 III: 191). If the forms of social organization manifest in individual behavior, rules of conduct must be its foundation. "It is essential for any collective life to lay down rules" (Piaget 1928/1: 12). Like Durkheim, Piaget defined moral rules as the cement that bonds society together. "All morality consists in a system of rules, and the essence of all morality is to be sought for in the respect which the individual acquires for these rules" (Piaget 1932: 7).

Durkheim had described social change as development of an anarchic society with a collectivist-religious morality into a modern society with an individualist-secular morality. Due to population increase, a greater division of labor and higher specialization had occurred which has enhanced the social importance of the individual. The individual's dependence has shifted from smaller communities to society as a whole, and has become more abstract, whereupon the individual has began to question his subordination to tradition and to society. "Only a more condensed society and the resulting differentiation can explain the liberation of the personal consciousness" (Piaget 1932: 433). Piaget did not only follow Durkheim's description of social change (Piaget 1932: 374f.), but also adopted Durkheim's fear that, if the differentiation of labor became too extensive, and individualization progressed too rapidly, society would be in danger. Consequently, it would be

> our first duty to create a morality for ourselves. Our equilibrium is in danger: we must find an inner equivalent for the outer solidarity that is a characteristic of conformism. What we lose in the way of material constraint from traditional institutions, we shall have to gain in the way of an inner morality and a personal consciousness of solidarity. (Piaget 1932: 387)

The family, according to Piaget, plays a central part in forming morality, besides fulfilling managerial and juristic functions. Durkheim had shown, however, that families were getting smaller in the course of social development, therefore losing part of their functions. This "progressive decrease of our elders' authority" was accompanied by "a gradual emancipation of the younger generations" (Piaget 1943/2: 87). This theory is, however, at cross purposes with regard to patriarchy. Like Durkheim, Piaget linked the reinforced power wielded by the father to the state's dependence on the family to pass on authoritarian values.

> These are precisely the values, which the family ought to transmit from father to son: hence the importance of the family, which grows in intensity, so to speak, while decreasing in size. In conclusion, the present crisis of the family seems like a natural result of a number of social transformations that would tend to explain the decreasing family size. The remedy, however, must be found in the transmission of values: we must create new values to transmit, as well as spiritual values (moral or religious ideals, political or social convictions, a vocation to perpetuate, intellectual or scientific work), in addition to material values, in order to strengthen the family unit and to provide it with vital and functional significance. (Piaget 1943/2: 88)

Should the transmission of values fail, we would be facing egoistical individualism, against which Durkheim opposed moral individualism. "It is a matter of completing, expanding and organizing individualism, and not a matter of limiting and fighting it. It is a matter of using the capacity of reflection, and not a matter of silencing it" (Durkheim 1898: 68). Individuals should become active partners within the collective consciousness, on the basis of reason and science, and with the help of the laicist school and of cooperative professional associations. In primitive societies, collective values are internalized through coercion, leading to a mechanical solidarity. In modern societies, on the other hand, moral discipline demands the understanding of having to subject ourselves to social rules. Reason guarantees that an organic solidarity will be formed. Up to this point, Piaget agreed with Durkheim's analysis.

In several articles, Piaget asked the question "whether logic was a social thing, and if so, in which sense. This question distracted me, I wanted to push it away, but it kept coming back" (Piaget 1928/2: 45). He could not contradict Durkheim's thesis of the collectivity of reason, because "language is more than a labelling system: it compels the individual to resort to classification, to a system of relationships, in short, to logic. And language presupposes a society" (Piaget 1928/2: 47). Durkheim, however, used reason in the sense of a fact as well as in the sense of an ideal. To Piaget, "the truth is not a factual law regarding society, but it is the law of equilibrium, towards which society strives, without ever fully achieving it" (Piaget 1928/2: 50). Because reason aspires to moral and intellectual equilibrium, development means moral progress. "Thus, the custom gradually purifies due to the influence of an ideal that is above the custom" (Piaget 1932: 76). According to Piaget, Durkheim's "collective consciousness" had presupposed, as fact, what was actually the aim of this development: the unity of all moral and mental phenomena. Because Durkheim was only focusing on social facts, he was unable to distinguish between duty and the good. Nor had Durkheim considered that "'common morality' did not consist of something that is given to individuals from the outside, but that it consisted of the total of relationships between individuals" (Piaget 1932: 398). His explanation, that morality was formed through constraint, was therefore not sufficient to understand how a sense of duty might emerge. A psychological complement was required: an insight into the affective relationship between individuals.

The Psychology of Morality

Piaget acknowledged Bovet's "paternity of our results" (Piaget 1932: 424) regarding the development of morality. Respect "comprises two things: fear and love, which support each other" (Bovet 1913: 155). Respect for a person is the basis upon which this person's instructions are accepted as rules. The sum total of all commandments and prohibitions, received and accepted, form the sense of duty. "The moral sense of duty is a phenomenon *sui generis*, presupposing a relationship between at least two individuals, whereby one person gives an order, a command, and the other person, who accepts this command, shows respect towards the one who gave it" (Piaget 1928/4: 106). The relationship is therefore the magical channel in which morality is transmitted. Because the sense of duty has no other source than the command, because the value of the command depends on admiration, and because the respected personality is characterized by the fact that he, himself, follows these rules, the perfect role model is the decisive psychological factor for the development of morality. In Christianity, this is Jesus.

Piaget refined Bovet's theory by differentiating between two types of respect: the unilateral respect "involves the inevitable constraint, which the superior imposes upon the inferior [. . .], which we shall call a *relationship of constraint*" (Piaget 1930/4: 34f.). It leads to a sense of duty, which is symbolized by the sacrosanct, which prevents autonomy. Individuals in a relationship of mutual respect, on the other hand, are "morally equal, for instance between two children of the same age" (Piaget 1928/4: 108). This reciprocity allows the development of an inner morality that leads to cooperation and self-reliance. Thus Piaget identified Baldwin's 'Ideal Self' with Bovet's concept of duty (Piaget 1932: 447f.).

These two kinds of respect correspond to two types of rules: "the outer, or heteronomous rule, and the internal rule" (Piaget 1931/11: 46). In order to explain the origin of respect for rules, Piaget and his colleagues observed boys who were playing with marbles, and asked them to explain the rules. The fact that such children's games develop and form traditions, independent of adults, was important to Piaget. Piaget noted a higher complexity in boys' games: "Even superficial observation shows that the juristic mentality is much less developed among girls than among boys" (Piaget 1932: 80f.). He found, nonetheless, that the course of development was the same for girls, but did not specify the reasons for the girls' "characteristic mentality."

Concerning the behavior of play, Piaget identified four stages, with fluctuating borders. Below the age of 3–4, the solipsistic child plays according to his own wishes and needs, disregarding any rules. Prohibitions would not be understood as moral rules but would simply be regarded as obstacles. Any emerging regularities in the children's actions are not yet linked to symbols. From the age of 3–4, the child adopts the rules from older children, but he uses these rules in an individual, rather than in a collective way. The child's fantasy imbues these rules with meanings of his own making, thus symbolization remains a private matter. The child bases his aims on the success of his actions (rewards or penalties). Not before the age of 7 will cooperation occur. At the same time, there is a growing desire to be better than the other players, hence the need to control adherence to the rules. The child's interest is now social (Piaget 1932: 59), but the rules are still interpreted in a rather subjective way. We are therefore only dealing with a "provisional morality." From 11 years onward, the rules become codified, but in such a way that they can still be modified, as long as all players agree.

After a premoral stage, in which the rules are not binding (Piaget 1932: 51), the consciousness of rules develops from heteronomous morality to autonomous morality. From the age of 4, children usually regard the rules as absolute and immutable (most pronounced around age 6).

> Strangely, almost all younger children, up to age 10 or 11, tend to regard the rules as sacrosanct and inviolable, although the children actually apply these rules rather at random. The rules, we were told, had been prescribed for the children in primeval times, at the time of Adam and Eve, by God, by the first Swiss, by the "town councilors" and so forth. Certainly, these rules could be changed, but "this would not be the right thing to do." (Piaget 1928/4: 109f.)

Once the children reach the age of 11–12, they see the rules as the result of a social contract, made on the basis of mutual respect. Moral ideas are now sought in 'higher' laws of reciprocity and of cooperative compensation, whereby the contents of the rules are rendered relative and are autonomously devised.

This research on moral development was consolidated by presenting children with stories containing relevant moral conflicts, in the same way that Alice Descoeudres interviewed children at the JJRI in 1919. Piaget's study showed that children up to age 7 model their judgment regarding lies, punishment and justice largely on the examples given by adults and on the reactions of adults. This is the first characteristic of moral realism. The second consists in the literal understanding of the rules, and the third regards the objective interpretation of duty (Piaget 1932: 121f.). Young children, for example, considered it to be a graver offence if a child were to accidentally break 15 cups than if a child broke one cup in the course of a forbidden action. Until around the age of 8, children focus mainly on the objective damage and tend to neglect the aspect of intention (Piaget 1932: 143). Piaget agreed with Friedrich Wilhelm Foerster (1869–1966) that children advocate severe punishment, but argued that this was only the case if the child's social relationships are dominated by heteronomy: "Constraint on the part of adults may not be the only source, but it is certainly the major source of the concept of justice through atonement" (Piaget 1930/4: 39). Constraint increases the child's spontaneous moral realism, whereas experiences of cooperation and solidarity with peers engender the preference of sanctions based on reciprocity, such as the temporary exclusion from the clique. This is the reason why children from the age of 12 consider lying to their mates to be a worse offence than lying to adults (Piaget 1932: 194f.). Thus they are approaching the internal norm of justice as a logical principle: "In contrast to rules [. . .] imposed from the outside, which the child does not understand, such as the command that one must not tell lies, the command of justice is a kind of immanent condition, or law of equilibrium for social relationships" (Piaget 1932: 224).

Socialization as Moral Development

According to Piaget, the theory of socialization must presuppose "three given factors: autism, social constraint and co-operation" (Piaget 1928/2: 66). The child is not born social (Piaget 1932: 210f.) but becomes social with the increasing number of his interactions. Piaget went as far as to claim that

the structure of behavior for a newborn baby would remain the same if the baby was nursed by a robot, whereas the [cognitive] structures are increasingly transformed through interactions with the environment.

These interactions start with the sensory-motor stage (smile, games involving voice and facial expressions, imitations etc.) and are consolidated in accordance with the child's overall mental evolution. (Piaget 1960/8: 165)

Socialization therefore means the progressive superposition of one's biological structures: "A phenomenon is always biological in its roots and social at its end point" (Piaget 1973: 7).

Moral ideas grow and change, because the child's relationships change. Once the original solipsism is overcome, the child is exposed to constraint:

From the baby's first smile onward, and especially once he utters his first words, he becomes subjected to a social influence, which, initially is only slight, but grows more and more constraining, until it simply begins to carve channels into his mind and will end up modelling it and will perhaps fundamentally alter it. (Piaget 1925/5: 204)

Because the child cannot yet develop any real consciousness of rules, the incomprehensible rules of adults "gain the value of ritual duties, and the prohibitions take on the meaning of taboos" (Piaget 1932: 150). In most of Piaget's expositions, constraint causes conformism, naïvety and dependence, so that we "accept [...] social injustices, national prejudices [and] place complete trust in our doctor like a savage trusts his witchdoctor" (Piaget 1930/9: 226). Thus, "the risk of social constraint is that this childlike attitude [...] may survive into adulthood" (Piaget 1932/1: 71). This has dramatic consequences, because only "an elite group of adolescents [...] will take up a disciplined life", while all the others "either refuse all discipline or, for the rest of their lives, will only be capable of an outer, legal morality" (Piaget 1932: 412). In other expositions, however, we learn that moral constraint is "of great practical value, for it is in this way that an elementary sense of duty is formed and the first normative control, of which the child is capable" (Piaget 1932: 458). Constraint compels the child to "elevate the will of the adult to having the highest value, when previously the child's own will held the highest value. Some progress, no doubt" (Piaget 1932: 459). It is necessary to have experienced duty, "in order to understand fully the value of this free ideal, which is the good" (Piaget 1930/4: 48). In any case, the parents cannot renounce constraint, because "egocentric individuals can only be guided thanks to external constraint" (Piaget 1933/2: 88). And "in the rational mood, in which the civilized child lives, it goes without saying that the child's progression [...] is facilitated considerably by the constant pressure of the adult mentality" (Piaget 1928/7: 300). But "the child becomes rational, despite, and not because of, the adults. There is a socialization process, other than constraint, which leads to norms" (Piaget

1928/3: 58). The relationship between constraint and egocentrism is not clear either. Sometimes, Piaget felt that the child's egocentrism "is always accompanied by constraint from adults" (Piaget 1932: 62), and that "there is indeed a kind of pre-established harmony [...] between the logic of ego-centrism and the logic of constraint" (Piaget 1928/3: 59). Sometimes, they "oppose each other and share the child's mind between each other" (Piaget 1930/9: 227). On another occasion he claimed that constraint "increases the child's egocentrism, intellectually as well as morally" (Piaget 1932: 215f.).

The ambivalence surrounding the idea of constraint stems from the fact that, for Piaget, "the spirit of discipline forms the starting point of any moral life" (Piaget 1932: 410). Discipline is the only remedy against egocentrism, because "we are egocentric on every occasion where no precise discipline imposes itself onto our behavior or thought" (Piaget 1930/9: 226). Yet the desirable kind of discipline is not directed from the outside, but is self-discipline. The problem is that self-discipline does not occur on its own. Piaget got tangled up in contradictions when he tried to explain why children bow to the rules. In most cases, he presupposed a child's spontaneous tendency towards cooperation, which is usually suppressed by parents and teachers (Piaget 1932: 215). Children even appear to be just as altruistic as their parents: "The child's relationship with his parents is certainly not only marked by constraint. There is a spontaneous mutual affection, which, from early stages onward, makes the child act magnanimously, even sacrificially" (Piaget 1932: 221). Yet it is not only cooperation that makes a spontaneous appearance (Piaget 1933/5: 143), but unilateral respect as well (Piaget 1932: 456). Although, in the latter case, the child subjects himself voluntar-ily, this still does not guarantee a harmonious atmosphere within the family: "Spontaneous submission, from the outset, will finally provoke generation conflicts" (Piaget 1960/8: 164). On the background of his own childhood, Piaget explained this ambivalence by postulating the intellectual superiority of adults: "In this social exchange, the child receives, from the beginning, the impression of being understood and dominated at the same time: hence the double feeling of communion with his parents" (Piaget 1930/9: 227).[8] On the whole, Piaget was less inclined to stress the spontaneous tendency to submit and was more inclined to emphasize the tendency to cooperate, and emphasized that "constraint transforms the individual much less deeper than co-operation" (Piaget 1945/3: 147).

Adults must therefore foster cooperation and must be "collaborators rather than taskmasters" (Piaget 1932: 461). Even though Durkheim had stressed that "co-operation especially [has] its own morality" (Durkheim 1893: 285), Piaget criticized this first full professor for sociology and pedagogy in France for the fact that due to his doctrine of unity, he could only differentiate between cooperation and constraint by degrees, and thus had overlooked the point that there are "two different types of morality" (Piaget 1932: 220), "that is to say, two ways of feeling and behaving" (Piaget 1931/11: 46), which "lead to different moral results" (Piaget 1932: 384). This duality is the reason why, during development, "a total transformation of the rule-consciousness takes place: heteronomy is followed by autonomy" (Piaget 1932: 66) thanks to "the beneficial work of co-operation" (Piaget 1928/2: 75). Since mutual respect is formed mainly between peers, "the foundation of welfare and youth societies (YMCA, ACSE, Blue Cross [the youth organization of the Catholic Church], etc.) progressively lessen dogmatic conformism, in favour of moral action" (Piaget 1928/1: 25). Piaget recognized "that, in our societies, constraint takes the form of solidarity within co-operation [...], but this continuity, which we are not disputing, by no means excludes qualitatively opposed results" (Piaget 1932: 393). Because society no longer forms a unit, there is no homogenous morality either. "The commands overlap, contradict each other more or less, and the more numerous the respected individuals become, the more one must bring diverging duties into harmony with each other. Consequently, our reason is compelled to create the necessary unity within our moral consciousness: this unifying task allows us to gain a sense of personal autonomy" (Piaget 1932: 428).

Piaget relied strongly on Kant: Autonomy is the subject's submission under maxims, which are self-constructed, critically examined (Piaget 1932: 72) and universally valid (Piaget 1932: 117). Yet the individual will not succeed in doing so, unless he cooperates with others: "Autonomy only becomes manifest [...] in reciprocity, when the mutual respect is strong enough to create, within the individual, an inner desire to treat the other person as he would wish to be treated himself" (Piaget 1932: 238).

Cooperation does not prescribe any content, "it is a method and nothing else" (Piaget 1928/2: 78). It contains "the rule of reciprocity, which enables individuals to redress that which remains unbalanced within themselves, and allows the manifestation of equilibrium, which is immanent in every conscious action" (Piaget 1933/2: 115). As mutual respect causes solidarity (Piaget 1928/4: 116) and sympathy (Piaget 1932: 238, 405) and because the need for mutual affection is "the first pre-requisite of a moral life" (Piaget 1932: 199), there is no real conflict between justice and love (Piaget 1932: 382f.). Once respect has become mutual, it "has become part of the personality of the child. Here we find true obedience, a true feeling for goodness" (Piaget 1931/8: 114).

In ignorance of Max Stirner (1806–1856) and Friedrich Nietzsche (1844–1900), Piaget claimed: "The moral good cannot have the singular for its object, because every morality rejects egoism" (Piaget 1932: 398). The good transcends the individual level, but not as a platonic idea in the sense of an outer ideal, but as an immanent ideal, leading "to the establishment of norms, which are immanent in their own functioning" (Piaget 1932: 437). This internalized kind of metaphysics remains, however, as speculative as the platonic one. Piaget therefore claimed that only those persons who "are capable of experiencing, within themselves, this higher and purely immanent duty, which forms the rational necessity, could grasp the value of the good" (Piaget 1932: 420). This is the same esoteric pattern as in the work of Piaget's youth, where he removed the right to enter the argument from anyone who had not undergone any mystical experience.

Since moral development of the universal norms is a divine process, it must run in an orderly way from heteronomy to autonomy. But both these moral stances can "coexist within the same age group and even within the same child" (Piaget 1932: 148), as the example of "Const" shows. Remembering her own clumsiness, the 7-year-old girl focused on subjective responsibility, but when she was told the story about the broken cups, she judged according to the objective damage (Piaget 1932: 138f.). Considering intention corresponds with a mature position, while "an evaluation, based purely on material damage, is more likely the result of adult constraint, which the child has taken on board, because of his respect for adults" (Piaget 1932: 145). Since Piaget excluded a synchronous development, we are left with the paradox of a "*co-existence of opposing tendencies*" (Vidal 1998: 587). According to Piaget, the decisive factor is the distribution of the two forms of morality, "whereby each difference in distribution becomes a qualitative difference for the whole, because the mind is a unit" (Piaget 1932: 91). Therefore, a change of moral paradigm is required in development, which Piaget expected to happen at the age of around 10 to 11. Since considerably younger children based their judgments upon intention, he claimed, as one of his typical ad hoc declarations, that this was due to the "parents, who bring up their children according to a morality of intention [allowing them to] reach their goal rather early" (Piaget 1932: 149).

In a few quotations, however, heteronomous and autonomous morality appear compatible: "These two forms of morality, which are more or less intricately combined in the adult [...], are quite distinct from each other during childhood, and will not be reconciled until later, during adolescence" (Piaget 1930/4: 33). Both the morality of constraint and the morality of cooperation are necessary, because relationships are based on duties and reciprocity. Piaget, however, never explained how such a "synthesis of the two groups of moral realities" (Piaget 1928/1: 23) into a third form of morality might become possible. Usually, Piaget presupposed antagonism or even a struggle between these two forms of morality, because "equality of individuals is not natural, but must be conquered little by little [...] Co-operation seems therefore to be the progressive victory of the social mind" (Piaget 1933/2: 87). This is reminiscent of the Zarathustrian idea that the world is dominated by a battle between good and evil.

A further problem area is the temporal difference between the manifestation of moral acts and moral consciousness. Following Claparède, Piaget established two laws: The first states that action precedes the grasp of consciousness. The second defines this process as a symbolic reconstruction of action "because every psychological operation in the different areas of acting and thought must be newly learned" (Piaget 1932: 91). Because action itself requires a cognitive process, Piaget differentiated between active, true and spontaneous thinking and verbal thinking (Piaget 1932: 124). In order to explain the fact that practical action and spoken judgments correspond despite the time lag (Piaget 1932: 130), Piaget used a metaphor from the field of music: the stages of mental development "are to be understood as consecutive phases of regular processes, which repeat themselves like rhythms, in areas of behavior and consciousness, lying one on top of the other" (Piaget 1932: 91).

Because the cognitive ability to distinguish between good and evil forms the basis of moral consciousness, cognitive development and moral development run parallel (Piaget 1930/7: 339). "To understand the other person and to respect him are one and the same, because objectivity implies the same unselfishness as altruism itself" (Piaget 1931/4: 116). Further confusion occurred, when Piaget attributed intelligence to object logic, and morality to affective logic (Piaget 1932: 454). Despite counterexamples like the intelligently engineered propaganda of Joseph Goebbels, he would adhere to his thesis of an analogous course of moral and intellectual development (Piaget cf. 1942/5: 16; 1954/6: 143f.), because "every progress [...] results from the fact that we have freed ourselves from egocentrism, and from intellectual and moral coercion" (Piaget 1933/5: 146). Piaget turned a blind eye to the fact that the ability to change perspective will allow not only cooperation but also deliberate deception and exploitation. But he claimed that development did not mean regress but meant progress, as Brunschvicg's law of development of moral judgment had demonstrated (Piaget 1932: 450f.). With this thesis of invariant progressive development, Piaget contradicted the ethnologist Lévy-Bruhl, because "we cannot regard, as contingent, the evolution which leads from a primitive mentality to a scientific mentality" (Piaget 1928/2: 56).

Primitive Morality and Civilized Democracy

Durkheim had postulated that primitive societies had a morality of their own:

They are characterized particularly by the fact that they are considerably religious. This means that the most numerous and the most important duties [. . .] do not consist in respecting and supporting one's neighbour, but consist in executing detailed, prescribed rituals, to render unto the gods that which is the gods', and, if need be, to sacrifice oneself for their glory. (Durkheim 1903: 61)

Piaget transferred this (questionable) assessment to the child: "The little one, who is dominated by unilateral respect, has the same mystical feelings towards the rules he receives from the outside, as the Australian aborigine [. . .] has for the tradition of his ancestors" (Piaget 1927/3: 1). He agreed with Durkheim's pupil, Paul Fauconnet (1874–1938), "that responsibility becomes individualized in the course of development. Whereas responsibility is collective and transferable in primitive societies, it is usually strictly personal in civilized societies" (Fauconnet 1912/1920: 330). The primitive peoples, like children, are subject to moral realism, although the conditions of moral development are quite different:

In the least evolved societies we know, children are, in fact brought up very liberally. During adolescence, on the other hand, severe educational constraint sets in, which culminates in initiation. From then on, the young men have to submit to their elders, and the elders, in turn, submit to tradition, which enslaves them in the same way as Church dogmas place the highest Church dignitaries under obligation. In our society, in contrast, the *strongest* intellectual and moral constraint happens during childhood. (Piaget 1933/2: 104)

In differentiated societies, it is therefore "the first duty of every modern adolescent, to revolt against any enforced truth, and to build his own mental and moral ideal, as freely as he might possibly do so" (Piaget 1947/8: 212). Thanks to this emancipation, "the morality of the good gains the victory over the morality of duty" (Piaget 1932: 400). Thus Piaget repeated the classical ethnocentric prejudices of Western societies: Because of "incomplete socialization" (Piaget 1945/3: 147) savages live in a retarded way, compared to civilized people: "We are more social than the non-civilized" (Piaget 1933/2: 115). The question, whether traditional tribal societies may be more cooperative than the competitive capitalist society, did not occur to him, because he understood development as an invariant process and equated socialization with moral development.

If adults remain bound by childlike realism, "their conservative attitude dwells on the idea of allowing eternal reason to triumph over present customs, while, in truth, they remain the slaves of past customs" (Piaget 1932: 75). Yet, unless the development is forcibly terminated, it will lead from "gerontocratic theocracy in all its forms to democracy, based on equality" (Piaget 1932: 368). In the classical theory of democracy, the citizen plays a paradoxical dual role of sovereign and subject. Piaget believed that children acquire the roles of legislator and law abider while playing games around the age of 10 to 11. A social game is therefore a democracy on a small scale, because through negotiation over the rules, the players learn that there can be no "offence through opinion," but only "illegal actions." "All opinions are tolerated as long as their protagonists urge their acceptance by legal methods" (Piaget 1932: 66), by which Piaget meant that an agreement is reached after a debate. The codified rules are only valid for as long as the concerned parties wish them to be. "We adults are no longer dominated by external rules. We feel that we have the right to judge the social group to which we belong, and its rules, its commands and its compulsions" (Piaget 1931/8: 112). Piaget interpreted this freedom as the result of cooperation among peers (Piaget 1932: 63), without abandoning Kant's moral definition of it: "Freedom is, in fact, autonomy, which means the submission of the individual under his self-chosen discipline" (Piaget 1944/1: 200). His concept of democracy referred to ideals of equality in the eyes of the law and cooperative division of labor, whereby he disregarded historical and political contexts.

Piaget did not concern himself with macro-social issues such as the functioning of the economy or politics, because "in the end, these depend on moral factors [...] The evil spirit of nationalism seems to make [people] blind towards each other. Seen from this point of view, the vicious circle of customs barriers, the arms race or the striving of national cultures for hegemony seems to be less of an economic or social phenomenon, than a human fact, and in its actual sense, a psychological fact" (Piaget 1931/4: 105). Piaget's psychologism led to fatalism, given the complexity of international networks, which became obvious during World War I and the worldwide economic crisis: "We are not psychologically adapted to our social condition, this is a fact. People were steam-rolled by these events, they happened too fast for our minds, for the individual mind and the collective mentality" (Piaget 1933/5: 130). Not only the citizen, but also the politician was affected by this situation:

Whereas in the 17th century, he could follow a plan, establish a line, from which he never deviated, in short, whereas he could still make real politics, he is nowadays unable to make any decision, which does not, at once, affect the entire world in completely unexpected ways. (Piaget 1933/5: 130f.)

This political idealism seems to have been the reason why there was no co-operation with the neo-Marxist Frankfurt School. Shortly after Hitler seized power in February 1933, Max Horkheimer's Institute for Social Research relocated to Geneva. For sponsorship, the International Society for Social Research was founded, and Piaget joined its board of directors, without leaving any track record of his position (for example in the *Journal for Social Research*). Since the Geneva authorities did not support these renowned intellectuals either, they soon relocated to Paris and to the USA (Wigger-shaus 1986: 152–70). Unlike most sociologists, Piaget was not interested in the role of a scientist in this society: "I would be very troubled if it were made a moral duty for me to be concerned about the social impli-cations of my work" (Piaget 1973: 59). He therefore had no qualms in applying psychology to industry and even to the military (Piaget 1970/5: 143f.).

Yet there were some analogies to the Critical Theory in Piaget's thinking. For instance, he assumed a dialectic progress of the state, according to which the state had been founded for the protection of man but was becoming a threat because of the human mind's own dynamics.

> The incredible treasures, such as solidarity, unanimous will and selfless-ness, which we human beings have amassed all over the globe in order to refine each nation's own cultural heritage, have become an obstacle for any kind of expansion. We have truly strived for co-ordination, but have declared the result as being inviolable. The motherlands that we created, by painstakingly keeping our egocentrism at bay and disciplining our-selves, are causing a revival of this very egocentrism, only now it is an even more tyrannical, collective egocentrism, which we consider sacrosanct. (Piaget 1931/4: 108)

Piaget termed this collective egocentrism sociomorphism (Piaget 1933/2: 99) or sociocentrism. Here, egocentrism merges with collective ideas, which are expressed in social symbols: myths, religious rites, dogmas, national flags and political ideologies.

> The vitality of these symbols is due to the fact each person can incor-porate them into his intimate affectivity and can fill them with the most individual content, although these symbols had been imposed upon every-one from the outside, causing a complete unification. (Piaget 1933/2: 102)

The egocentric structure of thought does not alter, because it is only a matter of replacing the individual contents with social symbols. These symbols express a superficial, nonreflected consensus, which is not the result of free negotiation but of social coercion and manifests itself in the acts of following a leader or following traditions. It prevents us from noticing any differences and from solving such differences in true debates. To counter symbolic thinking, Piaget postulated normative thinking. "The *norms*, the logical, moral and juristic principles" (Piaget 1928/2: 69), which can be attained by way of cooperation, guarantee the overcoming of sociocentrism.

This is apparently the privilege of the elite. Piaget had always been an integral part of scientific networks and had carried out most of his research and publications with the help of co-workers, but he described his own field of cooperation as being limited:

> When counting the small number of chosen ones, one is filled with silent horror. A few kindred souls, a few fellow students from school or university, a few colleagues in different countries, a few highly appreciated specialist authors, in short, a limited and select society, in which only we understand what it means to be a personality in solidarity with others. (Piaget 1931/4: 110)

For Piaget, cooperation was a purely intellectual activity, which excluded nonacademics as well as his own family. This, however, did not dampen his pedagogical purpose of "extending to the totality of human relationships the methods of co-operation, which function with great difficulty within small, highly refined subdivisions of the mind and in very few, limited circles of community life" (Piaget 1931/4: 111).

The most important factor responsible for forming both the kind of morality and the structure of society, is education, because there is "no morality without moral education" (Piaget 1930/4: 32).

> Social constraint and conformism go along with an authoritarian education, which, in each new generation, reinforces the symbols of transcendence and a morality of heteronomy. Social differentiation and co-operation go along with a more liberal education, which allows mutual respect to dominate over unilateral respect and thus fosters the development of a morality of autonomy and a religion of immanence. (Piaget 1928/1: 25)

With his work, *The Moral Judgment of the Child*, Piaget reached the goal he had set for himself in 1917: to find a scientific foundation for the Christian morality, which would save the world (cf. Vidal 1998). If cooperation prevails over constraint in socialization, immanent norms will develop, which allow peace, freedom and justice. Piaget's social and moral psychology is a description of transformation, through which the child and the society develop from a heteronomous morality, which obeys tradition, to

Table 7.1 Piaget's dualistic concepts of education

Authoritarian education	New education
Parents–child relationship	Relationship between peers
Constraint	Cooperation
Unilateral respect	Mutual respect
Hierarchy	Equality
Egocentrism, Sociocentrism	Objectivity
Egoism	Solidarity
Conformism (outer duty)	The good (inner duty)
Heteronomy	Autonomy
Gerontocracy, Theocracy	Democracy
Taboo, ritual	Critique, discussion
Conservatism	Liberalism
Tradition	Freedom
Primitive society	Civilization
Consensus	Social contract, free negotiation
Verbalism	Understanding
Symbol	Norm
Ideology	Science
Affective dependence	Love
Objective responsibility: damage	Subjective responsibility: intention
Expiatory punishment	Mutual punishment
Realism	Relativism
Transcendence	Immanence
Disequilibrium	Equilibrium
Self	Personality

an autonomous morality, where mutually accepted rules are negotiated. The decentration of perspectives and the individualization and differentiation of social roles correspond to the transition from egocentrism and sociocentrism to objectivity, from unilateral respect to mutual respect, from transcendence to immanence, and from theocracy to democracy (cf. Table 7.1).

In bringing to the fore the inferiority of a heteronomous morality, Piaget also took revenge on his parents and teachers. On 12 February 1930, shortly before publication, he wrote to his friend, Ignace Meyerson: "I am pleased with the Moral Judgement, in which I could work off all my bad temper against adult authority" (in Vidal and Parot 1996: 64).

Critique and Formalization

The Moral Judgment of the Child has been translated into ten languages and is probably Piaget's most widely read book. It has been highly praised as a "mine of queries for the thoughtful parent, teacher, or research worker" (Smith 1933: 237) and as a "vein of gold in the mountains of his thoughts" (Aebli 1983: 13). Soon Piaget's studies were followed up, and his essential findings were confirmed (Lerner 1937; Smith 1937). At the same time, however, fundamental doubts were expressed regarding his theory of stages (Harrower 1934). Susan Isaacs (1934) criticized Piaget for choosing the situations in such a way that the options for the children's answers were too limited: thus it became possible for 11-year-olds to give the same answers as 7-year-olds and they could therefore be judged to be at the same stage. In a subsequent study in 1943, Igor H. Caruso noted a gradual development, without breaks or stages. Moreover, he argued that Piaget's method of questioning hardly bore any resemblance to test procedures. Initially, Piaget did not take this criticism seriously (Piaget 1943/1: 170) but at a later stage, he viewed the insights gained from his early works in child psychology in more relative terms, not without emphasizing their pioneering aspect, however. "These five studies were limited to verbal questions and answers, and the children were not given any concrete objects to handle. The results of these first studies were, therefore, limited and only served to formulate the problems, which were new at the time" (Piaget 1968/9: 357).

In the USA, Piaget was regarded as a sociologist rather than a psychologist, whose theory would be suitable for social-scientific research. Elton Mayo (1880–1949) used Piaget's clinical interview approach to design interviews for the famous Hawthorne experiment (Hsueh 2002). The Russian psychologists objected to the abstract and intellectualist term of the social and to the dualistic conception of his theory: "The social works as an external force, through coercion, it suppresses the child's own thought processes, which would befit his nature, and replaces them by schemes of thought, which are imposed from the outside and are alien to the child" (Vygotsky 1934: 108). Cognitive development, therefore, was nothing but the mechanical suppression of one's own self. Mikhail Jaroshevsky (in Veer 1996: 220) considered Piaget a dualist, because he understood the individual world as being in opposition to the social world. Sergej Rubinstein (in Veer 1996: 221ff.) also considered Piaget's theory to be ambivalent because he had mixed up the psychoanalytical interpretation of the autistic child with the objectivity of Durkheim's social experience.

George Davy's criticism concerned the construction of an autonomous morality as "a redoubling that subjects the individual to a rule or a principle, which the individual has voluntarily rendered independent of himself, as well as superior to him" (Davy 1939: 227). Furthermore, mutual respect is only one aspect of a relationship, upon which one cannot base an entire morality. Piaget insisted, however, that "this kind of respect is not a random form of mutuality, but is, strictly speaking, a particular form, in which the respective points of view are mutually recognized" (Piaget 1954/12: 121). Charles Blondel criticized that children were likened to primitive peoples and pointed out that the children in Piaget's theory could not have any collective ideas, whereas "the ideas we encounter among primitive peoples are collective" (in Piaget 1933/2: 129f.). Piaget had also idealized coopera-tion, which, according to Blondel, was simply a different form of coercion. Marcel Mauss (1872–1950) was of the opinion that Piaget was not practicing general child psychology, but "psychology of the most civilized child" (in Piaget 1933/2). And he thought that the difference between primitive and civilized peoples was much less pronounced than one might like to assume. Piaget admitted that there was no difference from the functional point of view but insisted that, from the structural point of view, primitive people think on a pre-operative level (Piaget 1950 III: 243).

In 1943, Piaget was confronted with Marxism, when Lucien Goldmann (1913–1970) arrived at Piaget's door and declared that he wanted to work with him, because he was the most authentic dialectician in the Western world. This praise referred to Piaget's statements that intelligence develops through interaction with one's environment and through a growing aware-ness of contradictions. Piaget was surprised and admitted to Goldmann: "I have never read a single line of Marx, nor of the Marxist theorists, and I have no intention of doing so" (Piaget 1973/14: 546). Yet Goldmann man-aged to convince Piaget, and was offered a position among his staff one hour later. Piaget began to study Marx and was fascinated by the dialectic materialism, although he distanced himself from Marx's "political passions" (Piaget 1950 III: 232). Since Marx's philosophy of history was based on an immanent logic of development, Piaget tried to identify parallels between the genetic psychology and the "concrete sociology of behavior" founded by Marx (Piaget 1950 III: 187).

To do so, Piaget broadened his earlier postulate after which the cog-nitive aspect (operations) and the affective aspect (values) of the mental facts correspond to the social facts. "Every society is a system of obligations (rules), of exchanges (values), and of conventional symbols, which serve to express the rules and the values (signs)" (Piaget 1941/4: 100). Social exchange requires the reciprocal acceptance of values: when one agent renders a service to another, the second one is expected to compensate this non-equality. This compensation of the debts contains a valuation of the service, which depends on the aspect of time as well. The longer the time between service and compensation is, the less the second one estimates the first one. This is why "the transfer of values is based [...] on a large credit, perpetually maintained" (Piaget 1950 III: 110). Piaget (1945/3) formalized these expectations of reciprocity in terms of equilibrium that form an order of values. For Piaget, signs are arbitrary and neutral conventions for communication, while symbols are the basis for ideologies. Piaget's psychology explained that ideologies derived from egocentric thinking, whereas actions are based on sensory-motor thinking and science on operational thinking. The sociological explanation comprises three levels as well (Piaget 1950 III: 224ff.):

- real action (work and technique form the basis of society)
- ideology (the symbolic conceptualization of conflicts), and
- science (which explains the actions and expands them into operations)

This middle position of ideology contains the whole problem of the ambivalent concept of egocentrism. Ideologies play, in fact, "a dual role in preparing the way for scientific thinking, as well as obstructing scientific thinking; on the one hand, ideological thinking leads to an elaboration of general ideas (causality, legality, substance)" (Piaget 1951/6: 154), on the other hand, it remains sociocentric (racism, disrespect for women, nationalism).

Once symbolic thinking is overcome, thanks to cooperation, the "state," for example, would be understood as nothing more than a "juristic order, seen as a whole, and any attempt to attribute to the state an order other than a purely normative one, exceeds the law and belongs to the realm of political ideology" (Piaget 1950 III: 221). While Piaget succeeded in avoiding a hypostasis of the state, this very flaw of reasoning occurred when dealing with the concept of law: "The law completes transpersonal rules, i.e. relationships that permit the substitution of individuals through identical functions or services" (Piaget 1950 III: 215). By disengaging the contents of the law from the legislators, he removed from the law its political dimension, and replaced history by evolution. Thus, moral individualization and judicial elaboration are "the same constructive process" (Piaget 1944/4: 185). Because Piaget believed that all developments follow invariant tendencies, his sociology regressed into a "19th century unilinear evolutionism" (Berthoud 1976: 488).

8

The Pedagogic Work

The International Bureau of Education

In 1929 Piaget was able to return to Geneva as a professor of history of scientific thought, whereupon Jean de la Harpe, who had been bypassed four years earlier, took up Piaget's chair in Neuchâtel. Piaget not only became a member of the science faculty at Geneva University, but was appointed Director of the International Bureau of Education and Deputy Director of the Jean-Jacques Rousseau Institute. Both institutions had undergone some changes.

In 1928 the Geneva parliament had again debated the issue of subsidies to the JJRI, because its experimental school was said to have neglected discipline, and the institute was allegedly undertaking speculative research and acting as a propaganda machine for 'Red Vienna'. One year earlier, a member of their staff, Robert Dottrens (1893–1984), had published a praising book about the New Education in Austria, which contained a preface by Bovet, underlining Vienna's model character for the reform of Geneva schools. Piaget also agreed that "what is happening in Vienna appears to us as an ideal, which we would like to put into practice in Switzerland" (Piaget 1928/3: 55). The JJRI considered the school to be a political instrument for the reform of society. "History teaches us that revolutions generate progress in school education. Revolutions establish new principles, and the necessity to instruct the younger generation in accordance with the revolutionary ideal, soon becomes obvious" (Dottrens 1927: 192). This revolutionary rhetoric set alarm bells ringing among the conservatives. Even though its political intentions met with harsh criticism, the JJRI was annexed to the university in 1929, and became the Institute of Education Sciences. Because teacher training was undergoing a crisis in the canton, the professor of pedagogy and newly elected social democratic director of public education, Albert Malche (1876–1956), had decreed in 1928 that teacher training should consist of a three-year course of studies at the JJRI and proposed its affiliation to the university. Dottrens, who had great influence on the actual work done at the JJRI, and Piaget, as a member of the administrative council, favored the affiliation, in opposition to Claparède who worried about the JJRI's independence. The contract of cooperation with the university safeguarded the autonomy of JJRI/IES with regard to finance and administration and improved the economic situation. However, the following years remained difficult because the emerging economic crisis caused the number of students to drop from 120 in 1931 to 61 in 1934 (Lussi, Muller and Kiciman 2002: 405).

The International Bureau of Education, which the JJRI had founded in 1925, also became affiliated. Since 1880, there had been at least 15 initiatives to establish an international institute of education (Rossello 1943). As early as 1899, Ferrière had established the International Bureau of New Schools, following Edmond Demolins' instigation, and this Bureau had become an important center of documentation for pedagogical reform schools and homes, which were rated by Ferrière according to a list of points. In 1918, however, the major part of Ferrière's archives was destroyed by a fire, and the one-man enterprise was short of funds. In 1923, this Bureau was therefore integrated into the JJRI, after the 3rd Moral Congress of 1922, held at Geneva and chaired by Ferrière, had decided to initiate a new international bureau of education in The Hague. With the approval of the executive committee, Ferrière undertook the task of organizing such a bureau in the autumn of 1924. Meanwhile the second conference of the New Education Fellowship, held in 1923 at Montreux, had asked Henri Bergson to commend a bureau on behalf of the League of Nations. Bergson was the president of the International Institute of Intellectual Cooperation (IIIC), which, in fact, excluded educational issues, in order to avoid conflicts arising from infringement upon the sovereignty of the states. Because of this limitation, the JJRI decided to establish a private bureau of education, after the Rockefeller Foundation pledged support in 1925. The Bureau's committee of patrons included, among others, Albert Thomas, the director of the International Labour Office and Albert Einstein, a member of the IIIC. Among the members of the initiative committee were Dottrens, Malche, Piaget and Pedro Rossello (1897–1970). Bovet was appointed as director, and the deputy directors were Ferrière and Elisabeth Rotten (1885–1974); Marie Butts became the secretary general, and Claparède's son, Jean-Louis (1901–1937), was put in charge of the archives. The extensive information department of the JJRI was integrated into the new IBE that was housed in the buildings of the JJRI.

Faced with a *fait accompli*, the 400 participants of the Fourth International Moral Education Congress of 1926 in Rome approved the transfer of the IBE from The Hague to Geneva. Together with the Teacher's College in New York (where John Dewey, William H. Kilpatrick and Edward Thorndike worked), the London Day Training College (later called the Institute of Education in London, run by Percy Nunn) and the Haute Ecole de Pédagogie in Brussels (with Tobie Jonckheere and Ovide Decroly), Geneva was one of the most important centers of the New Education (Oelkers 1996a: 165), which were in competition with one another. The new independent IBE cooperated closely with the New Education Fellowship, which created tensions with the International Moral Education Congress. These difficulties were compounded due to financial bottlenecks and the differing views regarding how to rescue the dwindling pedagogical reform movement. Some optimists had hoped that perhaps one million teachers worldwide might be persuaded to pay an annual subscription of 5 SFr. each, but despite huge efforts only about 400 members could be recruited. Three years later, during which time exhibitions, congresses and conferences were organized, the IBE had accrued such serious debts that its very existence was in jeopardy. When Germany offered to fund the IBE, with the proviso that it must relocate to Berlin, the Rockefeller Foundation decided to grant another subsidy, but demanded that the Bureau should work on an intergovernmental level, in order to prevent nationalist tendencies (Vidal 1997: 87). At the same time, Pedro Rossello, who was appointed assistant director in 1928, succeeded in convincing the Geneva Canton to cofinance it. Once again, facts had to be created swiftly, to outsmart the opposition of the IIIC (cf. Piaget 1952/1: 131). The Education Ministries of Poland, Ecuador and Geneva Canton, as well as the JJRI, signed the agreement for the new foundation on 25 July 1929. Rossello became both the driving force of the IBE and its main chronicler.

The way in which Piaget later described his own appointment as director of the IBE, on 15 August 1929, creates the impression that he had no ambitions: "I imprudently accepted the duties of director [...] on the insistence of my friend Pedro Rossello" (Piaget 1952/1: 130). Nevertheless, Piaget led the IBE for the next 39 years, represented the Bureau at New Education congresses and the conferences of the League of Nations and UNESCO, organized its research, publications and annual conferences, and wrote the final summary reports thereof. He did all this in the hope of "contributing toward the improvement of pedagogical methods and toward the official adoption of techniques better adapted to the mentality of the child" (Piaget 1952/1: 131). Piaget did not merely wish to place New Education upon the scientific footing of his child psychology but also to encourage its political implementation on an international level. "Piaget hoped to exert his influence upon the Ministers for State Education, and felt, along with Bovet and Claparède, that educational reform required the combined action from schools and government departments, from top management down and from the grassroots up" (Xypas 1997). Hitherto, there had been no division of tasks between the IBE and the JJRI. Now Piaget announced an independent remit for the IBE, by charging them with the "co-ordination of the national departments of education themselves and of their efforts regarding the progress of education" (Piaget 1936/1: 23). Due to cross-staffing, however, the two institutes retained a close relationship.

Since 1928, the IBE had been organizing the summer course entitled "How to make the League of Nations known and how to develop the spirit of international co-operation," which was aimed at teachers, school directors, inspectors and government officials. To help with the propaganda for the League of Nations, a permanent exhibition was set up, and a collection of children's books about other countries was published. Like Bovet, Piaget was convinced that teaching children about the League of Nations and about international solidarity only makes sense if the children experience the meaning of solidarity in their everyday school life. To do so, one should encourage party games, discussions, pen pals, student exchanges, activities of youth organizations such as the Red Cross or the Scouts, lecture about different countries, and integral teaching (Piaget 1930/1: 54; 1930/4: 76; 1931/4: 116). According to Piaget, the pacification of the world is unthinkable without the school, provided that the adults themselves behaved in a cooperative manner. "Only a pedagogy, which is founded on social relationships and which implements the unity between adults, will permit the development of a morally sane, international attitude and will permit the child to surpass us" (Piaget 1932/1: 76).

The central aim of the IBE consisted in providing and processing information to help the education departments to implement reforms, which were in accordance with the League of Nations: improved education opportunities, international cooperation and securing peace. For these purposes, surveys were conducted among the member states, concerning the conditions of teaching and learning. Studies were carried out regarding

- child labor among children who left school before the age of 14
- youth literature
- relationships between school and family
- family relationships
- self-government and teamwork
- problems due to bilingualism

Every four months, a bulletin was issued that published the research results and documented the work done. Yet five years after its foundation, the IBE was still not widely recognized. At the Fifth International Moral Education Congress in Paris, a participant proposed the founding of an international bureau, whereupon Piaget had to remind him that "this Bureau already exists" (Piaget 1930/5: 277). As a member of the executive board of the New Education Fellowship, Piaget was actively involved in the last congresses of the movement in Elsinor (1929), Paris (1930), and Nice (1932), where he held speeches about his pedagogical views. But in Krakow (1934), Alina Szeminska read his speech about the development of the moral ideas.

Educational Aims and Problems

According to Piaget, the prime aim of education was that the children should become self-determined personalities, capable of cooperation. "Personality is the disciplined self that contributes to the laborious evolution of society, whereas the pre-social self is nothing but the anomic conscience of the infant, which needs to be tamed through education" (Piaget 1935/4: 185). This feature of disciplined contribution was matched by Piaget's own lifestyle:

> Piaget shows great discipline. He gets up early in the morning, sometimes as early as four o'clock, and in his small, neat handwriting, fills four or more pages of square white paper with words, ready to be printed. Later in the morning, he teaches or he attends meetings. In the afternoons, he takes long walks, on which he reflects upon the problems with which he is constantly confronted [...] In the evenings he reads and then retires early. Even during his international travels, he adheres to this daily routine. (Elkind 1968: 25)

Discipline is the result of the insight into the necessity of norms, which develops through mutual respect. Children have to discover the discipline "for themselves, in action, rather than adopting a ready-made discipline without understanding" (Piaget 1949/6: 54). He felt that the goal of educating children into autonomous citizens had hitherto scarcely been reached: "One knows how few autonomous adults there are, how inadequate our pedagogy is, when one contemplates life as one's criterion" (Piaget 1928/2: 73). Because children are obliged to obey, they neglect their potential for reflection and critique, and because they have to adopt existing solutions, their creativity atrophies. A further goal must therefore be "to create human beings, capable of achieving new things rather than simply repeating the acts of previous generations—human beings, who are creative, innovative and full of joy in discovering things" (Piaget 1964/2: 5).

Piaget identified several reasons why education had failed in achieving these goals. One of the obstacles was the ignorance or the wrong interpretation of the radical difference between the thinking of the child and of the adult: "The child has his own interests, his own activities, his own thoughts, and we must use this as our starting point for the child's education" (Piaget 1925/2: 464). The crucial mistake of traditional pedagogy was "to expect that the child's mental structure was identical to that of an adult, but that it functioned in a different way [...] In fact, the reverse is true" (Piaget 1939/3: 155f.). Children and adults both act according to their needs and interests. Their way of thinking, however, undergoes a dramatic mutation: "Like a tadpole, who can already breathe, but uses organs that are different from those of the fully developed frog, the child acts like the adult, but uses a mentality with varying structures, depending on the stage of the child's development" (Piaget 1939/3: 156). The human being, therefore, has an amphibian psyche, which undergoes transformation in accordance with the biological conditions of development.

Despite this Rousseauism, Piaget tried to avoid Rousseau's positive anthropology, according to which the child's natural goodness had to be protected from society. "The psychological nature of the individual is itself the source of the worst excesses, as well as the source of all imaginable positive developments" (Piaget 1930/4: 32). This, however, does not imply that the human condition is neutral, since Piaget assumed a "child's original psychological tendency for co-operation" (Piaget 1932: 325). But this tendency is not manifest in relationships with adults because cooperation requires reciprocity and equality. But "equality of adults and children is not possible" (Piaget 1932: 317). Even if parents and teachers try to respect the child like an adult, they cannot bypass dos and don'ts, and thus produce moral heteronomy, as Piaget demonstrated with the example of his daughter (Piaget 1932: 201ff.). Conflicts arise due to the hierarchic relationship and are amplified through the educational actions of adults. Furthermore, "the child feels inferior to the adult in every way, and, for a long time, labours under the delusion that the adult understands everything he himself says" (Piaget 1924: 205). Therefore, the child cannot be himself in the presence of parents or teachers, but has to suppress his spontaneity. This is why "the concepts of justice, solidarity and generosity [...] are, to a considerable extent, conquests that are made independently from adults, and often even despite adults" (Piaget 1928/1: 23). Hence the rebellion, which allows the adolescent "to escape, at least in his innermost depth, from the authority of adults, in order to find in relationships with his peers the life source of his future activity" (Piaget 1933/2: 99).

In many passages, Piaget equated the sociological term of coercion with the hierarchic parent–child relationship, while he considered relationships between children as egalitarian and cooperative. Only in cooperative relationships, such as he experienced in the Friends of Nature Club, can true moral feelings and attitudes come about. Piaget remained trapped in the romantic view that children, left to themselves, harmonize on an egalitarian basis: "the first 'buds' of equality can be found in the earliest relationships between children" (Piaget 1932: 322). There are only a few statements where he considered the possibility that true morality emerges "according to the parents' ability to be friends, rather than simply being legislators" (Piaget 1928/4: 114). Normally, he disregarded the fact that most parents cooperate with their children. He therefore thought that educators should be rather passive and confine themselves to respect the child's activity.

The Active Child and the *Ecole Active*

According to Piaget, the central question, which must be asked by the New Education, was whether spontaneous activity, arising from self-interest, was enough to acquire "superior adult behavior" (Piaget 1939/3: 155), or whether enforced work was required. "Spontaneous activity" was regarded to be the central criterion for a child-adapted education, since the child is not a passive being. Bovet had coined the expression *école active* for a school that focuses on the child's own inquisitive initiative. "In a school that considers the child to be an *active* organism, [...] in an *active school*, as we shall call it for short, everything is changed [...] The function of the lesson is to stimulate activity, the child's activities, so that they can be perfected through exercise" (Bovet 1919: 53). With his concept, Bovet combined the principles of the *Arbeitsschule* of Georg Kerschensteiner (1854–1932), the *méthode active* of Henri Marion (1846–1896) and the problem-orientation of John Dewey (1859–1952), together with the theories of child activity (of Spencer and James) and of active self-development (according to Bergson). Bovet advocated the abolition of schoolbooks, which, according to him, reduced the learning process to a consumption of pre-digested knowledge. Instead, he suggested that the children should research for themselves, with the help of encyclopaedias, dictionaries and documents, whereby the teacher's function should be limited to stimulating research, while trusting in the child's nature. "It will be less a matter of learning, than of learning how to 'learn', learning how to work" (Bovet 1919: 54). In his book *L'école active*, which appeared in 1922, Ferrière processed Bovet's outline into a didactic theory, which attracted much interest and was translated into 13 languages. Based on a six-step developmental psychology, he integrated several different methodological approaches into a system that combined the child's present needs with the future-oriented demands of life and society. He recommended the Montessori method for the elementary level, the didactics of Ovide Decroly for the intermediate level, and the Winnetka-Plan of Carlton Washburne for the advanced level. As long as the child's inclinations and interests were in accordance with the teacher's instructions, the immanent law of reason would unfold, leading from egocentrism to a sense of the social, from heteronomy to autonomy, and from an animal-like unconsciousness to consciousness of the universal laws.

Initially, Piaget understood activity to be of a physical nature: "Teaching must be based on personal, muscular activities (games of construction, calculation and modelling, etc.) and not on spoken words" (Piaget 1925/2: 464). Two years earlier, Claparède (1923) had criticized his friend Ferrière for using the term activity in an ambivalent way, i.e. in a "functional sense" as well as in an "effectual sense." Reception was also a form of activity, which ought to have been considered in its functional context. Since the goal of activity was to satisfy certain needs, the "active school" should use these needs as its basis, whereby one might have to arouse the children's interests initially. Piaget adopted Claparède's view. The modern school addressed "genuine activity, the spontaneous work, which is based on needs and personal interest" (Piaget 1939/3: 155). The child does not want to be taught, but wants to explore the world for himself. Piaget did not vote for the abolition of lessons, "but lessons should be reduced to a more modest role and should be subordinated to individual work: now it becomes a matter of finding the answers to questions the pupils ask themselves" (Piaget 1935/4: 182). Later, however, Piaget returned to his idea of manual activity.

> It is absolutely necessary that learners have at their disposal concrete material experiences (and not merely pictures), and that they form their own hypotheses and verify them (or not verify them) themselves through their own active manipulations. The observed activities of others, including those of the teachers, are not formative of new organizations. (Piaget 1973/16: ix)

Compared to teacher-centered approaches, he considered audio-visual methods, such as films, to be a slight progress. "They are, however, by no means sufficient to develop operative activity" (Piaget 1965/1: 81). The child must "grasp" things, "it is the materials he should learn from" (Piaget 1973/15: 23). Piaget too used the term "active" ambiguously and embedded in a dualist argumentation, in which

- active, exciting research and passive, boring reception
- new, progressive school and old, conservative school
- pupil-centred, cooperative lessons and teacher-centered, authoritarian lessons
- understanding of problems and rote-learning of material

were opposed to one another. Piaget was convinced that only those contents that were actively learned would be retained in the long term. "The things that will evaporate are all the things which have been merely taken over from external sources, or which were copied down or memorized, without true motivation" (Piaget 1935/4: 195). Obviously, activity and intrinsic motivation are mutually conditioning, because "the very principle of activity leads to [...] the stimulation of effort" (Piaget 1931/12: 46).

Spontaneity, a relic of Bergsonism, is the second key word in Piaget's pedagogical anthropology. "In all of my pedagogical writings, old or recent, I have [...] insisted that formal education could gain a great deal, much more than ordinary methods do at present, from a systematic utilization of the child's spontaneous mental development" (Piaget 1962/1: 250). One of the models for active and spontaneous learning is the playing of games, a model "which the new pedagogy uses as an essential lever of interest and effort, and which all too often is confused with useless amusement. It is therefore important to define the true character of children's games, if we want to protect the active school from a childish and softened pedagogy" (Piaget 1959/2: 315). The other model is experimental science, because pupils should not learn from books, but through research and verification. Piaget (1972b: 89) had to admit, however, that it is impossible to use experimental methods in subjects like Latin or history.

Pedagogical Errors

The core of Piaget's critique concerning the school system was directed against artificial and superficial methods of presentation and conveyance. Traditional schools present

> the knowledge to be acquired, without relating it to the child's interests or to any proper action. Moreover (and this increases the lack of meaning for the pupil), the matter is presented in isolation and in an analytical way. There are lessons in grammar, arithmetics, geography etc., but they remain without connections, so that the child cannot understand the inner links between these fields, and thus cannot understand their reference to life itself. To crown it all, the timetable is fragmented: after every hour one must totally change one's orientation. (Piaget 1939/4: 4)

This statement repeated the criticism made by Flournoy, Claparède, Bovet, Ferrière and Dottrens, who had accused the teacher-centered state schools of neglecting the potentials of pupils and of fostering uneducated human beings who lack self-reliance and live in awe of authority. Piaget compared the role of educators to that of the tribal elders in primitive cultures, who are in charge of the often gruesome "initiation of the adolescents, although their present-day 'masks' will no longer induce the same horror, but seem to have become a symptom of our pedagogues' occupational disease, and the sacred mysteries they transmit are no longer magic procedures, but are simply pre-fabricated truths" (Piaget 1947/8: 214).

Because of the "mysticism of the word of an adult" (Piaget 1932: 458), the pupil accepts the teaching as a higher truth, without having understood it, and he settles for learning the theorems off by heart, so that, when the occasion arises, he can rattle them off like dogmas. This "sad reality in schools" was called "verbalism" and meant that "spurious concepts, linked to words without true meaning, are getting out of hand" (Piaget 1939/3: 168), thus causing the usual shallow education of school leavers. The teacher-talk-dominated lesson consolidates the child's egocentrism, because it prevents cooperation with peers. This does not mean that the teacher's questions can be dispensed with. "One has to lead the child to the point where he reaches the correct awareness of the consequences of his actions" (Piaget 1926/1: 55). To this end, the teacher must be able to distinguish between practical questions and questions that aid understanding, because the first kind must be asked before the second: "I'd rather ask questions that lead to a practical task and then, once the child has succeeded in this, go on to the question of how it happened" (Piaget 1973/15: 24).

On the whole, lessons seem to have only a limited effect "because although the school indoctrinates the child with the contents of collective ideas, following a certain time schedule, his language and his general way of thinking are nonetheless defined by the environment in its entirety" (Piaget 1950 III: 179). This is why Piaget supported institutions such as the Scouts or the League of Goodness, where "the child simply promises to ask himself every morning what good deeds he might do today. In the evening, the child tallies up for himself an account of his efforts and remembers his observations of other people's good deeds" (Piaget 1930/4: 62). The results are recorded, posted anonymously into a box and discussed during the ethics lesson. According to Piaget, these pedagogical designs of Robert Baden-Powell and Gérôme Périnet are also suitable for sex education:

The Scout's appeal to personal honor and to mutual respect, the promise of good deeds demanded by the League of Goodness and, above all, the targeted mobilization of spontaneous interest and the provision of opportunities for co-operation are of crucial importance for mastering one's physical urges. We may say that sexual disorders among children are almost always due to the fact that the individual has not found a ruling ideal to which he could commit himself. (Piaget 1930/4: 67)

Piaget hoped for sublimation through good deeds and thus recommended, like Rousseau before him, that the child's curiosity in this respect should not be stimulated but that he must be furnished with objective information when the occasion arises. Piaget clearly spoke out against coercion and intimidation in sex education and advocated coeducation.

For obvious reasons, his own children did not receive any sex education. Despite the open and humorous atmosphere in the family, sexuality was a taboo (L. Piaget). Piaget scarcely involved himself in the education of his three children. "They have received an excellent education, thanks to the fact that I did not concern myself with their education at all. My wife was in charge of the children's education. I mainly observed them" (in Altwegg 1983: 152). He spent time with his children at the dinner table, during their weekend hiking tours and during their family holidays at the Spanish seaside or in the Valais mountains but at any other time the children were not allowed to disturb him at his work. His relationship with his children was more of an intellectual nature, and his son has nothing but good memories of his father; he nonetheless used to feel "a little intimidated" (L. Piaget) by him. The Piagets kept a maid, and while the three children were still young they also had a nanny. Despite having staff, Valentine dedicated herself fully to the role of mother and stayed at home. The children were brought up according to the ideas of New Education and were sent to private pedagogical reform schools, such as the Ecole Internationale de Genève. "When they started school, the teachers were surprised to see that my children were completely normal pupils. They had been convinced that I had subjected my children to some kind of traumatizing experiments. Today, my son is a librarian, one daughter lives in Holland and the other daughter is a secretary" (in Altwegg, 1983: 152f.).

Piaget criticized "the parents' great number of psychological absurdities", such as

> the multitude of instructions (the "average parents" are like bad governments, who simply pile law upon law, disregarding any contradictions between them or disregarding the mental confusion resulting from the sheer number), their enjoyment of giving out punishments, their enjoyment of using their authority, and that kind of sadism, which is found even among the most righteous people, who have made it their principle that "the child's will must be subdued" or that the child must be made to feel that "there is a higher will than the child's." (Piaget 1932: 217f.)

He condemned coercion as "the worst of all pedagogical methods" (Piaget 1949/8: 28). In the field of pedagogy as well, Durkheim was Piaget's major enemy, despite his unconventional views in matters of education.

According to Piaget, Durkheim had wanted to educate free and self-reliant personalities but, having failed to apply any adequate child sociology, he had defended the authoritarian method. His method did not work because "the issue of obedience is ultimately reduced to the question of whether one's judgement is due to one's obedience or whether one obeys due to one's judgement" (Piaget 1950 III: 213).

Piaget denounced any form of one-sided punishment as barbaric (Piaget 1928/1: 28) because "from the child's point of view, atonement is the same as revenge" (Piaget 1932: 262). Instead, he advocated a form of "punishment which is based on reciprocity [...], based on the concept of equality" (Piaget 1932: 226). A simple telling off, an explanation as to the consequences of the child's action, and in extreme cases, a punishment that involves compensation are "much more useful than corporal punishment" (Piaget 1932: 227). It was therefore important "to replace punishment itself by a system of measures, based on reciprocity, which merely illustrates that the ties of solidarity have been broken, to which the misdemeanour bears witness" (Piaget 1934/2: 164). The guilty person will then be stripped of honorary offices or of a responsibility, or he will be temporarily excluded from the group. His daughter, for instance, "had never been punished, in the usual sense of the word. At most, if she flew into tantrums, she was left alone for a moment, and was told that we would come back once she was ready for a talk" (Piaget 1932: 200). Piaget also had reservations regarding rewards: "Firstly, reward, like punishment, is doubtless a sign of moral heteronomy [...]. Moreover, and above all, a reward is the supplementing element of this competition between individuals, which our classical moral education has turned into the great driving force of the entire pedagogy" (Piaget 1930/4: 71).

Active education accepts the idea of competition between working groups or teams, but rejects egoistical rivalry, which leads to a hierarchy. Inequality and isolation are further generated through grades and exams, which corrupt the child's tendency towards cooperation. The usual tests are not deemed useful instruments for assessing performance, because too many distorting influences like the emotions are involved. Since, in addition, their prognostic value was perceived as being low, the JJRI/IES would not set exams in order to test knowledge, but the students had to prove their abilities in a practical way. "We do not want to examine knowledge which is rote-learned" (Bovet 1932: 118). Qualifications put into words, "have been proven to be more stimulating and ultimately more objective than any type of grade average, whose numerical and pseudo-mathematical character is known to everyone as being utterly symbolic" (Piaget 1965/1: 114). The new methods therefore focus less on the final product than on the mechanism through which performance is generated.

The New Methods and the Historiography of Pedagogy

According to Piaget, the child cannot be supported to the optimum level, unless one is "'guiding nature in following it', which means that one must follow the insights gained from child psychology" (Piaget 1931/3: 101). Yet it is a difficult task to turn the motto of Francis Bacon (1620: I: 3) into a practical methodology:

> The lessons must be timed to match the child's current development-psychological stage, to make sure that the child's interest is already engaged [...] A lesson will not yield results, unless it meets a need, and a need is only met when the knowledge transmitted corresponds to a reality, which the child has spontaneously experienced and tested. (Piaget 1931/3: 78f.)

Successful teaching can only make the child aware of his practical skills. The teacher therefore has to wait until the child has acquired a competence, before he can turn it into a central theme for consolidation. In order to solve this paradoxical situation, Piaget recommended creating as "natural" surroundings as possible, which, "while not 'spontaneous' in themselves, evoke spontaneous elaboration on the part of the child, if one manages both to spark his interest and to present the problem in such a way that it corresponds to the structures he had already formed himself" (Piaget 1962/1: 251f.). For Piaget, the "American question" (Piaget 1967: 30) as to what kind of training might accelerate development, was basically pointless, because learning processes require equilibration, which cannot be learned. Thus, Piaget defined the methods of the active school to be those that use the child's autonomous development and spontaneous activity as their base.

As precursors of the new methods, Piaget named Socrates, Comenius, Rousseau, Pestalozzi, Fröbel and Herbart (Piaget 1939/3; 1957/1). Although Piaget conceded that they had not been able to present any adequate theory of mental development, he believed that they had all emphasized the importance of pupil activity and autonomy, and of a true community within the classroom, perceiving therefore the issues intuitively, which later were analyzed and verified empirically by twentieth-century psychology. It was not until the appearance of genetic psychology that a "true embryology of intelligence and consciousness" (Piaget 1939/3: 145) emerged and served as the foundation of the New Education. Thus Piaget constructed a history of pedagogy that amounted to the conclusion that pedagogy had overcome its unscientific approach with the help of psychology, whereby his own theory appeared to be a point of culmination and intersection of pedagogical and psychological findings. According to this historical account, the milestones of applying psychology to pedagogy were set by William James, Stanley Hall, Baldwin and Dewey in the USA, Bergson, Binet and Janet in France, the Würzburg School around Karl Bühler in Germany, as well as by Flournoy, Claparède and Bovet in Switzerland.

Piaget insinuated that the New Education movement was developing toward a coherent theory that was implemented in the methods of individualization of Maria Montessori (1870–1952) in Italy, of Ovide Decroly (1871–1932) in Belgium, and in the Maison des Petits. He also identified important impulses for the emergence of these methods in the American "progressive movement": the Dalton Plan by Helen Parkhurst (1887–1959), the school in Winnetka under the management of Carleton Washburne (1889–1968), and the project method, inspired by Dewey. Individualization, however, was not the only principle, because "any appeal to free activity will necessarily lead to group work and to *self-government*" (Piaget 1939/4: 10). Autonomy and reciprocity were the two supplementary aspects of the New Education. "On the one hand, we must follow the child's natural development [. . .], on the other hand we must prevent any potential deviation at each stage of the development" (Piaget 1951/14: 263). The only sensible solution for these paradox challenges is found in self-government and group work because here the children "educate" themselves.

The IBE examined the practice of allowing children to work in groups throughout 16 countries, and reported on 518 experiments (Jakiel, Piaget, Petersen and Cousinet 1935). The main advantage of this method was seen in the acquisition of working techniques and in more efficient learning: "The greater the amount of activity, put into the acquisition of knowledge, the more solid and well-founded the knowledge will become, and group work is generally more 'active' than individual work" (Piaget 1935/4: 196). With younger children, below the ages of 8–10, however, group work was deemed impossible, due to the children's "confused contacts" (Piaget 1939/3: 179). However, Piaget did not advocate permanent group work but recommended "the necessary balance between collective and individual aspects of mental work" (Piaget 1965/1: 87).

What was achieved, on an intellectual level, through mutual stimulation in group work, was meant to be achieved, on a social and moral level, through self-government: by negotiating their own rules and sanctions, the pupils would develop "a new solidarity, a sense of equality and justice" (Piaget 1939/4: 13). The JJRI/IES propagated "turning the school class into a miniature society and turning the school into a federation of little, more or less autonomous republics" (Ferrière 1921: 10). In a democratic society, there was no place for a school under absolutist rule. "If we want to safeguard the progress of democracy, we must gradually introduce democracy into our schools. If we want people to know how to use their freedom, we must make sure that they learn this at school" (Dottrens 1933: 13). Piaget, too, emphasized that freedom and practical experience were preconditions for an education towards autonomy. One could therefore easily "sacrifice the school subject of 'civics' to practical lessons [. . .], because this would bring about a greater civic sense than the most brilliant lessons, which usually have no lasting effects to speak of, unless they are underpinned by social experience" (Piaget 1949/6: 59). The IBE also published a study on the method of *Self-government at School* (Heller and Piaget 1934). In his contribution, Piaget tried to structure the multitude of self-government methods, by distinguishing between three areas of application: between teachers and pupils, between older and younger pupils (for example, in the Scouts) and in the leadership principle between pupils of the same age. For Piaget, the leadership principle did not contradict self-government, because "for each of these social structures, there is potentially a corresponding form of *self-government*" (Piaget 1934/2: 164). Democratic states, as well as fascist ones, would therefore be able to implement this method in their programs of education. Fours years earlier, Piaget had still been linking this method to the "need of equality" (Piaget 1930/2: 57). The public announcement of his change of position was not only due to the fact that the fascist representatives of the IBE distanced themselves from the Genevans' political intentions. The German representative, for example, had stressed in his contribution that "it is not a parliamentary democracy any more, which governs the *Jugendbünde* [youth associations], but it is the authoritarian principle of leaders" (Heller 1934: 33). A further reason was that, in Geneva itself, there had arisen new resistance against the JJRI/IES's political aims.

The Change of Power at the Institute

As a result of world economic crisis, Geneva experienced a radicalization of the political groups. During left-wing demonstrations against the fascist Union Nationale, on 9 November 1932, the army killed 13 people in a shooting and injured a further 62, whereupon Pierre Bovet heavily criticized the police action. Very quickly, the finger of blame was pointed at the youths and at the school, who were made out to be the main culprits of the prevailing "moral and intellectual anarchy." The banker, Gabriel Bonnet, accused the JJRI/IES in parliament of having polluted primary schools with subversive theories. He held the "new methods" to be responsible for the lack of discipline among the youths, and the institute's internationalism and pacifism were branded as Bolshevism. After a lengthy debate, the parliament decided to continue their subsidies to the JJRI/IES, albeit with the proviso that the Institute must restrict itself to science only (cf. Vidal 1988).

It was not only the politicians who distanced themselves from the JJRI/IES, but also the teachers who had formerly sympathized with the institute withdrew their allegiance. At the Twelfth Congress of the Teachers' Association, which 12 years earlier had saved the JJRI from ruin, the ties were officially severed. The bottom line of their criticism was that the propagandists of the *école active* were theorists, incapable of judging whether their theories were manageable in practice. Because of this separation, Bovet's *Intermédiairs des éducateurs* had to be discontinued. His attempt to save the journal met with resistance from Piaget, whereupon Bovet felt betrayed and refused any further cooperation with his former favorite. The university delegated an academic commission to investigate the situation at the JJRI/IES. They demanded that it should "limit its activities to those which befit a scientific research and teaching institute" (in Vidal 1988: 66). Bovet (1933) considered this as an affront against the socio-political visions of the institute and Piaget, together with Dottrens, opposed his long-time mentor and supported the recommendations of the commission, among whose members was his school friend, Rolin Wavre. Moreover, Piaget met with influential delegates, in an effort to carry out the institute's reform, which Bovet had rejected (minutes JJRI, 1 July 1933: 142f.). Thus, Bovet called Piaget a representative of the "fascist clan" (ms 7 March 1933, in Vidal and Parot 1996: 71). Despite Claparède's wish to the contrary, Bovet resigned from his position as managing director of the institute, whereupon Piaget was appointed Co-Director of the JJRI/IES. Once the conflict was resolved, the JJRI/IES was jointly led by Piaget (responsible for administration), Bovet (pedagogy) and Claparède (psychology). Piaget's influence was, in fact, considerable as the institute abstained from further political statements. He directed more funds to psychology, to the detriment of pedagogy, which meant that the institute's research projects and courses became increasingly psychological and theoretical (see Table 8.1), and that a gradual dissociation between the institute's departments occured.

In December 1933, Piaget announced the launch of the *Cahiers de pédagogie expérimentale et de psychologie de l'enfant*, a publication that was to replace the *Intermédiaire*. This publication no longer addressed teachers in the main but was geared for experts and researchers. Topics such as school reforms according to New Education and practically oriented contributions dwindled, whereas specialized and theoretical articles on child psychology and developmental psychology increased, due to Piaget's research (Hofstetter 2004: 677ff.). The number of issues published decreased too, because of the difficult economic situation.

At the university, Piaget continued to lecture on the history of scientific thought, which created great interest among the more advanced students. At the JJRI/IES, he taught three courses on child psychology, one of which

Table 8.1 Proportion of psychology and pedagogy at JJRI/IES 1912–1948

	1912–1921	1921–1929	1930–1938	1939–1948
Research projects in				
Psychology	13 (15.1%)	62 (42.7%)	214 (73.3%)	36 (75%)
Applied psychology	33 (38.4%)	39 (26.9%)	46 (15.8%)	3 (6.3%)
Experimental pedagogy	15 (17.4%)	22 (15.2%)	18 (6.2%)	7 (14.5%)
Other	25 (29.1%)	22 (15.2%)	14 (4.7%)	2 (4.2%)
Courses in				
Psychology	42 (8.8%)	83 (14.1%)	144 (20.9%)	148 (19%)
Applied psychology	45 (9.4%)	81 (13.8%)	85 (12.3%)	142 (18.3%)
Experimental pedagogy	23 (4.8%)	24 (4.1%)	29 (4.2%)	52 (6.7%)
Teaching practice	132 (27.6%)	132 (22.4%)	117 (17%)	108 (13.9%)
Other	237 (49.4%)	268 (45.6%)	315 (45.6%)	338 (42.1%)

SOURCE: Adapted from Lussi *et al.* (2002: 392, 404)

was a course on current research, which "is the most characteristic one for the institute. All students attend it" (AJJRI BR 1/52: 2f.).

War and Reconstruction

Initially, Piaget countered the political and economic crisis with his faith in education. "With the war looming, our civilization has reached a more critical point than ever before [...] I am more convinced than ever that education is the only remedy against evil" (Piaget 1931/7: 42). When the Law on the Restitution of Professional Civil Servants of 7 April 1933 removed Jewish and left-wing intellectuals from their posts in Germany, and institutions were "cleansed," some of Piaget's colleagues were arrested and convicted and many fled into exile. As late as the summer of 1933, Piaget still clung to his hopes: "These hostile conditions have not managed to shake our faith in the future" (Piaget 1933/1: 39). He wrote to the Rockefeller Foundation to say that the JJRI/IES had become the last independent centre of education in Europe, whereupon, in 1934, the foundation pledged to maintain its subsidies (Vidal 1997: 94). In the face of political developments, however, it became difficult to believe in the effectiveness of educating children towards peace. The title of an essay, "Is education towards peace possible?" was not merely a rhetorical question. "The fact that this question must be asked is, in itself, significant [...] The feeling is beginning to spread that one had better be honest and admit the bankruptcy of such an education" (Piaget 1934/3: 171). Piaget considered that there might have been too great a sense of complacency. "The teaching of international co-operation [...] was exceedingly superficial and avoided the real psychological motives for action" (Piaget 1934/3: 172). Therefore "this education has not failed, since it has never been seriously undertaken" (Piaget 1943/3: 173). This allowed Piaget to adhere to his tenet "that only education is capable of saving our society from its potential violent or gradual dissolution" (Piaget 1934/1: 31). Once again, Piaget individualized political problems because, in his view, our everyday social situation was "the same" (Piaget 1934/3: 175) as our political one. His goal therefore, was not political enlightenment, but he simply pursued the aim "that everybody should find a way towards understanding and reciprocity" (Piaget 1934/3: 176f.).

Piaget changed the public appearance of the IBE in the same way as he had changed that of the JJRI/IES: it should no longer be regarded as the voice of the New Education but should be seen purely as a supplier of information that acted "without bias, for, or against, any particular educational methodology" (Piaget 1934/2: 148). In fear of becoming a plaything of the hostile member states, he emphasized the IBE's concern with pedagogical problems, which the different countries had in common:

"Indeed, no matter what social ideal one tries to instill in the pupils—ranging from individualistic liberalism to authoritarian systems—the generation conflict remains the same" (Piaget 1934/2: 149). Thus stressing the Institute's neutrality, he tried to safeguard its financial subsidies. In addition, in an effort to demonstrate the IBE's independence from the JJRI/IES, the IBE moved out of the institute's premises and was accommodated in the Palais Wilson, in 1937. All this did not mean that Piaget's political convictions had changed, even though his opportunistic strategy went so far as to allow fascist ideas to circulate under the seal of the IBE (Hameline and Vonèche 1996: 146). No member state was ever reproached or excluded on the grounds of politics, not even after the end of World War II. For instance, Piaget duly opposed the exclusion of Portugal, under attack because of its brutal colonial wars, and in protest, he resigned his presidency over the assembly in 1964, which led to the collapse of the conference (Piaget 1964/8: 78).

Piaget hoped that a comparison of school systems would be an adequate instrument for the nations to improve their education systems. To this end, Rossello produced the *International Annual of Education* from 1933 to 1968. This documentation contained the annual reports of the Ministries of Education, a retrospective summary report, as well as with suggestions for discussion at the next Members' Assembly (International Conference on Public Instruction), for which the IBE was charged with the preparations. As a result of these discussions, nonbinding *recommendations* for the organization of schools and lessons were issued to the governments of member states.

By 1939, the number of the IBE's member states had grown to 16, while the League of Nations comprised 54. Once World War II was under way, the warring nations would no longer sit at the same table, and assemblies had to be suspended. Thanks to the support of several countries and to the sale of postage stamps, the bulletin could continue to appear, and prisoners of war could be supplied with a total of 587,000 books, and even POW universities could be organized.

Piaget would not allow himself to be preoccupied with the war and concentrated on his work. In a letter of 24 November 1939 to Meyerson, he was "rather worried about the fate of this manuscript [on the logic of grouping], which must be published for the sake of my future work" (in Vidal and Parot 1996: 67). Meyerson helped German intellectuals to leave their country, and in 1941 joined the secret army of Résistance. In one case, Piaget took concrete action, too: on Valentine's instigation, he visited their Jewish friend Käthe Wolf (1907–1967) in Vienna in 1938, when he was returning from Warsaw, and managed to help her to obtain an exit permit (L. Piaget, interviewed by R. Kohler on 17 January 2006). After having worked several semesters at the JJRI/IES, she was called to Yale Child Study Center by René Spitz (1887–1974). With the help of Henri Piéron, Piaget held a series of lectures at the Collège de France in 1942 in occupied France and described this as an act of solidarity with his friends (Piaget 1947: 2). Meyerson was very disappointed when Piaget, after a few visits to Piéron, was appointed at the University of Paris. Further advancement of Meyerson's own academic career was denied him because of his political views, while Piaget was awarded the title of Doctor h.c. in 1946 and lectured as professor of Genetic Psychology at the Sorbonne from 1952 to 1963, and at Princeton in 1953/54. Around this time, their friendship broke up.

Shortly after the outbreak of war, Piaget was already reflecting upon the subsequent reconstruction, convinced that "education will once more be the decisive factor" (Piaget 1940/1: 12). The IBE's rallying call was to work, above all, for the time after the war. On 19 December 1943, a committee of experts was set up for the "task of the spiritual and educational reconstruction of the world" (Piaget 1944/2: 1), whose remit was to examine what possible help could be given to pedagogical and scientific libraries, how teaching resources might be delivered or how foreign teachers could be hired, as well as probing into possible school reforms. One month after the Americans had started their conquest of Europe in Normandy, Piaget held a lecture about "Education Towards Freedom" at the Elementary School Teachers' Congress in Bern. Although he spoke about freedom of thought and the freedom of morality and political views, he avoided any mention of totalitarian regimes. He treated the problem on a micro-sociological level, despite using political vocabulary.

> Traditional school life [...] does not do enough to prepare the pupils for this freedom, because it is often governed by a kind of autocracy or absolute monarchy, whereby the latter, at times, almost appears to come in the guise of divine right. The schoolmaster, who will not fight against this spontaneous tendency [...] embodies the mental authority and the tradition of the "elders" [...], and in an authoritarian regime, it is impossible to learn how to think. (Piaget 1944/1: 201)

Everything depended on the teacher's decision whether to use authoritarian or democratic methods. At the same time, Piaget still believed "that certain totalitarian states have recognized the benefits of some of these educational methods so clearly, that they have copied parts of it for their youth organizations" (Piaget 1944/1: 207). In reality, however, the totalitarian regimes had robbed the idea of self-government of its democratic meaning and had only retained its form.

After Piaget had been appointed professor of sociology at the University of Geneva in 1939, Claparède fell ill and died in 1940, whereupon Piaget took over his chair of experimental psychology, as well as the directorship of the Psychology Department at the JJRI/IES. From 1940 to 1943, he presided over the Swiss Society for Psychology, and from 1940 until his death, he held the posts of director of the Geneva Laboratory for Psychology, and of co-editor of the *Archives de Psychologie* and the *Revue Suisse de Psychologie*. After Bovet's resignation in 1944, the Department of Pedagogy was led by Dottrens, who opened a new laboratory for experimental pedagogy in 1945. However, the war, the end of subsidies from the Rockefeller Foundation and the low student intake had bled the institute dry. The University of Geneva helped again by integrating it as Institut Interfacultaire des Sciences de l'Éducation (ISE) in 1948, which guaranteed job security for the personnel and allowed the Institute to award degrees (licenciates) and doctorates, in addition to teaching qualifications. Piaget expanded Bovet's series of books, *Collection d'actualités pédagogiques* into *Actualités pédagogiques et psychologiques*. Samuel Roller (1912–2003), who was, in fact, an admirer of Piaget, regarded co-direction beside Piaget as a difficult job. Like his predecessor, Dottrens, and his successor, Laurent Pauli (1911–2001), Roller resigned out of protest against Piaget's neglect of pedagogy (Xypas 2001: 22).

The IBE also joined a more powerful institution. On 28 February 1947, a contract of cooperation was signed with the United Nations Educational, Scientific and Cultural Organization, founded in 1945 in london, where Piaget attended the constitutive conference as an observer in the name of the IBE. In 1947 he gave lectures at the Sèvres Semina of UNESCO and was nominated president of the Swiss delegation at UNESCO's General Assembly (1948–53). At a conference in Rio de Janero in 1949 he represented the general secretary of UNESCO, Jaime Torrès-Bodet (1902–1974), who offered him a position as General Secretary of UNESCO's education department. Piaget accepted this post in 1949/50, but only on a temporary basis, so that his research should not suffer. But as vice-president of the programme and Budget commission in 1949 and as a member of the Executive Council of UNESCO (1950–4), Piaget influneced the policy of UNESCO. Furthermore he collaborated as an expert at the 'Generul History of Civilization' of Lucien Febvre and took a Seat (1951–7), together with Maria Montessori (1951–2) at the board of the Institute of Education in Hamburg which was built up by UNESCO (Weindling 2005). According to his son, Piaget loved his work at the IBE, his international contacts with diplomats and his travels, even though he wrote: "This job has certainly cost me a good deal of time I might possibly have spent more advantageously on research in child psychology, but at least I have learned from it quite a bit about adult psychology!" (Piaget 1952/1: 131).

After the war, it was business as usual for the IBE. They summarized the reports from member states and processed them along with the Bureau's own suggestions into recommendations to the annual conferences. In addition, the Bureau accepted the task of regulating the exchange between offices for pedagogical documentation of UNESCO member states. In 1952, the Bureau also became responsible for comparative studies in the field of educational sciences and for providing state education ministries with information.

In his comment on the Declaration of Human Rights, Piaget disputed the ability of traditional schools to develop the human personality, as the Declaration demanded. To this end, a period of information and orientation would have to be introduced into a comprehensive school system, to facilitate subject changes. The pupils should delay their decision regarding their future occupation, until after "they have been observed, and the actual work which they have produced has been assessed" (Piaget 1949/6: 29), whereby this assessment should not be based on the result of one single exam. A higher school for all pupils should combine theory and practice, in order to "unite the various practical, technical, scientific and artistic aspects of social life into one organic whole, that should be linked to an understanding of history that deals with culture in the most comprehensive way possible, rather than focussing only on political and military events" (Piaget 1949: 25). In addition, the school must approach the parents, so that "joint parent and teacher councils [form] the desired synthesis of school and family, as the true upholders of the new pedagogy" (Piaget 1949: 34).

During the Cold War, Piaget, together with his assistant, Anne-Marie Weil (-Sandler), investigated the emergence of national stereotypes on behalf of UNO. The analysis showed a complementarity of intelligence and affectivity in the development of the concept of "fatherland," which represented a paradox as far as this concept does not develop until the age of 11or 12, by which time egocentrism and sociocentrism should have been overcome (cf. Piaget and Inhelder 1955: Chapter 18). Before this age, according to Piaget, the child identifies "native country" emotionally with family and tradition, without understanding this concept. The adolescent, who is emancipating himself from his family, sees himself as a member of a superior nation (or "race," religion, or political group). Piaget explained this atypical continuity of sociocentrism and lack of reciprocity through the individual's resistance against decentration (Piaget and Weil 1951/3: 125). This strange interpretation is due to Piaget's biological and mathematical reconstruction of his psychology. After 1935, he increasingly excluded the social influence—and with it education—as a causal factor of development and occupied himself less and less with sociological and pedagogical issues.

Despite the IBE's effort to introduce principles of New Education in the reconstruction of school systems, their last remnants collapsed during the mid-1950s. Even Ecole du Mail had to stop its activities as an experimental school, because "the general public of Geneva had a low regard for pedagogical experiments" (Piaget 1959/2: 314). The IBE propagated the new methods until 1968 with more than 320 publications, with little success. Piaget expressed his disappointment about the schools' reluctance to implement the active method (Piaget 1951/14: 271; 1965/1: 13). He therefore talked of a crisis in pedagogy, for which he saw several reasons (Piaget 1951/14: 19): experimental pedagogy, teacher training and educational policies had failed, and apart from that, there had been no more outstanding pedagogues after 1935.

Didactics, the Role of the Teacher and Role Models

Most of the articles Piaget wrote after the war dealt with the teaching of subjects, especially mathematics. He identified the passivity of pupils as the main problem in the didactics of mathematics, due to premature operations with numbers, premature abstraction, verbal teaching (Piaget 1949/6), premature formalization (Piaget 1965/1), premature introduction of the set theory (Piaget 1966/12) and incorrect linking, such as introducing numbers with colors (Piaget 1976/9). Observing the sciences, he demanded that the unity of physics, chemistry and biology should be preserved and that inductive and active methods should be applied (Piaget 1949/5). History should start with spontaneous attitudes, should be an instrument of critique and should generate an atmosphere of international understanding (Piaget 1933/4). Languages should be learned as directly as possible. Only in a second step, the language should be reflected in order to uncover the grammar (Piaget 1965/18: 48), while "teaching spelling is a waste of time" (Piaget 1970/9: 30). Regarding classical humanities, he advocated a closer connection between cultural history and languages, whereby the languages should contain less teaching of grammar (Piaget 1937/7). Art lessons must certainly not inhibit creativity, but must bring about a "synthesis between expressing self and subjecting it to reality" (Piaget 1954/16: 244). He considered philosophy to be in a permanent crisis because its branches would split off as soon as they reached a scientific level. Some lessons of philosophy should therefore be given over to psychology (Piaget 1965/1: 65; 1972b: 90). Piaget saw the main reason for the lack of a comprehensive education as the fact that education was divided into subjects, which, taken in conjunction with the worrying increase in student numbers and overcrowding of the humanities faculties, would make it necessary to revise the educational system. This would include an expansion of preschool education, the end of educational mollycoddling and a university education for all teachers (Piaget 1972b: 72ff.).

In active lessons, the teacher still has the task of

> providing stimuli and suggestions, i.e. he must first introduce the situations and create the basic conditions, in which the child is confronted with useful problems, whereupon the teacher will supply examples to the contrary, to make the child think and reconsider any rash judgement. We have no desire for the teacher to disappear, but it is desirable that he should stimulate the child's inquiring mind, rather than lecture and supply ready-made solutions. (Piaget 1972b: 78)

Thus Piaget toned down his resentment towards teachers (e.g. 1944/1: 203; 1950 III: 212), which might be illustrated by the following anecdote: at a meeting of the IBE, a Canadian recounted that his province had decided that each school class should be provided with two school rooms—"in one of them the teacher is located, and in the other one he is not. Piaget quoted this as the best idea he had ever heard from a teacher!" (Pulaski 1971: 170).

Nevertheless, he was convinced that teachers would shape the future society (Piaget 1949/6: 15); for this reason he repeatedly demanded that schools should be changed into active schools. His demands were high indeed: despite the large classes common at the time, the teacher, in his role as mediator between the child and the world, should provide documentation tailored to each child's individual needs. At the same time, he should provide opportunities for cooperation, discussions, experiments and research, he should keep the pupil's interest alive by asking questions leading to further discoveries, he should suggest counterexamples in order to generate cognitive conflicts and he should be a moral and social role-model (Piaget 1939/4: 4; 1948/9: 22; 1972b: 78). When he was asked whom he most admired, Piaget answered: "Einstein impressed me profoundly, because he took an interest in everything. He asked me to tell him about our experiments in conversation" (Piaget 1973: 38). Thus, what had really impressed him was that the famous physicist was interested in Piaget's research. When he was further questioned about his significant contacts, Piaget cited neither his teachers, nor thinkers who had influenced him, nor his favorite authors, François Mauriac (1885–1970), Charles Ferdinand Ramuz (1878–1947) or Marcel Proust (1871–1922), whose 3,000-page work *In Search of Lost Time* he had read six times, but he mentioned Robert Oppenheimer (1904–1967). This "father" of the nuclear bomb had accepted Piaget's theory of perception.

Piaget had no doubt that the teacher's personality "was by far the most important factor" (Piaget 1930/4: 51) for successful teaching. This image of the ideal teacher had origins in the Protestant tradition (Baader 2005: 178ff.) and meant that children respect and admire personalities because they represent a moral perfection. In its recommendation for elementary teacher training, the IBE had stated "that it is necessary to take full account, not only of general and pedagogical knowledge, properly so called, but also, and especially, of moral values" (IBE Recommendation No. 4, 1935). One has to be predestined for the teaching profession because "the educator's personal vocation, his pedagogical talent and his more or less innate qualities of authority, his contact etc. are what makes a good teacher" (Piaget and Meyer 1937/2: 5).

In addition to all these fundamental qualities, the teacher must have specialized subject knowledge and detailed knowledge of developmental psychology. Teacher training must be integrated in the university, because

> child psychology can only be learned by working on research projects and by participating in experiments [...] Only thus can teachers become researchers and can rise above the state of merely being transmitters of knowledge. The same is true for experimental pedagogy itself, the actual discipline *par excellence* of teachers. (Piaget 1965/1: 130f.)

A course of studies at the university would help to dismantle the hierarchy between types of schools and to counteract the feeling of inferiority that teachers experience when faced with academics. For Piaget, this also implied that teachers' salaries and their training, as well as the employment conditions of nursery and pre-school nurses, would have to be re-evaluated (Piaget 1965/1: 105). In the same article, Piaget expressed a low opinion of trained pedagogues. In a synopsis (Piaget 1965/1: 19) he gave an account of the fact that almost all great pedagogues, from Comenius to Claparède, were not trained teachers, but had a different profession. He felt that teachers could not be expected to join in with any scientific debate because of their weak intellectual capabilities. Therefore, he advocated the "constructive lie [...]: psychologists have known for a long time, that, if they want to be heard by teachers or government employees, they will have to guard against creating the impression of referring to psychological doctrines; instead they ought to act as if they were purely referring to common sense" (Piaget 1954/15: 28).

Pedagogy and Psychology

Piaget (1928/12: 261) understood pedagogy as a temple of "tribal idols". The *idola tribus*, one of Francis Bacon's four great illusions of mankind, is rooted in human nature and is projected upon the things of nature. In the case of pedagogy, this means that adults disregard the child's own logic. Since only psychology could make this understanding possible, and since psychology provided the basis for all other sciences, Piaget considered psychology to be "imperialist" (Piaget 1928/12: 261). According to him, the superiority of psychology lay in its objectivity, of which pedagogy, which is necessarily normative, is devoid. In contrast to logic, mathematics, physics, biology and sociology, Piaget did not regard pedagogy as a scientific discipline, but as a "field of application, albeit perhaps the most important one, of psychology" (Piaget 1970/5: 190). Like James and many others, he was of the opinion that "pedagogy is an art, whereas psychology is a science" (Piaget 1948/9: 22). Occasionally, he also compared pedagogy with medicine, thus attributing to it a double status of it being an art as well as a science. For him, experimental pedagogy has to apply the basic mechanisms, which the psychologist has researched, to classroom situations (Piaget 1933/4: 119). Through putting education and teaching on a scientific basis, the school should be improved. As late as 1973, Piaget still demanded (Piaget 1973/15: 26) that teachers should undergo experimental training, on the basis of in-depth studies of genetic psychology. But if his psychology was applied too rashly, Piaget saw a "great danger. I have the impression that very few people have understood" (Piaget 1973: 52).

Piaget used the platform of the IBE to propagate his research results among educators. Between 1946 and 1968, the conference decided to issue a further 47 recommendations, which Piaget regarded as "a body of pedagogical doctrines, the effectiveness of which cannot be underestimated" (Piaget 1970/11: ix). Yet this entire process was futile. The nation's surveys of their school systems resulted in whitewashed reports, full of optimism. The increasing number of member states had led to a "disproportion between the aims and the means. Thus the international conference had become a kind of huge editorial committee, which no longer allowed any detailed dialogue" (Egger 1979: 113). The IBE's recommendations were not binding and no efforts were made to monitor their implementation. Because educational policies disregarded the recommendations from Geneva, Piaget moaned: "Ministries and their conferences make laws, but they do not make scientific and pedagogical truths" (Piaget 1965/1: 126). Since the renewal of the contract of cooperation with UNESCO in 1952, every member state of UNESCO could take part in, and benefit from, the IBE's activities. More and more states joined UNESCO, but not the IBE. In the long run, a financial crisis was inevitable. A commission, set up in 1966, found that not only the financial situation but also the overlapping functions of UNESCO and the IBE had to be resolved. Only one sensible solution offered itself, therefore Piaget met with the General Secretary of UNESCO, René Maheu, and suggested that the IBE should, despite its integration, remain an independent organization within UNESCO. Yet, on 14 December 1967, before the problem could be resolved, Piaget handed in his resignation, which contained two conditions: "1. I do not want to hold the office of Director-in-Charge any longer, only as the provisional deputy of my future successor. 2. Above all, I do not want to participate in negotiations which concern the future" (in Egger 1979: 111). Deputy Director Rossello, who was opposed to the integration that left the IBE as an independent institution, resigned too. Piaget's successor, René Ochs, was appointed only as an interim director because all parties concerned agreed that there should be a limited term of office in the future (Stock 1979: 121). In 1968 Piaget also resigned from his post as Director of the JJRI/ISE, which then fell under the direct control of the University's Vice-Chancellorship.

Towards the end of his life, Piaget did not want his name to be associated with pedagogy any more. A characteristic example of this is Piaget's reaction, when he met Constantin Xypas in February 1980, who had written him three letters, which had remained unanswered:

> "Professor, allow me to introduce myself," I said. Piaget gave me a friendly smile and inclined his body a little, as a sign that he was listening; I informed him that I had his entire writings in my possession, and that I was very honored to make his acquaintance. His smile became increasingly cordial, so I plucked up my courage and thought that this was a good moment to announce my project to him. "I have already written to you concerning my PhD thesis on your pedagogical thoughts." His friendly smile disappeared abruptly, and Piaget seemed to be annoyed. He curtly interrupted me with an "excuse me," turned round to Cellérier and started a conversation with him! I waited for a moment or two because I could not, and would not, believe that our talk had ended like this but in vain. (Xypas 2001: 23f.)

Although Piaget had published around 40 articles on education and had published as many speeches and reports within the IBE, he stated: "I have no opinion on pedagogy" (Piaget and Bringuier 1977: 194). It is true that less than 3 per cent of Piaget's texts deal with pedagogy, but even these amount to roughly 1000 pages.[9] Piaget hoped, nevertheless, to change the school through his psychology:

> EVANS: What would be your hope, with respect to the future influence of your work, on the field of education? Would you think the time will come when it will really revolutionize our entire educational system?
> PIAGET: Oh, I hope so very much. (Piaget 1973: 53)

Because Piaget wanted to change society by reforming the school, he committed himself for almost 40 years to educational policy, working from within the IBE and UNESCO. Under the cloak of scientific neutrality, he tried to exert his influence upon government ministers and officials, so that these might implement school reforms in the spirit of New Education. Whether the recommendations encouraged such reforms is difficult to gauge. Any such effects, if they did take place, were more likely coincidental. Certainly, Piaget's hope that the states would use these recommendations to underpin their educational policies was as naïve as his entire political judgment.

His attempt to become the theoretician of the New Education also failed. Even though Piaget occupied a central position as director of the BIE, held speeches on congresses, and wrote articles in journals of French- and English-speaking countries since 1930, he has never been accepted as a founding figure of the reform-pedagogical canon (cf. Oelkers 1996a: 168). Marc-André Bloch (1948: 778ff.), for example, quoted Piaget only briefly in connection with moral development and, in *The Story of the New Education* by Boyd and Rawson, he received only a casual mention. This might be due to the fact that Piaget never wrote a book on pedagogy and that the majority of his statements coincided with those of Claparède, Bovet and Ferrière. But Piaget's psychology was less manageable to translate into didactics than was Ferrière's genetic psychology. Furthermore, experimental psychology, to which Piaget always referred without actually practicing it, had, in the field of reform-pedagogy, already been superseded by psychoanalysis. Finally, Piaget's comments on pedagogy remained superficial, and this included key concepts, such as cooperation. No detailed definitions or deeper analyses of this term were given anywhere, and it never became a catchword, in contrast, for instance, with Bovet's and Ferrière's *école active*.

Up until the mid-1930s, Piaget had considered cooperation, and thus the social environment, to be the causal factor in moral and cognitive development. "Depending on the education a child receives, he can be very different from what children generally are" (Piaget 1932/1: 72). But this assumption, that the environment had a determining influence on the individual, contradicted two other of Piaget's central beliefs. Following the tradition of Pierre Maine de Biran (1766–1824), Bergson and Kant, he presupposed a free will. "The individual is free to choose isolation within his self (his 'self' at each stage of socialization) or to hold his own, as a human being" (Piaget 1931/4: 109). This freedom of choice challenged his belief in an invariant cognitive development, leading to the universal norms of "noncontradiction" and reciprocity (Piaget 1930/3). Piaget tried to solve this fundamental conflict between the anthropological, psychological and sociological postulates with the help of biology. Due to Wallon's criticism as well, Piaget concentrated on the "analysis of the inner driving force of intellectual development" (Piaget and Leuzinger-Schuler 1947/9: 92). Over time, the social and educational factors lost more and more of their significance while the child's autonomous development gained ever greater importance, without Piaget being able to resolve the conflict properly.

9

The Biological Work

Experimental Study on Kinetogenesis

In his dissertation of 1918, Piaget had demanded a dual approach to biological research: one approach being the experimental study of genetics, and the other being "a kind of indirect genetics" (Piaget 1921/2: 2), which compares morphological characteristics with those of the environment. To this end, he resumed his research on mollusks, shortly after he arrived at Neuchâtel in 1925, and using biometrics, he studied the influence of an organism's activity upon the hereditary character. At the same time, Piaget, who had just become a father, observed the reflexes and the habit-forming behavior of his daughter Jacqueline. Moreover, he read the *New Theory of Life: Organic Psychology*, which appeared in 1925 under the pseudonym of Pierre Jean. With Pierre Janet Piaget discussed the attempt to combine biology and psychology, in order to find an explanation for adaptation of the organism (Ducret 1984: 623). Piaget's former teacher criticized the generalizing and metaphorical use of terms like "intelligence" or "memory" in this "book which I found rather seductive" (Janet 1935: 12). Piaget, however, concluded that "psychology [...] is a biological science" (Piaget 1928/5: 103).

In 1928, Piaget conducted his first experiments on Mendel's Laws, in order to determine whether the *Limnaea stagnalis* is formed by its environment or "preformed in the polymorphism" (Piaget 1928/6: 17). This water snail has an oblong shell when located in a habitat of stagnant water. If the snail is exposed, during its growth period, to waves, the result is that the spiral of its shell is shorter, because the mollusk flattens itself against the ground. Back in the aquarium, most of the snail's descendants will revert to an oblong shell (this characteristic was therefore phenotypic). The *Limnaea lacustris*, however, will pass down its shortened form to its descendants. Piaget concluded from this discovery that this was a case of genetic retention of the organism's active adaptation to its environment. The morphological change was the result of "purely psychomotor factors" (Piaget 1929/3: 447). This "psychoanalysis of the motor behavior of animals" (Piaget

1929/3: 445) confirmed the phenomenon of "kinetogenesis." This term was coined in 1896 by the American Lamarckist Edward Drinker Cope (1840–1897), and signifies that an animal's structures have been produced by the animal's movements. "The functioning of the animal in relation to its environment" has an effect "on the hereditary mechanism of (psycho-morphological) reflex organization" (Piaget 1929/1: 518). Following Rabaud, Piaget concluded that "beside random mutations, adaptation processes exist, which imply that a characteristic structure of the organism, as well as environmental effects, must be present, whereby the two poles, environment and organism, are irrevocably joined" (Piaget 1936: 26). Through relocating, crossing and studying more than 80,000 snails allegedly, Piaget attempted to prove his theory of "interactionism" (Piaget 1950 III: 115). He also used the *Sedum morganianum* (*crassulacae*), known as "burro's tail," to refute neo-Darwinism. On his many journeys, he collected 150 varieties of this plant, studied the characteristics of its offshoots in other environments and named a new variety (*Sedum sediforme* var. *parvulum*) (Piaget 1967: 202; 1974a: 42).

Piaget had already dreamt of a third theory when he wrote *Recherche*, and he still believed that there must be a "third stage between integral mutationism and the hypothesis of continual heredity of acquired traits" (Piaget 1929/3: 455). He claimed to be "pleased to bury the hatchet on this issue and to recognize the superficiality of our former work, compared to the solid thesis of this Polish zoologist" (Piaget 1929/1: 489), but he nevertheless queried Roszkowski's findings regarding the two species, *L. ovata* and *L. auricularia*, on the grounds of a variety which Roszkowski himself had identified, and he felt that "this study must be taken up again" (ibid: 490). This did not happen, however, because Piaget was able to return to Geneva in the same year. His further studies no longer involved empirical work, but "original orchestrations based on multiple borrowing" (Buscaglia 1985: 113).

Theoretical Studies and the Concept of Development

Piaget was fully aware that Lamarck's theory cannot explain the relative stability of the species and that this theory has never been proven, "despite thousands of experiments" (Piaget 1950 III: 99). He saw the reason for this failure in the fact that the inquiries relate to "long-term and quantitative dimensions, which hitherto have been impossible to measure under laboratory conditions" (Piaget 1950 III: 99). Thus Piaget could concentrate on the organism's active adaptation and interpret the behavior of the mollusks as "an interesting case of sensory-motor adaptation [...], which, contrary to appearances, is closely related to developmental psychology" (Piaget 1956: 299).

From 1957 on, Conrad Hal Waddington (1905–1975) introduced the concepts of "epigenetic system," "genetic assimilation," "homeorhesis" and "chreod" to biology, as well as the distinction between genotype and epigenotype. Piaget was thrilled, and in his subsequent publications, he largely assimilated the concepts, arguments and examples of this British embryologist.

> Waddington is the first to deliver an actual synthesis, by distinguishing within an evolutionary system four large subsystems, each of which is regulated separately, and the regulatory circuits are necessarily linked to one another; 1. the genetic system, 2. the epigenetic system, 3. the utilization of the environment and 4. the effects of natural selection. (Piaget 1967: 122)

The regulations maintaining the subsystems, and the system as a whole, do not create a static equilibrium (homeostasis) but represent a permanent process towards equilibrium (homeorhesis). In Piaget's terminology, the word "epigenesis" referred to the formation of the organism (phenotype), as a result of the joint effects of genotype and environment. The environment is "utilized" through "genetic assimilation." This is a term that Waddington borrowed from Piaget's biological observations, which he described as "the most thorough and interesting study of genetic assimilation under natural conditions" (Waddington 1975: 92). He criticized, however, Piaget's underestimation of the role of natural selection and his overestimation of the importance of individual adaptation, because Piaget's thinking was too individualistic. Waddington did not believe in an evolutionary necessity of logic, unlike Piaget, who regarded the "chreod" (necessary path) to be the missing link between the theory of biological maturation and the theory of cognitive learning (Piaget 1967: 19ff.). The construction of cognitive structures follows "the laws of the chreods which is a constant and necessary progress and happens in a way that allows the endogenous reactions to find support from the environment and from experience" (Piaget 1970/2: 43). Piaget concluded from this "that learning is subject to the developmental stage of the child" (Piaget 1970: 53).

In the 1970s, the phenocopy thesis became the focus of Piaget's intensive occupation with the theory of evolution. This term of the German zoologist Richard Goldschmidt (1878–1958), refers to the copying of a genotypic adaptation by the phenotype. Piaget inverted this definition and postulated that information could also be passed on from the phenotype to the genotype. A copy of the phenotype in the genotype is therefore a genetic assimilation. Piaget integrated this thesis into Baldwin's theory of "organic selection": ontogenetic development runs through a series of organizational levels, starting with the DNA and including enzyme production, cell formation, growth of tissue, formation of organs, organization of behavior, and, on the highest level, cognition. Development at every level occurs in interaction with the internal and then external environment. At every level, variation is possible, having an ascending effect, and the further variation on the next level will then select out the former. Piaget assumed that there might also be a descending effect of disequilibria, which would create new variations on the lower level. A phenocopy results when the disequilibrium descends all the way down to the genome and replaces it by an exogenous formation.

Disequilibria arise, because the behavior constantly exceeds the biological limits (Piaget 1967: 372; Piaget and Bringuier 1977: 172). The environment does not induce changes, but only disequilibria, which, in turn, induce the active subject to reinstate equilibrium (Piaget 1967: 121). If this re-adaptation fails, so-called regulator genes are activated, which transmit error messages to the genotype, as a result of which mutations will occur. The new variants of the genome are not only subject to external selection, but also to internal selection. Piaget described an organism's internal environment as a hierarchical system of regulatory circuits. In the course of the regulatory readaptation activity, accommodates will form, which are phenotypic, non-hereditary changes. A phenocopy is the internal reconstruction of an accommodate, which overcomes the disequilibrium. "We define phenocopy as the replacement of a phenotype, formed through environmental pressure, with a genotype, caused by the organism's genetic activity and now endogenously reproducing the traits of the original phenotype" (Piaget 1975: 181). "The general process is thus a *replacement* of exogenous knowledge by an endogenous reconstruction" (Piaget 1975/8: 806). With this, Piaget believed that he could "connect the formation of endogenous knowledge with biological mechanisms" (Piaget 1975/8: 806, 809).

According to Piaget, cognitive structures are equivalent to phenocopies, because the interaction between experience and the forming of structures is "isomorphous to the relationship between genotype and phenotype" (Piaget 1974a: 75). Thinking does not only reflect bodily regulations, but has, in itself, an organic function: "*Cognitive processes seem then to be, at one and the same time, the outcome of organic auto-regulation, reflecting its essential mechanism, and the most highly differentiated organs of this regulation at the core of interactions with the environment*" (Piaget 1967: 27). This logico-biological continuity forms the basis for Piaget's system: "As vast as the difference of dignity between intellectual structures and crustaceans and mollusks may be, [...] in both cases, we are nevertheless dealing with the developing organization of the living" (Piaget 1950 I: 20). Psychological and physiological structures merged with Piaget's notion of knowledge.

> *J.P.*: In my opinion, there is no demarcation line between the living and the mental, between psychology and biology. As soon as an organism reacts to a prior experience and adapts to a new situation, psychology is involved to a large extent.
>
> *J.-Cl. B.*: If sunflowers, for example, turn towards the sun, would this be psychology? (He smiles, reflects and nods).
>
> *J.P.*: I believe that we are, indeed, dealing with behavior.
>
> *J.-Cl. B.*: Is there no demarcation line between sunflowers and ourselves?
>
> *J.P.*: No. (Piaget and Bringuier 1977: 25)

With this global concept of behavior, Piaget tried to overcome Cartesian dualism. But this monist understanding led to the subjectivation of plants. Thus Piaget psychologized biology while he biologized psychology. Piaget had no misgivings in drawing inferences from biology into the field of psychology, as his criticism of the principle of selection illustrates:

> This thought process does not seem clear to me, when it is transferred to the field of psychology. It would amount to the statement that all knowledge starts with chance, and that our science would be the result of a sequence of selections of coincidental insights, whereby the useful ones are kept and the remaining ones discarded. Knowledge is thus stripped of all inner necessity. (Piaget and Bringuier 1977: 166)

The fortuitousness in evolution and in cognitive development is a category that Piaget always excluded.

> Let's suppose that the events occurring in our existence, and above all, the values, which have been successively worked out through thought, were a product of chance; and let's consequently assume that there was no connection between our thinking and the universe, nor any direction at the very core of the development of thinking, then life would no longer make sense. Let's further assume that values resulted from completely subjective decisions of one's individual consciousness, and there was no norm to govern the world of obligations, everything would dissolve into nothing. To affirm the meaning of life means to affirm that values go beyond chance and subjectivity, which means affirming an absolute and affirming God, whichever way we imagine Him to be. (Piaget 1930/3: 42)

Piaget could not deny the contingency of mutation, so he had to reduce this at least to the point where "the role of chance is reduced to proportions which are not negligible but modest" (Piaget 1974a: 108). Therefore one of Piaget's core ideas was that evolution overcomes contingency by its organizational and constructive powers.

It is therefore not surprising that Piaget was disturbed by the theses of the molecular biologist, Jacques Monod (1910–1976), who declared chance to be the "central concept of modern biology" (Monod 1970: 112). "The biologists are wrong, taking chance for an explanation as Monod does" (Piaget 1982: 1: 85). Piaget could not resist making a polemic comment: "If J. Monod tells us that the entire evolution is due to unfortunate disturbances or 'imperfections', which change preservation, being the one and 'only privilege' of life, then he has forgotten his own ontogenesis, in which a series of truly unfortunate events made him a Nobel Prize winner" (Piaget 1974a: 104).

Piaget turned the tables and considered chance as a religious concept: "once more, only 'divine coincidence' remains" (Piaget 1974a: 105) to explain adaptation.

> *J.-Cl. B.*: Should this adaptation be seen as something like a biological progress and almost as finality?
> *J.P.*: Certainly, finality as far as the teleonomy is concerned, of which Jacques Monod speaks. Every epigenetic system is based on a program, and this program follows a direction, of course. (Piaget and Bringuier 1977: 169)

On the one hand, Piaget maintained the tradition of the German embryologist, Caspar Friedrich Wolff (1733–1794), who, in 1759, declared in his epigenetic *Theoria generationis* that the formation of organisms occurs as self-production through the accumulation of substance. Piaget therefore criticized all forms of finalism, determinism, or preformism. On the other hand, he adhered to the tradition of Rousseau, who, in 1762, presented in *Emile* a preformist theory of child development. Piaget combined these traditions with his claim that cognitive development was dependent on biological maturation. It is significant that Piaget used the expressions "evolution" and "development" as synonyms: "Every psychological evolution is, at once, construction and development" (Piaget 1930/8: 43). Piaget assumed a homogenous and immanent tendency in ontogenesis and phylogenesis as well as in nature and culture, so he did not follow the development of the theory of evolution, which lost its metaphysical character in the second half of the nineteenth century. He typically never queried his own quasi preformist concept of development but showed amazing obstinacy in several attempts to disprove Darwinism.

Nearly all biologists rejected Piaget's theory of phenocopy and none of them would undertake to write a contribution regarding Piaget's biological work for the homage in *Archives de psychologie* of March 1982. The assistant, who, in the end, reluctantly wrote the contribution, considered Piaget's theories outdated (Xypas 2001: 32). Since "cognitive adaptation is an extension of general biological adaptation" (Piaget 1967: 188), Piaget's psychology also suffered from the obsolete biological paradigm.

10

The Main Psychological Work

Basic Concepts

"Psychology, as a science of the forms of behavior and of mental reactions, has its roots deep in biology and represents a continuation of biological research" (Piaget 1950 III: 124). Piaget's basic psychological concepts are not subject and action but rather organism and behavior (Piaget 1967: 6ff.). The behavior of human beings, however, is not determined by fixed urges and instincts but is controlled by actively developed schemata and structures.

Piaget was less interested in the contents of thinking than in its underlying regularities. "The development of thought manifests the existence of certain systems or 'schemata', that can be isolated, and whose history or genesis can be reconstructed" (Piaget 1933/3: 148). A schema allows the recognition of things and situations by abstracting from differences and contexts. It is an instrument, which links a specific activity to a situation and implies that the same activity will yield the same result. "A schema is a mode of reactions susceptible of reproducing themselves and susceptible, above all, of being generalized" (Piaget 1954/12: 94).

A cognitive structure consists of a group of schemata, which form a whole. This "form of organization of experience" (Piaget 1931/2: 149) is self-regulating insofar as it follows certain rules of construction in interaction with the environment. "While thinking adapts to things, it structures itself, and while it structures itself, it also structures things" (Piaget 1936: 18). Structures are the results of activities and define the competence of an individual to understand the world. They fix the scope of interpretation and thus change reality. To comprehend an object "means to construct transformation systems which can be applied to this object" (Piaget 1970a: 23). The structures contain regulated links between the contents of thought, and, like the contents, will never be fully developed. During childhood and youth, however, law-governed reorganization occurs of the cognitive structures, which results in a qualitative increase in intelligence.

Piaget faced the problem of how to put together the discontinuity in development, which arose from his postulate that the child was different from the adult, with the continuity in development as a cumulative process of knowledge. He solved this difficulty by differentiating between the variable structural pole and the invariant functional pole. Intelligence, therefore, consists of changeable schemata, structures and contents, as well as of the unchangeable functions assimilation and accommodation.

Spencer had used the term "accommodation" to denote the alignment "of internal relationships with external ones" (Spencer 1863 I: 96). In 1871, the German linguist and psychologist, Heymann Steinthal (1823–1899), employed "assimilation and accommodation" as a terminological combination, and Baldwin was the first to use both terms systematically in 1901. He referred to Johann Friedrich Herbart's (1776–1841) definition of 1825, according to which any cognition is assimilation to a cognitive schema. James had employed this term in 1907 to describe the integration of a new, but related, opinion or experience into the existing organization. "Assimilation" replaced the term association, thus Piaget (1923: 176) agreed with Bergson who, in 1896, had criticized the psychology of association. The combination of live activity and functional assimilation remained the foundations of Piaget's theory: "Bergson's psychology and Le Dantec's biology are the same thing. There is no doubt that the idealism of the one philosopher and the realism of the other are one and the same" (Piaget 1928/11). Assimilation is the "basic fact of psychological life" (Piaget 1936: 53) and identical to the definition of life itself.

Assimilation means the active integration of objects, by using the existing schemata and concepts. The external world is transformed in such a way as to render it an integral part of oneself. At the start of his development, the child manipulates the objects relatively freely in order to strengthen his innate or acquired schemata. If a wooden log becomes a ship for the child, then the child has assimilated the log to his cognitive concept of a ship. The quantity and quality of the acquired cognitive structures determine the potential of possible interpretations and experiences. Each time, as the internal framework of theories and expectations permits the assimilation of a phenomenon, its usefulness is confirmed. If assimilation fails, the structures must be changed. The reactive function of accommodation occurs in the case of a discrepancy, or disruption, for which the organism has no tried-and-tested schema or concept as yet. If a child, who is in the habit of putting his finger into the sugar bowl and licking it with gusto, happens to put his finger into a bowl of salt, he is forced, by the environment, to learn the difference between these two white, grainy substances. Accommodation, which adapts the organism to the environment, is a "source of changes" (Piaget 1937: 339), whereas assimilation, which adapts the

environment to the organism, is conservative. Depending on the requirements of objects and situations, accommodation reorganizes, generalizes,
differentiates, integrates and coordinates the assimilation schemata.

> Accommodation is the principle by which an organism comes to adapt
> itself to more complex conditions of stimulation, by performing more
> complex functions [...] Learning to act is just accommodation, nothing
> more and nothing less. Speech, tracery, handwriting, piano playing, all
> motor acquisitions, are what accommodation is, i.e. adaptations to more
> complex conditions. (Baldwin 1906: 454f.)

Following Baldwin, Piaget replaced Le Dantec's term of imitation through
accommodation, at first speaking of "the dualism of motor accommodation
and autistic assimilation" (Piaget 1927/2: 213). He then postulated that
the child was "driven in two opposite directions" (Piaget 1939/3: 157).
"Assimilation and accommodation are initially antagonistic, because the
former functions largely in an egocentric way, while the latter is mainly
directed by the environment. Gradually, they begin to complement each
other while differentiating themselves at the same time" (Piaget 1936: 421).
Later Piaget based his theory on the assumption that both aspects form
part of each act of cognition (Piaget 1950 III: 263). "Since there is no
assimilation without (prior or simultaneous) accommodation, there can be
no accommodation without assimilation: this means that the environment
does not simply induce the organism to register impressions or to make
copies, but induces the organism to actively reshape itself" (Piaget 1967: 9).

The importance of these two functions, however, contains a dilemma.
Piaget considered assimilation "as the primordial fact" (Piaget 1936: 412)
because it guarantees the elementary autonomy of the child. But with regard
to the imitation of, or the respectful admiration for, a personality, this autonomy seems questionable. Assimilation also contains a danger: "If assimilation *surpasses* accommodation (i.e. if the characteristics of an object are
only considered to the degree which meets the present interests of the subject), thinking will develop along egocentric, or even autistic lines" (Piaget
1970/2: 35). If, on the other hand, accommodation is too strongly marked,
development would become dependent on the environment, which would
have contradicted his thesis of immanent logic of development. Piaget therefore could not equate adaptation with accommodation, but had to search
for another mechanism, which he found in the striving for equilibrium
between the two functions. Biological adaptation consists "in equilibrium
between the accommodation of schemata of behavior to things, and the
assimilation of things to the schemata of behavior" (Piaget 1936: 378). The
driving force for development lies in a dynamic constraint: the organism

must constantly apply its schemata to new objects, and thus has constantly to improve its schemata.

Piaget understood the alignment between schemata and things as an approach of cognition and reality. A relationship of identity is "the ideal equilibrium, towards which the entire biological development is striving, because only this relationship can bring about the full harmony between assimilation and accommodation" (Piaget 1936: 373).

According to Rousseau, too, learning not only serves external purposes, but also helps to create equilibrium between the internal and external nature, from which one's own strength is meant to grow. If the child's interests were not respected during the various stages of his development, then "one would truly depart from the order of nature, and [...] the equilibrium would be destroyed" (Rousseau 1762: 338). Claparède understood equilibrium to be the most generally applicable principle for all that is living.

> *Every living organism is a system, which wants to keep intact. As soon as its inner equilibrium is (physically/chemically) upset, as soon as it begins to dissolve, it puts into operation all the actions necessary for its reconstitution.* This is what the biologists call *self-regulation* [...] An upset equilibrium is what we call a "need". (Claparède 1931: 56f.)

This statement was based on the theory of exchange, proclaimed by the evolution theoretician, John Fiske (1842–1901), according to whom thought develops as an autonomous construction process in the exchange with the environment. Piaget adopted the idea that development, in particular mental development, implied a striving for equilibrium, whereby adaptation is seen as the result of the equilibrium achieved. "The essence of intelligence is the mind's adaptation to things, a sort of intellectual accommodation prepared by the motor accommodation" (Piaget 1927/2: 202). In this realistic definition of reason, accommodation plays the central part. Adaptation leads to an internal-external equilibrium that shows up in the coherence of motor and mental structures (Piaget 1936: 16f.) To this realistic aspect of intelligence, Piaget added the "differentiation between real and ideal equilibrium" (Piaget 1936: 21) within the organism. "Reason is an ideal, immanent to every act of thought as well as to every practical operation [...] Being an ideal, reason is a form of equilibrium towards which all cognitive systems tend" (Piaget 1933/2: 98). This idealistic dimension of reason is in line with Fouillée, for whom intelligence "is an organizing form, which reacts to representations and puts them in order, in accordance with a rule of harmony" (Fouillée 1893: 226). This aspect of intelligence is dominated by assimilation and finds its completion in the "principle of noncontradiction" (Piaget 1936: 13), which is manifest in the reversibility of thinking

(Piaget 1950 I: 41). The idealistic and realistic components unite in the equilibrium as being the "place of specific junction between the possible and the real" (Piaget 1950 I: 40). Reason, then, is a harmonic relationship between assimilation and accommodation: "As assimilation partners with accommodation, the former will result in deductive activity and the latter in experimentation; the joining of the two becomes this inseparable relationship between logical conclusion and experience, by which reason is characterized" (Piaget 1939/3: 161).

In a few passages, there is a pragmatic dimension of intelligence, which Piaget had borrowed from Dewey via Claparède (cf. Tröhler 2005). "Intelligence has two clearly distinct functions: to invent (hypotheses, theories etc.) and to verify" (Piaget 1931/9: 494). But by biologizing intelligence, this component was pushed into the background. Piaget only elaborated this aspect 40 years later (Piaget 1974c), although failed assimilation attempts, contradictions or cognitive conflicts refer back to these functions. The reason for this nonelaboration lies in the fact that the cognitive system itself is responsible for the perception of disturbances.

For Piaget, intelligence was a broad and transitory concept because any activity is intelligent, ranging from the behavior of a greenfly to the discovery of the theory of relativity. Under the influence of Janet, Piaget considered intelligence to be more than a continuation of organic adaptation with more refined means because he postulated a genetic continuity between instincts and intellectual types of behavior. This functional continuity, and the breaches in its structure, forms the core of the theory of stages.

The Theory of Stages

"My problem was to find out what differences there are between children and adults, or what differences there are from one stage to another" (Piaget 1973: 35). Piaget assumed radical discontinuity and qualitative transformations of intelligence in development, which distinguished him from most other psychologists. His model was significantly influenced by the theories of stages of Baldwin (1894), Binet and Simon (1905), Stern (1907), Ferrière (1922), Wallon (1925) and, above all, Janet (1926), because "every time Piaget deals with the question of whether the stages truly exist in the form of continual, defined steps of development, he refers to Janet" (Meili-Dworetzki 1978: 517).

Piaget's stance regarding the stages was ambivalent. As with his taxonomy of mollusks, Piaget maintained "that a classification is always artificial" (Piaget 1933/3: 148). But psychologists have "to construct stages because this is an *indispensable instrument for the analysis of formative processes*" (Piaget

1956/7: 817). He therefore did not understand the stages to be static or fixed units. "The ages I have mentioned are only averages. Any child may be a year or so beyond or behind the average capabilities reached by most children his age" (Piaget 1973/15: 25). Despite this skepticism, all of Piaget's research is based on qualitatively distinguishable forms of thought, which appear in the course of development and remain stable over a certain period. Thus, his approach comprised a constant sequence of coherent, general cognitive structures (Piaget 1960/8: 172; 1967: 18).

Stages are not defined by learned forms of behavior or by a certain stock of knowledge but it is the underlying cognitive organization or deep structure that determines what insights and skills can be acquired, if any. The more advanced stages include the structures of the previous stage, which continue to be applied in the relevant situations. There is, however, a tendency towards giving preference to hierarchically higher ranging structures. From infancy to adolescence, every child undergoes four stages (exceptions are the models in 1943/6: 189ff.; 1956/7):

1. In the sensory-motor stage, from birth to 1½–2 years of age, the sensory-motor schemata develop. The first transition is due to the development of language and the use and recognition of symbols and their functions.
2. During the pre-operational (symbolic-intuitive) stage, age 2–7, the sensory-motor schemata are internalized. The second transition is defined by the appearance of operative structures, accompanied by a detachment from direct perception.
3. During the concrete-operational stage, age 7–10/11, mental acts with concrete contents are performed. The third transition is characterized by the abstraction from concrete contents.
4. During the formal-operational stage, age 11–15/16, hypothetical, combinatory and complex proportional operations are formed.

Sensory-Motor Development

Piaget was not the first to study his own children's development. In 1787, Dietrich Tiedemann (1748–1803) was the first to publish his observations regarding his own son's development from birth to age 2½, followed by Johann Elias Löbisch (1795–1853) in 1851, and by Adolf Kussmaul (1822–1902) in 1858. At the beginning, Piaget still based his work on the thesis that the child's egocentrism sprang from the infant's solipsism. He therefore advocated the use of a "regressive method" (Piaget 1927/2: 199) to reach the "solipsism in which the self identifies completely with the world" (Piaget

1927/2: 213). After Wallon's criticism (in 1928/5: 133), Piaget abandoned the terms of autism and solipsism and thenceforth spoke only of a sensory-motor stage, thus agreeing with Wallon's emphasis upon the neurological base for thinking. It was standard knowledge that the necessary coordination between the senses and movement forms part of the early stages of the development of intelligence (e.g. Bergson 1907: 299f.).

Observing his own children in everyday situations allowed Piaget to verify theories of development and offered a dual research strategy. On the one hand, Piaget investigated the development of an infant's cognitive capability as the subjective and logical pole of cognition. On the other hand, he researched the construction of reality, as the objective and ontological pole. Alongside the sensory-motor schemata, corresponding spatial and temporal reference systems are formed, as well as the categories of object and causality.

At a lecture in England in 1927, Piaget would have liked to have spoken about the "object." He refrained from doing so, because he had promised not to set himself in competition with Meyerson, who had been working on this topic for a long time. "I therefore look forward to your thesis, before I write my book, 'Jacqueline or How Girls Acquire Their Minds'" (unpublished letter dated 14 January 1927, cited in Vidal and Parot 1996: 68). Piaget promised, however, that he would not plagiarize his friend's ideas, because he did not intend to write from the perspective of perception but from the perspective of causality. Meyerson did, indeed, base his theories on Gestalt psychology, whereas Piaget's concept of object permanency referred to the studies of the Polish psychologist Stefan Szuman (1889–1972). In 1932, Piaget edited his observations on his children and wrote to his friend: "This is the first time that I have written something serious" (unpublished letter, cited in Vidal and Parot 1996). He received permission from Meyerson in 1933 to publish his "object" studies. *The Origins of Intelligence in Children* and *The Construction of Reality in the Child* appeared in 1936 and in 1937, not by Alcan in Paris, as had been intended, because this publishing house wanted to publish both books in one volume, but in the *Collection d'actualités pédagogiques* of the JJRI/IES, in order to mend his relationship with Bovet, "with whom I had a reconciliation" (letter dated 5 March 1935, cited in Vidal and Parot 1996: 71).

Piaget started from Baldwin's thesis (1897) that the infant's consciousness was adualistic. For the newborn child, objects do not exist for themselves, he is not conscious of himself and knows no boundaries between his inner world and the outer universe. The dualism between the subject (the pole of logical action) and the object (the ontological pole) will form only gradually, in a dual development. During the first stage, the child acquires his sensory-motor capability of action and a uniform reference system regarding space, time and causality. "Intelligence thus begins neither with knowledge of the self nor of things as such, but with knowledge of their interaction, and by orienting itself simultaneously toward the two poles of that inter-action, intelligence [=mind] thereby organizes the world by organizing itself" (Piaget 1937: 341). Piaget subdivided the nascent intelligence into an invariant sequence of six substages with flowing transitions:

  a. training of reflexes (birth to 6 weeks)
  b. first habits (up to 4 months)
  c. coordination of vision and prehension (up to 8 months)
  d. coordination between means and goals (up to 12 months)
  e. experimental stage (up to 18 months)
  f. internalization (up to 24 months)

(a) Immediately after birth, the infant begins to use his innate, still uncoordi-nated, reflexes (sucking, swallowing, gripping, focusing on objects, turning his head towards sounds, making sounds, etc.). Spontaneous practice and consolidation of these reflexes occurs largely in an autonomous and auto-centric way. By screaming, kicking and moving his head and his limbs, the infant differentiates his genetically programmed mechanisms. Repetition and generalization of the movements and recognizing their effects causes assimilation to the mechanisms and their accommodation to the environ-ment. The sucking reflex, for example, soon adapts to the mother's nipple (Piaget 1936: 40ff.). Initially, most infants can only feed if the breast is brought into their mouths. Within a short time, however, they learn to find the breast. In addition, the sucking reflex will be applied to other things, such as the thumb, but the infant's recognition of these "things" results in a purely sensory-motor reaction, and does not yet contain any concept of object. Thus, Piaget distinguished three interrelated forms of assimila-tion: the functional (or repetitional), the generalizing, and the recognitory assimilation (Piaget 1936: 42ff.).

(b) Many experiences (sucking his thumb, producing sounds), which accompany the spontaneous movements, are pleasurable for the child, and he attempts to repeat them. Piaget (1945: 37) interpreted this body-oriented repetition as the first form of imitation and, following Baldwin, named it pri-mary circular reaction. One example of this kind of self-sustaining sequence of actions is the infant's continuous kicking, in order to hear little bells ring, which are attached to his cot. "A circular reaction is a reproductive assim-ilation. It is the mechanism by which a schema is developed. The child performs an action, is interested in the result, and repeats the same action again" (Piaget 1973: 22). From such rhythmical circular reactions, the first elementary habits will form. On the basis of, say, the sucking reflex, the baby will develop a sucking schema, which is then systematically applied to the thumb, the dummy teat or the bottle. Piaget made a difference between this active habit forming and the passive form of conditioned reflexes, which are imposed from the outside. But here too, assimilation to an inherent need is required, "like in the case of Pavlov's dog, who salivates at the sound of a bell, as long as the bell corresponds to a signal for food, but will stop salivating when no more actual food follows the signal" (Piaget and Inhelder 1966: 14). The requirements for forming a schema are therefore an active and a generalizing assimilation of objects to a reflex.

The infant's world is still completely chaotic. Any object which appears will cause certain effects, but remains meaningless, once the direct sensory contact stops. The baby can already coordinate hearing and sight and will turn towards the direction of the source of sound, especially towards his mother's voice. However, "the infant will, of course, not yet perceive the person as the cause of the sound [...]; we rather have to assume that the visual and auditory schemata assimilate each other: the child is trying to hear the face and see the voice" (Piaget 1936: 95). Piaget did not consider the infant's first smiles to be a social phenomenon, but rather an emotional reaction to pleasant conditions experienced. What fascinate infants are, above all, objects of medium novelty.

(c) Between 4 and 8 months, the secondary circular reactions initiate the next phase of development. These sequences of action are no longer concerned with the infant's own body but try to reproduce phenomena that had been discovered incidentally (e.g. pushing and grabbing an object). The baby now employs sensory-motor schemata to make interesting phenomena last. He is interested in "things that can be shaken, swung to and fro, rubbed, etc., depending on the various differentiations of manual and visual behaviour schemata" (Piaget 1936: 179). Thus, hand-eye coordination forms the core of this phase.

> In front of Jacqueline, 0; 7 (16), a doll is attached to a string, which runs from the roof of the cot to the bar. By grabbing the doll, Jacqueline can shake the roof. She immediately notices this effect and repeats her movement at least 20 times in succession, pulling harder each time, laughing, as she watches the roof swing. (Piaget 1936: 179)

Claparède (1931: 7) termed such repetitive actions as "the law of reproduction of same." The baby discovers that specific actions always lead to a specific result, which introduces a separation between action (means) and result (purpose). Through his activities, the child experiences the elementary characteristics of objects (things can be sucked, grabbed, squeezed, bitten, swung, heard, etc.). Sensory-motor causality develops parallel and synchronously to the acquisition of a repertoire of sensory-motor behavior. Laurent, 0; 3 (12), for example,

> looks at his hands and keeps moving them back and forth, after having realized that the rattle no longer moves, or after having lost interest in the rattle. He then carefully examines his right hand, shaking it back and forth, and he looks at his hand with the same expression as before, when he still held the rattle. He proceeds as if he was trying to examine what power he had over his own hand. (Piaget 1937: 224, obs. 128)

This magico-phenomenalist causality is still utterly subjective and entirely linked to one's own actions.

(d) From 8 months onwards, the baby becomes capable of intentional actions, thanks to his coordination of means and purpose. If necessary, he can reach objects by removing obstacles or by utilizing familiar means (string, stick).

> At 0; 8 (8), I take hold of her celluloid raven as Jacqueline reaches for it. She now holds on to the toy with her right hand, and with her left hand she pushes my hand away. I repeat this test by only holding the raven by the end of its tail; again she pushes my hand away. (Piaget 1936: 225, obs. 124)

For Piaget, the execution of intentional actions and the (emergent) anticipation of events are "the very core of intelligence" (Piaget 1936: 235), because available schemata are applied to new situations.

Now, trained motor skills permit confident and precise seizing. The environment is gaining substance, which allows the forming of object permanency. This is the belief that things continue to exist, even if they are not perceived. The child is actively looking for a hidden object, which means that he must have a mental image of the disappeared object. Flexibility is, however, still rather limited at this early stage: if the experimenter repeatedly hides a toy under a cloth at one end of the table (location A), the child will immediately retrieve the toy. If the experimenter then removes the object from underneath A and hides it under a different cloth, at the other end of the table (location B), the child will nonetheless look under the cloth at A, where he himself last found the object. In the case of changes of location, object permanency is not yet fully stabilized. But the moving of things, the child's crawling and standing up, help him to orientate himself in space.

At 0; 10 (7) and over the next few days, Lucienne slowly moves her face towards objects she holds in her hand (rattles, dolls etc.), until her nose touches the object. Then she distances herself again from the object, watches the object with great interest, and starts the whole process over and over again. (Piaget 1937: 155, obs. 86)

Through his own movements, the child experiences different perspectives and size ratios, whereby the concept of space still remains self-centered. Once a child begins to search for hidden objects, a first concept of time emerges: parallel to the concepts of "in front of" and "behind" the child gains an understanding of "before" and "after" (Piaget 1937: 323ff.). His subjective understanding of causality is expanded and becomes more objective by taking into consideration external causes. "At 0; 9 (13), Laurent is lying in his four-poster cot, and I rock the cot three or four times by pulling a string. Then Laurent takes my hand and places it on the string" (Piaget 1937: 252, obs. 144). Imitation also begins to incorporate external sources, although it is still linked to the child's own repertoire of actions. "From 0; 11 (15) onwards, J. imitates yawning, by intentionally reproducing the hand movement and the sound, rather than finding the yawns of those around her infectious (Piaget 1945: 56, obs. 23).

(e) At the fifth substage, tertiary circular reactions occur, which deal with the targeted examination of objects and their characteristics. It is now no longer simply a matter of reproducing effects that have been discovered incidentally, but the "young scientist" experiments with objects by changing his actions (throwing, rubbing, hitting, shaking, etc.), in order to see what happens:

At 0; 10 (12), Laurent [. . .] drops a number of objects. In doing so, he varies the conditions, in order to study the fall. He is sitting in an oval basket and drops the object over the edge of the basket from different locations, sometimes to the right, sometimes to the left. Each time, he tries to retrieve the object, by leaning forward as far as possible, even if the object fell as far as 40 or 50 cm from the basket. (Piaget 1936: 272, obs. 141)

These trial-and-error variations lead to the discovery of new correlations and of new means of achieving a purpose: for instance, the baby can pull the object within his range, by pulling the mat on which the object lies (Piaget 1936: 283ff.). Because of his experiments, new schemata are formed and his coordination is expanded to many other schemata, so that Piaget spoke of a creative intelligence (Piaget 1936: 283ff.).

By the end of this phase, objects are considered to be independent items. The infant takes into consideration all displacements of an object and looks for a lost object where it was seen last. Therefore, a practical concept of space emerges. The objectivation of causality now leads to an understanding of cause and effect "through actuation," and to a correct imitation: "At 1; 0 (28), I place a cork stopper on the edge of her cot and push it down with a stick. I pass the stick to Jacqueline and replace the cork. She takes the stick, and immediately hits the cork until it falls down" (Piaget 1945: 76, obs. 39).

(f) Between the ages of one-and-a-half up to two, the transition occurs from sensory-motor thinking to representational thinking. According to Piaget, mental images are formed through the internalization of motor activities. Actions do not have to be carried out physically any more, because the relevant conditions, methods and means can be mentally conceived. Internalization also means setting a reflective distance to one's own actions. The internal actions are tied to the here-and-now, but become reversible. The most well-known example for this transition is that of the watch chain inside a matchbox.

> I put the chain back into the box and reduce the opening to 3 mm. It is understood that Lucienne is not aware of the function of the opening and closing the matchbox and has not seen me prepare the experiment. She only possesses the two preceding schemata: turning the box over in order to empty it of its contents, and sliding her finger into the slit to make the chain come out. It is of course this procedure that she tries first: she puts her finger inside and gropes to reach the chain, but fails completely. A pause follows, during which Lucienne manifests a very curious reaction, which shows that she tries to analyze the situation and visualize, through mental processing, the operations to be performed [...]. She looks at the slit with great attention; then, several times in succession, she opens and shuts her mouth, at first slightly, then wider and wider [...] Soon after this phase of plastic reflection, Lucienne confidently puts her finger in the slit and [...] pulls, so as to enlarge the opening. She succeeds and grasps the chain. (Piaget 1936: 339f., obs. 180)

Visualization of how the box can be opened is supported, in this example, by a motor imitation schema, which serves as a "symbolic substitute" (Piaget 1936: 345). Internalized imitation is a central prerequisite for the transition to symbolic thinking, which does not depend on the presence of realia and enables the child to anticipate the results of his actions. Piaget termed the internalization of actions a "reversal of the course of consciousness" (Piaget 1936: 155) and a true, small-scale Copernican revolution: while, at the start of this development, the child refers back to himself, or, to be more precise, to his body, he will, in the end, once language and thought commence, integrate himself as an element or body among the others, into a world he constructs bit by bit and which he will regard, from then on, as something which exists outside of himself. (Piaget 1943/6: 193)

Intelligence is now "systematic" (Piaget 1936: 283), because practical problems can be solved without actually having to execute all the actions in their proper sequence. Object permanency is now stabilized to the extent that the imperceptible displacement of objects (for example, bricks hidden in the hand of the experimenter) can be followed mentally. The child is now able to return to his starting point and to take detours. Analogous to the displacement in space, time-related sequences are forming, "which enable the child to recall memories, independent of direct perception" (Piaget 1937: 336): to say, for instance, that a dog goes "woof, woof," even if there is no dog (Piaget 1937: 333, obs. 173b).

Through his own activity, the child has constructed an understanding of the world and of himself, which allows him to act successfully. By postulating that "actions always precede thought" (Piaget 1976/9: 244), Piaget followed Fouillée, whose idea that action was the primary factor had strongly influenced Bergson and Janet. Because action has its own logic, Piaget did not concern himself with the kind of objects used for action. In this process, intelligence has constructed primitive forms of the categories of space, time and causality. However, at the end of the sensory-motor phase, the infant is not yet able to reflect, and cannot yet reach any rational insights. In this subsequent stage "he has to reconstruct, in conceptual terms, everything that he has constructed so far in terms of schemata" (Piaget 1973: 23). Piaget (1956/7: 49 cf. 1924: 121, 123; 1928/2: 79) called this law of higher recapitulation "vertical displancement" (décalage vertical).

The Preoperational Stage

Starting with the preoperational stage, regulation of the child's behavior begins to shift from the sensory-motor level to the symbolic level. "Without a doubt, the most decisive turning point in the mental development of the child is that which marks the beginning of representational thought" (Piaget 1962/4: 508). Piaget studied this transition by observing his own children, and he published his findings in the book *Play, Dreams and Imitation in Childhood* (1945), which he had been working on since the early 1930s (Piaget 1933/6: 283).

The child's repertoire of practical schemata is now being expanded and partially replaced by mental representation. He therefore acts faster and more flexibly. Action, perception and thinking differentiate, and the child becomes able to reflect upon his own actions. The child's growing ability to represent actions is supported by the development of speech, whereby mental images receive verbal meanings. The acquisition of language enables the child to recall past actions and to anticipate future ones.

These structural changes will be the effect of four achievements (Piaget 1945: 302): the acceleration of movement and the grasp of consciousness about the actions are the individual factors. The acquisition of a system of signs and the socialization are the interindividual factors. Within the stage of preoperational thinking, two substages can be identified:

(a) Symbolic thought (2 to 4/5 years)
(b) Intuitive thought (4/5 to 7/8 years)

Symbolic thought

Between the ages of one-and-a-half up to four, the child acquires the ability to represent things that are not directly perceived with the help of symbols and signs. Piaget borrowed the differentiation between signal, symbol and sign from the Genevan linguist, Ferdinand de Saussure (1857–1913). "The only signifier known to sensory-motor forms of behaviour is the signal" (Piaget 1954/10: 272). When sensory impressions join together, a phenomenon can become a signal: approaching footsteps, for example, indicate the arrival of the mother. Thus, signals consist of a part of a phenomenon. Once signals differentiate from the signified objects, they function as signifiers, and representational intelligence begins to develop. A representation consists of "linking a 'sign' to the 'signified', through evocation of the signified, which is delivered by thought" (Piaget 1945: 342). As thought functions with the help of these signifiers, Piaget termed the mechanism of representational intelligence "symbolic function," changing it later to "semiotic function."

The founder of structural linguistics distinguished two forms of signifiers: a symbol is a "motivated" signifier, because there is a rational connection between the signifier and the signified, whereas a sign is an "arbitrary" thing (Saussure 1916: 85). Symbols, as opposed to signs, usually show a similarity to the object signified, for instance if a child uses a piece of wood to represent a boat. Analogous to this differentiation between symbol and sign, Piaget postulated two forms of logic: symbols contain a prelogic, which is individual, affectively charged and usually unconscious, whereas the linguistic signs represent social conventions (Piaget 1945: 218; Piaget and Inhelder 1966: 48). "A sign can therefore only be created through social life, whereas a symbol can be created by an isolated individual" (Piaget 1947: 141). Piaget now abstained from linking symbolic thinking to autism, but its affectivity remained the basis for the development of morality (Piaget 1945: 268ff.). For Piaget therefore, symbols, which emerge before verbal signs, played the relevant role in development. "The origin of thought lies in the semiotic function" (Piaget 1954/10: 272) and not in the language. Piaget identified the following steps and manifestations as part of the semiotic function:

1 deferred imitation
2 symbolic play
3 drawings
4 mental images
5 dreams and fictions
6 verbal signs of language

The semiotic function forms a whole, because due to these symbols and signs, intelligence is now no longer subject to direct perception. Once the child realizes that a symbol, picture or sign can represent an object, an event or a relationship, a fundamental psychological change takes place. The reason for this process is neither the symbol itself, nor the language, but the interiorizing of action through imitation.

1. Since 1927, Piaget had understood imitation to be a result of accommo-dation (Piaget 1927/2: 214; 1935/5: 13), for which he found support in the theories of Henri Delacroix and Paul Guillaume (1878–1962). Imita-tion emerges during the fourth stage of sensory-motor development, and the schemata thus conceived are applied to new models during the fifth stage, and interiorized during the last stage. "Imitation depends upon schemata, which, of course, are sensory-motor intelligence in action. But imitation becomes a separate function, to the extent that these actions are carried out in the interest of accommodation for its own sake" (Piaget 1973: 21f.). At 1; 4 (4), Jacqueline imitated with precision the angry behavior of a young boy who had called at the house the day before (Piaget 1945: 85, obs. 52). Such "deferred imitation" presupposes the pattern of the acting boy as a symbol of rage. This kind of imitation is therefore a spontaneous and largely unconscious symbolic act. Between the ages of 2 and 7, imitation becomes more general, more detailed and comes under the control of conscious intelligence (Piaget 1945: 105). Once imitation is completely interiorized, motor symbolization is redundant.
2. If imitation is transferred to other contexts, it results in symbolic play. The transition between imitation and symbolic play fluctuates, because "there is a bit of imitation in every symbolic game" (Piaget 1945: 352). Based on the studies of Pérez (1886), Groos (1899), Stern (1914) and

Bühler (1928), Piaget differentiated between practice games and functional games, symbolic games and rule games, which all develop in this order. Sensory-motor functional games, like hopscotch, form the first step of this development. When several of these fun actions are coordinated towards a goal (for example, to pile building blocks on top of each other), the practice game becomes a construction game, and the fun of moving is now replaced by the fun of "being the cause" (Piaget 1945: 149). Symbolic games begin at around the age of one year, when the child imitates familiar actions like eating, drinking or sleeping. In order to pretend that she was sleeping, Jacqueline used various objects as symbolic substitutes for a pillow (Piaget 1945: 128, obs. 64). Thus, imitation, not language, is the essential cause of the development of fantasy games. "Symbolic play emerges at around the same time as speech, but is independent of speech, and plays an important role in the thinking of the young child, through being the source of individual (both cognitive and affective) representations and (also individual) representational schemata construction" (Piaget 1954/10: 270). During symbolic play, the child learns to attribute meaning to things. In contrast to the accommodating imitation, however, symbolic play is dominated by reality-distorting assimilation. Like Freud, Piaget regarded games as belonging to a realm that is detached from reality and follows its own laws. Specific features from reality are imitated, it is true, but "the composition of these features is imaginary" (Piaget 1945: 170). If a child pushes a box along the floor, imagining this box to be a car, the child dwells in a world of fiction, because the relationship between the sign and the signified remains utterly subjective. This "distorting assimilation" (Piaget 1945: 148), however, is the source of creative imagination, and play is "the precursor of art" (Piaget 1945: 196). The symbol is the instrument of assimilation, in order "to satisfy the desires of the self, through transformation of the real" (Piaget 1943/6: 208). In games, conflicts are solved fictitiously, without having to yield to reality. The child transfers his own mood to the symbol, by, for example, making the dolls quarrel with each other. Thus the child can process events and actions from his own life and "take his revenge on reality" (Piaget 1945: 174). The lack of the necessity of accommodation creates a feeling of freedom, and the child experiences the joy of being the cause and the master of the events. "It is therefore important for the child's affective and intellectual equilibrium, that he is allowed a range of occupations, in which he is not motivated by adapting to reality, but is, on the contrary, motivated by adapting reality to the self, without constraints or sanctions" (Piaget and Inhelder 1966: 49). But there is a danger: "To compensate for reality, by inventing stories, is typical of the little ones, and this regulation is salutary. But the same attitude among adults will lead to isolation and 'autism" (Piaget 1943/10: 168). In contrast to Groos, Piaget regarded symbolic games, played until the end of the preoperational stage, as "individual thinking in its purest form" (Piaget 1939/3: 159) because children take a long time to become cooperative. "Between two and seven years of age, every child still plays for himself, even at social games" (Piaget 1954/12: 117). From age 6 onwards, symbolic games are replaced by rule games, such as the game of marbles. The rules of competition or cooperation imply responsibilities and sanctions, which oblige the child to adapt his symbols to this reality. Rule games therefore are "the playful activity of the socialized human being" (Piaget 1945: 183).

3. Piaget ranked children's drawings somewhere "between symbolic play, which contain the same functional enjoyment and self-centeredness also found in drawings, and the mental image, the visualization, which shares, with the drawings, the attempt to imitate the real" (Piaget and Inhelder 1966: 52). Because a drawing depicts the "inner model" (Piaget 1945: 104) of an object, the drawing is primarily a work of imitation. Piaget agreed with Luquet's theory, according to which the first scrawls represent an "accidental realism." This is followed by a phase of "failed realism," for example pictures of human "tadpoles." The subsequent "intellectual realism," from which the perspectives are missing and in which overlapping objects do not cover the underlying ones, is supplanted, at around the age of 8, by "visual realism," in which the drawings are in the correct perspective.

4. For Piaget, the mental image, like the drawing, is not a result of perception, but of imitated action. In order to think, actions must be "symbolically translated into words and images" (Piaget 1967: 389). A mental image is a representation of an external (auditory, visual, olfactory, and so forth) object and contains "a sketch of a potential imitation" (Piaget 1945: 94). In its function as a symbol, it is a "differentiated signifier, because it is detached from the perceived object [and] is only accessible to individual thought" (Piaget 1945: 210). The mental image is neither an element of thought itself, nor is it a direct continuation of perception, but an instrument to help evoke and think of the object which has been perceived. The mental image emerges in the sixth phase of the sensory-motor stage. According to Piaget, there are "only moving perceptual pictures" (Piaget 1954/12: 39) during the first few months in a child's life; pictures "which appear, dissolve, and occasionally reappear" (Piaget 1970/2: 27). At the preoperational stage, however, the mental images remain static, and once the stage of concrete operations is reached, the child also succeeds in reproducing movement and transformation mentally.

5. Piaget described children's dreams and "unusual" fictions as "secondary symbolism." "C.G. Jung has correctly recognized that dream symbolism is a kind of original language" (Piaget and Inhelder 1966: 52). For Piaget, dreams are comparable to symbolic play because both use images as a means of expression. The dream, however, lacks consciousness (Piaget 1945: 258; 1954/12: 147), and merges symbols with images. From the observations on his own children, Piaget described an example of how Jacqueline, barely six years old, used her dolls to take symbolic revenge on her father, after a conflict: "Zoubab cut off her daddy's head" (Piaget 1945: 224, obs. 96). A month and a half later, she dreamt that a certain Dr M. had shot a man, who resembled her father: "He had a fat tummy like you; he was just like you" (Piaget 1945: 229). Piaget concluded from this that the father was an "object of ambivalent feelings" (Piaget 1945: 226), in contrast to the mother, because one day later, Jacqueline dreamt to be "afraid of the fox. So I crawled into mummy's body and hid there. Then the fox could not get me" (Piaget 1945: 229). Fears, according to Piaget, manifest themselves more easily in dreams than in play, because in dreams the self can exert less control.

6. The transition from using individual symbols to using collective signs is a central step in the development of semiotic functions. In this new phase, the child develops the ability to manipulate his environment by using the language. "As language develops, the use of symbols becomes increasingly unnecessary. In fact, the child resorts to symbols each time that his language is insufficient for communicating his experiences. The child will only gradually be able to put his thoughts into words and will only gradually acquire enough inner language to express his experiences. From then on, the child is content to express his thoughts by way of this collective instrument" (Piaget 1954/12: 139).

Piaget had an ambivalent attitude towards language. On the one hand, it is the most important means of thinking:

> The acquisition of language profoundly modifies behavior, from an emotional as well as from a mental point of view. In addition to all real and material actions, which the child is already capable of, language now enables him to recall all his past actions in the form of reports, and to anticipate future actions [...]. As soon as the child can speak, he is no longer dealing only with the physical universe, but is confronted also with two new and closely related worlds: the social world and the world of representation. (Piaget 1943/6: 202)

On the other hand, Piaget asserted that "the acquisition of language is not a sufficient explanation as to why logical thinking overrides sensory-motor intelligence" (Piaget 1945: 301). Even before semiotic functions constitute themselves, the infant's activity during the sensory-motor phase is meaningful. Language is only one of the representational possibilities and offers no "transfer of ready-made operational structures" (Piaget 1963/1: 100). Moreover, it is a deficient system of communication, because "it does not reflect reality directly, but has to make use of general terminology, through which experiences cannot be adequately communicated" (Piaget 1954/12: 146). Piaget borrowed the idea from Janet (Piaget 1914/15: 81) that language cannot be formed until the corresponding cognitive structures are in place. Language is a secondary phenomenon, because "there is a logic of co-ordination of actions, which is much more fundamental than language-based logic" (Piaget 1963/1: 93). Thought does therefore not depend on linguistic structures. "It is language that is influenced by operations, and not our operations that are influenced by language" (Piaget 1970/9: 31). Piaget's thesis was supported by studies carried out with deaf children, by researchers such as Pierre Oléron (1915–1995) in 1950: although lagging slightly behind, the mental development of deaf children runs largely parallel with that of children who can hear, whereas the development of blind children lags considerably further behind that of sighted children.

In his considerations regarding the development of language, Piaget largely referred back to Clara and William Stern. The phase of spontaneous babbling, between 6 and 11 months of age, is followed by a phase in which phonemes are differentiated through imitation (11 and 12 months of age). Proper speech begins with one-word sentences, followed, nearer the age of two, by two-word sentences. The child starts with "pseudo concepts" such as "woof woof," which can refer to all sorts of objects and activities. For one of his daughters, this meant "successively, dogs, cats, the pattern on a rug, people working in a garden (whom she saw from her balcony, just as she had seen the dogs), and finally any kind of spectacle observed from this balcony" (Piaget 1933/2: 113; cf. 1945: 276, obs. 101a). Such "initial verbal schemata are intermediate forms between sensory-motor intelligence and conceptual schemata" (Piaget 1945: 278). On the next level, "pre-concepts" with simple and imprecise meanings are formed. For Jacqueline, at 2; 7, any snail she encountered on her walks with her father was "the slug" (Piaget 1945: 287, obs. 107). She was not yet able to distinguish between the various specimens of a class and the class itself, and this included her own self. When she was looking at an old photograph of herself, she said: "This is Jacqueline when she was still Lucienne" (Piaget 1945: 286, obs. 106b). It is a relatively long process for words to be understood as pure signs, and Piaget associated the acquisition of language with social constraint, as the child is "compelled to adopt an increasing number of binding truths (fully-fledged ideas or actual norms of thinking)" (Piaget 1947: 180). But this is not true for babies. In the beginning, the child will only adopt those elements which match his cognitive stage, and he will "blithely ignore everything that surpasses his mental stage" (Piaget 1947: 179).

According to Piaget, social influence only begins when the child learns to speak (Piaget 1947: 181ff.). "Behavior in the first year of life cannot legitimately be considered as social" (Piaget 1927/2: 213). In the 181 records of observations on infants in *The Origins of Intelligence in Children*, the mother or other persons of reference were mentioned only nine times and only played a passive role in the instances recorded (Jalley 1981: 354). The first observation regarding the first attempts at feeding already neglects to mention the mother's supporting activity (Piaget 1936: 35, obs. 1). She is nothing but an interesting picture, or she means "as much as an occult spirit means to a magician: she is prepared to return, if one does all the right things, but she does not obey any objective law" (Piaget 1937: 23). Even when children react angrily, because their bottle has been hidden (Piaget 1937: 40, obs. 25), or when they show a joyful reaction to "peekaboo" (Piaget 1937: 53, obs. 35), there seems to be no social significance attached to this:

Sensory-motor intelligence is an adaptation of the individual to things or to the body of another person, but it does not involve any socialization of the intellect per se [. . .]. Even if the baby imitates an intelligent action that somebody else had carried out, or if the baby understands somebody else's intention, because of a smile or a discontented frown, we cannot yet talk of any exchange of thoughts which would lead to a structural modification of these thoughts. (Piaget 1937: 346f.)

Yet certain observations, regarding imitation (Piaget 1945: 27, obs. 2; 39f., obs. 9; 45, obs. 14; 53, obs. 19; 85, obs. 52), do indeed bear witness to a structured exchange. But there are passages where Piaget even spoke of "social instincts [. . .] From two months onwards, [the child] smiles at people and is looking for contact; one knows how demanding babies already are in this respect and how much they insist on having company, unless one gets them used to keeping themselves amused during specified hours" (Piaget 1939/3: 177). Despite all this, the child "begins his life in a purely individual state—the state of his first few months, when no kind of social interaction with others is possible" (Piaget 1939/3: 177).

After Henri Wallon's earlier criticism of Piaget's theory that the development of logic was entirely dependent upon socialization, he now reproached Piaget for neglecting the relationship of the individual with his social environment. For Piaget, as for Rousseau, pure individualism dominated the start of the child's development. "It appears that the child, like Robinson on his island, has all the necessary aptitudes to obtain directly from nature the needed material resources and instruments" (Wallon 1942: 47). Objects were supposed to be solely responsible for the child's education, because Piaget did not include the social environment until a very late stage and in a fashion that was much too abstract. "Nothing could correspond more to the alternative between *Emile* and the *Social Contract*" (Wallon 1947: 12). Piaget responded that "Wallon must have understood very little of our postulation" (Piaget 1943/12: 312). Both Piaget and Wallon "would not succeed in using the same words with the same meanings" (Piaget 1951/6: 157) because Wallon was a "victim of Durkheim's sociology, which considers social life to be a single block" (Piaget 1951: 160). But "'society' is neither a thing nor a cause, but is a system of relationships [...] For a psychologist, 'social life' is therefore only a statistical term" (Piaget 1945: 91, 275). By eliminating the concept of society, Piaget also eliminated the structuring function of interaction partners. He assigned this function to the internalization of one's own actions. Piaget therefore had difficulty with understanding why the child followed the expectations of his social environment. "Is it not astounding that a baby, who has scarcely grasped the first words of his mother tongue, will accept orders and feel bound by them, at an age when everything is still playful and spontaneous?" (Piaget 1949/6: 50).

In sum, there might be five reasons for Piaget's ambivalent approach to social interaction and language. First, he started from the assumption of inequality between parents and child, with the consequence that he saw no mutual action. Either the child is spontaneous and active and the parents are respectful and passive, or the parents dominate the child, who has to obey. Secondly, Piaget's concept of action and interaction relate to the physical environment, as "the simplest actions deal with solid and extended matter" (Piaget 1950 III: 119). This focus upon objects led to a systematic sidelining of the social, which became clear in his lectures on *The Psychology of Intelligence* of 1942. In Chapter VI, Piaget described the social factors of mental development without drawing any connection to the previously described development of logic. Thirdly, he supposed that there were two sources to thinking and never went beyond the dualism of inner and outer. He regarded symbols as individual, spontaneous and authentic manifestations of intelligence, whereas language appeared to be an external system of ready-made conventional meanings. Fourthly, being hamstrung by his theological convictions, he subjected everything that came from the outside to an immanent logic. Finally, he reduced language to semantics and disregarded its function for negotiating the interpretation of situations. Language therefore appeared to be disconnected from action and simply superimposed upon "layers, which have existed long before their symbolic function itself, and which are of a sensory-motor nature" (Piaget 1954/10: 279). Thus, Piaget constructed the emergence of representational thinking as an internalization of one's own "outward" actions. The resulting devaluation of language and the enhanced status of action sometimes took grotesque forms:

> In our opinion, thinking is in no way restricted to speaking, classifying or abstracting. Thinking means having an influence on the object and changing it. To grasp the situation regarding the breakdown of a car does not mean that one is able to describe the misfiring of the engine, but rather that one is able to take the engine apart and reassemble it. (Piaget 1960/7: 79)

The same problem that Piaget faced with language reappeared with perception. In this area, too, he had to prove that mental images are not determined by the outside, but that "intelligence proceeds from action as a whole" (Piaget and Inhelder 1966: 29). Despite innate reflexes like the pupillary reaction, seeing must first be trained. Sensory images have no meaning for the newborn baby, because the relationships to other actions and the coordination of the isolated schemata of perception are yet to be constructed (Piaget 1936: 74). Visual perception is enhanced through accommodation of the schemata to the objects and through assimilation of the objects to the action. Initially, the child can only perceive one dominant aspect in his field of vision. Perception is, therefore, in accordance with the Gestalt theory, centered on global features such as good shape, continuation or closure (Piaget 1947: 69).

Piaget "was strongly influenced by the Gestalt theory" (Piaget 1973: 10), although he often gave the impression of having reached a similar theory all on his own: in the second edition of *Language and Thought of the Child*, published in 1930, Piaget claimed to have written the chapter on "verbal syncretism" "before we had any knowledge of 'Gestalt theory'. One will immediately notice the extent to which our results agree with the leading hypotheses of this now well-known doctrine" (Piaget 1923: 174). Yet Piaget had already quoted Christian von Ehrenfels (1859–1932), Karl Bühler and Ernst Mach (1838–1916) in the first edition, and had postulated "that we do not recognize objects by prior analysis and perception of every detail, but rather by 'forms as a whole', which are constructed by us, in the same way as they are set out by the individual parts of the perceived objects, and which could be termed as the 'schema' or the '*Gestalt quality*' of these objects" (Piaget 1923: 172f.). Moreover, Bergson and James had already advocated a theory of perception which came quite close to Gestalt psychology.

Piaget was fascinated by the concept of Gestalt as a holistic structure, characterized by laws of organization and by its tendency towards equilibrium. The schemata of the sixth stage of the sensory-motor phase, for example, embodied "the characteristics of a 'gestalt'" (Piaget 1938/2: 178).

"Gestalt" was the archetype of the "grouping," since "all the characteristics, which the Gestalt theory ascribed to a good form of perception (simplicity, regularity, symmetry, similarity, proximity etc.) are also essential characteristics of logico-mathematical structures (except that of proximity [...])" (Piaget 1954/3: 116). Having studied Brunschvicg, however, he had criticized "that the psychology of 'form' of Wertheimer, Köhler and Koffka constitutes a renewal of apriorism" (Piaget 1927: 291) or of empiricism (Piaget 1938/2: 181). Piaget also agreed with Eugenio Rignano (1870–1930), who reproached Gestalt theory for having neglected the role played by action in perception. For Piaget therefore, "wholes" were structures that had been worked out, while the Gestalt theory "does not take into account any prior experience" (Piaget 1936: 383).

In order to prove his rationalist thesis that perception depended on sensory-motor intelligence, Piaget, together with Marc Lambercier (1890–1972) and others, conducted many studies between 1939 and 1960 that were published in 33 articles and two books (Piaget 1961a; Piaget *et al.* 1963c). One of the results was that the constancy of size and form develops from six months onwards and steadily improves until the age of 10 to 12 years. The irritating points were that perceptual constancy occurs three months before object permanency, and that 5-year-olds were much better at estimating lengths than are 8-year-olds (Piaget *et al.* 1943/4; Piaget 1961a: 315). Piaget concluded that the perception of length developed in a different way from the concept of length. He thus differentiated between the primary perception as a direct process and the secondary perception which stems from perceptual activities consisting of "transferences, comparisons, transpositions, projections in space and time, and, generally speaking, of an increasingly flexible analysis, which strives towards reversibility" (Piaget 1947: 96). Primary perception leads to "gestalts," which are primitive forms of equilibrium (Piaget 1952/1: 126) because they remain static and irreversible. Perceptual activity, on the other hand, transfers the data of perception into intellectual operations, which lead to superior and dynamic equilibrium. Piaget believed that he now could explain the contradictory results: "The great difference between a child of between 4–6 years of age and a child of between 8 and 10 consists in the fact that the thinking of the younger child casts itself upon perception-based *configurations* or 'gestalts', while the older child reflects upon *transformations*, which lead from one gestalt to the other" (Piaget 1954/3: 110). But Piaget *et al.* (1958) believed that there exist partial isomorphisms between perceptual and logical structures.

During the 1950s, Piaget further elaborated his dualistic model, especially during his time at the Institute for Advanced Studies in Princeton, when he worked on *The Mechanisms of Perception*. He concluded that knowledge always contains two different aspects: the figural aspect results from the

Table 10.1   Piaget's model of basic representations

Aspect	Signified	Signifier
Figural	Objects	Images
General	Concepts	Verbal Signs

SOURCE Piaget 1966b: 502

internalization of imitation, which enables perception to create "copies" of reality, in the form of mental images. The role of these figurations consists in "imitating, not in constructing or producing" (Piaget and Inhelder 1966b: 491). The operative aspect is the result of "transformations" of reality and leads, via the internalization of actions, to cognitive operations. Perception is characterized by the fact "that it depends on the figural aspect of knowledge of the real, while action in its entirety (and also already in its form of sensory-motor action), is fundamentally operative and transforms the real" (Piaget and Inhelder 1966: 29). Both aspects are derived from sensory-motor action (Piaget 1960/7: 71), which enabled Piaget to maintain his thesis of internally controlled development. As complementary components of every cognitive act, the respective structures have to rely on each other. "Operative structures supply knowledge of transformations from one configuration to another, and figurative structures supply knowledge of states which are linked by transformations" (Piaget 1961a: 284). Mental images are predominantly figurative, insofar as their content is considered; but using or changing the images involves the operative aspect. Since operations are characterized by reversibility, they form conserving structures, as opposed to figurations, which form modifying or distorting structures. Because a figuration, as a whole, is worth more than the sum of its parts, it cannot reach the ideal equilibrium of an operation. "Gestalts" therefore have a subjective and illusionary character and are a danger to the individual. Operations must perform corrective action upon perceptions, in order to overcome their centering and their static images, which prevail until the end of the preoperative stage (Piaget and Inhelder 1966: 34). The children cannot correctly represent or anticipate movement (such as upending a pole), or transformations (transfer liquid into cups of different sizes), until they start performing concrete operations. Only operations guarantee therefore the objective grasp of reality. Because of the dualism between perception and intelligence, there remains, however, a radical difference between the mental image and concepts (Table 10.1).

By introducing the figural and operative (general) aspects, Piaget effected a radical change in the meaning of Gestalts: from the universal structure of perception towards illusions and mistakes. This changed his estimation of the Gestalt theory altogether, as its concept of the field had a "detrimental influence, even if it has been inspiring" (Piaget 1968: 53).

Intuitive thought

This second part of the preoperational stage is the period that Piaget has most thoroughly researched, because it constitutes the basis for the development of logical thinking. Analogous to the decentration of practical intelligence, at the end of the sensory-motor stage, a decentration of intuitive intelligence occurs. The interiorized schemata of sensory-motor intelligence had enabled symbolic thinking. Now, between the ages of four and seven, "intuitive thinking takes an exact middle position [. . .] between the image and the concept" (Piaget 1945: 270). The number and quality of preconcepts increase considerably and will be transformed to real concepts and the end of the preoperational stage. Preconcepts are still dominated by figurative aspects. Four- to five-year-old children believe, for example, that an amount of pebbles suddenly contains more pebbles if they are spread over a larger area. The child now learns to form simple and concrete classes (for example, all cuddly toys) yet these classes are not systematic, because no generic classes or subclasses are possible.

Young children can represent objects and results of actions, but they have difficulties in grasping spatial, temporal or logical relations. Intuitive thinking imitates real actions through visual representation, so it is obstructed by the fact that one cannot do two things at the same time (Piaget 1947: 151). Children therefore have difficulties in understanding that an object can belong to two classes simultaneously, as demonstrated in the test with 18 brown and two white wooden beads:

> OLI 5; 2. Are all these beads brown?—*No, there are two white ones.*—Are they all made of wood?—*Yes.*—If we were to put all the wooden beads in here, would there be any left over?—*No.*—If we were to put all the brown beads in here, would there be any left over?—*Yes, the two white ones.*—Well, which chain would be longer then, the one made of the brown ones in this box, or the one made from the wooden beads in the other box?—*The one made from the brown ones.* (Piaget and Szeminska 1941a: 216)

In 1933 Piaget had asked Alina Szeminska (1907–1986) to examine the phenomenon regarding the beads more closely. She had been studying child psychology under Wolfgang Köhler (1887–1967), Kurt Lewin (1890–1947) and Max Wertheimer (1880–1943) in Berlin, and, following Köhler's recommendation, had come to Geneva in 1928, where she collaborated with Meili. In the following year, she began to investigate the development

of the numeric concept and created a vast number of experiments, which
were concluded in 1935, and which formed the basis of the book *Genesis of
Number in the Child* (Bideaud 1991).[10]

Szeminska and Piaget followed Stern and Kurt Koffka (1886–1941),
according to whom the number is composed of groups and series.

Early constructions of series occur already during the sensory-motor
phase (Piaget and Szeminska 1941a: 169). Infants at 10 to 12 months of
age can place three elements maximally, such as sticks, in order of increasing size. From the age of five onwards, children manage to form a "staircase"
out of a selection of sticks, by placing them in order of size, by trial and
error. Difficulties arise when they are required to introduce new sticks into
an existing order, because "prior to the operational formation of series,
the child can only achieve empirical series" (Piaget 1970: 57). Beginning
at the age of 7, children can determine the relations between three sticks
of different sizes, without the need for putting them into place. One great
problem is encountered in double seriation. When children are given two
collections (for example, ten dolls and walking sticks of different sizes) they
can place the items in order of size (single seriation). If they are asked,
however, to find the corresponding walking stick for each doll—to form
two corresponding series (double seriation)—the task often turns out to be
impossible at the preoperational stage.

Piaget had been working for some considerable time on the issue of "class
as foundation of relations" (Piaget 1927: 334). In order to make sense of the
world, children sort the phenomena by grouping similar features into a class.
Initially, simple, concrete classes are formed, such as all objects of the same
colour. From the age of 5 onwards, class inclusion begins to become rational,
without being systematic yet. If children at their intuitive stage are shown
a picture of three roses and eight tulips and are asked whether the picture
showed more flowers or more tulips then the children will answer that there
are more tulips. Although they can subdivide the basic category of flowers
into roses and tulips they are unable to revert their differentiation and
mentally file the tulips once more under the larger class of flowers.

Numbers contain a relation of order, because they denote a series of
consecutive sets, whereby each subsequent set contains one more object
than the previous set. This ability to ascribe objects as similar units, to
sets is a feature class formation. Numbers are therefore a logical synthesis of classes (cardinal number) and relations (ordinal number) (Piaget
and Szeminska 1941a: 240). Only with the fusion of these two aspects will
the number receive operational significance, which is still missing when a
5-year-old child rattles off numbers in sequence. Class, series and number
are "constructed together, in consecutive steps, whereby they follow the
same structuring stages synchronously" (Piaget *et al.* 1960a: 63). Initially,

children perceive numbers as a constituent part of objects, i.e. they attribute qualities to objects, as Aristotle did. In the course of development, numbers are understood as an application of the subject and are now "no longer an object, but an operation" (Brunschvicg, in Piaget 1924/1: 593). Yet Piaget did not conclude from this that numbers are subjective constructions, but postulated "an isomorphism between the operative structures and the objective qualities, discovered thanks to these employed structures" (Piaget and Garcia 1971: 68).

By deriving the concept of numbers from interiorized actions, Piaget opposed the English philosophers Bertrand Russell (1872–1970) and Alfred N. Whitehead (1861–1947), for whom the concept of numbers was purely due to logical cogitation. "If logic is taken in the narrow sense, the logic of classes defined as concepts and qualitative relations, then number is not at all reducible to logic" (Piaget 1942: 256). According to Piaget, the concept of number will only become independent from tangible collections around the age of 10–12, and become an infinite quantity. However, it turned out that certain simple formalizations are already possible at the age of 7 (Piaget *et al.* 1960a: 149–213; Gréco and Morf 1962). The transition from the concrete to the formal stage is therefore not as unambiguous as was originally assumed.

Most of the research regarding the development from preoperational to formal thinking was carried out by Bärbel Inhelder (1913–1997). She had grown up in the German-speaking Sankt Gallen and arrived at the JJRI/IES as a student in 1932, studying for six years under Claparède, Bovet, Piaget, Rey and Meili, but also under Brunschvicg, Wallon, Janet and Piéron in Paris. As an unpaid assistant, she had the opportunity to cooperate in numerous experiments at an early stage in her studies.

> On the day of my 20th birthday, Piaget suggested conducting a little study, which later gained tremendous importance and inspired numerous further studies: in this study, the children observed how a sugar cube dissolved in water and we tried to find out the children's ideas on the process of dissolving and the various stages of a substance [...] The youngest children thought that nothing was conserved, except perhaps the taste of the sugar in the water. The older ones, on the other hand, believed that part of the sugar was conserved in some invisible form [...] One child, aged 10, said: 'the sugar is entirely in the water. It consists of minute particles, so small and so spread out that one cannot see them any more, but in my mind I can combine them, and then I know that the same amount of sugar must be in there." This was the first time that we recorded the explicit expression of some kind of reversibility, which came from the mouth of a child. (Inhelder 1989: 36, 38f.)

Inhelder occupied herself intensively with the child's understanding of the conservation of quantity. Piaget's interest in this subject had been kindled by Emile Meyerson (1859–1933), the uncle of his friend. Building upon object permanency, children begin to understand the conservation of quantities between the ages of 4 and 7, even though the concepts of amount, weight, and volume generally do not yet reach stability at this stage. The most well-known experiment regarding quantity variation consists of changing the shape of one of two balls of clay into a coil, observed by the children. Then, they are asked whether the ball and the coil contained the same amount of clay. One typical example: "Do they have as much clay as each other?—*Yes, because you didn't take any off*.—Are they as heavy as each other?—*No, because this one* (the coil) *is smaller*" (Piaget 1941: 23ff.). The child can see that no clay has been added or removed but he is swayed by the change of shape and intuitively concludes that the weight has changed, too, because he is disposed to think in terms of conditions, not in terms of transformations. Although he can imagine spatial or social relations, he still understands them from one aspect only. For Piaget, the preoperational phase was characterized by cognitive deficits: the lack of invariance of amount, weight, volume and number, the lack of understanding of the relation of part and whole, the inability to adopt the perspectives of others, and the absolutist comprehension of rules create "a lack of equilibrium between assimilation and accommodation, which has not yet been overcome" (Piaget 1947: 180).

The critical method

Because of criticism of his clinical method from experts such as Janet (1935: 26, 167), Piaget tried to examine the child's logic "not any more on a verbal, but on an experimental level" (Piaget 1943/6: 215). "I believed in language too much. I had the children talk instead of the experiment" (Piaget 1973: 70). Further experiments, with carefully arranged material and observable situations, along with the subsequent questioning, were termed the "mixed" or "critical method." Children could point to objects or manipulate them, and the experimenter could ask the children for the reasons for their actions or false predictions. After the 1930s Piaget, who found it difficult to establish a direct line to children, left the empirical verification of his theories largely to his assistants. In 1943, after having established special classes for the disabled in her hometown, Inhelder was appointed "Chief of Studies" at the JJRI/IES. "Piaget tried to convince me that he needed my presence in order to counteract his tendency to become a completely abstract thinker" (Inhelder 1989: 56). She was to become Piaget's chief collaborator and to remain in Geneva for the rest of her life.

During the summer holidays, their work took place in mountain chalets, where the results of experiments were evaluated and interpreted and further research was planned. "Piaget formulated the epistemological problems, and I, either on my own, or together with selected advanced students, suggested the experiments" (Inhelder 1989: 64f.), which she then carried out.

As soon as all the results from observations and experiments were available, I wrote detailed reports on all the experiments, and together we decided to draft a book. Every chapter was written twice in those days: Piaget wrote a first version, as if this was the definitive one (he hated notes or preliminary drafts), and I made my comments, or, if necessary, carried out further studies. (Inhelder 1989: 64f.)

Still, the reader can only glimpse small excerpts from these experiments, which probably were often conducted with small groups of children. Despite the methodological criticism, data regarding the number of participants, their average age, their social backgrounds or the timescale of the experiments were still missing in the publications. Piaget refused to keep to the scientific standards of testing hypotheses.

If you start out with a plan, you necessarily falsify everything. Everything that is really interesting to you necessarily must fall outside any plan you have in advance. The reason I don't have experimental plans is that I am looking for new things. For me, an experiment is successful when I find something unexpected, totally unanticipated. (Piaget 1973: 35)

This mystification of spontaneity was intended to give him the appearance of a pioneer (cf. Piaget 1949/7: 241) and stood in contrast to the empirical method to which he referred in connection with psychological research. "All that matters is the trilogy of reflection—deduction—experiment; reflection represents the heuristic function, deduction and experiment represent the cognitive verification, which alone can constitute 'truth'" (Piaget 1968/6: 285). Whatever "cognitive verification" might be, Piaget increasingly limited himself to the axiomatic and deductive method, in parallel with his mathematical and logical approach to thought and his epistemological interests.

Thought in terms of mathematics and biology

In the middle of the 1930s, Piaget took a mathematical turn, and he tried to interpret the structures of thinking within axiomatic categories. Janet criticized the resulting formalization of Piaget's explanations: "You are becoming abstract; this is a fault you always had, and it is getting worse . . ."

(in Piaget 1960/1: 111). Piaget met Janet almost daily during Piaget's guest semester in Paris in 1942, where many lengthy discussions ensued.

During his time in Neuchâtel, Piaget's interest, aroused by the mathematician, Henri Poincaré (1854–1912), had already begun to turn to the theory of groups. Starting with spatial layouts, Piaget transferred the mathematical concept of group to the field of cognitive psychology. When objects are moved, the sum of positions forms a group of displacements. Every group is a closed structure of transformations and possesses some definite properties. An object moved from A to B can be moved back from B to A (reversibility). It is also possible to get from A to B via C (associativity). Every change of position produces a new position that is an element of the same sort as the others (identity), and which is combined with the others (composition). Children learn to coordinate their movements and the displacement of objects with the help of groups, because "every intellectual organization tends to take the form of a group" (Piaget 1937/3: 50).

Piaget was strongly influenced by the group theory of a French team, who published their work under the allonym of Nicolas Bourbaki. These mathematicians pursued the aim of unifying the entire field of mathematics on the basis of the set theory. Developed by Georg Cantor (1845–1918) and Felix Klein (1849–1925), the set theory was intensively discussed by mathematicians such as David Hilbert (1862–1943) and Luitzen Brouwer (1881–1966) during the 1920s. Brouwer founded the doctrine of mathematical intuitionism that viewed mathematics as the formulation of mental constructions governed by self-evident laws. On the basis of these theories, enhanced by the ideas of Brunschvicg, Wertheimer and Juvet, Piaget presented his first work on "grouping" at the International Congress of Psychology in 1937. In analogy to the mathematical term group, the psychological term grouping describes a sum of operations like classifications or seriations that have been grouped into a system. Each act of logical thinking refers to a closed system of coordinated operations (Piaget 1949: 330ff.). "A grouping is a system fulfilling the conditions of composition, associativity, and reversibility belonging to groups, but such that each element plays the role of identity operator with respect to itself" (Piaget 1942: 11). Such a system forms an equilibrium and "constitutes the fundamental law of the spirit and the things" (Piaget 1941/3: 46). Piaget believed that he had observed that groupings are the basis of logical behavior and thinking. They are not only the core of logical thought, but also of social behavior. "Intellectual co-operative exchanges necessarily form a reciprocal system of operations, and consequently of 'groupings'" (Piaget 1945/3: 166). Logic and social relations are therefore "two indissoluble aspects of one and the same reality, social and individual at the same time" (Piaget 1945/3: 159).

Since the early 1940s, Piaget had termed the relational totalities arising out of the interactions and operations as *structures d'ensemble*.

My one idea, developed under various aspects in (alas!) twenty-two volumes, has been that intellectual operations proceed in terms of structures-of-the-whole. These structures denote the kinds of equilibrium toward which evolution in its entirety is striving; at once organic, psychological, and social, their roots reached down as far as biological morphogenesis itself. (Piaget 1952/1: 141)

Biological principles not only guarantee "the harmony of mathematics with the real world" (Piaget 1967: 339), but also show the rise of logico-mathematical structures to be a necessary crowning of the evolutionary process. According to Piaget, classification and quantification take place on all levels of mental development, among humans and animals, so that "a certain amount of logic and mathematics is found in every co-ordination of living forms of behavior" (Piaget 1950 III: 268). In 1942, in order to combine biology and mathematics, Piaget extended the groupings by two more elementary types of structure: the sensory-motor rhythms and the preoperational regulations.

Groupings are produced by regulations and regulations, in turn, are produced by the rhythms. Because of this hierarchic interdependence, Piaget postulated "an isomorphism between the operative psychological structures and certain neural structures" (Piaget 1953/6: 388). Spencer (1863 I: 310) already believed that instinctive behavior was directed by rhythmical needs, such as thirst, which Piaget recognized in the circular reactions. "The circular reaction therefore constitutes a 'rhythmical' circle, leading to the automation of new acquisitions" (Piaget 1942/5: 10). Due to the coordination of such stereotypical habits, more complex actions develop during the preoperational stage, which are regulated symbolically. Following Janet, Piaget included among these regulations any accelerating and decelerating affects, unconscious compensation, and values. While "these regulations only lead to a semi-reversibility" (Piaget 1953/6: 380), groupings include reversibility. "Due to these three essential momentums of rhythm, regulation and grouping, intelligence finally manages to free itself from inferior sensory-motor activities, in accordance with an evolutionary principle, which is controlled by the internal laws of equilibrium" (Piaget 1942/5: 15). These laws guarantee the development of knowledge, affects and morality and thus "a strong unity of this development" (Piaget 1942/5: 16). These three types of structures are real psychological quantities "in the minds of the thinking subjects" (Piaget 1941/5: 217), especially because form and contents of psychological operations are inseparable (Piaget 1941: 180).

Concrete Operations

With the beginning of operations, a revolution of thought takes place: thinking becomes logical. Like the Stoics, Piaget believed that the onset of reason occurs at the age of 7: the intuitive explanations of phenomena turn into logical understanding, once the preconcepts coordinate themselves into coherent systems. "The change, which is decisive for the start of operations, manifests itself in the establishment of an equilibrium, which always happens very swiftly and sometimes quite suddenly, whereby this equilibrium comprises the totality of concepts within a whole system" (Piaget 1947: 157). This sudden grouping of the intuitive representations is possible, because logico-mathematical structures at the root of the child's thinking are now coming to the fore. During this stage of development, which for Piaget was the most significant one, the situation-specific and centered conclusions expand to become logico-rational, stable and coherent judgments.

"Operation" is an old term to describe mental activities (cf. Locke 1689: II, 1, §4). For Piaget, operations are still symbolically represented actions, but they "are not only *internalized* but are also *integrated* with other actions to form general *reversible systems*" (Piaget and Inhelder 1955: 6). This coordination of static representations into a dynamic system of concepts is a huge task for children, which takes at least five years. As mentally reversible transformations, operations are able to establish logical relations between several aspects of a phenomenon. If a liquid is poured from one beaker into a taller and narrower beaker, the dimensions of the beakers have to be taken into account and must be compensated for, and one must be capable of mentally reversing the action of pouring to understand that the amount of liquid remains the same. Apart from the three features of identity, compensation and negation, the groupings must include inner unity to enable the flexibility of logical thinking. This is necessary to understand complex systems like, for example, family relations, because one's relation to one's uncle, grandmother, cousin or sister-in-law only makes sense within the context of an entire family. During the next four years in the child's life, operations still deal with concrete objects, such as family members.

According to Piaget, no relevant social influence occurs before the stage of concrete operations. "The internal, operational activity and the external co-operation are actually nothing more than the two complementary sides of one and the same structure, because the equilibrium of the one depends on the equilibrium of the other" (Piaget 1947: 187). In contrast to Piaget's earlier discourses, logic was no longer a product of socialization, but to an equal degree, a consequence of logico-mathematical deduction. Because operations and cooperation are mutual conditions, logic, as the duty not to contradict oneself, follows a dual imperative: the dictates of conditional necessity ("hypothetical imperative"), and the social norm ("categorical imperative") (Piaget 1947: 183). In a next step, however, cooperation was reduced to act as a catalyst: The "normative character of logic is derived from the effectiveness of actions, which were interiorized to become operations, once these are carried out jointly, in the form of co-operation" (Piaget 1950 III: 257). Over time, Piaget placed an increasing emphasis upon the pre-dominance of the immanent coordination, and logic became a product of "an important spontaneous development of deductive operations" (Piaget 1973/6: 728). Piaget defined logic in terms of mathematics, so he neces-sarily had to abstract from the social logic of everyday life and to restrict himself to formal descriptions.

Logico-mathematical operations describe the relations between objects but not their construction. In 1941, Piaget therefore introduced the differ-entiation between logico-mathematical and infralogical operations. Logico-mathematical operations involve classes, relations and numbers and refer to objects without considering their position in space and time. Based on notions of resemblance (or of difference) (Piaget and Inhelder 1948: 511) and of equivalence (or of inequivalence) (Piaget 1976/9: 257), the objects are combined into classes, sorted into a series, or counted together to form numerical totalities. Intelligence, however, does not operate with relations of objects alone, "but its activity concerns itself also with the construction of the objects as such" (Piaget 1947: 53). Infralogical (also termed sublogical, physical or spatio-temporal) operations deal with the conditions of specific objects in space and time. They are based on the notions of neighborhood (or the difference in position) and they "transform correspondences of classes into sections, the asymmetrical relations into displacement, and num-bers into measures, permitting the quantification of the first two" (Piaget 1941: 216). Infralogical operations are therefore not prelogical or illogical but refer to the objects themselves and thus "to a different level of real-ity" (Piaget and Inhelder 1966: 79). Nor are they fundamentally different, because "in their elementary stages, all operations are both logical and phys-ical" (Piaget 1941: 279). Later on, Piaget even postulated the existence of an "isomorphism between the logico-arithmetical operations and the spatial or infralogical operations" (Piaget 1970: 62).

Analogous to these operations, there are two types of experience. Physical experience "consists in acting upon objects in a fashion so as to discover the properties which are abstracted from these objects as such: for example, to weigh an object in order to evaluate its weight" (Piaget and Gréco 1959b: 24). Logico-mathematical experience, on the other hand, includes "general actions proceeding by abstraction from co-ordinations between the actions" (Piaget *et al.* 1957: 33). In this case, the information is not derived from the objects, but from the actions (Piaget 1971/2: 33). Yet in both types of experience, the step which leads to knowledge involves abstraction, either of actions with concrete objects, or of operations, with the help of symbols or signs.

Abstraction and knowledge

Analogous to the operations and experiences was Piaget's differentiation between the abstraction from the operations of the subject and "the abstraction from the properties of the object" (Piaget 1950 III: 266). "Empirical abstraction concerns observable things, and reflective abstraction concerns co-ordination" (Piaget 1977a: II: 319). John Locke (1632–1704) had already postulated that "*abstract ideas are derived from sensation, or reflection*" (Locke 1689: II, 12, §8). As for Locke, Piaget's notion of empirical abstraction concerned the isolation and generalization of the perceptible properties (e.g. colour, temperature) when objects are experienced.

Piaget used Johann Gottlieb Fichte's (1762–1814) term "reflective abstraction" to designate those generalizations which do not only entail mere realization of an object but lead to its understanding, which involves the awareness of the action with the object (cf. Locke 1689: II, 4). One well-known example is that of the little boy who placed pebbles in a row and counted them from left to right and then from right to left. Even after placing the pebbles in a circle, he arrived at the same number. Thus he discovered that the sum is independent of the order of the elements. "The order was not inherent in the pebbles, but he, himself, had produced it [. . .] This realization [. . .] was therefore not due to the properties of the pebbles, perceived with his senses, but was due to the actions he carried out on the pebbles" (Piaget 1970a: 25). Most logical and mathematical concepts develop from reflective (or constructive) abstraction, whereby this abstraction organizes the general actions into formal categories.

Empirical (or simple or physical) abstraction, on the other hand, coordinates one's experience of the properties of objects into figurative categories. Yet "the figurative is always subordinate to the operative" (Piaget 1956: 88). This is a central postulate, because Piaget interpreted the two types of abstractions as being controlled in a different way, "depending on their exogenous or endogenous origins" (Piaget 1974a: 81). Piaget was convinced that "the logical structure is not the result of physical experience. It cannot be obtained by external reinforcement" (Piaget 1964/2: 25), but emerges "from a largely endogenous development, the contents of which, however, are not programmed in detail" (Piaget 1967: 314). Number, for example, originates in abstraction from the subject's operations because neither zero nor the negative numbers would have been recognized as numbers if they were abstracted from objects. One could understand the logico-mathematical structures as the "rules" of reality that intelligence abstracted from experience, like the grammar children intuitively learn while speaking. But for Piaget, logico-mathematical structures, although the result of experience, are preconditions of experience. "No learning and no empirical knowledge is possible, unless there exists a logico-mathematical framework" (Piaget 1967: 320). Because of the immanent laws within the logico-mathematical structures, "the acts of combining or sorting, ordering etc. by no means occur as a result of a learning process" (Piaget 1967: 317).

Piaget supposed that there was a radical difference between infralogical and logico-mathematical operations, between physical and logical experience, and between empirical and reflective abstraction, so his notion of knowledge was dualistic as well. It is true that his approach was actually based on three kinds of knowledge: "Innate knowledge, whose prototype is instinct, knowledge of the physical world, by which learning is extended in terms of the environment, and logico-mathematical knowledge" (Piaget 1967: 375). Innate knowledge, however, exerts nearly no influence on the psychogenetic level (Piaget 1967: 276), because "abstraction is a precondition of all new knowledge" (Piaget 1974a: 81). But the separation of physical knowledge from the logico-mathematical knowledge contains a problem. Logico-mathematical knowledge is not innate but depends on logico-mathematical experience and reflective abstraction. Since logico-mathematical structures are supposed to make object experience possible in the first place (Piaget 1957a: 16), one wonders how these structures and the world fit together. "The reasons for the remarkable accord between logico-mathematical structures and reality are to be sought within the very laws governing the functioning of the living organization in its permanent continuity" (Piaget 1967: 187). Piaget therefore assigned reality to logico-mathematical structures and a logico-mathematical structure to reality. Reality could therefore be accessed with the help of logic and mathematics, as postulated by Plato or Kant. Kant, however, had based his approach on an organized organization, while Piaget based his approach on an "organizing organization" (Piaget 1967: 333), with the consequence that reality has to be reconstructed by the mind. This reconstruction is, at the same time, a construction of the intelligence itself, and this dual process is destined to lead to congruency. With regard to form, Piaget equated this ideal with the total consistency of logic, and with regard to content, it would correspond with "the scientific thought which is accepted today" (Piaget 1970: 24). In order to connect the construction of logic to reality, Piaget needed the empirical abstraction, based on a positivist concept. However, objects or properties cannot be observed as such, because they are the results of conclusions, drawn from earlier abstractions.

From space to time

Following his studies of logico-mathematical operations (concepts of number, class and quantity), Piaget concentrated on the development of the concepts of space and time as these categories are preconditions for infralogical operations. At the JJRI/IES, it was mainly Edith Meyer (1904–1984) from Leipzig who, in the 1930s, researched the development of the concepts of space and time in children. When Meyer migrated to the USA in 1938, Inhelder continued her work, becoming Piaget's most important collaborator and his lifelong lover.

The concept of space emerges at a very early age, because every schema of action contains an aspect of space. During the first two years of his life the infant learns the practical groupings of displacement while he constructs the concept of object permanency. At the preoperational stage, an intuitive and static notion of space develops. But children have great difficulty in copying simple geometrical figures because they only pay attention to topological properties. Topology means the perception of concrete objects in space, based on proximity and distance. Along with topological structures, there is the emergence of projective structures, such as lines, shapes, positions, or distances. Yet the child is subject to a spatial egocentrism, as demonstrated by the three mountains test (Piaget and Inhelder 1948: 249–90) that had been invented by Meyer in 1935. A child is positioned in front of an arrangement of three model mountains and has to select, from a number of pictures, the one that reflects the scenery as seen from his own perspective. Then he is asked what the scene would look like from a different perspective. Most children select, once again, the picture that reflects the view from their own position. The child is then led to the location from where he has this different perspective, and succeeds in choosing the correct picture. When the child is once more placed in his original position, and again is asked to select the previous view, the probability is high that he will, once more, select his own, present view. At the operational stage, the perspective becomes decentered, leading to more dynamic notions, if concrete objects can be manipulated. Now the Euclidian space of geometry becomes accessible, due to abstraction from the observable neighborhood and due to orientation towards the vertical and horizontal planes. The child will no longer draw the chimney in a right angle to a sloping roof, but in a right angle to the horizontal plane.

This development from topological to Euclidian geometry contradicted Piaget's thesis of the analogy between ontogenesis and the history of science because topology was used for the first time by Leonard Euler (1707–1783) and it only became a scientific discipline in the twentieth century. Piaget tried to tone down this anomaly by explaining that "the order of the grasp of consciousness reverses the order of genesis: what is first in the order of construction appears last in reflexive analysis" (Piaget 1955/6: 14).

Euclidian geometry is based on an abstract reference system and on the idea of a displaceable unit of measurement. Measuring presupposes the notion of invariance of distances between two points, a notion that becomes possible around the age of 6. Younger children gauge the distance between two objects as being smaller, if the stretch is interrupted by an obstacle:

And (5; 3). Two dolls, no umbrella.—*They are close to each other.*—(The umbrella is placed between the dolls). Are they as close to each other as before?—*They are closer to each other.*—(The little window on the cardboard umbrella is opened): And now?—*They are even closer, because there is a hole.* (Piaget *et al.* 1948 a: 104)

Once a distance is recognized as an invariant length, it becomes a unit of measurement that can be displaced along the stretch to be measured. The measuring of space is therefore a synthesis of displacement and addition, through which points in an otherwise empty space can be clearly defined. This child is no longer dealing with intuitive relations between points, but is carrying out operations that permit a mental change of position and the subdivision of lengths. Space is now a coordination of changes of position.

While the spatial order emerges from the relations between proximity, exclusion and inclusion, etc., temporal groupings are based on the act of ordering sequences. The infant does not differentiate between the concepts of space and time because all his movements in space take their own time and remain uncoordinated. In contrast to Sabina Spielrein, who concluded in 1922 that the concept of space was formed first, followed by the concept of causality, and finally by the concept of time, Piaget believed, until the early 1940s, that the concept of time derived from a combination of interior experience (duration) and external experience (simultaneity of temporal sequences) and developed "parallel to that of space and complementary to that of objects and causality" (Piaget 1937: 310). Subsequently, however, he rejected "this Bergsonian metaphysics" (Piaget 1946: 275). Neither the notion of time nor the notion of space result from "primitive" intuitions, but both are constructed operations: children perceive a person's age by looking at how tall the person is (physical property). And because they do not recognize the duration of an event as an independent value, they equate the duration of a movement with the distance covered. The sequence of time is not differentiated from the order of space until the ages of 6 or 7. Up until then, children believe that a stopwatch runs faster if one measures a faster movement.

At a congress in Davos in 1928, Einstein asked whether the concept of time developed dependent on speed or vice versa. Motivated by this question, Piaget started experiments and found that the concept of time results from the coordination of movements and their speeds (Piaget 1946:

357). Speed, however, is a two-dimensional concept of quantity, because it combines distance with duration. According to Piaget, the child initially develops an intuitive notion of speed by comparing two movements carried out at different speeds. But "he does not yet make the connection between these speeds and a common or homogenous time" (Piaget 1950 II: 27). He learns this through the phenomenon of overtaking, which "is based on the temporal sequence (before and after) and on the spatial sequence (behind and in front of)" (Piaget 1964/6: 267). During the operational stage, temporal and spatial operations are coordinated into a system by comparing the increase or decrease of gaps with the duration. This leads to a metrical concept of time developed at the ages of 10 or 11, when the "synthesis of the two preceding quantitative groupings" (Piaget 1946: 247) is achieved. The measurement of time results from the fusion of the seriation of successive events and the addition of successive duration. Thanks to these operations (Piaget 1970a: 86), the irreversible time becomes reversible, which allows a mental detachment from the course of events: the present can be transcended. "To understand time means [...] to go beyond the spatial, through mental agility" (Piaget 1946: 365), which is a feature of the formal operations.

Formal Operations

In 1948, Inhelder was appointed as Professor of Child and Youth Psychology at the JJRI/ISE and continued with experimental studies, while Piaget concentrated his efforts on epistemology and logic. Piaget (1949: 6) knew that he was not competent enough to publish a *Traité de logique*, and thus the reviews were devastating: "This book abounds with errors, on the elementary level as well as on the superior level" (Beth 1950: 264). Nevertheless, Evert Beth (1908–1964) was invited by Piaget to discuss their differences, and became a collaborator for some years.

In order to discover the mechanisms of formal thinking, Inhelder conducted, amidst other research, interviews with pupils at the Collège de Genève. Piaget "worked out the academic tools needed to interpret these results. It was after we had compared notes and were making final interpretations that we saw the striking convergence between the empirical and the analytical results" (Inhelder 1989: 223). According to these results, formal thinking starts at the age of 11 years and is characterized by propositional logic. In contrast with concrete operations, formal-logical operations "are [...] no longer carried out on the object itself, but on statements and on verbally formulated propositions" (Piaget 1963/1: 101). As a consequence of the ability to use abstract symbols, the realm of facts is relativized, and the possible and the ideal become accessible. Formal operations "are, in their structure, nothing but concrete operations, albeit transposed into terms of propositions" (Piaget 1946a: 192). They can therefore become detached from their contexts, and can refer to hypothetical objects, or to the operations themselves. Adolescents can reflect upon their own thinking and upon the form of their argument. Such thought "exclusively constitutes the structure of final equilibrium, towards which tend the concrete operations, when they are reflected in more general systems, combining the propositions they express" (Piaget 1947: 170). During adolescence, young people become interested in hypothetical and theoretical issues. "Compared to the child, the adolescent is an individual who establishes systems and theories" (Piaget 1943/6: 248). He now examines whether the contents of statements are correct, by taking into account their logical form, which improves his ability hugely to make critical judgments. "To work with hypotheses, one must be capable of carrying out operations on operations. The content of any hypothesis is already a form of concrete operations; and thereafter to make some relationship between the hypothesis and the conclusion, is a new operation" (Piaget 1973: 26). According to Piaget, hypothetical-deductive thinking corresponds to the highest form of logical thinking, because its mechanisms are liberated from their contents (Piaget 1966: 100). The formal notion of premise enables deductive thinking to become free from contradictions, as Heinrich Joseph Ormian had observed in 1926. The adolescent is able to form logical systems, to abstract and combine variables, and to draw conclusions irrespective of concrete and real situations.

By emancipating itself from the given, his thinking achieves a final fundamental decentration. The first decentration was achieved by the infant when he differentiated between the world and the self and constructed object permanency. The second step was taken at the beginning of the stage of concrete operations when the child overcame his egocentrism by filing his notions into objective reference systems. At the end of the last stage, "possibility no longer appears merely as an extension of an empirical situation, or of actions actually performed. Instead, it is reality that is now secondary to possibility" (Piaget and Inhelder 1955: 251). In this last qualitative restructuring of thinking, the formal operational faculties (combinatorial analysis, proportions, dual reference systems, multiplicative probability, etc.) become established and enable the adolescent to experiment and to lead scientific proof.

The studies regarding *The Origin of the Idea of Chance in Children* (Piaget 1951) had already shown that the idea of chance can only be truly understood with the use of combinatorial analysis. Young children have no notion of chance, probability or necessity. At the stage of concrete operations, chance is what cannot be explained in terms of logical necessity. During the stage of formal operations, a systematic delineation of the range of possibilities develops, together with the ability of specifying relative probability. Probability mitigates the contrast between chance and causality, by introducing the idea of a regular overall distribution. Combinatorial analysis is a prerequisite for understanding the necessary (such as a law of physics), because the possible causal factors must be distinguished. The experiment of "equilibrium in the balance," for example, was designed to let the test persons discover the indirect proportionality of weight and distance. Different weights in bags had to be placed along the arm of the balance, at varying distances from the centre. Children between 5 and 7 years tried to get a balance but did not succeed in equalizing either distances or weights in a systematic way. This aim was achieved at the level of concrete operations with equal weights and equal distances. During the second substage, the "law of balance" is discovered:

> the heavier the weight, the closer it is to the middle [...]. ROL (10;10): *We have to hang the bag at a different location, because it weighs heavier nearer the end.* He pushes the lighter weight away from the pivot of the arm. (Piaget and Inhelder 1955: 165)

Increasing the distance *q* on one side of the arm is equivalent to increasing the weight *p* on the other. However, since the metrical propositions are still missing, the children cannot predict what will happen if the weight, as well as the distance, is changed. The discovery of simultaneous proportionality will not be made until the formal stage is reached:

> In order to compensate for weight *P*, placed at the very tip of one arm, measures the distances, and says: *That makes 14 holes. It's half the length. If the weight (C + E) is halved, that duplicates (P).*—How do you know that you have to bring the weight toward the centre? (to increase the weight)—*The idea just came to me, I wanted to try. If I bring it in half way, the value of the weight is cut in half. I know but I can't explain it. I haven't learned it.* (Piaget and Inhelder 1955: 167)

Logical proportionality results from the discovery of quantitative proportionality. Piaget described these operations with the help of propositional logic and the mathematical group theory. Logical operations such as implication (if then), disjunction (or–or as well–or both of them), exclusion (either or) or incompatibility (neither nor) are shown as propositions which contain a value of truth (Piaget 1949: 213). With regard to the example: simultaneously increasing the weight *p* and decreasing the distance *q* on one side of the arm is equivalent to decreasing the weight p and increasing the distance q on the other.

$$p \cdot \overline{q} = R(\overline{p} \cdot q)$$

Yet, changing either the weight or the distance on one side can be counteracted by changing the weight or the distance on the other side. Propositional logic contains more operative possibilities than simple groupings of class or relations, because it is a logic of all possible combinations of thinking. It forms a system of operations to the power of 2, making it possible to operate with operations. In this example we are dealing with direct and indirect proportionality.

$$\frac{p \cdot q}{\overline{p} \cdot \overline{q}} = \frac{p \vee q}{\overline{p} \vee \overline{q}}$$

In the next step, which is hard to understand, Piaget equated propositional logic with the commutative INRC group. Analogous to the reversibility of concrete operations, Piaget used the mathematical transformations as a criterion for formal operational intelligence. Logical statements therefore form a coherent group of four transformations: a direct transformation (I = Identity), an inversing transformation (N = Negation), a reciprocal transformation (R = Reciprocity), and an inversing reciprocal transformation (C = Correlativity). The above statement is equivalent to

$$\frac{I}{R} = \frac{C}{N}$$

In the case of our example, the four transformations mean:

Identity: Simultaneously increasing weight and distance on one arm.
Negation: Decreasing the distance and increasing the weight, or vice versa, or decreasing both.
Reciprocity: Compensating for *I*, by increasing weight and distance on the other arm.
Correlativity: Compensating for *R*, by decreasing the weight and increasing the distance, or vice versa, or by decreasing both, on this second arm. (Piaget and Inhelder 1955: 171f.)

The INRC transformation group is an application of the group theory of Klein. It is based on the thesis that any result, achieved through the combination of operations, can also be achieved in a different way. Because these transformations contain all combinations possible, Piaget considered them to be suitable instruments for describing formal operations. They constitute perfect reason, because all relevant factors pertaining to a problem are taken into account. According to Piaget, formal operational thinking there-fore guarantees scientific, stable and autonomous thought, even though the adolescents are not aware of the operations they carry out successfully.

According to the writings of the 1940s and 1950s, this last stage was supposed to end at the age of about 15 years. This period is, nevertheless, not an age of perfect thought. Because of the "change of mind between the real and the possible" (Piaget and Inhelder 1955: 238), adolescence is the "age of metaphysics *par excellence*" (Piaget 1943/6: 251). As was the case in his own youth, Piaget associated this change with dreams of large messianic projects, such as the "reconciliation between natural science and religion" (Piaget and Inhelder 1955: 332). Inhelder also seems to have interpreted her own experiences as a general pattern: "Young girls are, of course, more interested in marriage, but the husbands they dream of are often 'theoretical', and their ideas about married life frequently also have the aspect of 'theories'" (Piaget and Inhelder 1955: 328). It is not puberty, but integration into the social life of adults that "causes a total transformation of personality" (Piaget and Inhelder 1955: 323). Both agreed with Charlotte Bühler that adolescents are not only trying to adapt to their social environment, but are equally trying hard to adapt their environment to themselves. This manifests itself in a more intensive reflection upon the society they live in, upon alternative ways of living, and upon philosophical questions regarding the meaning of life, truth and morality.

Affectivity without Emotions

In 1952, Piaget was appointed to succeed Maurice Merleau-Ponty (1908–1961) at the Sorbonne. At this old and reputable university, he was the first professor to conduct a seminar in person, breaking with the aristocratic tradition of delegating any contact with students to one's assistants. Thus, he was all the more surprised to find himself the target of strong criticism from the students. One of the reasons for their displeasure was that he, unlike his predecessor, was not in tune with contemporary trends (existentialism, phenomenology, Marxism and psychoanalysis). Piaget experienced a "complete aversion with respect to existentialism, which blurs all values and degrades man by reducing freedom to arbitrary choice and thoughts of self-affirmation" (Piaget 1968/6: 269). Secondly, the students argued that his mathematical theory was so abstract and formal that it contained very little of substance (Piaget 1959/3: 8). A third reason was Wallon's criticism, launched at Piaget ten years previously, that Piaget had neglected to address the motivational and emotional factors in cognitive development, as well as the influence of the social environment. In his habilitation, Wallon's pupil,

Philippe Malrieu, described Piaget's theory as intellectualist. Published in 1952, *Emotions and Personality of the Child* was so successful that Piaget found it necessary to defend his position in his course of lectures of 1953/4, which was broadcast on the radio.

For Piaget, affectivity included not only feelings and emotions, but also instinctive tendencies and the will. Intelligence and affectivity are by nature "two entirely different things, although in concrete behavior, they do not occur in isolation from one another. Behavior, which is only determined by feelings and devoid of any cognitive component, is as much an impossibility as the converse" (Piaget 1954/12: 19). With this approach, Piaget changed his earlier belief that "feelings obscure thinking" (Piaget 1928/2: 59) and that intelligence was required "to eliminate the emotional factors" (Piaget 1932: 296). Shortly afterwards, he had postulated "a parallelism between affective development and cognitive development" (Piaget 1933/3: 147). Feelings and mental operations therefore constitute the complementary aspects of any psychological activity. Once reason has reached its equilibrium "it forms a unit of intelligence and feelings" (Piaget 1943/6: 258). In the interim, Piaget had assimilated Janet's theory of 1928, according to which feelings like effort, tiredness, the joys of success or the sadness of failures represent the energetic aspect of one's behavior and regulate the equilibrium of the psychological forces. Affects are the source of energy, "like gasoline, which activates the motor of an automobile, but does not modify its structure" (Piaget 1954/12: 23). Intelligence brings structure (order, laws) to behavior, while affectivity is its driving force.

In his lecture, Piaget divided affective as well as cognitive development into six stages. According to this model, the presocial phase of sensory-motor development consists of three stages. In the first one, inherited traits (tendencies and emotions on the affective side; reflexes and instincts on the cognitive side) are trained. During the second stage, perception-dependent feelings emerge, such as joy and sorrow, or ease and uneasiness, which accompany the actions of the subject. These feelings are based on the affective components of the schemata, which serve as the carriers of feelings (Piaget 1945: 265). Piaget agreed with Wallon's findings that emotions, such as joy or fear, have an effect on the development of cognitive functions but he opposed Malrieu's thesis, which stated that emotions could become a source of cognition (Piaget 1954/12: 46f.). At six months of age, intentional affects arise and the stage of sensory-motor intelligence begins. Janet had differentiated between "primary" and "secondary" actions, whereby the latter are reactions of the subject and regulate the effort of the former with the help of feelings. Piaget considered this kind of behavior control to be only appropriate for the first few months of the child's life, after which a second regulatory system starts playing its part. Based on Claparède, Piaget postulated that feelings now express the interests and values of actions and regulate their energy. The affective aspect of assimilation describes the self-oriented interest in one's environment, while the affective aspect of accommodation refers to the object-oriented interest, especially the interest in all new phenomena.

Once the child acquires language, during the fourth stage, conceptual intelligence begins to develop, which entails an affective exchange with other persons. Piaget distinguished between object-oriented behavior, based on logico-mathematical structures, and person-oriented behavior, based on "interests, effort, intra-individual feelings and their regulation" (Piaget 1954/12: 128). According to the Finnish ethnologist, Edward Westermarck (1862–1939), moral judgments are made on the basis of moral emotions, mainly of indignation and approval. Thus, reciprocal attitudes determine values, which, if they are lasting, lead to feelings such as gratitude. The feelings themselves do not last, but "*are repeatedly reconstructed*. The thing which lasts is not the feeling itself, but a certain schema, in accordance with which we react to other people" (Piaget 1954/12: 93f.). At the stage of concrete operations, semi-normative feelings, such as one-sided respect, become normative feelings, directed by will. On the basis of James, Janet and Claparède, Piaget defined will as "a regulation of regulations, which is comparable to an operation" (Piaget 1954/12: 33). If one's sense of duty (for example to do one's work) is weaker than one's present wish (to go for a walk), the will has to intervene. An act of will consists in reinforcing the weak tendency and in thwarting the strong desire, by calling upon the conservation of values. "Having will is to possess a permanent scale of values" (Piaget 1962/8: 144). It is not a matter of condemning any constellation of feelings, but to go beyond it and "change one's perspective" (Piaget 1954/12: 114). Here, the idea of conversion resurfaces once more, which turns the self into a personality. Piaget still worked on the assumption that the child of 7 years of age is able "to make his own moral assessments and to decide freely, in accordance with his own will" (Piaget 1954/12: 116). Intelligence and free will organize the moral feelings into a "system of relatively fixed values, which becomes a duty to maintain" (Piaget 1954/12: 117). The logic of feelings consists in being coherent in one's attitude and affective reactions (Piaget 1962/8: 138), so as to become a reliable partner for others, because "affective structures have to do with an intellectualization of the affective aspect of our exchanges with other people" (Piaget 1954/12: 127). Ideal values will become fully developed during the sixth stage of formal operations, when social feelings are extended to collective ideals. The notion of "fatherland," for example, now receives "an adequate affective value" (Piaget 1966: 110). A sense of justice emerges with the desire to uphold the rules that serve society. In finding one's role and purpose within a moral system, the personality is formed. With his approach, that "morality as a whole is an apparatus of conservation of affective values, by means of obligations" (Piaget 1962/8: 138), Piaget could embed affectivity into his earlier theory.

His thesis of the "isomorphous parallels" (Piaget and Weil1951/3: 126; cf. Piaget 1954/12: 28, 127) of intelligence and affectivity did, however, show some inconsistencies (cf. Herzog 1991: 220). Firstly, he sometimes described this relation as being symmetrical (Piaget 1954/12: 75) and complementary (Piaget 1954/12: 115), but sometimes as being interactionist (Piaget 1954/12: 54), whereby "cognitive and affective components are closely interwoven in the most varied situations" (Piaget 1954/12: 29). Secondly, feelings and cognition are "inseparable, albeit different" (Piaget 1947: 8; cf. 1954/12: 53) in their nature, although "there is as much construction in the affective domain as there is in the cognitive" (Piaget 1947: 32). Thirdly, affectivity can "disrupt the activity of intelligence, or can change the contents of intelligence, but affectivity itself can neither build structures nor modify them" (Piaget 1947: 126). A fourth point is that Piaget claimed that there were "schemata that have to do with people and schemata that have to do with objects. Both are cognitive and affective at the same time" (Piaget 1947: 51). Yet, on the other hand, he understood "*affective structures' as the cognitive aspect of one's relationship with persons*" (Piaget 1947: 127). A fifth point is that, despite the parallel, conflicts between feelings and intellect can arise. Since he could not explain them, he resorted to a regression model: conflicts always occur "between basic processes, assigned to the different stages of development" (Piaget 1947: 126). The sixth point concerns the significance of providing emotional care for infants. According to the findings of the hospitalism research by Spitz, published in 1945, affective neglect significantly obstructs mental development. Piaget queried these findings and speculated that this phenomenon could have "something to do with the genetic constitution, and, above all, with the surroundings" (Piaget 1947: 80). He must have been aware of how unsatisfactory this explanation was, because he asked the Americans who were editing the lecture, to extract the section dealing with emotions, since it was outdated (Leber 1994: 9). Emotions were always a secondary topic for Piaget: "It is simply the case that I am not interested in this. I am not a psychologist. I am a cognitive theorist. (He smiles mischievously)" (Piaget and Bringuier 1977: 85). It is worth noting that Piaget never conducted one single experiment in connection with affectivity. On the contrary, the elements of interaction between the experimenter and the interviewee were disregarded, because the child's thinking was to be seen as being autochthonous. In fact, Piaget reduced affectivity to the drive to act, which led to a multiple motivation theory: beside affects, Piaget assumed that the human being possessed fundamental activity and a compulsion for development, caused by disequilibria. A genuine theory of emotions is absent, however. Because of Piaget's need for deliberate rational disciplining, one may assume that he must have felt threatened by feelings and therefore ignored them as much as possible, in practice and in theory.

Consciousness and the Limits of Psychology

Reaching the formal stage is dependent on the grasp of consciousness, in the affective as well as in the cognitive domain.

> *Awareness of obligation* is in the area of affectivity what *awareness of necessity* is in the cognitive field [...] affective and cognitive consciousness are parallel, rather than opposed to each other. These two aspects of consciousness can, of course, never be separated, even though they are distinct from each other. (Piaget 1954/6: 144)

As early as 1920, Piaget adopted Janet's rejection of a radical distinction between the conscious and the unconscious, and instead emphasized the continuity between conscious and unconscious processes. "Rather than being a reservoir of memories, the 'unconscious' now appears to be a system of active operations and schemata, whose genesis and interlinking" (Piaget 1933/3: 152) cannot be equated with affectivity, because "there are unconscious intellectual processes as well as unconscious affective ones. This means, however, that the unconscious is not a section, in the sense of an 'area'; the difference between 'conscious' and 'unconscious' is a gradual one, or one that depends on the degree of reflection" (Piaget 1945: 222f.). Piaget therefore criticized psychoanalysis, because for Freud "*the unconscious remains tied to the past*" (Piaget 1954/12: 93). His concept of repression, on the other hand, "immediately convinced everybody" (Piaget 1945: 244) because there can be inhibitions that prevent the person from becoming aware of contradictory schemata (Piaget 1971/8: 34). Repression blocks the mutual assimilation of schemata because some tendencies are stronger than others. Psychoanalysis could therefore build a bridge between isolated schemata and integrate them with the self. The resulting equilibrium allows conscious regulation of the schemata. "Equilibrium consists in preserving the living aspects of the past by continual accommodation to the manifold and irreducible present" (Piaget 1945: 263).

Consciousness is a particular form of behavior (Piaget 1950 III: 256, 1970/5: 109f.) and a "rather wide-spread phenomenon" (Piaget 1967: 48) even among animals. Yet, he regarded it nonetheless as "a reality in its own right, unique in its nature" (Piaget 1967/7: 50), and "not a by-product of physiological processes" (Piaget 1965: 195). Piaget agreed with the thesis of

Janet (1929), that the grasp of consciousness is linked to the updating of schemata of action and cognition. We "reconstitute, on a higher level, that which already exists on the lower level" (Piaget 1971/8: 38f.). Conceptual knowledge always lags behind the knowledge of action, as Goethe aptly put it: "In the beginning was the deed" (in Piaget 1941/3: 42; 1960/7: 79). Children are always able to do more than they know, because "the grasp of consciousness of one's actions happens always only partially" (Piaget 1970: 41). In a study, children were asked to crawl on all fours along the floor, after which they had to explain how they had done it. Children up to the ages of 7 or 8 claimed to have moved simultaneously both legs, and subsequently both arms, or they had simultaneously moved one arm and one leg on one side. Only children above this age realized that they had simultaneously moved their left arm and their right leg, and vice versa. At a symposium in Geneva, the same experiment was conducted, just for fun, with the scientists. The physicists and psychologists succeeded instantly in describing their movements correctly, whereas the mathematicians and logicians failed in this task. Nobody, of course, doubted that these mathematicians had reached the stage of concrete operations, because Poincaré had already assumed that there was a logico-mathematical unconscious. Piaget explained these results through the fact that physicists and psychologists are experienced observers, "whereas mathematicians construct that model which appears to be the simplest and the most logical one" (Piaget and Bringuier 1977: 136). Piaget took this example as proof that "the process of becoming conscious of action schema transforms it into a concept; thus becoming conscious consists essentially in conceptualization" (Piaget 1974: 261). There is a twofold and parallel movement of conceptualization: an increasing self-awareness as subject and an increasing knowledge of objects. Consciousness therefore means to distinguish between the subject and the object even if these two kinds of knowledge go hand in hand. There is "an agreement between thought and the real, because action proceeds from the laws of an organism, which is, at the same time, a physical object among others, and the source for the subject acting, and thereafter thinking" (Piaget 1974: 282).

Although Piaget considered the grasp of consciousness as a crucial mechanism in cognitive development, he excluded the investigation of consciousness from psychology. The activity of consciousness consists in "assigning or linking meanings" (Piaget 1967/7: 51) to the concepts formed by abstraction. In contrast to perception, where the meanings are linked to "cues," and thus to the object, the consciousness assigns meanings with the help of symbols and signs. We therefore can only become conscious of what can be represented. States of consciousness can consist either of "'meanings' of the cognitive kind (translated into the concepts of true or false), or of the affective kind (values), or which is probably the case—of both kinds simultaneously" (Piaget 1968/13: 188). Consciousness cannot be researched in a causal-scientific way, because only "neurophysiology is exclusively *causal*" (Piaget 1961a: XXIII). The contents of consciousness are a matter of philosophical reflection: "Psychology is not a science of the consciousness, but it is a science of the behavior!" (Piaget and Bringuier 1977: 26).

Piaget defined the structure of consciousness as a "system of implications" (Piaget 1970/4: 93). Implications are logical links and form "*the basic relationship between two states of consciousness*" (Piaget 1954/6: 143). A concept always implies other concepts, and every value implies other values. On the level of formal operations, implication becomes an intellectual "logical necessity" and an affective "moral obligation." "In affectivity, consciousness constitutes a system of values [. . .] It deals with implication of value rather than knowledge, but is otherwise as irreducible, specific, and original as consciousness of cognitive implication" (Piaget 1954/6: 144). Piaget not only believed in a parallelism of affective and cognitive implication, but also in an isomorphism between conscious implication and physical causality. "Far from modifying or contradicting its material causality, consciousness completes it, because it elucidates" (Piaget 1954/6: 147). Behind this statement, there is still the same basic idea that Piaget expressed in his first book: "Life is a force, an élan, a stream of consciousness, which permeates matter, organizes it, and imbues it with harmony and love" (Piaget 1915/1: 17).

Development Factors and Stage Transitions

From 1950 on, Piaget defined four mechanisms effecting the transitions from one stage to the next, as: maturation, physical experience, social influence and equilibration:

1. Organic growth forms the foundation for cognitive development. Maturation of the nervous and hormone systems is especially important, because progress in behavior depends on the correct functioning of the organs and the central nervous system. Taken by the research regarding neuron networks by Warren S. McCulloch (1899–1969) and Walter Pitts (1923–1969), who, in 1943, established an analogy between binary computer logic and the impulse transmission of neurons, Piaget declared that operational structures "can all be causally explained by neurological processes" (Piaget 1954/6: 141). Later, however, he denied that there was a "direct relation between the 'logic of neurons' and the logic of thought" (Piaget 1970/2: 63), and instead postulated an isomorphous relation.

Piaget agreed with the common thesis that human beings behave largely independently of instincts (Piaget 1967: 375ff.) and emphasized that "nothing is innate, but rather everything has to be gradually and painstakingly acquired" (Piaget 1962/5: 18). With regard to possible aptitudes, Piaget made contradictory statements: "I do not believe in aptitudes and non-aptitudes in mathematics and science that differentiate children at the same intellectual level. What is usually involved is either aptitudes or non-aptitudes in the teacher's approach" (Piaget 1973/15: 26). With regard to perceptions, he felt that "aptitudes" were possible. "I think that in the artistic world there exist people who are more or less visual, or more or less audio-motor [...] I would not be surprised if it were innate. It is possible, though, that experiences have to be taken into consideration. I myself am not visually orientated at all" (Piaget 1973/15: 26). On occasions, he talked of "people who are more gifted than others; every now and then we encounter a genius" (Piaget 1962/5: 26). On another occasion, however, he stated: "There are no innate structures: every structure has to be built" (Piaget 1965/7: 332), because the development of aptitudes depends upon one's relationship with one's environment.

In October 1975, Noam Chomsky and Piaget made opening speeches at a symposium near Paris. Once the French biologists discovered that Piaget was a Lamarckist, a heated debate ensued between the biologists, on the topic of neo-Darwinism. Piaget's alleged debate with Chomsky was "invented by the Harvard University Press, in the face of strong reservations from all concerned" (Chomsky, in Barsky 1997: 224), in order to promote the book *Language and Learning: The Debate between Jean Piaget and Noam Chomsky*, published by Massimo Piattelli-Palmarini. Piaget expressed his admiration for Chomsky's work and declared: "I see no significant conflict between Chomsky's linguistics and my own psychology. The question of heredity or innateness seems rather secondary to me" (Piaget 1979/5: 95). Yet significant differences did exist: Chomsky (1979: 85) also considered Piaget's work as important but he refuted Piaget's understanding of "innatism." He considered the generative structure of language to be hereditary, whereas for Piaget "it is the operations that lead and direct the progress of language, and not the inverse" (Piaget 1970/13: 13). Chomsky rightfully demanded that Piaget should prove the formation of syntax from the operative structures and not simply maintain that language was a secondary phenomenon.

2. The second factor comprises the training of innate abilities and physical and logico-mathematical experiences. In order to distance himself from empiricism, Piaget claimed that "the forming of logico-mathematical structures (from the sensory-motor stage until formal thinking) precedes physical knowledge" (Piaget 1966: 115). Therefore the crucial factor is not the child's

exploration of physical properties of objects, but the "deeper" structures, because experience "always implies an assimilation to previous structures" (Piaget 1952/3: 7).

3. From the 1940s onwards, Piaget also applied this reservation to the social influence. It is true that Piaget never denied the importance of one's fellow human beings after the age of 7 years. Yet "everything must be constructed from that which is given and from that which has been acquired in a sensory-motor way, the instruments of exchange as well as the internal representational links" (Piaget 1960/8: 183). The only effect of the social environment that Piaget always acknowledged was that it accelerated or retarded cognitive development. And even this influence seemed fraught with problems, because "an assimilative process can be neither accelerated nor much retarded, without harming it" (Piaget 1974/3: x).

4. The most complex and most general development factor, which increased in importance from the 1950s, is equilibration. The analysis of the tendency towards equilibrium and its relation to the other factors became the main topic of Piaget's contribution to the "Research Study Group on the Psychological Development of the Child" (Tanner and Inhelder 1960), sponsored by the World Health Organization. Between 1953 and 1956, Ronald Hargreaves, head of the mental health section, organized annual meetings, where Piaget and Inhelder, for two weeks, discussed children's development with other scientists including Konrad Lorenz, Margaret Mead, John Bowlby, Erik Erikson, Ludwig van Bertalanffy, Julian Huxley and René Zazzo.

The "equilibration factor" plays a role in more than one area and upon two levels, because "each of the previously mentioned three factors is, in itself, subject to the laws of equilibrium and [...] their interaction also contains an aspect of equilibrium" (Piaget 1956: 311). Even organic growth is already controlled by tendencies towards equilibrium. Piaget tried to make this plausible by referring to the second law of thermodynamics, which, in his opinion, "could be applied to the phenomena of life" (Piaget 1959/8: 285). Just as mechanical systems approach a thermodynamic equilibrium by dissipating their energy, organic systems conserve their form by adapting to new conditions. This tendency towards preservation is inherent in all organic systems, "because any kind of behavior strives for equilibrium between internal and external factors, or, more generally speaking, between assimilation and accommodation" (Piaget 1959/8: 284). Adaptation to the physical and social environment is not achieved purely through assimilation and accommodation, but these two functions also need to be coordinated. Coordination is a process of equilibration, which enables the organism to continue its assimilation. The stages of development form "successive steps of equilibration" (Piaget 1952/3: 8), whereas the cognitive equilibrium becomes increasingly stable and more mobile.

The neurological, the physical and the social factor superimpose one on another, and they require "constant equilibration" (Piaget 1956: 311). Tarde had used this expression in 1893 to designate the coordination of individual logic and social logic through the elimination of contradictions. Piaget adopted this idea (1950 III: 230) and formulated the thesis that a cognitive equilibrium "always consists of a system of probable compensations of external perturbations, by the activities of the individual" (Piaget 1959/8: 291). Any emerging contradictions or failed assimilation attempts compel the child to reorganize the relevant cognitive structures. Thanks to reversibility, the individual can anticipate perturbations and conflicts and prevent them from happening. In his late works, Piaget distinguished three types of contradictions (Piaget 1974c), which correspond to three types of equilibrium (Piaget 1975):

- Contradictions between the schemata and external objects are external perturbations, which prevent assimilation. These disequilibria leave us with a "feeling that something still has to be done" (Piaget 1975: 169). Equilibration consists of "successive constructions with a constant elaboration of new structures" (Piaget 1975: 7).
- A lack of coordination among the various subsystems manifests itself in contradictions regarding the various properties of objects or circumstances. Equilibration occurs through reciprocal assimilation and accommodation of the schemata, whereby reciprocal accommodation means mutual assimilation of structures (Piaget 1975: 13f.).
- Contradictions between the properties of subsystems and the total system manifest themselves as incoherencies in behavior and thinking. Equilibration means that the parts are simultaneously differentiated and integrated into the whole.

By defining these three types, Piaget came back to the same forms of equilibrium he had identified 57 years earlier.

Equilibration occurs with the help of regulations and reflective abstraction. Perturbations trigger regulations, which occur on three different levels of development, depending on the ability to compensate. An *alpha-reaction* ignores the perturbation, or removes it through a simple change. For instance, a child may realize that lions are bigger than dogs, but because both have four legs, the child would still call a lion "woof-woof." A perturbation must actually perturb the subject to have impact (Piaget 1975: 84). In a *beta-reaction* the system is modified, whereby perturbing elements are integrated by means of accommodation. Lions would then be big "woof-woofs," and dogs would be small "woof-woofs." This partial compensation is completed in a *gamma-reaction*, which, applied to our example, would mean that felines are recognized as being a separate species. Equilibration is successfully executed when schemata are differentiated and integrated in higher order structures, so that similar classifications no longer appear to be contradictory.

The second mechanism, which became increasingly important for Piaget, is reflecting abstraction, whereby schemata, representations, actions and operations are "reconstructed on a higher level, reorganized, and thus extended" (Piaget and Garcia 1983a: 14). The increased control, which results from abstraction, allows more complex operations and creates a higher resistance against perturbations.

Piaget termed the improving equilibrium as *équilibration majorante* (Piaget 1975: 166), derived from Tarde's term of "majoration." An absolute equilibrium can never be achieved (Piaget and Bringuier 1977: 78), although the logico-mathematical structures mark the end of the qualitative changes in the general process of equilibration. This end is a "kind of necessity a priori" (Piaget 1965/7: 341), because external perturbations only stimulate the formation of logic, without controlling it. "The logical structure is reached only through internal equilibration" (Piaget 1964/2: 25).

The connection between equilibration and self-organization became increasingly important to Piaget. Since "life is essentially auto-regulation" (Piaget 1964/2: 26), his concept of self-regulation comprised any form of control, from the genome to behavior and thought. Yet "the auto-regulatory function of the cognitive mechanism produces the most highly stabilized forms of equilibrium, found in any living creature" (Piaget 1964/2: 37). Piaget attempted to explain this self-regulation with the help of cybernetics, which allowed a forecast of processes. In the 1940s, the mathematician, Norbert Wiener (1894–1964), established cybernetics as a theory of self-regulation for technical systems. As a means of investigating information processes, it was soon applied to the field of biology (for example for bee colonies). Disregarding that cybernetics is only useful in connection with pre-set machines, Piaget applied it to the internal control of the organism: "*Feedback* particularly helps us to understand the importance and general significance of operational reversibility" (Piaget 1954/6: 141), because, in Piaget's opinion, the equilibrium of a group structure corresponded to complete reversibility. The central idea of "internal environment" had been published as early as 1866, by the French physiologist, Claude Bernard (1813–1878), and formed the basis upon which Walter Bradford Cannon (1871–1945) established his concept of homeostasis, in 1932. Piaget was primarily fascinated by the approach of William Ross Ashby (1903–1972):

We have homeostasis at every level within biology [...] so at the level of human conduct, we simply have another self-regulatory system. But homeostasis is not required instantly. It is an arrival point, the result of a process. I translate this arrival point into operational terms—logical, mathematical operations. (Piaget 1973: 46f.)

Piaget never succeeded in going beyond postulating that there were similarities between equilibration and cybernetics. By associating the term of self-regulation with equilibration, Piaget hoped to "avoid finality" (Piaget 1965: 251). In actual fact, he used "equilibration" not only as a causal (Piaget 1968/13: 177) or empirical (Piaget *et al.* 1957a: 40), but also as an intentional (Piaget 1961a: XXIII) explanation (cf. Mischel 1976: 335ff.). This mixture of categories is the result of a fixed direction ("vection") towards which development must strive, due to the immanent logic of development. Lucien Sève (1971), therefore, reproached Piaget for advocating a new variant of genetics, in form of heredity of the construction processes of structures.

Memory, Learning and Development

From the mid-1950s onwards, Inhelder's and Piaget's fields of work became increasingly different. While Piaget was working on genetic epistemology, her research concentrated on the strategies of thinking, memory and the mental image. Together with the Dutch linguist, Hermina Sinclair-de Zwart (1919–1997), and with Magalie Bovet, she devoted herself to establishing a genetic psychology, which placed the central focus on learning processes and problem-solving processes.

Together with Gérard Noelting (1921–2004), she also conducted long-term case studies, in order to observe the development of structures. Her occupation with the pragmatic aspects of development enriched Piaget's formal and mathematical theory.

With regard to memory, Piaget and Inhelder identified several steps: recognition, evocation, and reconstruction. In the course of evolution, recognition occurs already among invertebrates, and during ontogenesis it already occurs when the nipple is recognized. Memory depends on activity but not every stored item corresponds to a symbolic form of memory because the sensory and motor schemata themselves are preserved due to their functioning. Piaget criticized Freud's theory of repression of early experiences, because at this stage "there is no memory of evocation, which would be able to organize any recollections" (Piaget 1945: 240). The evocative memory, on the other hand, stores mental images, which Piaget attributed to deferred imitation (Piaget 1966b: 477ff.). The function of evocative intelligence consists in presenting these images as stable and adequate reflections of the past. Young children can only retain static situations; changes are beyond their ability. To remember processes is part of conceptual thinking. Piaget's colleague, Jean Larguier de Bancel (1876–1961), understood memory to be a mental reconstruction, and for Janet, memory was "recitation," comparable to an interiorized report. Piaget gave a striking example of this: when his nanny took the two-year-old Jean for a walk on the Champs-Elysées, they were attacked. The nanny successfully fought off the attacker, who wanted to snatch Jean from the pram:

> Even today I can see the entire scene before me, as it happened, near the Metro station. Yet, when I was 15 years old, my parents received a letter from this nanny, in which she informed them that she had entered the Salvation Army, and wished to confess her past transgression. Above all, she wanted to return the watch, which she was given as a reward for this totally invented incident, complete with self-inflicted scratches. (Piaget 1945: 240f.)

Piaget concluded from this that "memory operates like a historian, who deductively reconstructs parts of the past from few, always incomplete documents" (Piaget 1971/8: 41). The studies concerning *Memory and Intelligence* (Piaget and Inhelder 1968a), which were based on an information-theoretical paradigm, showed that the ability to remember depends on the level of understanding and that it develops in line with this level. Surprisingly, 24 out of 30 children between the ages of 6 and 8 remembered an arrangement of sticks better after eight months than they did after one week. Piaget and Inhelder concluded that this result was due to the development of the operational structures between the two sessions. Thus, memory is dependent on the cognitive structures, and not vice versa. With regard to learning, Piaget reached the same conclusion:

> Learning is not a primary mechanism and cannot adequately explain development [...] One can hold that, along with the mechanism of learning, the presence of which we have never denied, there are internal mechanisms of development, endogenous mechanisms, such as the mechanism of equilibration. (Piaget 1970/13: 2)

This view, however, was challenged, when Jan Smedslund (1955, 1961) managed to teach children as young as 5–6 about the conservation of weights, which, according to Piaget, should only be possible five years later. In order to explain these results, Piaget (1959b: 36) distinguished between learning in the narrow sense (experience) and learning in the wide sense (experience plus equilibration = development). While the first kind of learning is supposed to be focused on 'content', the second gives rise to the 'form'. In the beginning, form and content are not separated, and logical structures will "only become complete by dissociating forms from contents" (Piaget 1959b: 56). Formal operations are independent of specific contents and can therefore be applied to all contents. "If one can easily learn the 'content' of a conservation of weight, the logical 'form' of this conversation requires, by contrast, an active reorganization on the part of the subject: It is this reorganization that cannot be taught just like that" (Piaget 1959a: 169).

Piaget understood learning in the narrow sense as verbal acquisition of cultural knowledge, and development as an endogenous construction of logico-mathematical structures.

> The development of knowledge is a spontaneous process, tied to the whole process of embryogenesis.[...] Learning presents the opposite case. [...] It is provoked, in general, as opposed to spontaneous. In addition, it is a limited process – limited to a single problem, or to a single structure. So I think that development explains learning (Piaget 1964/2: 20).

Piaget was amazingly sure that only spontaneous development could have long-term effects. "If a structure develops spontaneously, once it has reached a state of equilibrium, it is lasting, it will continue throughout the child's entire life" (Piaget 1964/2: 26). Teaching should therefore follow this spontaneous development. Piaget warned teachers "that every time a child is prematurely taught something which the child could have discovered on his own, he is deprived of the opportunity of discovery and thus of the opportunity of proper understanding" (Piaget 1970/2: 49). Since development is manifested through spontaneous thinking, Piaget did not research cognitive development among trained adults. "For our purpose, studies of adults are completely worthless. For when one asks them questions, they do not give you spontaneous thoughts" (Piaget 1970/13: 8f.). Because of this association of spontaneity with real development, Piaget was immune to contradicting evidence and never gave up his maturation paradigm:

> *J.P.*: Twenty-five children, whom I do not know, all say the same! At the same age!
> *J.-Cl.B.*: Because they all come from the same social background and from the same town?
> *J.P.*: I don't think so.
> *J.-Cl.B.*: Because they all are at the same level of development?
> *J.P.*: Yes! (Piaget and Bringuier 1977: 55)

Piaget's universal model of stages was queried by comparative studies in anthropology. Margaret Mead (1901–1978) knew Piaget's first books when she observed that the children on the Manus and Admiral Islands thought in less animist terms than the adults, which she attributed to the fact that the relevant patterns are missing in the Manus language and that the young people are barred from religious rites until after their puberty (Mead 1932). During the late 1950s, cross-cultural studies demonstrated that the age at which children reach the formal level depends on their social backgrounds. Piaget had to accept that children from Teheran reached the operative level two to three years before children from rural areas, that children from Martinique were four years behind the children of Geneva (Piaget 1962/5: 27f.) and that many did not reach the formal level (Piaget 1966/6: 122, 134). Since these results put Piaget's theory into question, he discussed three possible explanations:

- The different pace of development does not call into question the sequence of the stages, and does not mean that the development of "the formal structures is exclusively the result of social arrangements, because the factor of spontaneous and endogenous constructions, which every normal human being possesses, must, of course, be taken into account. This means, however, that the acquisition of cognitive structures involves an entire process of social exchange and mutual stimulation" (Piaget 1970/8: 54).
- It is possible that emerging skills are due to a talent that will only manifest itself in later years. Should this be the case, however, the universality of the fourth level would have to be radically questioned.
- Formal competences do not manifest themselves in all areas.

In his solution, Piaget combined the first and third explanation, by declaring "that all normal individuals will eventually reach the stage of formal operations, if not between the ages of 11 and 12, or between 14 and 15, then at least between 15 and 20. This stage is, however, reached in different areas, in accordance with individual skills and vocational specialization" (Piaget 1970/8: 57). Consequently, development leads to differentiation, because "six-year-old children are much more alike and similar to each other than children of 12 or adolescents of 18 [...] There is no reason why the same structures should carry over to any and all activities beyond those of his profession and his specialization" (Piaget 1970/13: 10). This statement, however, contradicted the thesis of a universal structure at the basis of all cognitive processes. Piaget, therefore, differentiated the social developmental factor into the universal social patterns and the culture-specific influences. The first aspect comprises verbally coded interactions, in which "we continually encounter the same laws of co-ordination and regulation"

(Piaget 1966/6: 125). The second aspect concerns the learned contents of concepts, which differ in accordance with the respective culture. Because of the universal laws of general coordination of actions in the first aspect, Piaget believed that he could identify an underlying logic of development within the external influences. This, however, led to a bizarre understanding of individuality and the social domain: "Thus, logic, understood as the final form of equilibration, could be seen as being individual and social at the same time; individual in as far as all individuals have it in common, and social, in as far as all societies have it in common" (Piaget 1966/6: 125). This Platonic figure of thought is the logical consequence of an assumed immanent logic of development, which is supposed to prevail against the coincidental circumstances of one's social background.

11

The Epistemological Work

Genetic Epistemology

From the end of World War II, Piaget worked ardently on his ambitious project to set up a scientific theory that would explain the genesis and functioning of thought and therefore lay the foundation for all sciences. Sometimes, Piaget was overtaxed with this task and his "difficulty to write was insurmountable" (letter to Ignace Meyerson, 13 January 1947, International Bureau of Education, Box 186). This major work was published in three volumes in 1950, entitled *Introduction à l'épistémologie génétique*.[11] Five years later, he was granted funds from the Rockefeller Foundation, for the purpose of establishing an interdisciplinary centre of research, enabling him to found his own school. The International Centre for Genetic Epistemology, which he used, above all, to support his own research, was located at the Science Faculty of the University of Geneva. From 1962 onwards, the ICGE was financed by Swiss National Funds and the Ford Foundation.

Interdisciplinary cooperation was by no means common practice in those days, but Piaget exaggerated the problems at the beginning in order to appear as a pioneer.

> During the first year of our Centre for Genetic Epistemology, nobody understood anybody else for the first six months. Any problem that one person enunciated was totally incomprehensible to everybody else. So we spent those first six months creating a [...] translation system. (Piaget 1973: 49)

Nonetheless, logicians, biologists, physicists, linguists, psychologists, science historians, cognitive theorists and mathematicians from all over the world were discussing the development of logic, causality, perception, inconsistency, awareness, abstraction, structures, etc. in the history of thought and in ontogenesis.

Over the following 25 years, a new topic of research was suggested every autumn. Every Monday morning, experimental methods and possible interpretations of results were discussed, and every summer some especially important symposium would take place, to which experts from different countries were invited, in order to discuss the theories advanced by the Genevans. (Inhelder 1989: 71)

Piaget usually wrote the preliminary drafts of manuscripts for the discussions, which led to "additional controls and new projects" (Piaget 1976: 33). The results were published in the series *Etudes d'Epistémologie Génétique*, which eventually amounted to 37 volumes. In total, around 300 authors (including Leo Apostel, Evert Willem Beth, Pierre Gréco, Jean-Blaise Grize, Seymour Papert and William Van Orman Quine) participated in these studies. Piaget invested much time and energy in the ICGE's events, research and publications, to secure his breakthrough as an epistemologist. Moreover, his centre allowed him to put into effect his ideas of cooperation, understood as "self-transcendence in the sense of feeling oneself to be a part of a greater totality" (Chapman 1988: 194).

The interdisciplinary program for a genetic epistemology had been devised by Baldwin in 1909, and Piaget had adopted it in the 1920s (cf. Piaget 1924/1: 607; 1932: 76; 1965: 44ff.).

To establish a scientific epistemology does not only mean the construction of a theory of the forms of knowledge, pertaining to the various sciences, but it also means the construction of this theory by using the material of the strictly positive sciences, without referring to metaphysical hypotheses, which characterize the various philosophies. (Piaget 1946/3: 2)

In contrast to the philosophical tradition, Piaget emphasized the evolutionary nature of cognition (Piaget 1970a: 7) and epistemology's claim of being scientific (Piaget 1968/9: 359). According to Piaget, a scientific approach has to use two complementary methods: "the logical analysis and the historical, or genetic, analysis" (Piaget 1947/4: 137). The logical method operates deductively, by analyzing the axiomatic basis of operations (classes, relations, and propositions). The genetic analysis examines the historical and individual development of knowledge. To answer the core question of "how the human mind proceeds from a state of less satisfactory knowledge to a state of superior knowledge" (Piaget 1970a: 20), it would be most useful, if human thought could be reconstructed from its first historical beginnings. Since no such resources are available, the historical-critical method comprises "only concepts, which are formed and applied by an already fully developed thinking" (Piaget 1950 I: 21). Therefore, the history of the human mind can only be reconstructed indirectly, by comparing scientific knowledge and experimental research to the ontogenesis of cognition, "so that invariants and transformations can be identified in it" (Piaget 1947/4: 140). The laws, discovered in this way, are supposed to govern the individual, as well as the historical, development of thinking. "There can be no theoretical break between thinking, as it manifests itself in a child, and the scientific thinking of the adult; thus we have expanded developmental psychology into a genetic epistemology" (Piaget 1970/2: 30).

Following Einstein's theory of relativity, Piaget distinguished between a special and a general epistemology.

> Special genetic epistemology is the term we apply to any psycho-genetic or historical-critical research into the types of increasing cognition, as long as this research is supported by a reference system, which is in line with the latest scientific research. Yet, if the reference system itself is integrated in the genetic or historic process to be studied, we are dealing with a general genetic epistemology. (Piaget 1950 I: 49f.)

The genetic epistemology would be relativist, if the reference system itself was understood as a construct, as in Brunschvicg's theory. Piaget found it "worrying, when the theses of *a priori* necessity or of identity are reversed, until rational activity is characterized as arising from pure chance" (Piaget 1950 III: 285). He therefore limited the relativity of the human cognitive capacity, by assuming a specific direction of development, guided by a "mechanism, immanent in reason" (Piaget 1950 III: 289).

His friend, Ignace Meyerson, had warned him against taking rationality as being linear: "Do not invest it with a fixed character [. . .] There is not only one history of categories, but each category has a history of a different kind" (Meyerson ms 13.11.49, cited in Vidal and Parot 1996: 71). Piaget, however, did not understand this objection: "The epistemology will not be static" (document cited in Vidal and Parot 1996: 72). While Meyerson applied psychology to the historical and concrete human being, Piaget concentrated on the universal mechanisms of transformation in a general subject. These mechanisms create "an 'established' harmony, which gradually develops, in accordance with an organically rooted process that continues into infinity" (Piaget 1970: 98).

Piaget named his genetic epistemology "dynamic Kantianism" (Piaget 1972/12: 3). While Kant worked on the premise that the forms of sensibility (space and time) and the categories of reason (quantity, quality, relation and modality) were given, Piaget considered them to be the final destinations in the process of construction on the level of formal operations. Under the influence of Baldwin, Brunschvicg and Janet, Piaget repeatedly changed his list of categories. Among these, he counted the cognitive ability for drawing logical conclusions, as well as the classifying, modal, causal, temporal, relational, quantitative, numerical and spatial-geometric structures. Kant's transcendental subject became Piaget's epistemic subject, consisting of mechanisms, "which all individual subjects on the same level have in common" (Piaget 1968: 67). Because the Platonic idea of Kant's pure reason *a priori* was retained in the aim of development, "there is, beyond a certain level, pure logic and mathematics" (Piaget 1957/4: 25).

The genetic epistemology does not only concern the realm of facts, but the development of norms is also subject to the "directional laws [...]. The genetic epistemology is based on this possible collaboration between the genetic and normative analyses, but there is never any passage from the facts to the norm" (Piaget 1961/1: 168). Piaget made this statement defending himself against Gaston Bachelard's daughter, Suzanne, who had reproached him in 1958 for mixing up facts and norms. The historical-critical method, according to Piaget, was an "objective method" for the examination of "normative facts" (Piaget 1961/1: 170) and would therefore not psychologize the sciences. This, however, cannot be flatly denied as far as his historical expositions are concerned.

History and the Interdependence of the Sciences

Despite the counter-example of topological geometry and the criticism of Delacroix, Bourjade, Blondel and Mauss, Piaget cleaved to a close correlation between the history of science and ontogenesis. "The fundamental hypothesis of genetic epistemology is that there is a parallelism between the progress made in the logical and rational organization of knowledge and the corresponding formative psychological processes" (Piaget 1969/8: xlii). Piaget found similarity between the understanding of time, movement, speed and number in primitive societies and in the preoperative child (Piaget 1950 II: 75). He believed that the stage of concrete operations was reached by the Egyptians and the Chaldeans (Piaget 1950 II: 75), because of their knowledge of Euclidian geometry and astronomy (Piaget 1950 I: 58, 261; II: 77f.). Furthermore, the Pre-Socratics were the first to overcome phenomenalism, when they began to reflect upon the constructivity of concepts (Piaget 1950 II: 80ff.). Since reflexivity upon one's own concepts is already a characteristic of formal operations, and the thesis of "gradual progress" (Piaget 1950 II: 82) should therefore be questioned, Piaget resorted to an astonishing explanation: because of the speculations of the Pre-Socratic atomists, and because of "Plato's mathematism," Aristotle was compelled to return to "common sense," whereby he "had undergone a regression towards concrete operations" (Piaget 1950 II: 80). On the whole, Piaget believed that Greek thinking ranged between the concrete and the formal stage. Following Pierre Boutroux (1880–1922), Piaget thought that this latter stage was only reached with the philosophy of Descartes (Piaget 1950 I: 267ff.).

Piaget attempted to explain these common features with the term "intellectual mutation" of Gaston Bachelard (1884–1962) and Alexandre Koyré (1892–1962). This puzzling term describes an important historical step towards intellectualization (a change of paradigm), which "accelerates the psychogenetic process, whereby the sequence of stages remains relatively constant, but the speed at which one stage follows the previous one varies, depending on the social environment" (Piaget 1950 III: 184). The history of science is a resultant of the hereditary structure and two social factors:

> The first factor is the dissolution of the original social units into larger and denser totalities, which led to an economic division of labour, as well as to a psychological differentiation between individuals. The second factor is the progress of techniques, resulting from the division of labour and from mental differentiation. (Piaget 1950 II: 77)

But in the 1960s, more and more results of cross-cultural studies were published that contradicted his theory of the invariant development. In 1969, Piaget therefore conceded that "one should perhaps not exaggerate this parallelism between history and individual development, but, in general terms, there certainly are stages which resemble each other" (Piaget and Bringuier 1977: 82). Six years later, however, he was once more so convinced that the history of science recapitulated ontogenesis that he started to write a book about it (Piaget and Garcia 1983a).

> Beginning with the cognitive development of the child and throughout the entire course of the history of scientific thought, we can observe a more or less continuous passage from exogenous to endogenous knowledge. This is the nature of the case, since the general tendency of the mind is to pass beyond empiricism in the direction of deductive models. (Piaget 1975/8: 804)

Empiricism here means the primitive intellectual realism that will be overcome due to the progressive internalization of knowledge by "endogenous" reconstruction. This usage should not be confounded with the epistemological foundation of knowledge.

Scientific thinking proceeds in two "directions": the realistic direction concentrates on the object and the idealistic direction is characterized through the "predominance of deduction and conscious implication"

(Piaget 1950 III: 307). Realism is a precondition of empirical research, while idealism emphasizes the dependence of experience on subjective structures. The genetic epistemology does not conceive these two points of view as oppositions, but as necessary poles. Piaget had already, at an early stage, adopted a position "exactly midway between realism and idealism: there are no things independent of the mind, yet the reverse is true also, the mind is nothing independent of experience" (Piaget 1930/3: 38). This "circle of subject and object," Piaget explained with reference to Harald Høffding (1843–1931), is fundamental to all knowledge and to the unity of sciences.

> Physics [...] is a science of the object, but it can only reach the object via the intermediate step of the logico-mathematical structures, which spring from the activities of the subject. Biology is another science of the object, but the living creature, which is examined with the help of tools, partially borrowed from chemo-physics, is at the same time the starting point for a subject, forming behavior patterns and leading towards the human subject. In order to study a human subject, psychology and the other sciences dealing with the human being use some techniques of the sciences mentioned earlier, but the human being also forms logico-mathematical structures, which constitute a starting point for formalization within logic and mathematics. (Piaget 1970/4: 85)

In this circle of sciences, psychology, as a "natural science" (Piaget 1966/9: 12), occupies a position of prime importance, because it studies the logico-mathematical structures. Therefore "psychology is not just a science of the individual, but of the human being in general, and especially of the universal 'subject'" (Piaget 1966/9: 11). Psychology will have to mediate between biology and mathematics, because "only psychologists will truly understand" (Piaget 1947/4: 150) how the mind works.

Constructivist Realism

Piaget was convinced that the human being progressively constructs the forms and the contents of his thinking. "If the new structures—the development of which has been proven by history and psychogenesis—are not pre-formed in the ideal world of possibilities, nor in the objects, or in the subject, then their authentic constitution can only be due to a historic-genetic process of construction" (Piaget 1970: 142f.).

The term of constructivism was coined in 1909 by the biologist and philosopher Hans Driesch (1867–1941), whose theory of regulation was

Table 11.1 Piaget's classification of epistemological theories

	Non-genetic theories	Genetic theories
Primacy of the object	*Realism*	*Empiricism*
Primacy of the subject	*Apriorism*	*Pragmatism and conventionalism*
Indissociability of object and subject	*Phenomenology*	*Relativism*

SOURCE Piaget (1950 I: 31)

praised by Bergson (Piaget 1907: 42). Further sources for Piaget's constructivism were Kant, Brunschvicg, Goblot, Rignano, Janet, Emile Meyerson, and Brouwer, who understood intuition to be an operational construct. Piaget, too, maintained that there was "no direct inner experience" (Piaget 1950 III: 261), nor could there be any pure observation. This was also true if modern measuring instruments were used: "Even the reading of the results, and, moreover, their generalization, pre-suppose constant operational activity on the part of the subject: the physical 'fact' is only accessible by means of a mathematical set of tools" (Piaget 1970: 125). Knowledge is not a mental copy or image of reality. "To know an object is to act upon it. To know is to modify, to transform the object, and to understand the process of this transformation" (Piaget 1964/2: 20). The copy theory of empiricism "is founded upon a vicious circle: in order to make a copy, we must know the original we are copying, but according to this epistemology, the only way to know the original is by making a copy of it; thus we enter this circle, without ever knowing whether our copy is a true likeness of the original" (Piaget 1970a: 22f.).

Sensations and perceptions cannot sufficiently explain the forming of thought structures and knowledge. Cognition is neither preformed in the object nor in the subject, but arises "from the interaction between subject and object, which is initially triggered by spontaneous activity of the organism, as well as by external stimuli" (Piaget 1967: 29). Since Piaget's notion of interaction contained no social connotation whatsoever, and since his approach was always based on the idea of an active subject and a passive object, "transactionalism" would be a more appropriate term than "interactionism" (Kitchener 1985). Piaget classified the common epistemologies by considering the developmental aspect and the relation between subject and object, whereby he gave to his own theory the somewhat misleading name of relativism (Table 11.1).

Part of the subject's realm of objects is his own body, and "in contrast to inorganic bodies, any living being is simultaneously object and subject, because it is the origin of behaviour (and this includes plants, which also affect their environment)" (Piaget 1978/5: 257). At first, subject and object are identical, until cognitive development leads to the differentiation of body and mind. This process is never quite finalized because the object to be known will always remain a thing-for-us, just as the human being can never become a subject-in-himself (Piaget 1967: 371). For the subject, the objects are the "trigger (not the reason) for the form-giving regulations" (Piaget 1967: 121). It is therefore "from the interior that the subject is in interaction with the object as far as general coordination of his acts are concerned, and that is why these coordinations always agree with reality, from which they proceed their source" (Piaget 1950 I: 324). This means that the logico-mathematical structures form themselves, through the coordination of actions. Due to the developing of the subject's intellectual tools, his understanding of reality changes, too (Piaget 1950 I: 44). At the stage of formal operations, the constructions are logical, and therefore always agree with reality:

> Any cognition always means a new construction and the great problem of epistemology consists in the task of making the new creation agree with the facts: as soon as the new creations are made, they involve a formal necessity, and they become objective, i.e. corresponding with reality that they [...] allow to grasp. (Piaget 1967: 23)

Piaget's great epistemological problem was, in fact, that his arguments were realistic and constructivist at the same time. He believed that objective reality could be approached empirically, although reality is only a construction. "The object is a limit in the mathematical sense. One continually approaches objectivity, without ever reaching the object itself. The object one believes being reached is always the object represented and interpreted by the intelligence of the subject" (Piaget and Bringuier 1977: 104). Piaget's all-important problem was the equation between the objective object and the subjective object. Piaget found the solution in Bergson's *Matière et mémoire* (1926: 211) and remained true to it. "There are physical structures, which are independent of us, but correspond to our operational structures" (Piaget 1968: 43). With his postulate that a psycho-physical isomorphism was the destination of development, Piaget believed that he had overcome the antagonism between idealism and realism. These approaches, according to Piaget, simply "expressed the same thing in two different languages" (Piaget 1950 III: 309). A typical example for Piaget's position gives the anecdote of 1955, when he was invited by the Academy of Sciences in Moscow:

"Do you believe that objects exist before knowledge?" Piaget answered: "As a psychologist, I don't know, because I only know objects by acting on them, and I can affirm nothing before that action." Rubinstein then asked: "Do you believe that the world exists before knowledge?" He replied: "That's another story. To act on an object one needs an organism, and that organism is also part of the world. Obviously, I believe that the world exists before knowledge, but we can only cut it into specific objects during the course of our actions and by interactions between the organism and the milieu" (Piaget 1965: 253; cf. 1956/5; 1961/1: 182f.). Thus, the Russian scientists came to the conclusion that Piaget was no idealist. But this is only half the truth because Piaget always maintained a dual position and this conflict seems to have been one major motivation for his restless working. He agreed with the idealists that the possibility of experiences was dependent on *a priori* given ideas (the logico-mathematical structures), which would indicate a dominance of assimilation. He agreed with the empiricists that experience was the only source of knowledge and the concept of accommodation refers to an external reality. Since he considered reality to be objective, "there can only be one truth" (Piaget 1965: 260). But in the end of his argumentations, logico-mathematical structures, reflective abstraction, assimilation and immanent laws always dominated their counterparts. This was the reason for him to give up his project of a genetic ontology.

Genetic Structuralism

Piaget substituted a genetic ontology by the genetic structuralism, whereby he excluded a socio-historical view as well. He adopted a functionalist view and supposed that "the subject exists, because, on the whole, the 'essence' of the structures is their structuring" (Piaget 1968: 134). This position allowed him to maintain the claim of objectivity, with respect to physical, as well as to cognitive structures. He defined the physical-causal structures as "the *objective* system of operators" (Piaget 1968: 40), which corresponds to the operative structures of the subject because the structuring organism itself forms part of the structuring world. Piaget did not consider this to be a realistic position, with respect to the constructive activity of the subject. "The point of intersection between the subjective structures and those of material reality must therefore be found *within* the organism, and not (or not only) in the realm of experience" (Piaget 1970: 97). The cognitive structures, however, also have an objective existence (Piaget 1970a: 31). The structures are located "midway between the nervous system and conscious behavior" (Piaget 1968: 133) and consist of an inner construction "behind" the contents. A structure "is not something the subject thinks, it is something the subject knows how to do" (Piaget 1970/13: 4). Behind the phenomena, there is a structure, which can be formalized, whereby "the formalization may manifest itself directly in logico-mathematical equations, or may be imparted through a cybernetic model" (Piaget 1968: 8f.). Because of this formal approach, Piaget saw structuralism as a theoretical means of reconciling heterogeneous disciplines, such as linguistics (Saussure, Jacobson), psychology (Lewin), the social sciences (Mauss, Lévi-Strauss, Foucault), physics (field theory), biology (of Bertalanffy, Cannon) or mathematics ("Bourbaki").

Structures contain three essential properties: wholeness, transformations, and self-regulation. Piaget's notion of structures developed from the philosophical concept of wholeness was later shaped by the Gestalt theory and the mathematical concept of sets and was finally combined with cybernetics. He stressed that the relationships between parts and their relative orders were of primary importance. "Integers, for example, do not exist independently of each other, and were not discovered in a random sequence, to be ultimately combined into a whole; they only appear as a function of a number sequence" (Piaget 1968: 10). Structures are the results of the coordination of actions and reflective abstractions, which form a certain cognitive equilibrium, because of the universal laws of transformation that govern their composition. Following an intervention by the Neo-Platonist, Emile Bréhier (1876–1952), at the assembly of the Société Française de Philosophie in 1949, Piaget had begun to study the relationship between genesis and structure (Piaget 1965/7: 328f.). Ten years later, he chaired the *Colloque de Cerisy*, together with Maurice de Gandillac (1906–2006) and Lucien Goldmann, where discussions took place about the problem of how a structure can be a whole, and, at the same time, be a quantity which surpasses this whole.

J.-Cl. B.: This is the paradox of structure . . .

J. P.: Certainly.

J.-Cl. B. . . . that it also manifests itself as a closed whole.

J. P.: Yes, and at the same time it is also the starting point for new structures. The true problem is the construction of these structures. (Piaget and Bringuier 1977: 73).

For Piaget, a structure was not something static, and its construction was not devoid of order, but "*every genesis starts from a structure and leads to a structure*" (Piaget 1965/7: 329), which is more complex, more stable and more mobile. In genetic structuralism, therefore, "structure and function, genesis and history, individual subject and society are inseparable" (Piaget 1968: 122). Self-regulation is the mechanism of construction and self-preservation. This means "that transformations within a structure will not exceed the boundaries of the structure, but will only generate elements, which pertain to the structure and obey the laws of the structure" (Piaget 1968: 16). Regarding this third property, the organism, as a "physico-chemical system" (Piaget 1968 44), evidently served as a prototype of a structure.

When we are dealing with structures in society, things become more complicated: "If the concept of self-regulation or equilibration has any sense at all, the logic or pre-logic of the members of a given society cannot be adequately gauged by already crystallized cultural products" (Piaget 1968: 111f.). According to Piaget, logic is an individual achievement and must not be equated with cultural achievements, as Lévi-Strauss did. The history of intelligence "is a bundle of transformations, not to be confused with the transformations of culture, or those of symbolic activity, but antedating and giving rise to both of these" (Piaget 1968: 113). Lévi-Strauss had declined Piaget's qualitative distinction between primitive and modern thought, and considered the primitive's concern with concrete phenomena as a form of scientific thinking (in Gardner 1970: 80). Piaget criticized Michel Foucault (1926–1984) harshly for having negated the actual subject. Foucault's "irrationalism" was a "structuralism without structures", because his understanding of "reason transforms itself for no reason" (Piaget 1968: 129). His work *The Order of Things* "clearly shows that it is impossible to construct a coherent structuralism, by divorcing it from any kind of constructivism" (Piaget 1968: 130).

Piaget's disagreement with anthropological and discursive structuralism did not lead him to the historical individual. When Piaget spoke of constructed structures, he did not mean individual skills, but rather the universal competences of the epistemic subject, which are adapted to reality. Because the "bio-physical and organic co-ordinations are the actual sources of the structures" (Piaget 1970: 116), there is a "harmony between thinking and reality" (Piaget 1968: 67). And because the genesis of structures "is linked to immanent dialectics" (Piaget 1968: 137), genetic structuralism dovetails seamlessly with immanentism. Piaget believed that "God Himself had ceased to be immobile and keeps constituting stronger and stronger systems, which also have the effect of making Him more alive" (Piaget 1968: 135f.). The idea that God develops, and comprehends Himself in the evolution of thought, had been worked out by Georg Wilhelm Friedrich Hegel (1770–1831) in his *Phenomenology of Mind* of 1807, which had already inspired Baldwin's concept of an interdisciplinary genetic epistemology. It was not until 1977 that Piaget asked one of his co-workers to translate parts of this work into French, whereupon dialectics was elevated to an annual research topic at the ICGE. Piaget, too, understood dialectics as being a genetic principle, which "corresponds to a progression, which is inevitable, once thought turns away from false absolutes" (Piaget 1968: 118). In contrast to Hegel (cf. Kesselring 1981) he did not emphasize inconsistency but emphasized equilibration, which advances thought. Piaget used the term of dialectics with various meanings, such as interaction, interdependence, the circle or spiral of the sciences, the establishment of an equilibrium, and assimilation between systems (Piaget 1967a: 1156ff.). But all these significations contained the idea that thought frees itself, through evolution, from the compulsion of reality, by gaining a better understanding of reality, thanks to its formalization. "The outstanding characteristic of cognitive organizations is the progressive dissociation of form and content" (Piaget 1967: 153). Free from content, the decentrated logico-mathematical structures correspond to the universal laws of reality.

By systematically combining structuralism, developmental psychology, epistemology and the history and theory of the sciences, Piaget intended to found a holistic basis for all scientific disciplines. His genetic epistemology thus fulfilled his aim of 1918, of overcoming the traditional philosophical, religious and scientific opposites. He not only reconciled idealism and realism, by placing them, as corresponding results, at the end of an immanently driven process of construction—he also agreed with the reductionists that the mind is an aspect of behavior, and, therefore, a biological entity. This fruit of the mind is expressed in the functional continuity of adaptation. At the same time, he could agree with Brentano's thesis of the irreducibility of mind, because there is a structural discontinuity in the development from child to adult. Thus, he combined Spencer's monism with the dualism of Lalande and Bergson (1954/9: 135). The transition from monism to dualism in the development of the child occurs with the separation of body and mind, when practical intelligence becomes representative intelligence (cf. Mounoud 1996).

The Aversion against Philosophy

Despite numerous publications by Piaget and his co-workers at the ICGE, Piaget's epistemology was not widely received, because of its ambivalence. Piaget felt that he had been sidelined and misunderstood by his critics, such as Isaak Benrubi (1876–1943), Henri-Louis Miéville (1877–1963) or Merleau-Ponty. Thus, in 1965, he launched a polemic offensive.

Piaget took revenge on his teacher for his failed dissertation project. Despite the significance that Reymond's conjunction of logic and psychology had upon the theories of his pupil (Piaget 1965: 19f.), he accused him of having remained an absolutist speculator, who had hoped to dismantle

Einstein's theory of relativity, and who commented in lectures upon theories, without having informed himself of the basic facts. Because this kind of attitude was the great danger of philosophy, Piaget described his book as a "testimony of a man who had been lured into the spell of speculation and had almost succumbed to it" (Piaget 1965: 12). In a clearly derogatory tone, he called philosophers "wise men," who, in their search for the absolute, gained insights, but not scientific knowledge. While scientists occupy themselves with specific questions and limit their goals, the philosopher feels obliged "to combine everything with everything" (Piaget 1950 I: 14). This is why he speaks of everything "at the same time [...], whereas the scientist strives to work on only one thing at a time" (Piaget 1947/4: 133). Piaget declared that the objective of philosophy was to recognize "the whole of reality, considered as the co-ordination of all values, including knowledge" (Piaget 1983/1: 78), which supposes the aiming for a final harmony. He thus equated philosophy with metaphysics (Piaget and Bringuier 1977: 38).

According to Piaget, the only useful function of philosophy was to ask good questions. "It poses problems, but it never solves them." This is "at the same time very necessary and very dangerous" (Piaget 1970/13: 17) because if questions are kept too general the realistic dimensions are lost. Philosophy "does not contain its own controls. There is no method of verification; there is only thought" (Piaget 1983/1: 77). Piaget refuted that philosophers, with the exception of the logicians, had any credibility, because only theories that were based on experiments could be taken seriously. Therefore, "the psychologist is somehow compelled to ignore philosophy" (Piaget 1947/4: 130). The same applies to epistemologists, who can no longer do without verification of their theses, which he tried to prove with an irrefutable argument: "All epistemologists, of whatever school, are implicitly calling on psychology. Even if they maintain that they want to avoid any aspect of psychology that is already a psychological position" (Piaget 1973: 34).

For Piaget, it was obvious that philosophy would lose more and more of its domain due to the differentiation of the sciences. Hence he accused the philosophers of trying to save their threatened territory with the imperialist claim that epistemology was superior to the sciences. Piaget's "sounding of the alarm" (Piaget 1965: 12) was directed against this "intellectual gerontocracy" (Piaget 1965: 40), in the hope of breaking their institutional and public influence in France. The decisive turning point in the modern history of philosophy was to be the detachment of the epistemology, which Piaget put into effect with his scientific genetic epistemology: "It is true that I have taken epistemology away from philosophy" (Piaget 1970/9: 26).

Piaget constructed a radical contrast between philosophy and the sciences. His reduction of the sciences to verification compelled him to adhere to a naïve concept of truth and progress (Piaget 1965: 141f., 260, 263), which was not in harmony with a constructivist approach. Piaget was therefore repeatedly considered to be a positivist. Vygotsky had already noted that Piaget "keeps interrupting his train of thoughts with an amazing persistence, every time that these thoughts take him to a boundary with serious consequences—philosophy" (Vygotsky 1934: 103). And he had drawn the same conclusion as Piaget did, though with another connotation: "Deliberate avoidance of philosophy is itself a philosophy" (Vygotsky 1934: 103).

Because of the critique by Jean Lacroix (1900–1968) and Paul Ricoeur (1913–2005), Piaget admitted in the postscript to the second edition (Piaget 1968/6: 269) that the dichotomy of insight and cognition could not be maintained. But criticism did not change Piaget's views because he "even agreed with the American psychiatrist, Anthony, who had written that Piaget was far too narcissistic to respond to objections. No, critique really does not interest me, I will not waste my time on refuting it. I know that I am right" (in Altwegg 1983: 151).

12

Neither Retirement nor Resignation

In 1971, at the age of 75, Piaget resigned from his chair at the University of Geneva, after 50 years of teaching. At the end of the 1960s, a difficult situation had arisen at the JJRI/ISE, due to a massive rise in student numbers. Piaget, in charge of 80 assistants and 400 students, held a dominant position, which was severely criticized by striking students and by other professors during the protests of 1968. Although his own co-workers defended his position, whereby Inhelder even chose not to follow a call to Harvard, remaining in Geneva to support Piaget, he lost some of his assistants to other departments. After Piaget's retirement his chair was divided. Jacques Vonèche took over child and adolescent psychology, and Inhelder taught genetic epistemology and experimental psychology. She continued Piaget's studies and in 1974 established the Jean Piaget Archive. In 1970, the Jean Piaget Society had been founded in Philadelphia, which has been organizing annual congresses ever since. In 1972, Piaget was awarded the renowned Erasmus Prize, as one of eleven awards. Yet Piaget did not retire altogether. He retained the directorship of the ICGE, where further research on causality, necessity and possibility mainly, as well as logic, was conducted.

The Last Works

In the early 1970s, a new series of studies regarding causality appeared, in which Piaget advocated a theory of attribution. He took up Emile Meyerson's thesis of 1907, according to which causality is the result of ascribing a reason to physical changes. Thus, even at the operative stage, the idea of causality "must be understood as attributing one's own operations to the objects" (Piaget 1970: 63). He differentiated between operations regarding objects and those regarding the operations themselves, and called them attributed and applied operations, respectively. Attributed operations always refer to real, and thus causal, processes, and include (a) that the properties of objects exist in their own right, on a certain scale, before the subject discovers them; (b) that to find them the subject needs to construct operations applicable to these objects [...]; (c) [...] that it amounts to establishing an isomorphism between the operational structures used and the objective characteristics discovered because of them. (Piaget and Garcia 1971: 64)

Successful acting precedes understanding, even though the latter rapidly surpasses the former, whereby thinking no longer requires acting. "Understanding means exposing the reason of things, whereas success only consists in using things successfully" (Piaget and Amann 1974b: 242f.). Analogous to the understanding way and the acting way of dealing with the world, he differentiated between "two ways of abstraction, depending on exogenous or endogenous origins" (Piaget 1974a: 81). The exogenous origin of abstraction, however, does not mean that knowledge of objects is directed from the outside: "There can be no exogenous knowledge, except for the knowledge which is conceived as content, with the help of forms, which are of endogenous origin" (Piaget 1974a: 83). It is always the active subject who builds up his knowledge by way of abstracting his actions with objects, and by generalizing his experience. As usual, "generalization" was divided, too: Inductive generalization takes observable things into account whereas constructive generalization involves the generation of new forms and contents from actions and operations. This further development of his dual theory resulted in the postulate of two cognitive systems:

- The presentational system consists of stable schemata and structures. The presentational schemata contain the simultaneous properties of the objects and enable the knowledge of reality with the help of assimilation. This system is the epistemological and universal pole of thought and refers to the necessary, which is to be comprehended.
- The procedural system consists of mobile procedural schemata, which focus upon an aim and are context specific. This system contains the psychological and individual pole and refers to successful action. It is functioning due to accommodation and forms the source of creativity, because it is "the moulder of the 'possible', and, as such, constitutes the mechanism of 're-equilibration'". (Piaget 1978/5: 252)

These two types, the presentational and procedural schemata, are combined within the operational schemata. This is why the operations contain the properties of both systems. Procedures open up new possibilities, whereas understanding embraces the structural necessities. The possible and the necessary are not observable properties of the objects but the result of the increasing deductive construction of the subject.

The real, the necessary and the possible are in parallel development with one another, in three phases. Piaget (Piaget and Berthoud-Papandropoulou 1981; Piaget and Ackermann-Valladao 1983) tried to show that there is no possibility for the infant. Because "things" must be as they are, the physical world is the only possibility for the child, which means that there is no possibility but only pseudo-necessity. His procedural schemata are not based on understanding but on success and new possibilities emerge only as analogous consequences of prior phenomena. In a second stage, lasting from 7–10 years of age, the child understands those possibilities that can be implemented in a concrete way. As he begins to reflect upon the results of transformations, he begins to differentiate between the real (as merely one form of the possible) and the possible. During the third stage, these three modalities are integrated into a comprehensive system. After being transformed to formalized operations, the possibilities are without limitations, and the necessary is the only possibility that remains when all others have been excluded. "It appears that the real is finally absorbed at its two poles, by the possible and the necessary" (Piaget 1978/5: 257).

This differentiation of modalities changes the entire thinking. To understand the "reason of things" means to imbue things with meaning, whereby reason "expands to comprise the possible and thus surpasses the real" (Piaget and Amann 1974b: 242f.). This concerns all concepts, because the defining properties of a concept correspond to the necessity, whereas the nondefining properties belong to the possibilities. Moreover, the possible is the foundation for the abnormal, which surpasses reality, therefore "one can see in it the organic source of the 'cognitive normative'" (Piaget 1978/5: 257). During the mid-1970s, Piaget, inspired by the work of Ilya Prigogine (1917–2003), tried once more to elaborate similar developmental mechanisms in biological and cognitive systems. In order to solve the problem of how necessity can be acknowledged without assuming predetermination, Piaget (1980) postulated that cognitive development contained changing phases of dialectic and deductive constructions. New contexts of possibilities are recognized in dialectical phases, while the necessary relations among these new constructions are consolidated in the deductive phases. He believed that this development in phases applied to psychogenesis, as well as to the history of science: "The mechanisms of transition from one historical period to the next are analogous to those of the transition between one psychogenetic stage and that which follows" (Piaget and Garcia 1983a: 41).

Motivated by new tendencies in mathemathics (MacLane 1971) and by critics like Bryant, Donaldson or Markman, saying that his model was wrong in assessing the competencies of children, Piaget (Piaget and Berthoud-Papandropoulou 1980a; Piaget and Ackerman-Valladao 1990) reformulated his theory in terms of correspondences. These are instruments of comparison between variables like actions. A specific correspondence is called morphism. On the first level of development, the intramorphical niveau (= the preoperational stage), children are unable to classify adequately two black cats, two black dogs and three white dogs: the four black animals and the five dogs are only parts of seven animals. Generalizing and abstracting the correspondences leads to transformations. On the intermorphical level, "the transfomations and the correspondences are in interaction" (Piaget 1979/9: 20), which enables correct classifications. These classifications become systematized on the transmorphical level (= stage of concrete operations), because "transformations are based essentially on reversibility" (Piaget 1979/9: 26). Thus, in order to save his theory, Piaget added a new stage to his old model.

Having studied the theories of Allan Anderson and Nuel Belnap (Anderson and Belnap 1975), Piaget found a new orientation in the field of logic, too. His ultimate study, which he planned in 1979, together with Rolando Garcia (published in 1987), concerned the research of intensional logic. This logic is based on the meaning of concepts and takes its orientation from the natural usage of language, while extensional logic is based on the extent of concepts and corresponds to the formal-logical usage of language. Piaget concluded that the hitherto valid operatory logic was "too closely [...] linked to the more familiar extensional logic" (Piaget and Garcia 1987: 8). He hoped to prove that the underlying logical structure of life was intensional and extensional at the same time. According to Piaget, meanings are based on implications that have their origins in the relations among actions. The semiotic function transforms the action implications into implications among statements. If meanings are coordinated on the operatory level, a kind of grouping is formed (Piaget and Garcia 1987: 121). The elaboration of a theory of intensional logic would have meant a partial reorganization of his lifetime's work, but he could not progress beyond writing a sketch on the genesis of the capability of rational explanations any more.

The Missing Degree

Piaget had never obtained an official academic qualification to teach psychology, sociology, and epistemology. In 1976, the celebration of his 80th birthday was seized as an occasion to catch up with his missing exam in psychology. Just for fun, the professor emeritus subjected himself to a colloquium for PhD candidates (Inhelder, Garcia and Vonèche 1977). A jury, among whose members were Prigogine and Heinz von Foerster (1911–2002), asked him questions concerning his latest work, *The Development of Thought: Equilibration of Cognitive Structures* (1975). As this examination could not be held under the official authority of the University, Piaget commented: "I shall die without an actual degree and shall take the secret of my educational shortcomings to my grave" (Piaget 1976: 43).

In 1979, Piaget, who was a passionate pipe smoker, suffered an abscess in his lungs, and by the end of that year was so seriously ill that he had to be hospitalized. During mid-May in 1980, he also started to suffer from circulatory problems. He still attended the XXV symposium of the ICGE, which was held in June 1980, but which was foreshortened due to the state of Piaget's health. Shortly before his death, Piaget was asked whether he considered it possible that there was life after death. He answered that he had never thought about this and was

> amazed and appeared to be full of indignation over the fact that an enlightened journalist, working for a liberal newspaper, could still ask such a silly, irrelevant question, in the 83rd year of the Piaget era. He gave his reply in the reassuring knowledge of the fact that he would continue to exist, in spirit, in this world, after his eventual (biological) demise. (Altwegg 1983: 156f.)

This attitude accords with Piaget's thoughts in his first work:

> When a man of action dies, his work will only survive him long enough to bring forth some new, paler and weaker men of action. When a man of thought dies, his work will encourage a thousand men of action, all of them provided with new vigour. Honour be to the man who reflects, in the silence of his study, alone, and who then launches a new idea into the bright daylight, an idea that throws itself upon the world, like a storm churns up the ocean. (Piaget 1915/1: 11)

In July, Piaget had to be taken to a hospital in Geneva, where he died on 16 September 1980. Two days later, 800 people gathered for his memorial service in the university auditorium, which was named after him, and where music by Mozart, Piaget's favorite composer, was played.

Notes

1. This was not true for Bovet, Claparède, Piaget, and Raymond de Saussure (1894–1971).
2. The heading is mentioned in the congress report of the *Internationale Zeitschrift für Psychoanalyse* (1922: 478–505), but, unlike for other lectures, no summary is given. Piaget extended his lecture half a year later and published it with the title *La pensée symbolique et la pensée de l'enfant* (Piaget 1923/2).

3. In Moscow, Spielrein worked at the Polyclinic of the Psychoanalytical Institute until Stalin closed all psychoanalytical institutes in 1934. On 11 August 1942, she was gunned down by the Nazis, together with her two daughters Renata and Eva, just outside Rostow.
4. Piaget usually shortened the surnames of his test persons and noted their ages as (year; month; day).
5. This foreword was only published in the French edition.
6. In November 1925, the Laura Spelman Rockefeller Memorial promised subsidies to match the Institute's other income (to a maximum of $5,000). From 1926–27, the Rockefeller Foundation also supported the Bühlers' Institute in Vienna. Other institutes, such as the National Foundation for Educational Research, were supported by the Carnegie Foundation. While American foundations enabled the establishment of pedagogic networks and experiments, which attempted to counter-act fascism, American bankers, such as W. Averell Harriman, Clarence Dillon and Prescott Bush, the father and grandfather of the later presidents, helped finance the rise of Hitler (Tarpley and Chaitkin 1992). The Centre for Genetic Epistemology, which Piaget founded in 1956, was also largely financed by the Rockefeller Foundation.
7. Xypas showed that Piaget had violated numerous principles of formal logic in his speech (despite having studied logic under Brunschvicg and Lalande), such as "the sophism of declaring, as resolved, the very thing one is about to resolve" (Xypas 2001: 94).
8. According to Gregory Bateson (1972), double-bind situations cause schizophrenia, of which autism is a symptom (Bleuler 1911).
9. Piaget published:

	books	contributions	articles	reviews	introductions forewords	speeches interviews	reports	Number of pages
Biology	3	2	37	1		2		1,000
Religion	1		8	4		2	1	260
Philosophy	8	2	11	6	2	3		1,750
Psychology	35	72	192	26	41	27	2	17,000
Education		8	20	2	16	37	16	1,000
Social-psychology	1	7	8		1			810
Epistemology	40	14	28	5	4	7	1	7,860
Sum	88	105	304	44	64	78	20	29,680

10. Szeminska returned to Poland just one day before it was attacked by Nazi Germany. She committed herself to the Polish Red Cross and the antifascist resistance. In 1942, she was arrested, imprisoned for nine months, and subsequently deported to Auschwitz where she remained until 1945 and survived. After the war she worked in teacher training

and taught at the Warsaw Institute of Pedagogy where she became a professor in 1956. She translated texts by the Marxist psychologist Wallon but the communist regime did not permit her to translate Piaget's texts. In 1967, she was allowed to travel and went to Geneva several times, where she received the title of Honorary Doctor in 1979 for her work on the development of the concepts of series, classes and numbers.

11. Even though it is considered to be a synthesis of his previous theses, his most important work on epistemology and the theory and history of sciences has not been translated into English.

Part 3

The Reception and Influence of Piaget's Work

13

The Reception

In 1984, the Centre for Genetic Epistemology was closed. Piaget's hopes of a "possible great future" (Piaget 1966/9: 18) for the ICGE were not fulfilled. Despite 25 years of intensive research and extensive publications, genetic epistemology received very little attention from the science theorists and from the scientists. On the basis of his early work in psychology, Piaget was generally perceived as a developmental psychologist in the field of child thought and his holistic ambitions were disregarded. Although he no longer defined himself as a psychologist during the last decade of his life, he was praised as one of the "few giants in contemporary psychology" (Berlyne 1976: 15), "who has upset the world of developmental psychology [...] Sigmund Freud discovered the unconscious, it is said, and Piaget discovered the conscious" (Hall, in Piaget 1970/9: 28).

The Construction of a Genius

Through the subtle construction of his autobiography and with his statements given during interviews, Piaget had skillfully supported the general perception that he was a genius. Almost all biographical accounts report the legend of Piaget's early maturity, which he displayed in his "scientific" publication on an albino sparrow. "This short paper is generally considered as the start of a brilliant scientific career" (Smith 2000; cf. e.g. Heidbrink 2005). This observation report of the "child prodigy of science" (Altwegg 1983: 147) was elevated to be a sign of extraordinary predestination. The myth of Piaget being a revolutionary of psychology connects his early "scientific" education with the application of philosophical issues to the "new" field of child thought: "Piaget's genius combines the tenacity and skill of a precise scientist with his brilliant acumen for theory" (Elkind 1978: 584). Piaget liked to portray himself as an innovator, who generated new ideas on his solitary walks: "I have always preferred to reflect on a problem before reading on it" (Piaget 1952/1: 111). And he knew how to cultivate the impression of being a pioneer: "Well, I think my role has been, above all, to raise problems—problems which other people were not seeing, because they were not looking at things from this interdisciplinary point of view" (Piaget 1973: 33). His disciples adopted this self-appraisal:

> What never ceases to impress us is the fact that Piaget is always ahead; ahead of his time, ahead of topical problems, ahead of the accepted solutions, even ahead of train time tables and flight times. This psychologist has asked himself questions which, due to their genetic viewpoint, have revolutionized our view of the human subject. (Inhelder 1976: 199)

Part of the construction of a revolutionary is the attributed knowledge about the mission he had to carry out. Thus, Piaget "was totally aware of his break with the Western tradition of epistemology" (Glasersfeld 1994: 16). To build a legend, something amazing or surprising is required as well: "The fact that children said that the quantity of liquid changes merely through pouring it from one vessel into another of different proportions is a phenomenon that has played a large part in making Piaget's reputation. (What is the prophet without his miracles?)" (Lloyd 1983: 109). One of the most important characteristics of a prophet is the unity of his doctrine. "From the years of his education to his last writings, the same core of intellectual issues and the same general framework of concepts have given a rather exceptional unity to this work" (Ducret 1990: 5). Placing the emphasis on continuity does not only allow a reduction of the complexity, of the breaks and contradictions, but also allows the distillation of an original message. Considering the portrayal of Piaget in secondary literature and his numerous awards, his own stage management had been very successful indeed.

Geographical Reception

Piaget found a reception primarily in those countries that had close connections with the JJRI: France, Spain and Poland. But his theory gained its most lasting influence in the USA.

In 1931, Piaget was invited by Carl Murchison to write the entry about "Children's philosophies" (Piaget 1931/1) into the renowned *Handbook of Psychology*, whereupon he suddenly was well known in the English-speaking world. But a few years later, his name disappeared. On one hand, educators did not like his logical view and his too scientific and insufficiently child-centered approach. On the other hand, experimental psychologists, such as Florence Goodenough (1886–1959), criticized him for being too child-centered and insufficiently experimental. "Piaget was caught in the middle, during a period in which different psychologies were battling for supremacy within academe and for dominance in the world of the school and the nursery school, and different pedagogies were competing for control of the classroom" (Beatty 2004). The behaviorists were the most important factor behind the repression of Piaget in the USA in the 1930s. "None of Piaget's books were translated into English between 1933 and 1949" (Flavell 1963: 10), despite his lectures at Harvard University, Columbia University and Johns Hopkins University in 1936. Thanks to the support of Henry A. Murray (1893–1988), a biologist, psychologist and disciple of Jung, Piaget was awarded the first of 35 *honoris causa* doctorates at Harvard. This choice was a compromise, because the other well-known candidates Freud, Jung, Ivan Pavlov (1872–1951), eugenist Lewis Terman (1877–1956) and Edward Thorndike (1874–1949) were either unable to attend, or no clear decision in their favor could be reached (Hsueh 2004).

With the decline of behaviorism in the late 1950s, genetic psychology experienced a renaissance, thanks to Jerrold Zacharias, Jerome Bruner, David Weikart, J. McVicker Hunt, John H. Flavell, Richard Ripple, Verne Rockcastle, David Ausubel, and Millie Almy. The most widely read writings of Piaget concerned the development during early and middle childhood, while the logical and epistemological theories were normally ignored. Piaget was integrated in and reactivated the traditions of James, Baldwin and Hall as well as of the progressive education. But he had a low opinion of "the American question" about how to accelerate development and stage transition: "If the aim is to accelerate the development of these operations, it is idiotic" (Piaget 1973/15: 22). Nonetheless, it was primarily the pedagogues who referred to his psychology, a phenomenon he was at a loss to explain: "It's a mystery. I don't know what happened. In Geneva no one pays any attention" (Piaget 1973/15: 22). This success might be based in the fact that Piaget advocated a Protestant, individualistic and nonsexual view of the child, whereby the subliminal determinism eased the responsibility of the educator.

British educators gave more credit to the theories of John Dewey and Susan Isaacs than they did to Piaget (Weber 1971). Nevertheless, Piaget influenced the English primary school in the 1960s, mainly through the reception of his writings by the Froebel movement. In 1955, Nathan Isaacs, a prominent spokesman for science education in primary school, published *Some Aspects of Piaget's Work*, which moulded the way Piaget was understood. Based on this interpretation, the Nuffield Junior Science Project (1963–1967) produced three guides for teachers, while the Oxford Primary Science Project (1964) tried to combine the approaches of Piaget and Susan Isaacs (Hall 2000).

In Latin America, genetic psychology became an argument in the social and political fight for liberation. Piaget was most widely read in Brazil, where Helena Antipoff had been working since 1929, and where Paulo Freire (1921–1997) organized literacy campaigns for the poor in the early 1960s. Here, the model of stages was of less interest than the constructivist assumption that the human being creates himself through cooperation, and that his future is not determined by heredity or social background.

In the Soviet Union, several of Piaget's theorems found approval, such as the idea that cognitive development originated from actions, but his bio-logic reduction of reason met with criticism. It was argued that intellectual development was not fostered by intrinsic laws but through education. In 1955, when Piaget was in Moscow as President of the International Union of Scientific Psychology, he explained to Peter Galparin (1902–1988) that his skeptical position was based upon his observation of pedagogical reality whereas Galparin's approach was simply a theoretically possible education in an imaginary world. Galparin is said to have replied that the real was only a special case of the possible (in Veer 1996). In his report (Piaget 1956/5) on this journey, Piaget mentioned the other participants but not Galparin, whose statement was adopted by Piaget in his last works.

In the remaining European countries, and in Japan, the discussion of Piaget's work began later and with a greater hesitation. During the 1960s and 1970s, however, his developmental theory was integrated into the psy-chological canon, and its basic concepts were taught in the teachers' col-leges. In 1996, on the occasion of his 100th birthday, events were held in Argentina, Brazil, Canada, France, Great Britain, Japan, Mexico, Portugal, Spain, Switzerland, and in the USA.

Critique of the Developmental Psychology

From the 1960s onwards, comparative studies on Piaget's experiments were undertaken. Because Piaget's research had been qualitative, he was wor-ried and, because he did not speak English, asked his colleague, Jacques Vonèche, to enquire about the results of this new research. The first replica-tions still yielded the same results, but other researchers were soon criticiz-ing Piaget's experiments and began to modify them. These studies showed that Piaget had underestimated the abilities of newborn babies, toddlers and younger children, in most areas (Donaldson 1978; Harris 1983; Goswami 2001; Rauh 2002; Sodian 2002; Wilkening and Krist 2002). Shortly after birth, babies are capable of constant perception (Butterworth and Cochran 1980; Rose and Ruff 1987; Stern 1985: 47ff.), of hand-eye coordination (Hofsten 1982; 1983; Harris 1983; Lockman 1990) and imitation (Meltzoff and Moore 1989). Object permanency already appears at the age of three or four months (Uzgiris and Hunt 1970; Bower 1977; 1989; Bremner 1985; Baillargeon 1991), a result Piaget (1976a: 224) accepted with astonishment. As early as within the first six months, they seem to have an intuitive understanding of space, movement, causality and the stability of objects (Gelman and Baillargeon 1978; Bullock, Gelman and Baillargeon 1982; Leslie 1982; Anderson and Wilkening 1991; Spelke, Breinlinger, Macomber and Jacobson 1992; Spelke 2000). Two-year-olds are capable of discriminating, representing, and remembering small numbers of items (Starkey and Cooper 1980). Three-year-old children can distinguish between the mental and the physical world (Wellman and Estes 1986) and understand the difference between intention and chance (Shultz, Wells and Sardia 1980). From the age of four, they possess a "concept of belief," which enables them to differentiate between subjective convictions and reality (Wimmer and Perner 1983). Preschool children are more competent with numbers (Bryant and Trabasso 1971; Siegler and Opfer 2003), at measuring (Bryant and Kopytynska 1976), at estimating speed (Wilkening 1981), at drawing transitive conclusions (Braine 1959; Pears and Bryant 1990), at class inclusion (McGarrigle, Grieve and Hughes 1974; Povey and Hill 1975) and at understanding causality (Donaldson 1986) than Piaget had assumed.

Studies on egocentrism, which were resumed during the mid-1960s, revealed that "egocentric reactions were based relatively often on misunderstandings, rather than on the child's inability to identify the other person's point of view" (Aebli, Montada and Schneider 1968: 16). Children as young as three years of age consider, in appropriate settings, the other person's perspective (Borke 1971; 1975; Lemperers, Flavell and Flavell 1977; Hudges and Donaldson 1983) and begin to have empathy with the emotional situations of others (Bischof-Köhler 1988). From the age of four, they behave in a cooperative way (Charlesworth and Hartup 1967; Gelman 1979). The communicative competence of preschool children is also much greater than Piaget had assumed (Church 1961; Slama-Cazacu 1961). Moreover, egocentrism is much stronger at age 12 than in younger children (Elkind 1967; Donaldson 1978; Enright, Schukla and Lapsley 1980). Depending on situations, practically everybody thinks and acts egocentrically, especially in political-ideological areas (Buggle 1985: 104). Piaget did not take into account that the "forms and contents of egocentrism are culture-specific and also dependent on social strata" (Eck 1979: 103; cf. Völzing 1982). Cohen concluded from Piaget's insufficient recognition of the child's abilities that "it is not the children who lack decentration, but Piaget and his disciples!" (Cohen 1981: 115).

Children who are 6 to 8 years old can master simple formal operations (Karplus 1980) such as dealing with proportions (Brainerd 1976). Piaget's stages often fail to correspond to specific abilities, such as the capacity to draw analogous conclusions (Goswami 1992). Very different results are obtained from the operation tasks, depending on their complexity, clarity, abstractness or the degree of verbalization (Donaldson 1978), so that the results cannot be slotted into a global grid. Furthermore, the same child will solve different tasks on comparable subject matters in very different ways (Pinard and Laurendeau 1969; Seiler 1973; Gelman and Baillargeon 1983), which proves that cognitive structures are domain specific.

As Piaget had underestimated the preschool children, so he overestimated the logical abilities of older children. Children of working-class or middle-class backgrounds only reach the concrete stage at the age of 12, and the formal stage at the age of 16 (Sutherland 1992: 76, 110). One essential reason for this is that logical understanding depends to a great degree on linguistic competence (Johnson-Laird and Byrne 1991). Between 40 per cent and 60 per cent of adolescents and adults in the Western world never reach the stage of formal operations, or will only reach this stage in specific fields of knowledge (Neimark 1978; Dasen and Heron 1981; Scribner 1984). To solve complex tasks, even grammar-school pupils have to rely on illustrative material. In fact the experiments conducted by Inhelder only dealt with concrete-operational structures of thinking (Boden 1979: 83). Laux was therefore of the opinion that "visualizing thought" "is never abandoned, but becomes more refined, and remains functional alongside other forms" (Laux 1969: 180). Furthermore, expertise is not characterized by the application of formal logic but by the application of strategies (Polya 1954: 275ff.). Rather than using a formal system of stages, a model that concentrates upon the integration of skills should be more suitable (Brown and Desforges 1977). Because formal operations reveal nothing about the quality of knowledge and skills, the question frequently arose of whether formal operations truly were the highest form of development (for example, Galperin, cited in Van der Veer 1996: 215ff.). A fifth stage would grant the individual access to dialectic thinking (Riegel 1973; Meacham and Riegel 1978), or would describe problem-generating thinking (Arlin 1975). Piaget (1950 I: 215ff.; Piaget and Ackermann-Valladao 1983: Chapter 7) wondered about postformal operations in the thinking of experts but did not consider this to be a further stage. Basically, the transitions between the stages in his theory remain dubious because his theory cannot explain why each new step in the development occurs (Kagan 1984: 262).

Development is by no means a uniform process, as Piaget assumed, but there may even be setbacks: for example, 5-month-old babies can aim better when reaching for an object, after the light has been turned off, than older babies do (Bower 1979). Also, in Magalie Bovet's (1974) conservation experiments with Algerian children, unexpected results were obtained: 7- to

8-year-old children who had understood the conservation of fluids, relapsed into the preoperational phase one year later, and rediscovered the conservation of fluids between the ages of 9 and 10. Such phenomena and cultural differences cannot be explained with Piaget's theory (Dasen 1972; Carlson 1978).

Piaget supposed that "the child is the real primitive among us, the missing link between prehistorical men and contemporary adults" (Vonèche and Bovet 1982: 88). Since the 1960s, more than a thousand cross-cultural studies have been carried out (Oesterdiekhoff 1997: 36), which show that all children pass through the sensory-motor and preoperational stages (Werner 1979). According to Hallpike (1979), simple societies, as a rule, do not reach the concrete-operational stage, probably because the ability to draw syllogistic conclusions requires a school training of at least three years (Scribner 1984). But the results depend on the settings, as well. When 6-year-old children (of the Wolof people in Senegal) poured the liquids in the conservation test themselves, the rate of operative thinkers rose from 25 per cent to 67 per cent (Greenfield 1966). In any case, the level of cognition in primitive societies cannot be equated to the preoperational stage, because "ontogenesis and historiogenesis are two fundamentally different processes" (Damerow 1994: 314). Even in the industrial societies, the stage of concrete operation is not reached everywhere (Peluffo 1967). Buck-Morss (1975) criticized Piaget's theory as being ethnocentric because it reflects the capitalist industrial society. The Western scientific logic, which had been used as a standard, gave rise to a deficit-orientation, particularly regarding the pre-operational level (Cole and Bruner 1971). In addition, the Occidental logic is not a pure logic of the mind but must also be seen as a product of this culture (Damerow and Lefèvre 1998). Piaget's developmental goals were therefore rejected as unsuitable (Emler 1983: 145), together with the idea of a linear and uniform development. "We must not imagine a unique line of development emanating from any initial state, but rather picture a number of such lines radiating in all directions from the starting state toward end-points, both desirable and not" (Scheffler 1985: 57). Brown and Desforges (1977) concluded that the notion of stages created more conceptual problems than it solved, because each area of achievement is different from other domains. Piaget never devised a systematic theory to take care of the many abnormalities and contradictions, but "tended to amend the global and universal theory of stages" (Reusser 2006: 172).

The logico-mathematical structures, which control the experience of the individual, were criticized as a tautological concept: "Piaget adds an abstract generalization to the result of his studies, e.g. on the development of the concept of numbers, which is supposed to explain the object (the child's thinking) through processes, which in themselves are an arbitrary abstraction from the object" (Steeg 1996: 44f.). A general level of structures (competence), which forms the basis of any specific performance, cannot actually be identified (Krist and Wilkening 1991). Piaget, on the other hand, did not distinguish "between the acquisition of operational competence and the construction and expansion of categorical forms" (Dux 2000: 228), but based all of it upon a logico-mathematical structure. "We cannot claim that the objects and events of everyday life derive from operations of the algebraic group" (Dux 1994: 183f.).

The thesis of equilibration, the core of Piaget's system, was criticized for being undefined (Kesselring 1999: 81), not proven (Ducret 1984: 30), superfluous (Bruner 1959: 369; Bryant 1972; Boden 1979: 101) and paradoxical: "The equilibrium embodied in logic and mathematics is [...] the *telos*, the 'end' of development, and paradoxically, also its origin" (Jardine 2006: 68). The late assumption that development occurs through contradictions was deemed to be "simply wrong on an empirical level" (Ros 1994: 165). The concepts of assimilation and accommodation were judged as a "model which derives its power from forming analogies, and thereby descends into a completely meaningless teleology of adaptation" (Steeg 1996: 45). Many students, who have to learn Piaget's theory, confuse accommodation with adaptation, for obvious reasons. The parallel between organic and cognitive development has led to a "quasi theory of maturing" (Ausubel 1968) and was "a throwback to the 'nativism' of Rousseau, and the 'vitalism' of Henri Bergson" (Skinner 1980: 174).

Piaget's assumption that all knowledge is rooted in spontaneous action with objects turned out to be incorrect (Anthony 1977). Children with amputated or immobile limbs do not show any retardation in their development (Décarie 1969) and notions of phenomena which lie outside our range of action, such as sky and earth, would not be possible (Merleau-Ponty 1988: 250ff.). Concepts are "acquired through abstraction and therefore not interiorised" (Steeg 1996: 55; cf. Schwarz 1996: 115–119). It is true that Furth (1966) proved that the essential cognitive abilities do not depend on language because 14-year-old deaf children can classify or form generic terms equally well as hearing children of the same age. But sensory-motor activities cannot explain the linguistic constraints (Karmiloff-Smith 1992) because there is neither a direct link between action and language, nor between language and representation (Mandler 1990; 1991). Nehemia Jordan's report (1972) of a highly intelligent woman, who had not been able to move since birth, defeated Piaget's thesis.

It is not the case that the development of language begins once the sensory-motor coordinations are completed. A two-month-old baby already begins to communicate with his minders by making noises (Zimmer 1986). Smedslund (1966), Hamlyn (1978: 42ff.), Broughton (1981), Schaffer

(1989) and many others criticized Piaget's neglect of social, emotional and physical aspects in his studies. "Piaget believed that children are like scientists, working alone on the physical, logical, and mathematical material of their world to make sense of reality" (Tudge and Winterhoff 1993: 311). Thus, in Piaget's studies, social everyday life appeared as something alien, "which we have to 'add' to psychology in an interdisciplinary manner" (Rijsman 1996: 157). In fact, babies are much more interested in persons than in objects (Wells 1981), and the first things they recognize are human faces (Fantz 1961). Children achieve better results from teamwork than from individual work (Doise, Mugny and Perret-Clermont 1975; Bruner, Jolly and Sylva 1976: 282f.). Since Piaget defined the process of development as being formal, he "simply had no methodological motive to account for the fact that the constructive process takes place through communication" (Dux 2000: 219). Children, however, are strongly influenced by the experimenter and by the test setting. In the conservation experiments, 4-year-old children did much better when the experimenter dressed up as a bear (McGarrigle and Donaldson 1975). Because Piaget had felt no need for control groups or tests in different social or ethnical settings and because his information on the experiments was "anecdotal in character" (Boden 1979: 153) he obviously was not really concerned with the verification of his assumptions. The esotericism of his research practice, however, had an unexpected effect: "It is difficult to think of another theorist who has provoked quite so much comparative research" (Lloyd 1983: 36).

In contrast to Piaget's assumptions, 3-to 6-year-olds do not act because of possible sanctions (Nunner-Winkler 1992: 261), and "young children do make moral judgments that go well beyond heteronomous obedience to authority and rules" (Turiel 1983: 148). Whereas the connection between social constraint and conformism had been examined and confirmed by Serge Moscovici (1984), the link between constraint and transcendence, which Piaget had claimed (1928/1: 13), could not be established. Moreover, moral judgments are formed in a domain-specific way (Smetana 1981; Davidson *et al.* 1983) because children regularly evaluate behavior according to three distinct conceptual domains: moral, conventional, and personal rules. Piaget overlooked the fact that game rules are not moral rules, but conventions (Kölbl 2005: 242). This is why John Watt described the marble game as "a surprising choice of material for a book on *moral judgement*" (Watt 1989: 176). In contrast to Piaget's assumption, 5-year-olds think that game rules can be changed. As they get older, the children begin to believe that the rules are unchangeable and this belief grows stronger until the age of 12 (Colby and Kohlberg 1978: 354). Adolescents, on the other hand, consider these rules as conventions in order to regulate games (Brooks-Walsh and Sullivan 1973), but a similar notion concerning political rules within a democracy does not necessarily apply (Heidbrink 1991).

Contrary to Piaget's statements regarding the higher complexity of games played by boys, research has not identified any significant difference between the sexes, as far as moral judgments or moral actions are concerned (Döbert 1991: 132f.). Lickona (1976) believed that Piaget was only interested in moral competence of a general nature, and in intelligence. He had therefore failed to distinguish between action and moral judgment, which had been investigated by Jurkovic (1980). Among preschool children, there is a discrepancy between these two areas because knowledge exists before motivation and only in the course of development will they approach each other (Gerson and Damon 1978; Nunner-Winkler 2005: 180f.). There are enormous cultural differences: While Icelandic children act in an egoistical way for a long time, despite their moral knowledge, Chinese children show a much greater consistency between action and judgment (Keller 2005: 163f.). Furthermore, Piaget's thesis of an intellectual and moral parallelism cannot be maintained. Peters (1966: 326) observed that Piaget had failed to explain how autonomy becomes possible in a peer group. Research confirms the importance of the peer group for moral development, it is true (Doise 1978; Krappmann 1994), but parents and school also foster moral development, if they create an affectively positive climate (Hoffman 2000; Edelstein, Oser and Schuster 2001).

Critique of the Epistemology

Alberto Munari identified a contradiction between Piaget's psychological approach and his epistemological one. Piaget's psychological research assumed objective laws of development, which manifest themselves, for example, in clearly identifiable and biologically founded stages. His epistemological reflection, however, was based on the assumption that "the concept of a stage must be understood more as a kind of sudden structuring or re-structuring, which is partially unforeseeable, and always provisional and instable" (Munari 1994: 329). Other critics such as Moessinger (1981) also deplored the contradictory relation of Piaget's theory and his experiments. On the one hand, Piaget followed Galileo's tradition of *scienza nuova* (Fetz 1978; Wetzel 1978), in which a communicative validation of insights appears unnecessary (Rotman 1977: 180f.). Thus he had "claimed, in a fashion that appears naïve, that he could, with his method, decide issues of epistemology in an empirical way" (Kesselring 1999: 189). Since Piaget believed that his "experimental" research, which was carried out with the qualitative method of "clinical" interviews, would expose an objective nature of thought, he was called a "science realist" (Neuhäuser 2003: 213). Although he advocated a historio-critical method, his thesis of the parallelism between individual development and scientific history led to "a positivist interpretation of history [...] Piaget's history coincides with the history of formal transformations reduced to the universal mathematical laws" (Venn and Walkerdine 1978: 90). Piaget did not only disregard "the nature and the historical importance of mathematical *proof*" (Boden 1979: 100) but also the context in which scientific theories developed and the track record of problems within a discipline. His postulate that "genetic epistemology attempts to explain knowledge, and in particular scientific knowledge, on the basis of its history, its sociogenesis, and especially the psychological origins of the notions and operation upon which it is based" (Piaget 1970a: 7), was refuted as a genetic fallacy. Practically nobody accepted Piaget's concepts of parallelism or isomorphism, with which he believed to have overcome the gap between science theory and epistemology. On the other hand, Piaget was conceived as being "undoubtedly the pioneer of the constructivist-oriented cognition research of this century" (Glasersfeld 1994: 18). But with the notion of accommodation, Piaget had implicitly imported "a copy theory into his own explanation of the process of imitation [...] Imitation is an essential factor in the constitution of representative activity, whereas play is not" (Sutton-Smith 1966: 141f.). In his response, Piaget claimed to "have never said that representative or symbolic thought, including concept formation, is derived from imitation" (Piaget 1966/14: 515), although he had done (Piaget 1945: 94, 133; 1954/10: 271). Since Piaget argued in a realist, as well as in a constructivist way, it makes no sense to label him a representative of radical constructivism (Glasersfeld 1987: 99ff.).

Overall, Piaget's conciliating approach seems "like a resurgence of the problem situation of the 19th century" (Ottavi 2001: 274). His thinking was based on dualist concepts, such as spontaneous self versus social rules, constraint versus cooperation, empirical versus reflective abstraction, or reality versus construction, which are conciliated in the course of development. The notion of structural transformations "is an excellent example of what Rorty calls a *tertium quid*, a 'third thing' that dualistic theories require to mediate between an organism and its environment" (Russell 1983: 177). Due to his harmonizing target of development, Piaget's philosophy could be termed as monist finalism (cf. Brockmeier 1996: 139) or idealism. Gruber and Vonèche (1977: 785) identified four idealistic aspects: "the teleological note of auto-regulation, the assertion that cognitive processes are an organ, the claim of their universality and completeness, and the ultimate separation of form and content."

14

The Influence

Piaget had a considerable influence on psychology, particularly on developmental psychology and on the discourse in pedagogy in the 1960s and 1970s (Murray 1979). Twenty years after his death, he still occupied the third position, after Freud and Foucault, in the ranking of the most quoted social scientists (Kesselring 1999: 199).

Impacts on Psychology

Piaget, as a "prophet" and as an adversary as well, had an enormous impact on the research of developmental psychology. In 1975, he was identified as the most-cited psychologist in the world (Endler, Rushton and Roediger 1978: 1074) and in 2002, he was still number 4, after Skinner, Freud, and Bandura (Haggbloom 2002). Many psychologists like Erik H. Erikson (1902–1994) appreciated the genetic psychology as a promising alternative to behaviorism, and Piaget was one of the founders of cognitive psychology, together with Edward Tolman (1932), Donald E. Broadbent (1958), Ulric Neisser (1967) and others. But the alleged "cognitive revolution" (Gardner 1985; Miller 2003; O'Donohue, Ferguson and Naugle 2003) in the history of the social sciences is an exaggerated interpretation because there has never been a global change of paradigm (Andler 1998). Amazingly, Piaget hardly had any influence in the fields of cognitive sciences and in biological psychology (cf. Birbaumer and Schmidt 1996).

But he had a lasting effect on the theory of moral development, thanks to Lawrence Kohlberg (1927–1987). Kohlberg's model seems to be based on a combination of *The Moral Judgment of the Child* and a draft by Piaget's religious-psychological research group, who were searching for a normative reason for the judgment of values:

Individuals, as different as they may be, can, for instance, pass through stages which follow upon each other in a constant order. Let us assume the existence of six different types. Once type 6 has passed through types 1, 2, 3 etc., one could admit that these apparent types constitute the stages of the same evolution. Some reach stage 6, others stop at stage 2, or 4, or 5, and so forth. The question of what is normal would then simply be a question of constancy in the development, and would thus be a matter of psychology. (Piaget 1923/3: 50)

Kohlberg's system, to which other thinkers, such as George Herbert Mead (1863–1931), Dewey or Baldwin contributed significant impulses, contains six stages on three levels (preconventional, conventional and postconventional level). According to Kohlberg (1969), three trends within moral development could be confirmed:

- Shift of judgment away from objective damage towards intention. Judgments depend, however, on a great number of factors, and "the same child may judge by intentions in one case, and consequences in another" (Emler 1983: 141).
- Shift from absolute assessments (either true or false) towards relative judgments.
- Shift from punishment-orientation towards judgments independent of sanctions.

Kohlberg and Clark Power (1981) advocated the thesis that the attainment of the developmental stage of morality was a necessary, albeit insufficient, precondition for respective religious judgments. Elkind (1961) found a link between Piaget's cognitive stages and a child's identification of various religious communities. Ronald Goldman (1964) examined children's understanding of religious doctrines, such as the omnipotence of God and their interpretation of Bible stories. He reached the conclusion that children are only able to understand religious concepts adequately after the age of 13 and suggested that younger children should not be confronted with them. Like Kohlberg, Fritz Oser and Paul Gmünder (1992) constructed a theory of stages on the basis of how decisions in stories containing dilemmas were explained. Thus, the concept of God develops, as is the case in Piaget's thesis, from an absolute concept of God to an immanent one, which respects religious autonomy. Piaget's religious work had some influence on American sociology through Guy Swanson's (1967) use of the concept of immanence. James Fowler (1989) based his theory upon Piaget, Erikson and Kohlberg and postulated that development over six stages would lead to a universalistic, tolerant and committed faith. Heinz Streib (2001) added the "lifespan" approach to this theory, in order to break through the one-dimensional nature of Piaget's tradition. Lifespan theories expand Piaget's four stages and examine development until a ripe old age (Looft

1972; Whitbourne and Weinstock 1979; Baltes 1987). The fact that cognitive development is not completed with the formal stage is doubtlessly true (Alexander, Langer and Oetter 1986).

Several attempts were made to identify common features between Piaget and Freud (Anthony 1957; Wolff 1960; Haynal 1975; Sandler 1975; Peters 1978; Schneider 1981; Furth 1990). Because Piaget's earlier essays on the subject of psychoanalysis (1920/2; 1923/2; 1923/3; 1933/3) were largely unknown, these authors usually noted "a nice theoretical agreement between psychoanalytical and genetic-cognitive assumptions" (Liebsch 1986: 238). On the other hand, Leber (1995) saw in Piaget's theory on affectivity an instrument to revise problematic psychoanalytical concepts like narcissism or transfer.

Impacts on Pedagogy

Enthusiasm for Piaget's psychological work was stronger and more lasting in education than in psychology, although, in his later years, Piaget, as well as Inhelder, distanced themselves from pedagogical issues. Not one of 58 contributions in the 1,200-page encyclopaedia about Piaget (Steiner 1978) dealt with pedagogy. Furthermore, at the homage which took place at the University of Geneva on 3 November 1981, the Director of UNESCO, Amadou-Mahtar M'Bow, held a lecture on Piaget's contribution to the IBE that was the only one not published in the *Archives de Psychologie* in March 1982. Despite this shunning of pedagogy, repeated attempts were made to render Piaget's psychology useful for education (Aebli 1951; Sigel 1969; Gorman 1972; Charles 1974; Lowery 1974; Sprinthall and Sprinthall 1974; Sund 1976; Fuller 1977; Labinowicz 1980; Kubli 1983; DeLisi and Goldbeck 1999; Jardine 2006). In a first phase of application, the theory of stages was used as a means of diagnosis of learning capacities (Pinard and Laurendeau 1964; Beilin 1965). But tests based on Piaget did not show a better prognostic validity than others (Goldschmid and Bentler 1968). Then, in the early 1970s, direct instruction was replaced by active discovery learning in groups (Furth 1970; Sinclair and Kamii 1970; Schwebel and Raph 1973; Elkind 1976). At the same time, conflicts or contradictions were regarded as the main instrument in teaching (Langer 1969; Furth and Wachs 1974; Turiel 1974; Doise, Mugny and Perret-Clermond 1975; Moessinger 1977; Kuhn 1979; Smock 1981). This old principle of discrepancies as the motor of learning was used in Forman's School for Constructive Play (Forman and Kuschner 1977) and in Sigel's Child Care Research Center Program in Princeton, New Jersey (Copple, Sigel and Saunders 1979). Up to now, "Piagetian constructivism has been attractive to

educators because it emphasizes precisely those humanistic aspects of cognitive acquisition that behaviorism has denied—the creative activity of the
human agent organizing herself and her environment" (Bidell and Fischer
1992: 11).

The strongest impact of Piaget could be observed in preschool education:
The Early Childhood Curriculum (Lavatelli 1970) in Illinois and Missouri
tried to promote concrete operations with the help of concrete materials.
David Weikart developed the *Perry Preschool Project* in Ypsilanti, Michigan,
and the *Cognitevely Oriented Curriculum*, which served as the model of the
Head Start Planned Variation Study (Weikart, Rogers, Adcock and McClelland
1971). The *Piagetian Preschool Education Program* (Bingham-Newman, Saunders and Hooper 1976) offered 200 suggestions to foster operations like
seriation or classification in small groups. These programs were refuted as
misuse of Piaget's psychology. "Children do not have to learn to seriate little sticks or dolls in order to become capable of concrete operations [...]
Teaching this is ridiculous if our real aim is logical thinking" (Kamii and
DeVries 1972: 390). Rheta DeVries and Constance Kamii presented their
own program, which allowed the child free choice of activity in a wide
range of offered games and experiments, in three books. Piaget praised
their project as the best application of his psychology because "they have
well understood (unlike so many others) [its] essentially 'constructivist'
character" (Piaget 1978/1: VII).

In schools, Piaget's doctrine has had an enormous influence on curric-
ular reforms of "modern mathematics" and science education (Copeland
1970; Cambon 1977; Kubli 1981; Kamii and DeClark 1985; Aikenhead 1996;
Bryant 1996). The operative principle has been one of the main approaches
in the didactics of mathematics since 1960 (Fricke 1959; Wittmann 1982).
The application of Piaget's principles to science subjects led to the syllabi
Science 5–13 in the UK, to the *Australian Science Education Project* and to the
Science Curriculum Improvement Study in the USA (Mackay 1983).

Some schools, such as the Westfield Infants School in Leicestershire,
structured their lessons around spontaneous and pupil-directed learning,
with the help of concrete material (Pulaski 1971: 170f.). Pulaski felt that
"regarding the failings of traditional schools, Piaget has shown us how to
solve this problem—by allowing the teachers more initiative, more freedom and a better grounding in child psychology and research" (Pulaski
1971: 173f.). But the antiauthoritarian education movement referred much
more to other models of reform than to Piaget. Rémy Droz arrived at the
conclusion "that, in pedagogical matters, Piaget is hardly more than an
enlightened amateur; all Piaget's pedagogical texts are interspersed with
evidence of his ignorance in the world of pedagogical ideas and practices"
(Droz 1980: 23).

Piaget's assistant Hans Aebli, who was disliked by his patron because of his conservative stance (Fuchs 2002: 191), discovered that it was impossible to derive any didactics from genetic psychology: "If Piaget's genetic studies prove that an operation exists at a specific age, then the child *will not require* to be taught this operation *any more*. However, if this operation does not yet exist, the child cannot yet be instructed in it" (Aebli 1963: 88). This paradox (Droz 1980) deprives teachers of their legitimacy to teach and reduces their role to shaping the learning environment. Piaget's pedagogy was therefore called a "horticultural philosophy" (Brainerd 1978: 284), which contented itself with a "watering can methodology" (Schurz 1985: 350). Piaget's theory was reproached for having mainly served to find out what children could not yet do (Watt 1989: 176; Metz 1995), which, according to Egan (2002), had resulted in an intellectual impoverishment of Primary School. But Charles Brainerd reviewed comparative studies and concluded that there were hardly any differences between Piagetian settings and traditional instruction. "Those few comparisons which revealed differences tended to favor the traditional group" (Brainerd 1978: 293). Since the 1980s, Piaget's name disappears more and more from the literature on didactics but the fear of expecting too much at too early an age is still widely present (cf. Egan 2005). Nevertheless, Piaget remains one of the most often quoted authors of pedagogy (Horn 2001).

The Other Disciplines

While Piaget had a formative effect on pedagogy and developmental psychology, his influence upon other scientific disciplines and trends remained marginal. This may be astounding, at least as far as structuralism and sociology are concerned. Although the concept of structure was part of the core of his theory, although he introduced structuralism into developmental psychology, although his book on structuralism (Piaget 1968) was a huge success and attracted great public attention and although there are many theoretical analogies to Pierre Bourdieu (1930–2002) (Perrenoud 1976: 465ff.), Piaget never entered history as a structuralist (cf., for example, Dosse 1991). It is true that Thomas S. Kuhn (1962: vi) had been influenced by Piaget but his main source had been Ludwik Fleck's book of 1935. In science theory or in cultural history, Piaget's effect remained limited, extending only to individual exponents. Ulrich Oevermann (2002), for example, partially implemented Piaget's idea of an objective sociology with his project of objective hermeneutics, replacing Piaget's biologism with a conception of sociogenesis altogether (Oevermann 1979). Günter Dux attempted to overcome Piaget's biologist logic of development with his own historio-genetic theory of culture, because, according to Dux, Piaget had "systematically omitted to take up the trail of history, or [. . .] had, in fact, virtually denied its existence" (Dux 2000: 197). In philosophy, Piaget's theory on rule forming influenced political philosophers, such as John Rawls (1971) and Jürgen Habermas (1981; 1983).

In mathematics and logic, Piaget's influence was almost nonexistent, because he frequently put his own interpretation on technical terms, or sometimes misunderstood them (Quine 1943; Parsons 1960; Freudenthal 1973: 295; Ducret 1984: 82). In computer science, Seymour Papert and his colleagues at MIT used Piaget's theory in 1967 as a basis for the Logo Programming Language, a subset of LISP, designed as an educational aid for children (Sebesta 1996). Inspired by this project, Alan Kay, together with colleagues at the Xerox Palo Alto Research Center, developed the laptop computer (Gasch 2005). In 1954, the physicists, Jean Abele and Pierre Malvaux, put forward a theory of ordinal speed, which was based on Piaget's developmental theory regarding speed, but this remained an exception. Even biologists, such as Waddington, with whom Piaget was believed to be in agreement, refuted his central theses (Boden 1979: 150). Thus, despite outstanding successes in parts, Piaget's project of constructing a unified foundation for the sciences, through a combination of empirical psychogenesis, historio-critical sociogenesis and logico-deductive mathematics, must be considered a failure.

Part 4

The Relevance of Piaget's Work Today

15

The Relevance of Piaget's Work Today

After Piaget's death, his theory soon lost its appeal in the field of developmental psychology, and the rediscovery of Vygotsky began to take centre stage. Some of Piaget's theorems, however, were further developed by Neo-Piagetians and taken up by constructivists.

The Neo-Piagetians accepted the criticism that Piaget had sidestepped individual and cultural differences in development and that his theory was actually unable to explain these differences. Researchers, such as Robbie Case, Kurt Fischer and Juan Pascual-Leone therefore distanced themselves from Piaget's content-neutral logico-mathematical structures and abandoned the idea that formalization of these structures should be a criterion for successful development. Instead, they concentrated on the elaboration of process theories that describe the acquisition of area-specific competence and knowledge in the sociocultural context. For this purpose, they integrated theories of information processing, learning and social history into Piaget's model, while adhering to the invariant sequence of the stages of development (Case 1987; Biggs 1992; Ribeaupierre 1997), and thus to the core of Piaget's religion-determined logic of development.

Neo-Piagetians such as Juan Pascual-Leone, Robert Siegler, Seymour Papert, Phillip Johnson-Laird or Robbie Case adopted central concepts of information processing theories, like those by Richard Sternberg (1977). The arguments that most closely resembled Piaget's were propounded by Case, who still presupposed four stages in the development. He, however, understood the "representational stage," from the ages of 2 to 5, to be more than a mere forerunner of concrete-operational development. It is "an autonomous stage with its own sequences of operative structures and its own concluding operational system" (Case 1985: 126). According to Case, the driving forces of cognitive development are learning and the expansion of the capacity of the working memory, because he considered the limitations of the child's short-term memory to be responsible for the difficulties younger children experience in problem solving. Only the elaboration of "chunks," the summarizing and reorganization of information in a higher order, relieves the working memory and allows difficulties to be surmounted in a rational way (Laird, Rosenbloom and Newell 1986; Klahr and MacWhinney 1998). Problem-solving strategies are generalized once regularities have been discovered and form the core of human behavior (Siegler 1991). Jerry A. Fodor (1983) assumed a modularity of mind, whereby modules are seen as specific systems of information processing, which are activated through experiences and developed through area-specific learning. Kurt Fischer and Thomas Bidell understand psychological functions, as well as structures, to be variable and culture-determined, thus they consider the definition of the stages to be superfluous. They believe that their concept of "dynamic structuralism" offers the possibility to "illuminate the order within the variation" (Fischer and Bidell 2006: 389) despite the multiple levels of skills.

It is no longer the structures behind the knowledge but the knowledge itself and its changes during the process of its acquisition that have captured the interest of Chi (1978) and Wellman and Gelman (1998). Regarding the issue of how knowledge is acquired, there are two schools of thought, basing themselves on conceptual change or knowledge enrichment. Susan Carey (1985) assumes that children have various theories, which consist of a system of interdependent core concepts. At first, children develop an intuitive physics and an intuitive psychology, from which further (biological, economic, mathematical and so forth) "theories" are derived, through processes of differentiation. At the transition between stages, it is not a categorial change that takes place, as Piaget had assumed, but a change in the complex conceptual systems, as explained in Kuhn's change of paradigm. Liz Spelke (2000), on the other hand, supposes a continual enrichment of early core concepts. Cognition develops with perception and action, and "development leads to the enrichment of conceptions around an unchanging core" (Spelke, Breinlinger, Macomber and Jacobson 1992: 605).

At an early stage, George Kelly (1955) developed a personality theory based on Piaget, which claimed that behavior is directed by personal constructs. These consist of tried and tested hypotheses, which allow the anticipation of events. This constructivist psychology is continued by Maureen Pope (Pope and Denicolo 2001), who places her focus on education.

From the 1970s onward, papers on epistemology were published by constructivists such as Humberto Maturana, Francisco Varela (1946–2001), Gerhard Roth and Heinz von Foerster, whose neurobiological and system-theoretical approaches showed some parallels to Piaget, but only few references to him were made. Ernst von Glasersfeld, who directly referred to Piaget, termed his own stance as "radical constructivism" (Glasersfeld 1978), a term that soon applied to the ideas of an entire group. His interpretation of Piaget contributed significantly to the fact that a renaissance of Piaget as epistemologist occurred during the boom of constructivism in the

1990s. Pedagogues like Horst Siebert (2003) tried to deduct their theories of learning and didactics from constructivist epistemology.

Another reason for this renaissance is to be found in the various attempts connecting Piaget to Vygotsky made by co-constructivism or social constructivism. One of the most influential psychologists was Jerome Bruner (Bruner 1966; Bruner and Haste 1987), who refuted the concept of structure, and instead postulated three forms of representation (enactive, iconic and symbolic), which are formed successively. Language is an autonomous dimension, and its acquisition is dependent on social interaction. During development, the representations become translatable from one form into another, but they can also contradict each other. Doise, Dionnet and Mugny (1978) adopted Piaget's term *conflict de centrations* (1935/4: 185) and reformulated it into a sociocognitive conflict. Many authors like Bower believe that contradictions are the decisive factor in mental development. Changes "are not mainly due to some *process of imitation*, but to a *constructive elaboration* of new assessments and new forms of thought" (Doise, Mugny and Pérez 1995: 117). Youniss (1994) followed up Piaget's early work, especially his book on moral judgment (Piaget 1932), which is better suited for a synthesis with Vygotsky than Piaget's later works.

Although Piaget had neglected the reflection-forming function of co-operation and social interaction, after he had undergone his biological-mathematical turn, his late work (Piaget 1974; Piaget and Amann 1974b) nonetheless influenced the beginning of metacognition research (Weinert and Kluwe 1983), which, however, soon emancipated itself from the individualistic approach. In addition, the "theory of mind" (Astington, Harris and Olson 1988) recontextualized "Piaget's solitary thinker in a social world composed of enculturated and communicating human adults" (Fleisher Feldman 1992: 107). This theory of children's intuitive commonsense psychology became a central area within developmental psychology during the 1980s and 1990s (Perner 1991). Children were considered to be "little scientists" who develop coherent models of the world in a number of domains like psychology, biology or physics, based on a commonsense interpretation of their experience (Driver 1996). The role of the teacher is to challenge the students' models, and guide them to a better understanding. Constructivism led to new approaches in the field of didactics, such as "reciprocal teaching" (Brown and Campione 1998), the "community of practice" (Lave 1991), "cognitive apprenticeship" (Collins, Brown and Newman 1989), "guided participation" (Rogoff 1993; Mercer 1995) or "situated cognition" (Resnick 1987), none of which have much in common with Piaget's basic assumptions of his main works any longer.

To conclude, it is evident that Piaget's concepts have either been changed or abolished by the Neo- and Post-Piagetians since the 1970s. Therefore it comes as no surprise that his name is gradually disappearing from text books on developmental psychology and, somewhat more slowly, from pedagogical textbooks. Any mention of Piaget usually takes the form of a cursory reference to individual aspects or concepts, which appear to be isolated from his system. This leads to the conclusion that Piaget's theory has already entered the history of ideas, where it will keep its place as one of the last metaphysical systems. Even as an immanentist one, it cannot expect more.

Bibliography

Piaget's Works

References to Jean Piaget's books and articles correspond to the alphabetical classification of the *Archives Jean Piaget*, which may be found at www.unige.ch/piaget/publications/piaget.html. A chronological list of the works in French, German, and English is available at www.richardkohler.ch/piagetbiblio.htm.

1907/1 Un moineau albinos. *Le Rameau de sapin*, 41, 36, www.fondationjeanpiaget.ch/fjp/site/ModuleFJP001/index_gen_section.php?IDSECTION=746.

1912/5 La vanité de la nomenclature (ms 26 September 1912), www.piaget.org/piaget/6.6.html.

1913/3 Les mollusques sublittoraux du Léman recueillis par M. le Prof. Yung. *Zoologischer Anzeiger*, 42, 615–624.

1913/5 Premières recherches sur les mollusques profonds du lac de Neuchâtel. *Bulletin de la Société neuchâteloise des sciences naturelles*, 40, 148–171.

1913/6 Contribution à la faune de la Haute-Savoie: malacologie de Duingt et des environs. *Revue savoisienne* 54, 69–85, 166–180, 234–242.

1914/1 Bergson et Sabatier. *Revue chrétienne*, 61, 192–200.

1914/4 Notes sur la biologie des Limnées abyssales. *Internationale Revue der gesamten Hydrobiologie und Hydrographie. Biologisches Supplement*, 6, 1–15.

1914/5 Quelques mollusques de Colombie, in O. Fuhrmann and E. Mayor (eds), *Voyage d'exploration scientifique en Colombie*. Neuchâtel: Attinger, pp. 253–269.

1914/10 L'espèce mendelienne a-t-elle une valeur absolue? *Zoologischer Anzeiger*, 44, 328–331.

1915 ms Letter to the Amis de la Nature (25 septembre 1915), www.piaget.org/piaget/7.3.html.

1915/1 *La mission de l'Idée*. Lausanne: La Concorde 1916.

1915/3 Les journées d'Evilard. *Nouvelles de l'ACSE*, 5, 7, 198–200.

1916/3 Les mystères de la douleur divine (ed. F. Vidal). *Revue de Théologie et de Philosophie*, 1993, 126, 112–118.

1917 ms Lettre à Romain Rolland (4 août 1917). *Action étudiante*, 1966, 12, 7.

1918 *Recherche*. Lausanne: La Concorde.

1918/1 Biologie et guerre. *Feuille centrale de la Société suisse de Zofingue*, 58, 374–380.

1918/2 Compte rendu de R. Warnery: Via Crucis. *Nouvelles de l'ACSE*, 8, 120–122.

1918/3 Première neige/Je voudrais, in Fernando Vidal (ed.), Piaget Poète. Avec deux sonnets oubliés de 1918. *Archives de psychologie*, 1994, 64, 3–7.

1920/1 Corrélation entre la répartition verticale des mollusques du Valais et les indices des variations spécifiques. *Revue Suisse de Zoologie*, 28, 125–133.

1920/2 Die Psychoanalyse in ihren Beziehungen zur Kinderpsychologie, in S. Volkmann-Raue (ed.), *Jean Piaget. Drei frühe Schriften zur Psychoanalyse*. Freiburg: Kore, 1993, pp. 23–81.

1921/1 Essai sur quelques aspects du développement de la notion de partie chez l'enfant. *Journal de psychologie normale et pathologique,*18, 449–480.

1921/2 *Introduction à la malacologie valaisanne*. Sion: Aymon.

1921/3 L'orientation de la philosophie religieuse en Suisse romande. *La semaine littéraire*, 29, 409–412.

1921/4 Une forme verbale de la comparaison chez l'enfant: un cas de transition entre le jugement prédicatif et le jugement de relation. *Archives de psychologie*, 18, 141–172.

1922/1 Essai sur la multiplication logique et les débuts de la pensée formelle chez l'enfant. *Journal de psychologie normale et pathologique*, 19, 222–261.

1923 *Le langage et la pensée chez l'enfant* [*Language and Thought of the Child*]. Neuchâtel: Delachaux et Niestlé (second ed. 1930).

1923/2 Das symbolische Denken und das Denken des Kindes, in S. Volkmann-Raue (ed.), *Jean Piaget. Drei frühe Schriften zur Psychoanalyse*. Freiburg: Kore 1993, pp. 83–146.

1923/3 La psychologie et les valeurs religieuses, in Association chrétienne d'étudiants de la Suisse romande (ed.), *Sainte-Croix 1922*. Lausanne: La Concorde, pp. 38–82.

1924 *Urteil und Denkprozess des Kindes* [*Judgment and Reasoning in the Child*]. Düsseldorf: Schwann, 1974.

1924/1 "L'expérience humaine et la causalité physique" de L. Brunschvicg: étude critique. *Journal de Psychologie Normale et Pathologique*, 21, 586–607.

1924/2 Les traits principaux de la logique de l'enfant, *Journal de Psychologie Normale et Pathologique*, 21, 48–101.

1924/3 Compte rendu de L. Brunschvicg: L'expérience humaine et la causalité physique. *Archives de Psychologie,* 19, 88–89.

1924/9 Das symbolische Denken. *Praxis. Schweizerische Rundschau für Medizin,* 17, XIII (28 April 1924).

1925/2 Le développement de la pensée de l'enfant. *Pro Juventute,* 6, 464–469.

1925/5 Psychologie et critique de la connaissance. *Archives de Psychologie,* 19, 193–210.

1926 *Das Weltbild des Kindes* [*The Child's Conception of the World*]. München: Deutscher Taschenbuch Verlag, 1997.

1926/1 La naissance de l'intelligence chez l'enfant. *Pour l'ère Nouvelle,* 4, 51–55.

1927 *La causalité physique chez l'enfant* [*The Child's Conception of Physical Causality*]. Paris: Alcan.

1927/2 The first year of life of the child, in H.E. Gruber and J.J. Vonèche (eds), *The Essential Piaget.* London: Routledge & Kegan Paul 1977, pp. 198–214.

1927/3 Le respect de la règle dans les sociétés d'enfants. *Le Nouvel Essor,* 22, 1.

1928/1 Immanence et transcendence, in J. Piaget and J. de la Harpe, *Deux types d'attitudes religieuses: Immanence et transcendence.* Genève: Association Chrétienne d'Etudiants de la Suisse Romande, pp.5–40.

1928/2 Logique génétique et sociologie. *Cahiers Vilfredo Pareto. Revue européenne des sciences socials,* 1976, 38–39, 44–80.

1928/3 Psychopédagogie et mentalité enfantine. *Journal de Psychologie Normale et Pathologique,* 25, 31–60.

1928/4 Die moralische Regel beim Kind, in H. Betram (ed.), *Gesellschaftlicher Zwang und Moralische Autonomie.* Frankfurt: Suhrkamp 1986, pp. 106–117, http://pst.chez.tiscali.fr/svtiufm/educmora.htm.

1928/5 Les trois systèmes de la pensée de l'enfant: étude sur les rapports de la pensée rationnelle et de l'intelligence motrice. *Bulletin de la Société française de philosophie,* 28, 97–141.

1928/6 Un problème d'hérédité chez la limnée des étangs: appel aux malacologistes et aux amateurs en conchyliologie. *Bulletin de la Société zoologique de France,* 53, 13–18.

1928/7 La causalité chez l'enfant. Conférence donnée à Cambridge le 4 mars 1927. *The British Journal of Psychology,* 18, 276–301.

1928/11 Compte rendu de J. Sageret: La révolution philosophique et la science. *Journal de Psychologie Normale et Pathologique,* 25.

1928/12 Pour l'étude de la psychologie. *La Nouvelle Semaine Artistique et Littéraire,* 12–13.

1929/1 L'adaptation de la Limnaea stagnalis aux milieux lacustres de la Suisse romande : étude biométrique et génétique. *Revue Suisse de Zoologie*, 36, 263–531.

1929/3 Les races lacustres de la Limnaea stagnalis L. Recherches sur les rapports de l'adaptation héréditaire avec le milieu. *Bulletin biologique de la France et de la Belgique*, 63, 424–455.

1929/4 Pour l'immanence: réponse à M.J.-D. Burger. *Revue de Théologie et de Philosophie*, 17, 146–152.

1929/5 Compte rendu de E. Minkowski: La schizophrénie: psychopathologie des schizoïdes et des schizophrènes. *Archives de Psychologie*, 22, 117–118.

1929/6 Encore "immanence et transcendance". *Cahiers Protestants*, 13: 325–330.

1930/1 Le développement de l'esprit de solidarité chez l'enfant, in *Comment faire connaître la Société des Nations et développer l'esprit de coopération internationale: troisième cours pour le personnel enseignant*. Genève: BIE, pp. 52–55.

1930/2 La notion de justice chez l'enfant, in *Comment faire connaître la Société des Nations et développer l'esprit de coopération internationale: troisième cours pour le personnel enseignant*. Genève: BIE, pp. 55–57.

1930/3 *Immanentisme et foi religieuse*. Genève: Robert.

1930/4 Das Verfahren der Moralerziehung, in *Über Pädagogik*. Weinheim: Beltz 1999, pp. 30–77, http://pst.chez.tiscali.fr/svtiufm/educmora.htm.

1930/5 Le Bureau international d'éducation, in *Cinquième congrès international d'éducation morale, Paris Vol. II*. Paris: Alcan 1931, pp. 277–280.

1930/7 Le parallélisme entre la logique et la morale chez l'enfant, in *Ninth International Congress of Psychology, Yale University*. Princeton: The psychological review company, pp. 339–340.

1930/8 Psychologie expérimentale: la mentalité de l'enfant. *L'école Libératrice*, 2, 43–44.

1930/9 La vie sociale de l'enfant. *L'école Libératrice*, 2, 226–227.

1931/1 Children's philosophies, in C. Murchison (ed.), *Handbook of Child Psychology*. Worcester: Clark University Press, pp. 377–391.

1931/2 Le développement intellectuel chez les jeunes enfants: étude critique. *Mind*, 40, 137–160.

1931/4 Internationale Erziehung. Eine psychologische Einführung. *Über Pädagogik*. Weinheim: Beltz 1999, pp. 104–117.

1931/6 Post-scriptum de l'article d'Arnold Reymond "La pensée philosophique en Suisse romande de 1900 à nos jours". *Revue de Théologie et de Philosophie*, 19, 377–379.

1931/7 Rapport du directeur, in *Le Bureau international de l'éducation en 1930–1931*. Genève: BIE, pp. 20–43.

1931/8 On moral realities in child life. *New Era in Home and School,* 1930, 11, 112–114.

1931/9 La logique de l'enfant. 1. L'Egocentrisme. *L'école libératrice,* 2, 494.

1931/11 Sur l'existence de deux morales dans l'enfance. *Pour l'ère Nouvelle,* 9, 45–46.

1931/12 Sur les méthodes "actives". *Pour l'ère Nouvelle,* 9, 46–47.

1932 *Das moralische Urteil beim Kinde (The Moral Judgment of the Child).* Frankfurt: Suhrkamp 1973.

1932/1 Les difficultés psychologiques de l'éducation internationale, in *Cinquième cours pour le personnel enseignant.* Genève: BIE, pp. 57–76.

1932/4 Foreword, in *Rech i myshlenie rebenka.* Moscow-Leningrad: Uchpedgiz, pp. 55–56.

1933/1 Rapport du directeur, in *Bureau international d'éducation.* Genève: BIE, pp. 38–65.

1933/2 L'individu et la formation de la raison. *Cahiers Vilfredo Pareto. Revue européenne des sciences sociales,* 1976, 38–39, 81–123.

1933/3 Psychoanalyse und geistige Entwicklung, in S. Volkmann-Raue (ed.), *Jean Piaget. Drei frühe Schriften zur Psychoanalyse.* Freiburg: Kore 1993, pp. 147–153.

1933/4 Psychologie des Kindes und Geschichtsunterricht, in *Über Pädagogik.* Weinheim: Beltz 1999, pp. 118–127.

1933/5 Die soziale Entwicklung und die neue Pädagogik, in *Über Pädagogik.* Weinheim: Beltz 1999, pp. 128–147.

1933/6 Quelques remarques sur l'égocentrisme de l'enfant, in *Compte rendu du Congrès international de l'enfance.* Paris: Nathan, pp. 279–287.

1934/1 Rapport du directeur: cinquième réunion du Conseil, in *Le Bureau international d'éducation en 1933–1934.* Genève: BIE, pp. 3–31.

1934/2 Psychologische Anmerkungen zum self-government, in *Über Pädagogik.* Weinheim: Beltz, 1999, pp. 148–170.

1934/3 Ist eine Erziehung zum Frieden möglich?, in *Über Pädagogik.* Weinheim: Beltz, 1999, pp. 171–178.

1934/4 Discours du directeur, in *3e Conférence internationale de l'instruction publique.* Genève: BIE, pp. 27–30.

1935/4 Psychologische Anmerkungen zur Gruppenarbeit, in *Über Pädagogik.* Weinheim: Beltz 1999, pp. 179–198.

1935/5 Les théories de l'imitation. *Cahiers de pédagogie expérimentale et de psychologie de l'enfant,* 6, 1–13.

1936 *Das Erwachen der Intelligenz beim Kinde [The Origins of Intelligence in Children]* Stuttgart: Klett, 1975.

1936/1 *Le Bureau international d'éducation en 1935–1936: rapport du directeur à la septième réunion du Conseil.* Genève: BIE.

1937 *Der Aufbau der Wirklichkeit beim Kinde* [*The Construction of Reality in the Child*]. Stuttgart Klett 1974, www.marxists.org/reference/subject/ philosophy/works/fr/piaget2.htm.

1937/2 and Edith Meyer: Introduction. In *6e Conférence internationale de l'instruction publique: documents officiels sur l'enseignement de la psychologie dans la préparation des maîtres primaires et secondaires.* Genève: BIE, pp. 5–9.

1937/3 La philosophie de Gustave Juvet, in *A la mémoire de Gustave Juvet, 1896–1936.* Lausanne: Université de Lausanne, pp. 37–52.

1937/7 Les problèmes, in V. Broendal and K. Capek (eds), *Vers un nouvel humanisme: entretiens.* Paris: IICI, pp. 9–84.

1938/2 Le problème de l'intelligence et de l'habitude: réflexe conditionné, "Gestalt" ou assimilation, in *Onzième congrès international de psychologie, Paris, 25–31 juillet 1937.* Agen: Imprimérie Moderne, pp. 170–183.

1939/3 Die neuen Methoden und ihre psychologischen Grundlagen, in *Theorien und Methoden der modernen Erziehung.* Wien: Molden 1972, pp. 139–183.

1939/4 Examen des méthodes nouvelles, in C. Bouglé (ed.), *Encyclopédie française 15: éducation et instruction 28.* Paris: Société de Gestion de l'Encyclopédie Française, pp. 1–13.

1940/1 *Le Bureau international d'éducation en 1939–1940: rapport du directeur à la onzième réunion du Conseil.* Genève: BIE.

1941 *The Child's Construction of Quantities: Conservation and Atomism.* London: Routledge & Kegan Paul, 1974.

1941a and A. Szeminska: *Die Entwicklung des Zahlbegriffs beim Kinde.* [*The Child's Conception of Number*]. Stuttgart: Klett, 1965.

1941/3 Esprit et réalité. *Annuaire de la Société Suisse de Philosophie*, 1, 40–47.

1941/4 Essai sur la théorie des valeurs qualitatives en sociologie statique ("synchronique"), in *Etudes sociologiques.* Genève: Droz 1965, pp.100–142.

1941/5 Le mécanisme du développement mental et les lois du groupement des opérations: esquisse d'une théorie opératoire de l'intelligence. *Archives de Psychologie*, 28, 215–285.

1942 *Classes, relations et nombres: essai sur les groupements de la logistique et sur la reversibilité de la pensée.* Paris: Vrin.

1942/5 Les trois structures fondamentales de la vie psychique: rythme, régulation et groupement, in *Revue Suisse de Psychologie et de Psychologie Appliquée*, 1–2, 9–21.

1943/1 Le jugement moral de l'enfant d'après I.H. Caruso. *Archives de Psychologie*, 29, 170.

1943/2 Le développement sociologique de la famille. *Pro Juventute*, 24, 84–88.

1943/4 and Marc Lambercier and Renée Iturbide: Le problème de la comparaison visuelle en profondeur (constance de la grandeur) et l'erreur systématique de l'étalon. *Archives de Psychologie*, 29, 255–312.

1943/6 Die geistige Entwicklung des Kindes, in *Theorien und Methoden der Modernen Erziehung*. Wien: Molden, 1972.

1943/12 Compte rendu de H. Wallon: De l'acte à la pensée: essai de psychologie comparée. *Archives de Psychologie*, 29, 311–312.

1944/1 Erziehung zur Freiheit, in *Über Pädagogik*. Weinheim: Beltz 1999, pp. 199–207, http://pst.chez.tiscali.fr/svtiufm/educmora.htm.

1944/2 *Le Bureau international d'éducation et la reconstruction éducative d'après-guerre*. Genève: BIE.

1944/3 L'organisation et l'esprit de la psychologie à Genève. *Revue Suisse de Psychologie et de Psychologie Appliquée*, 3, 97–104.

1944/4 Les relations entre la morale et le droit, in *Etudes Sociologiques*. Genève: Droz, 1965, pp. 172–202.

1945 *Nachahmung, Spiel und Traum. Die Entwicklung der Symbolfunktionen beim Kinde* [*Play, Dreams and Imitation in Childhood*]. Stuttgart: Klett, 1993.

1945/1 Hommage à C.G. Jung. *Revue Suisse de Psychologie et de Psychologie Appliquée*, 4, 169–171.

1945/3 Les opérations logiques et la vie sociale, in *Etudes sociologiques*. Genève: Droz 1965, pp. 143–171.

1946 *Die Bildung des Zeitbegriffs beim Kinde*. [*The Child's Conception of Time*]. Frankfurt: Suhrkamp 1974.

1946a *The Child's Conception of Movement and Speed*. London: Routledge & Kegan Paul, 1970.

1946/3 Les trois conditions d'une épistémologie scientifique. *Analysis: Revue pour la Critique des Sciences*, 1, 25–32.

1947 *Psychologie der Intelligenz* [*The Psychology of Intelligence*]. Zürich: Rascher 1970.

1947/4 Du rapport des sciences avec la philosophie. *Synthese*, 6, 130–150.

1947/8 Die moralische Entwicklung des Jugendlichen in zwei verschiedenen Gesellschaftstypen: der "primitiven" Gesellschaft und der "modernen" Gesellschaft, in *Über Pädagogik*. Weinheim: Beltz, 1999, pp. 208–216.

1947/9 and A. Leuzinger-Schuler: Der Anteil der egozentrischen Sprache bei der verbalen Kommunikation mit Erwachsenen und unter Kindern, in 1923. Düsseldorf: Schwann 1972, pp. 55–92.

1947 ms Letter to Ignace Meyerson (13 January 1947). International Bureau of Education, Box 186.

1948 and B. Inhelder: *The Child's Conception of Space*. London, Routledge & Kegan Paul, 1956.

1948a and B. Inhelder and A. Szeminska: *Die natürliche Geometrie des Kindes* [*The Child's Conception of Geometry*]. Stuttgart: Klett, 1974.

1948/9 Discours du directeur, in *11e Conférence internationale de l'instruction publique*. Genève: BIE, p. 22.

1949 *Traité de logique: Essai de logistique*. Paris: Colin.

1949/5 Naturkundeunterricht in der Grundschule. Psychologische Bemerkungen, in *Über Pädagogik*. Weinheim: Beltz, 1999, pp. 217–235.

1949/6 Das Recht auf Bildung in der heutigen Welt, in *Das Recht auf Erziehung und die Zukunft unseres Bildungssystems*. München: Piper 1975, pp. 7–66.

1949/7 Die moderne Pädagogik, in *Über Pädagogik*. Weinheim: Beltz, 1999, pp. 236–241.

1949/8 Discours du directeur, in *12e Conférence internationale de l'instruction publique*. Paris: UNESCO, Genève: BIE, pp. 26–28.

1950 *Die Entwicklung des Erkennens. [Introduction à l'épistémologie génétique]. I: Das mathematische Denken. II: Das physikalische Denken. III: Das biologische Denken; das psychologische Denken; das soziologische Denken*. Stuttgart: Klett 1973.

1951/3 and Anne-Marie Weil: Le devéloppement, chez l'enfant, de l'idée de patrie et des relations avec l'étranger. *Cahiers Vilfredo Pareto. Revue européenne des sciences sociales*, 1976, 38–39, pp. 124–147.

1951/6 Pensée égocentrique et pensée sociocentrique. *Cahiers Vilfredo Pareto. Revue européenne des sciences sociales*, 1976, 38–39, 148–160.

1951/14 Plan d'action de trois ans, in *De la pédagogie*. Paris: Jacob, 1998, pp. 259–279.

1952/1 Jean Piaget, an Autobiography, in R.L.Evans (1973), *Jean Piaget. The Man and His Ideas*. New York: Dutton, pp. 103–142.

1952/3 Equilibre et structures d'ensemble. Leçon inaugurale en Sorbonne. *Bulletin de Psychologie*, 6, 4–10.

1953/6 Structures opérationnelles et cybernétique. *L'année Psychologique*, 53, 379–388.

1954/3 Die Gestalttheorie in der zeitgenössischen Psychologie der Intelligenz und der Wahrnehmung, in *Probleme der Entwicklungspsychologie. Kleine Schriften*. Hamburg: EVA, 1993, pp. 106–119.

1954/6 The problem of consciousness in child psychology: developmental changes in awareness, in *Problems of Consciousness: Transactions of the Fourth Conference 1953*. New York: Macy, pp. 136–147.

1954/9 Leben und Denken aus der Sicht der Experimentalpsychologie und der genetischen Epistemologie, in *Probleme der Entwicklungspsychologie. Kleine Schriften*. Hamburg: EVA, 1993, pp. 135–142.

1954/10 Sprechen und Denken in genetischer Sicht, in *Theorien und Methoden der modernen Erziehung*. Wien: Molden, 1972, pp. 269–280.

1954/12 *Intelligenz und Affektivität in der Entwicklung des Kindes* [*Intelligence and Affectivity: Their Relationship during Child Development*]. Frankfurt: Suhrkamp 1995.

1954/15 Discours du directeur, in *17e Conférence internationale de l'instruction publique*. Genève: BIE; Paris: UNESCO, pp. 27–28.

1954/16 Kunsterziehung und Psychologie des Kindes, in *Über Pädagogik*. Weinheim: Beltz, 1999, pp. 242–245.

1955 and Bärbel Inhelder: *Von der Logik des Kindes zur Logik des Heranwachsenden: Essay über die Ausformung der formalen operativen Strukturen* [*The Growth of Logical Thinking from Childhood to Adolescence: An Essay on the Construction of Formal Operational Structures*]. Olten: Walter, 1977.

1955/6 Les structures mathématiques et les structures opératoires de l'intelligence, in *L'enseignement des mathématiques*. Neuchâtel: Delachaux et Niestlé, pp. 11–33.

1956 Probleme der genetischen Psychologie, in *Theorien und Methoden der modernen Erziehung*. Wien: Molden, 1972, pp. 297–324.

1956/5 Some impressions of a visit to Soviet psychologists, in A. Tryphon and J. Vonèche (eds), *Piaget–Vygotsky. The Social Genesis of Thought*. East Essex: Psychology Press, pp. 201–206.

1956/7 Die Stadien der geistigen Entwicklung des Kindes und des Heranwachsenden, in *Probleme der Entwicklungspsychologie. Kleine Schriften*. Hamburg: EVA 1993, pp. 46–55.

1957 and W.E. Beth and W. Mays: *Epistémologie génétique et recherche psychologique. EEG I*. Paris: PUF.

1957a and L. Apostel and B. Mandelbrot: *Logique et équilibre. EEG II*. Paris: PUF.

1957/1 Die Aktualität des Johann Amos Comenius, in *Über Pädagogik*. Weinheim: Beltz 1999, pp. 246–282.

1957/4 Le mythe de l'origine sensorielle des connaissances scientifiques. *Actes de la Société helvétique des sciences naturelles*, 20–34.

1958 and J.S. Bruner, F. Bresson and A. Morf: *Logique et perception. EEG VI*. Paris: PUF.

1959a and M. Goustard, P. Greco and B. Matalon: La logique des apprentissages. EEG. X. Paris: PUF.

1959b and P. Gréco: *Apprentissage et connaissance. EEG VII*. Paris: PUF.

1959/2 L'Institut des sciences de l'éducation (Institut J.-J. Rousseau) de 1912 à 1956, in *Histoire de l'Université de Genève: annexes: historique des facultés et des instituts*. Genève: Georg, pp. 307–316.

1959/3 Les modèles abstraits sont-ils opposées aux interprétations psycho-physiologiques dans l'explication en psychologie? Esquisse d'autobiographie intellectuelle. *Bulletin de Psychologie*, 13, 7–13.

1959/5 Wahrnehmung, Lernen und Empirismus, in *Probleme der Entwicklungspsychologie. Kleine Schriften*. Hamburg: EVA 1993, pp. 80–92.

1959/8 Die Rolle des Gleichgewichtsbegriffs in der Psychologie, in *Theorien und Methoden der modernen Erziehung*. Wien: Molden, 1972, pp. 281–296.

1959/11 Lettre à Arnold Reymond. *Revue de Théologie et de Philosophie*, 3, 9, 44–47.

1960a and P. Gréco, J.-B. Grize and S. Papert: *Problèmes de la construction du nombre. EEG XI*. Paris: PUF.

1960/1 L'aspect génétique de l'oeuvre de Pierre Janet. *Psychologie Française*, 5, 111–117.

1960/7 Die kindlichen Praxien, in *Probleme der Entwicklungspsychologie. Kleine Schriften*. Hamburg: EVA 1993, pp. 56–79.

1960/8 Problèmes de la psycho-sociologie de l'enfance. *Cahiers Vilfredo Pareto. Revue européene des sciences socials*, 1976, 38–39, 161–197.

1961a *The Mechanisms of Perception*. London: Routledge & Kegan Paul, 1969.

1961/1 Défense de l'épistémologie génétique, in E.W. Beth, J.B. Grize, R. Martin and J. Piaget (eds), *Implication, formalisation et logique naturelle. EEG XVI*. Paris: PUF, 1962, pp.165–191.

1962/1 Comments on Vygotsky's critical remarks concerning "The language and thought of the child" and "Judgement and reasoning in the child", in P. Lloyd and Ch. Fernyhough (eds), *Lev Vygotsky. Critical Assessments*. London: Routledge, 1999, pp. 243–260.

1962/4 The role of imitation in the development of representational thought, in H.E. Gruber and J.J. Vonèche (eds), *The Essential Piaget*. London: Routledge and Kegan Paul, 1977, pp. 508–514.

1962/5 Der Zeitfaktor in der kindlichen Entwicklung, in *Probleme der Entwicklungspsychologie. Kleine Schriften*. Hamburg: EVA, 1993, pp. 7–30.

1962/8 Will and action. *Bulletin of the Menninger Clinic*, 26, 138–145.

1963c and P. Fraisse, E. Vurpillot and R. Francès: *La perception*. Paris: PUF.

1963/1 Sprache und Denkoperationen, in *Probleme der Entwicklungspsychologie. Kleine Schriften*. Hamburg: EVA, 1993, pp. 93–105.

1964/2 Development and learning, in R.E. Ripple and V.N. Rockcastle (eds), *Piaget Rediscovered: a Report of the Conference on Cognitive Studies and Curriculum Development, March 1964*. Ithaca, NY: Cornell University, pp. 7–20.

1964/6 Das Denken des Kleinkindes, in *Theorien und Methoden der modernen Erziehung*. Wien: Molden, 1972, pp. 259–268.

1964/8 Discours du directeur du Bureau international d'éducation, in *27e Conférence internationale de l'instruction publique*, 1964. Genève: BIE; Paris: UNESCO: 42–44, 74–78.

1965 *Weisheit und Illusionen der Philosophie* [*Insights and Illusions of Philosophy*]. Frankfurt: Suhrkamp, 1974.

1965/1, Erziehung und Unterricht seit 1935, in *Theorien und Methoden der modernen Erziehung*. Wien: Molden 1972, pp. 13–137.

1965/7 Genese und Struktur in der Psychologie der Intelligenz, in *Theorien und Methoden der modernen Erziehung*. Wien: Molden, 1972, pp. 325–342.

1965/18 Discours du directeur, in *Conférence internationale de l'instruction publique, 28e session*. Genève: BIE, Paris: UNESCO, pp. 46–48.

1966 and B. Inhelder: *Die Psychologie des Kindes* [*The Psychology of the Child*]. Frankfurt: Fischer 1977.

1966b and B. Inhelder: *Die Entwicklung des inneren Bildes beim Kind* [*Mental Imagery in the Child*]. Frankfurt: Suhrkamp, 1990.

1966/6 Notwendigkeit und Bedeutung der vergleichenden Forschung in der Entwicklungspsychologie, in *Probleme der Entwicklungspsychologie. Kleine Schriften*. Hamburg: EVA, 1993, pp. 120–134.

1966/9 Qu'est-ce que la psychologie? *I.S.E. Echo*, 1967, 9, 10–18.

1966/12 L'initiation aux mathématiques, les mathématiques modernes et la psychologie de l'enfant, in *De la pédagogie*. Paris: Jacob 1998, pp. 231–236.

1966/14 Response to Brian Sutton-Smith. In H.E. Gruber and J.J. Vonèche (eds) (1970), *The Essential Piaget*. London: Routledge & Kegan Paul, pp. 515–517.

1967 *Biologie und Erkenntnis. Über die Beziehungen zwischen organischen Regulationen und kognitiven Prozessen*. [*Biology and Knowledge: An Essay on the Relations Between Organic Regulations and Cognitive Processes*]. Frankfurt: Fischer 1974.

1967a *Logique et connaissance scientifique*. Paris: Gallimard.

1967/7 Das Bewusstsein, in *Das menschliche Wagnis: Enzyklopädie der Wissenschaften vom Menschen, V. Der Mensch und sein Ich*. Genf: Kister, pp. 48–52.

1968 *Der Strukturalismus* [*Structuralism*]. Olten: Walter, 1973.

1968a and B. Inhelder: *Mémoire et intelligence* [*Memory and Intelligence*]. Paris: PUF.

1968/9 Autobiographie, in H.G. Furth: *Intelligenz und Erkennen. Die Grundlagen der genetischen Erkenntnistheorie Piagets*. Frankfurt: Suhrkamp, 1976, pp. 356–359.

1968/13 Explanation in Psychology and Psychophysiological Parallelism, in P. Fraisse and J. Piaget (eds), *Experimental Psychology: Its Scope and Method*. New York: Basic Books, Chapter 3.

1969/8 Genetic epistemology, in R.L. Evans (1973), *Jean Piaget. The Man and His Ideas*, New York: Dutton, pp. xlii–lxi.

1970 *Abriss der genetischen Epistemologie* [*The Principles of Genetic Epistemology*]. Olten: Walter, 1974.

1970a *Einführung in die genetische Erkenntnistheorie*. [*Genetic Epistemology*]. Frankfurt: Suhrkamp 1973, www.marxists.org/reference/subject/philosophy/works/fr/piaget.htm.

1970/2 *Meine Theorie der geistigen Entwicklung* [*Piaget's Theory*]. Frankfurt: Fischer, 1983.

1970/4 Die Wissenschaften vom Menschen und ihre Stellung im Wissenschaftssystem, in *Erkenntnistheorie der Wissenschaften vom Menschen*. Frankfurt: Ullstein, pp. 13–103.

1970/5 La psychologie, in *Epistémologie des sciences de l'homme*. Paris: Gallimard 1972, pp. 131–250.

1970/8 Die intellektuelle Entwicklung im Jugend- und im Erwachsenenalter, in T. Schöfthaler and D. Goldschmidt (eds), *Soziale Struktur und Vernunft*. Frankfurt: Suhrkamp 1984, pp. 47–60.

1970/9 A conversation with Jean Piaget and Bärbel Inhelder. Interview by Elizabeth Hall. *Psychology Today*, 3, 25–32, 54–56.

1970/11 Introduction à la troisième édition, in *Conférences internationales de l'instruction publique: recommandations 1934–1968*. Genève: BIE; Paris: UNESCO, p. IX.

1970/13 Invited Seminar at the Catholic University of America, Washington D.C. June 6, 1970. Archives Jean Piaget.

1971 and R. Garcia: *Understanding Causality. EEG XXVI*. New York: Norton 1974.

1971/2 Hasard et dialectique en épistémologie biologique: examen critique des thèses de Jacques Monod. *Sciences: Revue de la Civilisation Scientifique*, 71, 29–36.

1971/8 Das affektive und das kognitive Unbewusste, in *Probleme der Entwicklungspsychologie. Kleine Schriften*. Hamburg: EVA 1993, pp. 31–45.

1972b Die Zukunft unseres Bildungssystems, *Das Recht auf Erziehung und die Zukunft unseres Bildungssystems*. München: Piper 1975, pp. 67–91.

1972/2 Lebendige Entwicklung. *Zeitschrift für Pädagogik*, 1974, 20, 1–6.

1973 Interview, in R.L.Evans (ed.), *Jean Piaget, the Man and His Ideas*. New York: Dutton, pp. 1–74.

1973/6 Comments on mathematical education, in H.E. Gruber and J.J. Vonèche (eds), *The Essential Piaget*. London: Routledge & Kegan Paul, 1977, pp. 726–732.

1973/7 Préface, in *Alfred Binet: Les idées modernes sur les enfants*. Paris: Flammarion, pp. 5–10.

1973/14 Bref témoignage. Hommage à Lucien Goldmann. *Revue de l'Institut de sociologie*, 3–4, 545–547.

1973/15 Piaget takes a teacher's look. Interview by E. Duckworth. *Learning: the Magazine for Creative Teaching*, October, 22–27.

1973/16 Foreword, in M. Schwebel and J. Raph (eds), *Piaget in the Classroom*. New York: Basic Books, pp. ix–x.

1973/17 Interview by J. Bofford (14 November 1973). Archives de la Radio Suisse Romande, Genève.

1974 *La prise de conscience* [*The Grasp of Consciousness*]. Paris: PUF.

1974a *Adaptation vitale et psychologie de l'intelligence: sélection organique et phénocopie* [*Adaptation and Intelligence: Organic Selection and Phenocopy*]. Paris: Hermann.

1974b and M. Amann: *Réussir et comprendre* [*Success and Understanding*]. Paris: PUF.

1974c *Recherches sur la contradiction. 1: Les différentes formes de la contradiction. 2: Les relations entre affirmations et négations. EEG XXXI, XXXII*. Paris: PUF.

1974/3 Foreword, in H.E. Gruber: *Darwin on Man: A Psychological Study of Scientific Creativity*. New York: Dutton, pp. ix–xi.

1975 *Die Äquilibration der kognitiven Strukturen* [*The Development of Thought: Equilibration of Cognitive Structures*]. Stuttgart: Klett 1976.

1975/1 L'intelligence, selon Alfred Binet. *Bulletin de la Société Alfred Binet et Théodore Simon*, 75, 106–119.

1975/8 Phenocopy in biology and the psychological development of knowledge, in H.E. Gruber and J.J. Vonèche (eds), *The Essential Piaget*. London: Routledge & Kegan Paul, 1977, pp. 803–813.

1976 Autobiographie, in *Cahiers Vilfredo Pareto. Revue Européenne des Sciences Sociales*, 38–39, 1–43.

1976a *Le comportement, moteur de l'évolution* [*Behavior and Evolution*]. Paris: Gallimard.

1976/9 Une heure avec Piaget à propos de l'enseignement des mathématiques, in *De la pédagogie*. Paris: Jacob 1998, pp. 237–257.

1977 and J.-C. Bringuier: *Jean Piaget. Ein Selbstporträt in Gesprächen*. Weinheim: Beltz 2004.

1977a *Recherches sur l'abstraction réfléchissante. EEG. XXXIV and XXXV*. Paris: PUF.

1977/14 Réponse de Jean Piaget au Dr Olivier Flournoy. *Journal de Genève* (5 February 1977).

1978/1 Preface. In C. Kamii and R. DeVries: *Physical Knowledge in Preschool Education: Implication of Piaget's Theory*. Englewood Cliffs: Prentice-Hall, pp. VII–VIII.

1978/5 Le réel, le possible et le nécessaire, in *Actes du 21e Congrès international de psychologie, Paris, 18–25 juillet 1976*. Paris: PUF, pp. 249–257.

1979/4–8 La psychogenèse des connaissances et sa signification épistémologique, in M. Piattelli-Palmarini (ed.), *Théories du langage, théories de l'apprentissage: le débat entre Jean Piaget et Noam Chomsky*. Paris: Editions du Seuil, pp. 53–64, 95–100, 247–251, 406–412, 510–512.

1979/9 Correspondences and transformations. In F.B. Murray (ed.), *The Impact of Piagetian Theory: on Education, Philosophy, Psychiatry, and Psychology*. Baltimore: University Park Press, pp. 17–27.

1980 *Les formes élémentaires de la dialectique*. Paris: Gallimard.

1980a and I. Berthoud-Papandropoulou: *Recherches sur les correspondances. EEG XXXVII*. Paris: PUF.

1981 and I. Berthoud-Papandropoulou: *Le possible et le nécessaire* [*Possibility and Necessity*], *I: L'évolution des possibles chez l'enfant*. Paris: PUF.

1982/1 Reflections on Baldwin. Interview by J. Jacques Vonèche, in J.M. Broughton and D.J. Freeman-Moir (eds), *The Cognitive-Developmental Psychology of James Mark Baldwin: Current Theory and Research in Genetic Epistemology*. Norwood NJ: Abelx, pp. 80–86.

1983 and E. Ackermann-Valladao: *Le possible et le nécessaire* [*Possibility and Necessity*], *II: L'évolution du nécessaire chez l'enfant*. Paris: PUF.

1983a and R. Garcia: *Psychogenèse et histoire des sciences* [*Psychogenesis and the History of Science*]. Paris: Flammarion.

1983/1 Piaget on Lévi-Strauss. Interview by J. Grinevald. *New Ideas in Psychology*, 1, 73–79.

1987 and R. Garcia: *Toward a Logic of Meanings*. Hillsdale: Erlbaum, 1991.

1990 and E. Ackerman-Valladao: *Morphisms and categories: comparing and transforming*. Hillsdale: Erlbaum, 1992.

Other Sources

Abele, J., and Malvaux, P. (1954), *Vitesse et univers relativiste*. Paris: Societé d'édition d'enseignement supérieur.

Adler, A. (1912), *Über den nervösen Charakter. Grundzüge einer vergleichenden Individual-Psychologie und Psychotherapie*. Frankfurt: Fischer 1972.

Aebli, H. (1951), *Psychologische Didaktik*. Stuttgart: Klett.

Aebli, H. (1963), *Über die geistige Entwicklung des Kindes*. Stuttgart: Klett 1982.

Aebli, H. (1983), Zur Einführung, in J. Piaget (ed.), *Das moralische Urteil beim Kinde*. Stuttgart: Klett, pp. 13–22.

Aebli, H., Montada, L., and Schneider, U (1968), *Über den Egozentrismus des Kindes*. Stuttgart: Klett.

Aikenhead, G.S. (1996), Science Education: border crossing into the sub-culture of science. *Studies in Science Education*, 27, 1–52.

Alexander, C.N., Langer, E.J., and Oetter, R.M. (eds) (1986), *Higher Stages of Develoment. Adult Growth beyond Formal Operations*. New York: Oxford University Press.

Altwegg, J. (1983), Jean Piaget—Systeme und Strukturen, in J. Altwegg, *Leben und Schreiben im Welschland. Porträts, Gespräche und Essays aus der französischen Schweiz*. Zürich: Amman, pp. 147–157.

Anderson, A.R., and Belnap, N.D. (1975), *Entailment: The Logic of Relevance and Necessity, I*. Princeton: Princeton University Press.

Anderson, N.H., and Wilkening, F. (1991), Adaptive thinking in intuitive physics, in N.H. Anderson (ed.), *Contributions to Information Integration Theory. III*. Hillsdale: Erlbaum, pp. 1–42.

Andler, D, (1998), (ed.), *Introduction aux sciences cognitives*. Paris: Gallimard.

Anthony, E.J. (1957), The system makers. Piaget and Freud. *British Jounal of Medical Psychiatry*, 30, 255–269.

Anthony, W.S. (1977), Activity in the Learning of Piagetian Operational Thinking. *British Journal of Educational Psychology*, 47, 18–24.

Arlin, P.K. (1975), Cognitive development in adulthood: A fifth stage? *Developmental Psychology*, 11, 602–606.

Astington, J.W., Harris, P., and Olson, D. (eds) (1988), *Developing Theories of Mind*. Cambridge: Cambridge University Press.

Ausubel, D.P. (1968), *Educational Psychology. A Cognitive View*. New York: Holt, Rinehart & Winston.

Baader, M.S. (2005), *Erziehung als Erlösung. Transformationen des Religiösen in derReformpädagogik*. Weinheim: Juventa.

Bachelard, S. (1958), *La conscience de rationalité. Etude phénoménologique sur la physique mathématique*. Paris: PUF.

Bacon, F. (1620/1863), *The New Organon or True Directions Concerning the Interpretation of Nature. The Works (Vol. VIII)*. Boston: Taggard & Thompson.

Baillargeon, R. (1991), Reasoning about the height and location of a hidden object in 4.5- and 6.5-month-old infants. *Cognition*, 38, 13–42.

Baldwin, J.M. (1894), *Mental Development in the Child and the Race. Methods and Processes*. New York: Macmillan.

Baldwin, J.M. (1897), *Social and Ethical Interpretations in Mental Development: A Study in Social Psychology*. New York: Macmillan.

Baldwin, J.M. (1906), *Thought and Things: A Study of Development and Meaning of Thought, or Genetic Logic*. New York: Macmillan, Putnam.

Baltes, P.B. (1987), Theoretical propositions of lifespan developmental psychology: on the dynamics between growth and decline. *Developmental Psychology*, 23, 611–626.

Barrelet, J.-M. (1996), L'arrière-plan neuchâtelois, in J.-M. Barrelet and A.-N. Perret-Clermont (eds), *Jean Piaget et Neuchâtel. L'apprenti et le savant*. Lausanne: Editions Payot, pp. 15–26.

Barsky, R.F. (1997/1999), *Noam Chomsky. Libertärer Querdenker*. Zürich: edition 8.

Bateson, G. (1972/1985), *Ökologie des Geistes. Anthropologische, psychologische, biologische und epistemologische Perspektiven*. Frankfurt: Suhrkamp.

Baumgarten, F. (1927), Besprechung: Le jugement et le raisonnement chez l'enfant. *Zeitschrift für Angewandte Psychologie*, 28, 537–542.

Beatty, B. (2004), A Brief Encounter: Piaget's Reception by Nursery School Educators and Child Psychologists in the United States, 1927–1935. Paper presented at ISCHE 26, Geneva, 16 July.

Beilin, H. (1965), Learning and operational convergence in logical thought development. *Journal of Experimental Child Psychology*, 2, 317–322.

Bergson, H. (1907), *L'évolution créatrice*. Paris: Quadrige/PUF 1998.

Berlyne, D.E. (1976), in *Hommage à Jean Piaget zum achtzigsten Geburtstag*. Stuttgart: Klett, p. 15.

Berthoud, G. (1976), L'identité et l'altérité. *Cahiers Vilfredo Pareto. Revue européenne des sciences socials*, 38–39, 471–494.

Besseige, P. (1926), Quelques observations sur la logique enfantine. *Revue pédagogique*, 89, 14–32.

Beth, E.W. (1950), A propos d'un "Traité de logique". *Methodos*, 2, 258–264.

Bideaud, J. (1991/1992), Introduction, in J. Bideaud, C. Meljac and J.-P. Fischer (eds), *Pathways to Number: Children's Developing Numerical Abilities*. Hillsdale: Erlbaum, pp. 1–17.

Bidell, T.R., and Fischer, K.W. (1992), Cognitive development in educational contexts. Implications of skill theory. In A. Demetriou, M. Shayer and A. Efklides (eds), *Neo-Piagetian Theories of Cognitive Development. Implications and Applications for Education*. London: Routledge, pp. 11–30.

Biggs, J. B. (1992), Modes of learning, forms of knowing, and ways of schooling, in A. Demetriou, M. Shayer and A. Efklides (eds), *Neo-Piagetian Theories of Cognitive Development*. London: Routledge, pp. 31–49.

Binet, A., and Simon, T. (1905), *La mesure du développement de l'intelligence chez les jeunes enfants*. Paris: Alcan.

Bingham-Newman, A.M., Saunders, R.A., and Hooper, F.H. (1976), *Logical Operation Instruction in the Preschool. Technical report, N. 354*. Madison: University of Wisconsin.

Birbaumer, N., and Schmidt, R.F. (1996), *Biologische Psychologie*. Heidelberg: Springer.

Bischof-Köhler, D. (1988), Über den Zusammenhang von Empathie und der Fähigkeit, sich im Spiegel zu erkennen. *Schweizerische Zeitschrift für Psychologie*, 47, 147–159.

Bleuler, E. (1911/1966), Dementia Praecox oder die Gruppe der Schizophrenien, in G. Aschaffenburg (ed.), *Handbuch der Psychiatrie*. Wien: Deuticke.

Bleuler, E. (1912), Das autistische Denken, in E. Bleuler and S. Freud (ed.), *Jahrbuch für psychoanalytische und psychopathologische Forschung 4*. Leipzig: Deuticke, pp. 1–39.

Bleuler, E. (1919/1976), *Das autistisch-undisziplinierte Denken in der Medizin und seine Überwindung*. Berlin: Springer.

Bloch, M.-A. (1948), *Philosophie de l'éducation nouvelle*. Paris: PUF 1968.

Blondel, C. (1924), Le langage et la pensée chez l'enfant, d'après un livre récent. *Revue d'Histoire et de Philosophie Religieuse*, 5, 456–480.

Boden, M.A. (1979), *Piaget*. Glasgow: Fontana.

Borke, H. (1971), Interpersonal perception of young children: egocentrism or empathy? *Developmental Psychology*, 5, 263–269.

Borke, H. (1975), Piaget's mountains revisited: changes in the egocentric landscape. *Developmental Psychology*, 11, 240–243.

Bourjade, J. (1927), *Essai d'interprétation psycho-pédagogique des formes enfantins de l'explication causale chez quelques écoliers*. Lyon: Rey & Alcan.

Bovet, M. (1974), Cross-cultural study of conservation concepts: continuous quantities and length, in B. Inhelder, H. Sinclair and M. Bovet (eds), *Learning and the Development of Cognition*. London: Routledge & Kegan Paul.

Bovet, P. (1913/1951), Le respect. Essai de psychologie morale, in *Le sentiment religieux et la psychologie de l'enfant*. Neuchâtel: Delachaux & Niestlé, pp. 152–169.

Bovet, P. (1917), *L'instinct combatif*. Neuchâtel: Delachaux & Niestlé.

Bovet, P. (1919), La tâche nouvelle de l'école, in D. Hameline, A. Jornod and M. Belkaïd (eds), *L'école active. Textes fondateurs*. Paris: PUF, pp. 51–56.

Bovet, P. (1920), Le sentiment filial et la religion. *Revue de théologie et de philosophie*, 8, 141–153.

Bovet, P. (1932), *Vingt ans de vie. L'Institut Jean-Jacques Rousseau de 1912 à 1932*. Neuchâtel: Delachaux & Niestlé.

Bovet, P. (1933), Aux membres collaborateurs de l'Institut J.-J. Rousseau. Letter written on 7 May 1933, in the archives of the University of Geneva, 5B1/45.

Bower, T.G.R. (1977), *The Perceptual World of the Child*. London: Fontana.

Bower, T.G.R. (1979), *Human Development*. San Francisco: Freeman.

Bower, T.G.R. (1989), The perceptual world of the new-born child, in A. Slater and G. Bremner (eds), *Infant Development*. Hove: Erlbaum, pp. 85–96.

Boyd, W., and Rawson, W.T.R. (1965), *The Story of the New Education*. London: Heinemann.

Braine, M.D. (1959), The ontogeny of certain logical operations: Piaget's formulation examined by nonverbal methods. *Psychological Monographs: General and Applied*, 73, 1–43.

Brainerd, C.J. (1976), The development of the proportionality scheme in children and adolescents. *Developmental Psychology*, 5, 469–474.

Brainerd, C.J. (1978), *Piaget's Theory of Intelligence*. Englewood Cliffs: Prentice Hall.

Bremner, J.G. (1985), Object tracking and search in infancy: a review of data and theoretical evaluation. *Developmental Review*, 5, 371–396.

Broadbent, D.E. (1958), *Perception and Communication*. London: Pergamon.

Brockmeier, J. (1996), Construction and interpretation: Exploring a joint perspective on Piaget and Vygotsky, in A. Tryphon and J. Vonèche (eds), *Piaget-Vygotsky. The Social Genesis of Thought*. East Essex: Psychology Press, pp. 125–143.

Brooks-Walsh, I., and Sullivan, E. (1973), Moral judgement, causal and general reasoning. *Journal of Moral Education*, 2, 131–136.

Broughton, J.M. (1981), Piaget's structural developmental psychology. *Human Development*, 24, 78–109, 195–224, 257–285, 320–346, 382–411.

Brown, A.L., and Campione, J.C. (1998), Designing a community of young learners: Theoretical and practical lessons, in N.M. Lambert and B.L. McCombs (eds), *How Students Learn. Reforming Schools through Learner Centered Education*. Washington D.C: American Psychology Association, pp.153–186.

Brown, G., and Desforges, C. (1977), Piagetian psychology and education: Time for revision. *British Journal of Educational Psychology*, 47, 7–17.

Bruner, J.S. (1959), Inhelder and Piaget's "The Growth of Logical Thinking". A Psychologist's Viewpoint. *British Journal of Psychology*, 40, 365–370.

Bruner, J.S., and Haste, H. (1987), *Making Sense. The Child's Construction of the World*. London: Methuen.

Bruner, J.S., Jolly, A., and Sylva, K. (1976), *Play—Its Role in Development and Evolution*. New York: Basic Books.

Bruner, J.S., Olver, R.R., and Greenfield, P.M. (1966/1971), *Studien zu kognitiven Entwicklung*. Stuttgart: Klett.

Brunschvicg, L. (1897), *La modalité du jugement*. Paris: Alcan 1964.

Brunschvicg, L. (1900), *Introduction à la vie de l'esprit*. Paris: Alcan 1911.

Brunschvicg, L. (1921), *Nature et Liberté*. Paris: Alcan.

Brunschvicg, L. (1922), *L'expérience humaine et la causalité physique*. Paris: Alcan.

Bryant, P.E. (1972), The understanding of invariance in very young children. *Canadian Journal of Psychology*, 26, 78–96.

Bryant, P.E. (1996), Children and arithmetic. In L. Smith (ed.), *Critical Readings on Piaget*. London: Routledge and Kegan Paul, pp. 312–364.

Bryant, P.E., and Kopytynska, H. (1976), Spontaneous measurement by young children. *Nature*, 260, 773.

Bryant, P.E., and Trabasso, T. (1971), Transitive inferences and memory in young children. *Nature*, 232, 456–458.

Buck-Morss, S. (1975), Socio-economic bias in Piaget's theory and its implications for cross-cultural studies. *Human Development*, 18, 35–49.

Buggle, F. (1985), *Die Entwicklungspsychologie Jean Piagets*. Stuttgart: Kohlhammer.

Bühler, C. (1928), *Kindheit und Jugend. Genese des Bewusstseins*. Leipzig: Hirzel.

Bühler, K. (1918), *Die geistige Entwicklung des Kindes*. Jena: Fischer 1921.

Bullock, M., Gelman, R., and Baillargeon, R. (1982), The development of causal reasoning, in W. J. Friedman (ed.), *The Developmental Psychology of Time*. New York: Academic Press, pp. 209–254.

Burger, J.-D. (1929), Pour la transcendance. *Revue de théologie et de philosophie*, 17, 33–40.

Buscaglia, M. (1985), La biologie de Jean Piaget (1896–1980)—cohérence et marginalité. *Synthèse*, 65, 99–120.

Butterworth, G.E., and Cochran, E. (1980), Towards a mechanism of joint visual attention in human infancy. *International Journal of Behavioural Development*, 4, 253–272.

Cambon, J. (1977), Jean Piaget et la recherche française en éducation. *Bulletin de psychologie*, 30, 159–165.

Carey, S. (1985), *Conceptual Change in Childhood*. Cambridge: MIT Press.

Carlson, J.S. (1978), Kulturvergleichende Untersuchungen im Rahmen von Piagets Theorie, in G. Steiner (ed.), *Die Psychologie des 20. Jahrhunderts, VII. Piaget und die Folgen*. Zürich: Kindler, pp. 709–728.

Carotenuto, A. (1986), *Sabina Spielrein. Tagebuch einer heimlichen Symmetrie*. Freiburg: Kore.

Caruso, I.H. (1943), *La notion de responsabilité et de justice immanente chez l'enfant*. Neuchâtel: Delachaux et Niestlé.

Case, R. (1985), *Intellectual Development*. London: Methuen.

Case, R. (1987), Neo-piagetian theory: retrospect and prospect. *International Journal of Psychology*, 22, 773–791.

Chapman, M. (1988), *Constructive Evolution. Origins and Development of Piaget's Thought*. New York: Cambridge University Press.

Charles, C.M. (1974), *Teachers' Petite Piaget*. Belmont: Fearon.

Charlesworth, R., and Hartup, W. (1967), Positive social reinforcement in the nursery school peer group. *Child Development*, 38, 993–1002.

Chi, M.T.H. (1978), Knowledge structures and memory development, in R.S. Siegler (ed.), *Children's Thinking. What Develops?* Hilldale: Earlbaum, pp. 73–96.

Chomsky, N. (1979), *Language and Responsibility*. New York: Phanteon.

Church, J. (1961), *Sprache und die Entdeckung der Wirklichkeit. Über den Spracherwerb des Kleinkindes*. Frankfurt: Fischer 1971.

Cifali, M. (1982). Entre Genève et Paris: Vienne. *Le Bloc-notes de la psychanalyse*, 2, 91–130.

Claparède, E. (1923), La psychologie de l'école active. *L'Educateur*, 59, 371–379.

Claparède, E. (1931), *L'éducation fonctionelle*. Neuchâtel: Delachaux et Niestlé 1956.

Cohen, D. (1981), *Faut-il brûler Piaget?* Paris: Retz.

Colby, A., and Kohlberg, L. (1978), Das moralische Urteil, in G. Steiner (ed.), *Die Psychologie des 20. Jahrhunderts, VII. Piaget und die Folgen*. Zürich: Kindler, pp. 348–366.

Cole, M., and Bruner, J.S. (1971), Cultural differences and inferences about psychological processes. *American Psychologist*, 26, 867–876.

Collins, A., Brown, J.S., and Newman, S.E. (1989), Cognitive apprenticeship: Teaching the crafts of reading, writing and mathematics, in L.B. Resnick (ed.), *Knowing, Learning and Instruction. Essays in the Honour of Robert Glaser*. Hillsdale: Erlbaum, pp. 453–494.

Copeland, R. (1970), *How Children Learn Mathematics: Teaching Implications of Piaget's Research*. New York: Macmillan.

Copple, C., Sigel, I., and Saunders, R. (1979), *Educating the Young Thinker: Classroom Strategies for Cognitive Growth*. New York: Van Nostrand.

Criblez, L., Jenzer, C., Hofstetter, R., and Magnin, C. (eds) (1999), *Eine Schule für die Demokratie. Zur Entwicklung der Volksschule in der Schweiz im 19. Jahrhundert*. Bern: Lang.

Damerow, P. (1994), Vorüberlegungen zu einer historischen Epistemologie der Zahlbegriffsentwicklung, in G. Dux and U. Wenzel (eds), *Der Prozess der Geistesgeschichte. Studien zur ontogenetischen und historischen Entwicklung des Geistes*. Frankfurt: Suhrkamp, pp. 248–322.

Damerow, P., and Lefèvre, W. (1998), Wissenssysteme im geschichtlichen Wandel, in F. Klix and H. Spada (eds), *Enzyklopädie der Psychologie, II: Kognition, VI: Wissen*. Göttingen: Hogrefe, pp. 65–113.

Dasen, P.R. (1972), Cross-cultural Piagetian research: A summary. *Journal of Cross-Cultural Psychology*, 3, 23–39.

Dasen, P.R., and Héron, A. (1981), Cross-cultural tests of Piaget's theory, in H.C. Triandis and A. Héron (eds), *Handbook of Cross-Cultural Psychology, IV*. Boston: Allyn & Bacon, pp. 295–341.

Davidson, P., Turiel, E., and Black, A. (1983), The effect of stimulus familiarity on the use of criteria and justifications in children's social reasoning. *British Journal of Developmental Psychology*, 1, 49–65.

Davy, G. (1939), Les sentiments sociaux et les sentiments moraux, in G. Dumas (ed.). *Nouveau traîté de Psychologie VI*. Paris: Alcan, pp. 224–236.

Décarie, G.T. (1969), A study of mental and emotional development of the thalidomide child, in B. Foss (ed.), *Determinants of Infant Behavior, IV*. London: Methuen.

Delacroix, H. (1924), Comte rendu de: Le langage et la pensée chez l'enfant. *Journal de Psychologie Normale et Pathologique*, 1–3, 17.

Delacroix, H. (1927), Comte rendu de: Le jugement et le raisonnement chez l'enfant et de la représentation du monde chez l'enfant. *Journal de Psychologie Normale et Pathologique*, 6, 561–569.

DeLisi, R., and Golbeck, S. (1999), Implications of Piagetian theory for peer learning, in A. O'Donnell and A. King (eds), *Cognitive Perspectives on Peer Learning*. Mahwah: Erlbaum, pp. 3–37.

Depaepe, M. (1993), *Zum Wohl des Kindes. Pädologie, pädagogische Psychologie und experimentelle Pädagogik in Europa und den USA, 1890–1940*. Weinheim: Deutscher Studien Verlag.

Döbert, R. (1991/1995), Männliche Moral—weibliche Moral? in G. Nunner-Winkler (ed.), *Weibliche Moral. Die Kontroverse um eine geschlechtsspezifische Ethik.* München: Deutscher Taschenbuch Verlag, pp. 121–146.

Doise, W. (1978), Soziale Interaktion und kognitive Entwicklung, in G. Steiner (ed.), *Die Psychologie des 20. Jahrhunderts, VII. Piaget und die Folgen.* Zürich: Kindler, pp. 331–347.

Doise, W., Dionnet, S., and Mugny, G. (1978), Conflit socio-cognitif, marquage social et dévelopment cogitif. *Cahiers de Psychologie*, 27, 231–243.

Doise, W., Mugny, G., and Pérez, J.A. (1995), Soziale Konstruktion des Wissens—soziale Markierung und soziokognitiver Konflikt, in U. Flick (ed.), *Psychologie des Sozialen. Repräsentationen in Wissen und Sprache.* Reinbek: Rowohlt, pp. 100–118.

Doise, W., Mugny. G., and Perret-Clermont, A.-N. (1975), Social interaction and the development of cognitive operations. *European Journal of Social Psychology*, 5, 367–383.

Donaldson, M. (1978), *Children's Minds.* New York: Norton.

Donaldson, M. (1986), *Children's Explanations.* Cambridge: Cambridge University Press.

Dosse, F. (1991/1996/1997), *Geschichte des Strukturalismus.* Hamburg: Junius.

Dottrens, R. (1927), *L'éducation nouvelle en Autriche.* Neuchâtel: Delachaux & Niestlé.

Dottrens, R. (1933), L'éducation nouvelle et la paix. *Supplément de L'école nouvelle*, 13, 13.

Driver, R. (1996), *Young People's Images of Science.* Philadelphia: Open University Press.

Droz, R. (1980), De la nécessité et de l'impossibilité d'exploiter les travaux de Piaget en pédagogie. *Education et recherche*, 2, 7–24.

Ducret, J.-J. (1984), *Jean Piaget, savant et philosophe. Les années de formation, 1907–1924. Etude sur la formation et du sujet de la connaissance.* Genf: Droz.

Ducret, J.-J. (1990), *Jean Piaget. Biographie et parcours intellectuel.* Neuenburg: Delachaux et Niestlé.

Durkheim, E. (1893/1977), *Über die Teilung der sozialen Arbeit. Studie über die Organiation höherer Gesellschaften.* Frankfurt: Suhrkamp.

Durkheim, E. (1898/1986), Der Individualismus und die Intellektuellen, in H. Bertram (ed.), *Gesellschaftlicher Zwang und moralische Autonomie.* Frankfurt: Suhrkamp, pp. 54–70.

Durkheim, E. (1903/1984), *Erziehung, Moral und Gesellschaft. Vorlesungen an der Sorbonne 1902/03.* Frankfurt: Suhrkamp.

Durkheim, E. (1924/1976), *Soziologie und Philosophie.* Frankfurt: Suhrkamp.

Dux, G. (1982), *Die Logik der Weltbilder. Sinnstrukturen im Wandel der Geschichte.* Frankfurt: Suhrkamp.

Dux, G. (1994), Die ontogenetische und historische Entwicklung des Geistes, in G. Dux and U. Wenzel (eds), *Der Prozess der Geistesgeschichte. Studien zur ontogenetischen und historischen Entwicklung des Geistes*. Frankfurt: Suhrkamp, pp. 173–224.

Dux, G. (2000/2005), *Historisch-genetische Theorie der Kultur*. Weilerwist: Velbrück.

Eck, C.D. (1979), Sozialpsychologische Aspekte der Religion, in G. Condrau (ed.), *Psychologie des 20. Jahrhunderts, XV*. Zürich: Kindler, pp. 93–108.

Edelstein, W., Oser, F., and Schuster, P. (2001), *Moralische Erziehung in der Schule. Entwicklungspsychologie und pädagogische Praxis*. Weinheim: Beltz.

Egan, K. (2002), *Getting it Wrong from the Beginning. Our Progressivist Inheritance from Herbert Spencer, John Dewey, and Jean Piaget*. New Haven: Yale University Press.

Egan, K. (2005), Students' development in theory and practice: the doubtful role of research, www.educ.sfu.ca/kegan/HER.html.

Egger, E. (1979), L'intégration de BIE à L'UNESCO, in B. Suchodolski (ed.), *Le Bureau International d'éducation au service du mouvement éducatif*. Paris: UNESCO, pp. 107–118.

Elkind, D. (1961), The child's conception of his religious denomination. *Journal of Genetic Psychology*, 99, 209–225.

Elkind, D. (1967), Egocentrism in adolescence. *Child Development*, 38, 1025–1034.

Elkind, D. (1968), Giant in the nursery—Jean Piaget. *The New York Times Magazine*, May, 25–27.

Elkind, D. (1976), *Child Development and Education: a Piagetian Perspective*. New York: Oxford University Press.

Elkind, D. (1978), Zwei entwicklungspsychologische Ansätze: Piaget und Montessori, in G. Steiner (ed.), *Die Psychologie des 20. Jahrhunderts. VII. Piaget und die Folgen*. Zürich: Kindler, pp. 584–594.

Emler, N. (1983), Approaches to moral development: Piagetian influences, in S. Modgil, C. Mogdil and G. Brown (eds), *Jean Piaget, an Interdisciplinary Critique*. London: Routledge & Kegan Paul, pp. 139–151.

Endler, N.S., Rushton, J.P., and Roediger H.L. (1978), Productivity and scholarly impact (citations), of British, Canadian, and U.S. departments of psychology (1975). *American Psychologist*, 33, 1064–1082.

Enright, R.D., Schukla, D.G., and Lapsley, D.K. (1980), Adolescent egocentrism-sociocentrism and self-consciousness. *Journal of Youth and Adolescence*, 9, 101–116.

Etkind, A. (1993/1996), *Eros des Unmöglichen. Die Geschichte der Psychoanalyse in Russland*. Leipzig: Kiepenheuer.

Fantz, R.L. (1961), The origin of form perception. *Scientific American*, 204, 66–72.

Fässler, H. (2005), *Reise in Scharz-Weiss. Schweizer Ortstermine in Sachen Sklaverei.* Zürich: Rotpunkt.

Fauconnet, P. (1912/1920), *La Responsabilité. Etude de sociologie.* Paris: Alcan.

Favre, L., Bachelin, A., and Guillaume, K. (1874), A nos lecteurs, *Le Rameau de Sapin*, 1 (January 1874), 1.

Ferrière, A. (1921), *L'autonomie des écoliers. L'art de former des citoyens pour la nation et pour l'humanité.* Neuchâtel: Delachaux & Niestlé.

Ferrière, A. (1922), *L'Ecole active.* Neuchâtel: Editions Forum.

Ferrière, A. (1928), Compte rendu de J. Piaget: La causalité physique chez l'enfant. *Pour l'ère nouvelle*, 7, 108–109.

Fetz, R.L. (1978), Piaget als philosophisches Ereignis, in G. Steiner (ed.), *Die Psychologie des 20. Jahrhunderts, VII. Piaget und die Folgen.* Zürich: Kindler, pp. 27–40.

Fetz, R.L. (1999), Whitehead, Cassirer, Piaget. Drei Denker—ein gemeinsames Paradigma. *Salzburger Theologische Zeitschrift*, 3, 154–168.

Fischer, K.W., and Bidell, T.R. (2006), Dynamic development of action, thought, and emotion, in W. Damon and R.M. Lerner (eds), *Handbook of Child Psychology. Theoretical Models of Human Development.* New York: Wiley, pp. 313–399.

Flavell, J.H. (1963), *The Developmental Psychology of Jean Piaget.* New Jersey: Van Nostrand.

Fleck, L. (1935), *Entstehung und Entwicklung einer wissenschaftlichen Tatsache. Einführung in die Lehre vom Denkstil und Denkkollektiv.* Frankfurt: Suhrkamp 1980.

Fleisher Feldman, C. (1992), The new theory of theory of mind. *Human Development*, 35, 107–117.

Flournoy, T. (1903), Les principes de la psychologie religieuse. *Archives de psychologie*, 2, 33–57.

Flournoy, T. (1916/1984), Religion et psychoanalyse. *Le Bloc-notes de la psychanalyse*, 4, 191–199.

Fodor, J.A. (1983), *The Modularity of the Mind.* Cambridge, MA: MIT Press.

Forman, G., and Kuschner, D. (1977), *The Child's Construction of Knowledge: Piaget for Teaching Children.* Monterey: Brooks & Cole.

Fouillée, A. (1893), *Psychologie des idées-force.* Paris: Alcan.

Fowler, J.W. (1981), *Stages of Faith: the Psychology of Human Development and the Quest for Meaning.* New York: HarperCollins.

Freud, S. (1914/1960), Zur Geschichte der psychoanalytischen Bewegung, in Freud, S., *Gesammelte Werke, X.* Frankfurt: Fischer, pp. 43–113.

Freudenthal, H. (1973), *Mathematik als pädagogische Aufgabe.* Stuttgart: Klett.

Fricke, A. (1959), Operatives Denken im Rechenunterricht als Anwendung der Psychologie von Jean Piaget. *Westermanns Pädagogische Beiträge*, 11, 99–114.

Fromm, E. (1941), *Die Furcht vor der Freiheit*. Frankfurt: Ullstein 1984.

Fuchs, M. (2002), *Hans Aebli—zwischen Psychologie und Pädagogik*. Aarau: Sauerländer.

Fuller, R.G. (1977), (ed.), *Multidisciplinary Piagetian-Based Programs for College Freshmen*. Lincoln, NE: University of Nebraska.

Furth, H.G. (1966), *Thinking Without Language: Psychological Implications of Deafness*. New York: Free Press.

Furth, H.G. (1970), *Piaget for Teachers*. New York: Prentice Hall.

Furth, H.G. (1990), *Wissen als Leidenschaft. Eine Untersuchung über Freud und Piaget*. Frankfurt: Suhrkamp.

Furth, H.G., and Wachs, H. (1974), *Thinking Goes to School: Piaget's Theory in Practice*. New York: Oxford University Press.

Gardner, H. (1970/1978), Piaget und Lévi-Strauss, in G. Steiner (ed.), *Die Psychologie des 20. Jahrhunderts, VII. Piaget und die Folgen*. Zürich: Kindler, pp. 74–85.

Gardner, H. (1985), *The Mind's New Science: A History of the Cognitive Revolution*. New York: Basic Books.

Gasch, S. (2005), Alan Kay, http://ei.cs.vt.edu/~history/GASCH.KAY. HTML.

Gelman, R. (1979), Preschool thought. *American Psychologist*, 34, 900–905.

Gelman, R., and Baillargeon, R. (1983), A review of some Piagetian concepts, in J.H. Flavell and E.M. Markman (eds), *Handbook of Child Psychology, III: Cognitive Development*. New York: Wiley, pp. 167–230.

Gelman, R., and Gallistel, C.R. (1978), *The Child's Understanding of Number*. Cambridge: Harvard University Press.

Gerson, R.R., and Damon, W. (1978), Moral understanding and children's conduct, in W. Damon (ed.), *Moral Development*. San Francisco: Jossey-Bass, pp. 41–61.

Glasersfeld, E. v. (1987), *Wissen, Sprache und Wirklichkeit. Arbeiten zum Radikalen Konstruktivismus*. Braunschweig: Vieweg.

Glasersfeld, E. v. (1994), Piagets konstruktivistisches Modell: Wissen und Lernen, in G. Rusch and S. J. Schmidt (eds), *Piaget und der Radikale Konstruktivismus*. Frankfurt: Suhrkamp, pp. 16–42.

Goblot, E. (1918), *Traité de logique*. Paris: Colin.

Godet, P. (1909), Letter to Jean Piaget (19 March 1909). Archives Jean Piaget, Geneva.

Goldman, R. (1964), *Religious Thinking from Childhood to Adolescence*. London: Routledge & Kegan Paul.

Goldschmid, M.L., and Bentler, P.M. (1968), *Concept Assessment Kit-Conservation*. San Diego, CA: Educational and Industrial Testing Service.

Gorman, R. (1972), *Discovering Piaget: a Guide for Teachers*. Columbus, OH: Merril.

Goswami, U. (1992), *Analogical Reasoning in Children*. Hove: Erlbaum.

Goswami, U. (2001), *So denken Kinder. Einführung in die Psychologie der kognitiven Entwicklung*. Bern: Huber.

Gréco, P., and Morf, A. (1962), *Structures numériques élémentaires. EEG XIII*. Paris: PUF.

Greenfield, P.M.(1966), On culture and conservation, in J.S. Bruner, R.R. Olver and P.M. Greenfield (eds), *Studies in Cognitive Growth*. New York: Wiley, pp. 225–256.

Groos, K. (1899), *Die Spiele des Menschen*. Jena: Fischer.

Gruber, H.E., and Vonèche, J.J. (eds) (1977), *The Essential Piaget*. New York: Basic Books.

Grünbaum, A.A. (1927), Die Struktur der Kindersprache. *Zeitschrift für pädagogische Psychologie*, 28, 446–463.

Grunder, H.-U. (1992), Jean Piaget als Reformpädagoge. *Pädagogische Rundschau* 46, 541–564.

Habermas, J. (1981), *Theorie des kommunikativen Handelns*. Frankfurt: Suhrkamp.

Habermas, J. (1983), *Moralbewusstsein und kommunikatives Handeln*. Frankfurt: Suhrkamp.

Haggbloom, S. (2002), The 100 most eminent psychologists of the 20th century. *Review of General Psychology*, 6, 139–152, http://psychology.about.com/od/historyofpsychology/p/topten.htm.

Hall, Jody S. (2000), Psychology and schooling: the impact of Susan Isaacs and Jean Piaget on 1960s science education reform. *History of Education*, 29, 153–170.

Hallpike, C.R. (1979), *The Foundation of Primitive Thought*. Oxford: Oxford University Press.

Hameline, D. (1995), L'anonyme et le patronyme, portraits et figures de l'éducation nouvelle, in D. Hameline, J. Helmchen and J. Oelkers (eds), *L'éducation nouvelle et les enjeux de son histoire. Actes du colloque international des Archives Institut Jean-Jacques Rousseau*. Bern: Lang, pp. 131–160.

Hameline, D. (1996), Les figures de Jean Piaget, in J.-M. Barrelet and A.-N. Perret-Clermont (eds), *Jean Piaget et Neuchâtel. L'apprenti et le savant*. Lausanne: Editions Payot, pp. 235–252.

Hameline, D., and Vonèche, J. (1996), *Jean Piaget. Agir et construire. Aux origines de la connaissance chez l'enfant et le savant*. Genève: FPSE.

Hamlyn, D.W. (1978), *Experience and the Growth of Understanding*. London: Routledge & Kegan Paul.

Harris, P.L. (1983), Infant cognition, in M.M. Haith and J.J. Campos (eds), *Handbook of Child Psychology. II: Infancy and Developmental Psychobiology*. New York: Wiley, pp. 689–782.

Harris, P.L. (1997), Piaget in Paris: from "autism" to logic. *Human Development* 40, 109–123.

Harrower, M.R. (1934), Social status and moral development. *British Journal of Educational Psychology*, 4, 75–95.

Haynal, A. (1975), Freud und Piaget. *Psyche*, 29, 242–272.

Hazlitt, V. (1930), Children's thinking. *British Journal of Psychology*, 20, 354–361.

Heidbrink, H. (1991), *Stufen der Moral. Zur Gültigkeit der kognitiven Entwicklungstheorie Lawrence Kohlbergs*. München: Quintessenz-Verlag.

Heidbrink, H. (2005), Jean Piaget, in H.E. Lück and R. Miller (eds), *Illustrierte Geschichte der Psychologie*. Weinheim: Beltz, pp.131–135.

Heller, J., and Piaget, J. (eds) (1934), *Le self-government à l'école*. Genève: BIE.

Helmchen, J. (1995), L'éducation nouvelle francophone et la Reformpädagogik allemande. Deux histoires? In D. Hameline, J. Helmchen and J. Oelkers (eds), *L'éducation nouvelle et les enjeux de son histoire. Actes du colloque international des Archives Institut Jean-Jacques Rousseau*. Bern: Lang, pp. 1–29.

Herzog, W. (1991), *Das moralische Subjekt. Pädagogische Intuition und psychologische Theorie*. Bern: Huber.

Hoffman, M.L. (2000), *Empathy and Moral Development. Implications for Caring and Justice*. New York: Cambridge University Press.

Hofsten, C. von (1982), Eye-hand co-ordination in the newborn. *Developmental Psychology*, 18, 450–461.

Hofsten, C. von (1983), Catching skills in infancy. *Journal of Experimental Psychology. Human Perception and Performance*, 9, 75–85.

Hofstetter, R. (2004), The construction of a new science by means of an institute and its communication media: the Institute of Educational Sciences in Geneva (1912–1948). *Paedagogica Historica* 40, 657–683.

Hofstetter, R., and Schneuwly, B. (2004), Introduction. Educational sciences in dynamic and hybrid institutionalization. *Paedagogica Historica* 40, 569–589.

Horn, K.-P. (2001), Abbild oder Zerrbild? Ergebnisse der Befragung zu den pädagogisch wichtigsten Veröffentlichungen des 20. Jahrhunderts, in K.-P. Horn and C. Ritzi (eds), *Klassiker und Aussenseiter*. Baltmannsweiler: Schneider, pp. 23–49.

Hsueh, Y. (2002), The Hawthorne experiments and the introduction of Jean Piaget in American industrial psychology, 1929–1932. *History of Psychology*, 5, 163–189.

Hsueh, Y. (2004), "He sees the development of children's concepts upon a background of sociology": Jean Piaget's honorary degree at Harvard University in 1936. *History of Psychology*, 7, 20–44.

Hubendick, B. (1951), Recent Lymnaeidae. Their variation, morphology, taxonomy, nomenclature, and distribution, in *Kungliga Svenska Vetenskapsakademiens Handlingar,* 3, 1–223.

Hudges, M., and Donaldson, M. (1983), The use of hiding games for studying coordination of viewpoints, in M. Donaldson, R. Grieve and C. Pratt (eds), *Early Childhood—Development and Education.* Oxford: Basil Blackwell, pp. 145–253.

Inhelder, B. (1976), Notre maître Jean Piaget. *Cahiers Vilfredo Pareto. Revue européenne des sciences socials,* 38–39, 199–201.

Inhelder, B. (1989), Autobiographie, in S. Volkmann-Raue (ed.), *Mit Jean Piaget arbeiten: Bärbel Inhelder.* Münster: LIT 1997, pp. 25–124.

Inhelder, B., Garcia, R., and Vonèche, J. (eds) (1977), *Epistémologie génétique et équilibration: Hommage à Jean Piaget.* Neuchâtel: Delachaux et Niestlé.

Isaacs, N. (1955), *Some Aspects of Piaget's Work.* London: National Froebel Foundation.

Isaacs, S. (1929a), Review: the child's conception of the world. *Mind,* 38, 506–513.

Isaacs, S. (1929b), Review: the language and thought of the child, judgment and reasoning in the child, and the child's conception of the world. *The Pedagogical Seminary and Journal of Genetic Psychology,* 36, 597–607.

Isaacs, S. (1930), *Intellectal Growth in Young Children.* London: Routledge & Kegan Paul.

Isaacs, S. (1931), Review: the child's conception of causality. *Mind,* 40, 89–93.

Isaacs, S. (1934), Review: the moral judgment of the child. *Mind,* 43, 85–99.

Jakiel, A., Piaget, J., Petersen, P., and Cousinet, R. (eds) (1935), *Le travail par équipes à l'école.* Genève: BIE.

Jalley, E. (1981), *Wallon, lecteur de Freud et Piaget.* Paris: Editions Socials.

Janet, P. (1914/15), Les tendances intellectuelles relatives à la recherche de la vérité. *Annuaire du Collège de France,* 14–15, 80–91.

Janet, P. (1926), *Les stades de l'évolution psychologique.* Paris: Maloine.

Janet, P. (1928), *De l'angoisse à l'exstase.* Paris: Alcan.

Janet, P. (1929), *L'évolution psychologique de la personnalité.* Paris: Maloine.

Janet, P. (1935), *Les débuts de l'intelligence.* Paris: Flammarion.

Jardine, D.W. (2006), *Piaget and Education. Primer.* New York: Peter Lang.

Jean, P. (1925), *Théorie nouvelle de la vie. La Psychologie organique.* Paris: Alcan.

Johnson-Laird, P.N., and Byrne, R.M.J. (1991), *Deduction.* Hove: Erlbaum.

Jordan, N. (1972), Is there an Achilles heel in Piaget's theorizing? *Human Development,* 15, 379–382.

Jurkovic, A.G. (1980), The juvenile delinquent as moral philosopher. *Psychological Bulletin,* 88, 709–729.

Kagan, J. (1984), *Die Natur des Kindes*. München: Pieper 1987.

Kamii, C., and DeVries, R. (1972/1977), Piaget for early education, in M.C. Day and R.K. Parker (eds), *The Preschool in Action. Exploring Early Childhood Programs*. Boston: Allyn & Bacon, pp. 365–420.

Kamii, C., and DeClark, G. (1985), *Young Children Reinvent Mathematics. Implications of Piaget's Theory*. New York: Teachers College Press.

Kant, I. (1781/1787/1968), *Kritik der reinen Vernunft*. Frankfurt: Suhrkamp.

Karmiloff-Smith, A. (1992), *Beyond Modularity. A Developmental Perspective on Cognitive Science*. Cambridge: MIT Press.

Karplus, R. (1980), Denkmuster. *Physica Didacta*, 7, 5–15.

Katz, D., and Katz, R. (1928), *Gespräche mit Kindern. Untersuchungen zur Sozialpsychologie und Pädagogik*. Berlin: Springer.

Keller, M. (2005), Moralentwicklung und moralische Sozialisation, in D. Horster and J. Oelkers (eds), *Pädagogik und Ethik*. Wiesbaden: VS Verlag, pp. 149–172.

Kelly, G.A. (1955), *The Psychology of Personal Constructs*. New York: Norton.

Kesselring, T. (1981), *Entwicklung und Widerspruch. Ein Vergleich zwischen Piagets genetischer Erkenntnistheorie und Hegels Dialektik*. Frankfurt: Suhrkamp.

Kesselring, T. (1999), *Jean Piaget*. München: Beck.

Kitchener, R.F. (1985), Holistic structuralism, elementarism, and Piaget's theory of relationism. *Human Development*, 28, 281–294.

Klahr, D., and MacWhinney, B. (1998), Information processing, in D. Kuhn and R.S. Siegler (eds), *Handbook of Child Psychology, II*. New York: Wiley, pp. 631–676.

Kleint, B. (1928), Besprechung: La causalité physique chez l'enfant. *Zeitschrift für Psychologie und Physiologie der Sinnesorgane*, 108, 455–457.

Kohlberg, L. (1969), Stages and sequences. The cognitive development approach to socialization, in D. Goslin (ed.), *Handbook of Socialization*. Chicago: Rand McNally, pp. 347–480.

Kohlberg, L., and Power, C. (1981), Moral development, religious thinking and the question of a seventh stage, in L. Kohlberg (ed.), *Essays on Moral Development, I: The Philosophy of Moral Development*. San Francisco: Harper & Row, pp. 311–371.

Kolakowski, L. (1985), *Henri Bergson. Ein Dichterphilosoph*. München: Piper.

Kölbl, C. (2005), Moral im Geschichtsbewusstsein. In D. Horster and J. Oelkers (eds), *Pädagogik und Ethik*. Wiesbaden: VS Verlag, pp. 235–257.

Krappmann, L. (1994), Sozialisation und Entwicklung in der Sozialwelt gleichaltriger Kinder, in K.A. Schneewind (ed.), *Psychologie der Erziehung und Sozialisation, I*. Göttingen: Hogrefe, pp. 495–524.

Krist, H., and Wilkening, F. (1991), Repräsentationale Entwicklung. *Sprache und Kognition*, 10, 181–195.

Kubli, F. (1981), *Piaget und Naturwissenschaftsdidaktik. Konsequenzen aus den entwicklungspsychologischen Untersuchungen von Jean Piaget.* Köln: Aulis.

Kubli, F. (1983), *Erkenntnis und Didaktik. Piaget und die Schule.* Basel: Reinhardt.

Kuenburg, M. von (1926), Besprechung: Le développement de la pensée de l'enfant. *Zeitschrift für Kinderforschung*, 32, 288–289.

Kuhn, D. (1979), The application of Piaget's theory of cognitive development to education. *Harvard Educational Review*, 49, 340–360.

Kuhn, T.S. (1962), *The Structure of Scientific Revolutions.* Chicago, University of Chicago Press.

Labinowicz, E. (1980), *The Piaget Primer: Thinking, Learning, Teaching.* Menlo Park: Addison-Wesley.

Laird, J.E., Rosenbloom, P.S., and Newell, A. (1986), Chunking in SOAR: the anatomy of general learning mechanisms. *Machine Learning*, 1, 11–46.

Lalande, A. (1893), *Lecture sur la philosophie des science.* Paris: Hachette 1907.

Lalande, A. (1899), *Les illusions évolutionistes.* Paris: Alcan 1930.

Langer, J. (1969), Disequilibrium as a source of development, in P.H. Mussen, J. Langer and M. Covington (eds), *Trends and Issues in Developmental Psychology.* New York: Holt, Rinehart & Winston, pp. 22–37.

Laux, J. (1969), *Die Bildung des Zahlbegriffs in den ersten drei Schuljahren.* Stuttgart: Klett.

Lavatelli, C. (1970), *Piaget's Theory Applied to an Early Childhood Curriculum.* Boston: American Science and Engineering.

Lave, J. (1991), Situating learning in communities of practice, in L.B. Resnick, J.M. Levine and S.D. Teasley (eds), Perspectives on Socially Shared Cognition. Washington: American Psychology Association, pp. 63–82.

Leber, A. (1994), Vorwort, in J. Piaget: *Intelligenz und Affektivität in der Entwicklung des Kindes.* Frankfurt: Suhrkamp, 1995, pp. 9–13.

Leber, A. (1995), Ein Schlüssel zum Verständnis menschlichen Verhaltens. Die Aktuaität der Sorbonne-Vorlesung Jean Piagets für Theorie und Praxis, in J. Piaget: *Intelligenz und Affektivität in der Entwicklung des Kindes.* Frankfurt: Suhrkamp, pp. 151–194.

Le Dantec, F. (1897), *Le déterminisme biologique et la personnalité consciente.* Paris: Alcan.

Lemperers, J.D., Flavell, E.R., and Flavell, J.H. (1977), The development in very young children of tacit knowledge concerning visual perception. *Genetic Psychology Monographs*, 95, 3–53.

Lerner, E. (1937), *Constraint Areas and the Moral Judgment of Children.* Menasta: George Banta.

Leslie, A. M. (1982), The perception of causality in infants. *Perception*, 11, 173–186.

Lévy-Bruhl, L. (1910), *Les fontions mentales dans les sociétés inférieures*. Paris: Alcan 1918.

Lickona, T. (1976), Research on Piaget's theory of moral development, in T. Lickona (ed.), *Moral Development and Behavior. Theory, Research, and Social Issues*. New York: Holt, Rinehart & Winston, pp. 219–240.

Lidz, C.W., and Meyer Lidz, V. (1976), Piagets Psychologie der Intelligenz und die Handlungstheorie, in J.J. Loubser, R.C. Baum, A. Effrat and V. Meyer Lidz (eds), *Allgemeine Handlungstheorie*. Frankfurt: Suhrkamp 1981, pp. 202–327.

Liebsch, B. (1986), Psychoanalyse und Genfer Konstruktivismus. *Psyche*, 40, 220–247.

Liengme Bessire, M.-J., and Béguelin, S. (1996), De la malacologie à a psychologie: la "conversion" de Jean Piaget s'est-elle jouée à la Faculté des lettre? in J.-M. Barrelet and A.-N. Perret-Clermont (eds), *Jean Piaget et Neuchâtel. L'apprenti et le savant*. Lausanne: Editions Payot, pp. 81–94.

Lloyd, P. (1983), Language and communication: Piaget's influence, in S. Modgil, C. Modgil and G. Brown (eds), *Jean Piaget, an Interdisciplinary Critique*. London: Routledge & Kegan Paul, pp. 105–121.

Locke, J. (1689/1997), *An Essay Concerning Human Understanding* (ed. R. Woolhouse). London: Penguin.

Lockman, J.J. (1990), Perceptumotor coordination in infancy, in C.A. Hauert (ed.), *Developmental Psychology. Cognitive, Perceptuo-Motor, and Neuropsychological Perspectives*. Amsterdam: Elsevier, pp. 85–111.

Looft, W.R. (1972), Egocentrism and social interaction across the life span. *Psychological Bulletin*, 78, 78–92.

Lowery, L. (1974), *Learning about Learning: Conservation Abilities*. Berkeley: University of California Press.

Lussi, V., Muller, C., and Kiciman, V. (2002), Pédagogie et psychologie: les frontières mouvantes du développement des sciences de l'éducation à Genève, in R. Hofstetter and B. Schneuwly (eds), *Science(s), et l'éducation 19e–20e siècles: entre champs professionnels et champs disciplinaires*. Bern: Lang, pp. 383–421.

Mackay, C.K. (1983), Piaget and education: a positive comment, in S. Modgil, C. Mogdil, and G. Brown (eds), *Jean Piaget, an Interdisciplinary Critique*. London: Routledge & Kegan Paul, pp. 61–68.

MacLane, S. (1971), *Categories for the Working Mathematicians*. New York: Springer.

Malrieu, P. (1952), *Les émotions et la personnalité de l'enfant*. Paris: Vrin.

Mandler, J.M. (1990), A new perspective on cognitive development in infancy. *American Scientist*, 78, 236–243.

Mandler, J.M. (1991), Prelinguistic primitives, in L.A. Sutton and C. Johnson (eds), *Proceedings of the Seventeenth Annual Meeting of the Berkeley Linguistics Society*. Berkeley: Berkeley Linguistics Society, pp 414–425.

Markman, E.M. (1978), Empirical versus logical solutions to part-whole comparison problems concerning classes and collections. *Child Development*, 49, 168–177.

McGarrigle, J., and Donaldson, M. (1975), Conservation accidents. *Cognition*, 3, 307–311.

McGarrigle, J., Grieve, R., and Hughes, M. (1974), Interpreting inclusion: a contribution to the study of the cognitive and linguistic development. *Journal of Experimental Psychology*, 26, 528–550.

Meacham, J.A., and Riegel, K.F. (1978), Dialektische Perspektiven in Piagets Theorie, in G. Steiner (ed.), *Die Psychologie des 20. Jahrhunderts, VII. Piaget und die Folgen*. Zürich: Kindler, pp. 172–183.

Mead, M. (1932), An Investigation of the thought of primitive children with special reference to animism. *Journal of the Royal Anthropological Institute*, 62, 173–190.

Meili-Dworetzki, G. (1978), Piaget in seinem Verhältnis zu seinen Lehrern Pierre Janet und Edouard Claparède, in G. Steiner (ed.), *Die Psychologie des 20. Jahrhunderts, VII. Piaget und die Folgen*. Zürich: Kindler, pp. 507–529.

Meltzoff, A.N., and Moore, M.K. (1989), Imitation in newborn infants: exploring the range of gestures imitated and underlying mechanisms. *Developmental Psychology*, 25, 954–962.

Mercer, N. (1995), *The Guided Construction of Knowledge*. Clevedon: Multilingual Matters.

Merleau-Ponty, M. (1988/1994), *Keime der Vernunft. Vorlesungen an der Sorbonne 1949–1952*. München: Fink.

Metz, K.E. (1995), Developmental constraints on children's science. *Review of Educational Research*, 65, 93–127.

Meyer, E. (1935), La représentation des relations spatiales chez l'enfant. *Cahiers de pédagogie expérimentale et de psychologie de l'enfant*, 45, 357–366.

Miller, G..A. (2003), The cognitive revolution. A historical perspective. *Trends in Cognitive Sciences*, 7, 141–144, www.cogsci.princeton.edu/~geo/ Miller.pdf.

Mischel, T. (1976), Piaget und das Wesen psychologischer Erklärungen, in *Psychologische Erklärungen. Gesammelte Aufsätze*. Frankfurt: Suhrkamp 1981, pp. 322–345.

Mitchell, L.S. (1927), Review of "The Language and Thought of the Child". *Progressive Education*, 4, 136–139.

Moessinger, P. (1977), Piaget on contradiction. *Human Development*, 20, 178–184.

Moessinger, P. (1981), Piaget on abstraction. *Human Development*, 24, 347–353.

Monod, J. (1970), *Chance and Necessity: An Essay on the Natural Philosophy of Modern Biology*. New York: Knopf 1971.

Moscovici, S. (1984), *Psychologie sociale*. Paris: PUF.

Moser, A. (1992), Switzerland, in P. Kutter (ed.), *Psychoanalysis International. A Guide to Psychoanalysis throughout the world. Vol.1, Europe*. Stuttgart: Frommann-Holzboog.

Mounoud, P. (1996), Comment naturaliser l'esprit, tout en lui conservant son irréductabilité. *Campus*, 33, 23–25.

Muchow, M. (1926), Besprechung: Le langage et la pensée chez l'enfant. *Zeitschrift für pädagogische Psychologie, experimentelle Pädagogik und jugendkundliche Forschung*, 27, 316–321 and 346–352.

Muchow, M. (1929), *Pychologische Probleme der frühen Erziehung*. Erfurt: Stenger.

Munari, A. (1994), Jean Piaget (1896–1980). *Perspectives: revue trimestrielle d'éducation comparée, XXIV*, 1–2, 321–337.

Murray, E. (1931), Review: "The Child's Conception of the World". *The American Journal of Psychology*, 43, 154–156.

Murray, F.B. (1979), (ed.), *The Impact of Piagetian Theory on Education, Philosophy, Psychiatry and Psychology*. Baltimore: University Park Press.

Neimark, E.D. (1978), Die Entwicklung des Denkens beim Heranwachsenden. Theoretische und empirische Aspekte der formalen Operationen, in G. Steiner (ed.), *Die Psychologie des 20. Jahrhunderts, VII. Piaget und die Folgen*. Zürich: Kindler, pp. 155–172.

Neisser, U. (1967), *Cognitive Psychology*. New York: Appleton-Century-Crofts.

Neuhäuser, G. (2003), *Konstruktiver Realismus. Jean Piagets naturalistische Erkenntnistheorie*. Würzburg: Königshausen und Neumann.

Nunner-Winkler, G. (1992), Zur moralischen Sozialisation. *Kölner Zeitschrift für Soziologie und Sozialpsychologie*, 44, 252–272.

Nunner-Winkler, G. (2005), Zum Verständnis von Moral-Entwicklungen in der Kindheit, in D. Horster and J. Oelkers (eds), *Pädagogik und Ethik*. Wiesbaden: VS Verlag, pp. 173–192.

O'Donohue, W., Ferguson, K.E., and Naugle, A.E. (2003), The structure of the cognitive revolution. An examination from the philosophy of science. *The Behavior Analyst*, 26, 85–110.

Oelkers, J. (1995), La Reformpädagogik au seuil de l'histoire, in D. Hameline, J. Helmchen and J. Oelkers (eds), *L'éducation nouvelle et les enjeux de son histoire. Actes su colloque international des Archives Institut Jean-Jacques Rousseau*. Bern: Lang, pp. 31–63.

Oelkers, J. (1996a), Piaget et l'éducation nouvelle, in J.-M. Barrelet and A.-N. Perret-Clermont (eds), *Jean Piaget et Neuchâtel. L'apprenti et le savant*. Lausanne: Editions Payot, pp. 165–176.

Oelkers, J. (1996b), *Reformpädagogik. Eine kritische Dogmengeschichte*. Weinheim: Juventa.

Oesterdiekhoff, G.W. (1997), *Kulturelle Bedingungen kognitiver Entwicklung. Der strukturgenetische Ansatz in der Soziologie*. Frankfurt: Suhrkamp.

Oevermann, U. (1979), Ansätze zu einer soziologischen Sozialisationstheorie und ihre Konsequenzen für die allgemeine soziologische Analyse, in G. Lüschen (ed.), *Deutsche Soziologie seit 1945.* Opladen: Westdeutscher Verlag, pp. 143–168.

Oevermann, U. (2002), Klinische Soziologie auf der Basis der Methodologie der objektiven Hermeneutik Manifest der objektiv hermeneutischen Sozialforschung, www.publikationen.ub.uni-frankfurt.de/volltexte/ 2005/540.

Ohlig, K.-H. (2001), Christentum—Individuum—Kirche, in R. van Dülmen (ed.), *Entdeckung des Ich. Die Geschichte des Individualisierung vom Mittelalter bus zur Gegenwart.* Köln: Böhlau, pp. 11–40.

Oléron, P. (1950), *Les sourds-muets.* Paris: PUF.

Ormian, H.J. (1926), Das schlussfolgernde Denken des Kindes. Eine psychogenetische Untersuchung auf experimenteller Grundlage, in C. Bühler and V. Fadrus (eds), *Wiener Arbeiten zur Pädagogischen Psychologie IV.* Wien: Deutscher Verlag für Jugend und Volk.

Oser, F., and Gmünder, P. (1992), *Der Mensch—Stufen seiner religiösen Entwicklung. Ein strukturgenetischer Ansatz.* Güterloh: Mohn.

Ottavi, D. (2001), *De Darwin à Piaget. Pour une histoire de la psychologie de l'enfant.* Paris: CNRS Editions.

Parrat-Dayan, S. (1993a), Le texte et ses voix: Piaget lu par ses pairs dans le milieu psychologique des années 1920–32. *Archives de psychologie,* 61, 127–152.

Parrat-Dayan, S. (1993b), La réception de l'oeuvre de Piaget dans le milieu pédagogique des années 1920–1930. *Revue Française de Pédagogie,* 194, 73–83.

Parsons, C. (1960), Inhelder and Piaget's "The Growth of Logical Thinking". *British Journal of Psychology,* 51, 75–84.

Pears, R., and Bryant, P.E. (1990), Transitive inferences by young children about spatial positions. *British Journal of Psychology,* 81, 497–510.

Peluffo, N. (1967), Culture and cognitive problems. *International Journal of Psychology,* 2, 187–198.

Pérez, B. (1886), *L'enfant de trois à sept ans.* Paris: Alcan.

Perner, J. (1991), *Understanding the Representational Mind.* Cambridge, MA: MIT Press.

Perrenoud, M. (1990), Eléments de l'histoire sociale des Montagnes neuchâteloises (1871–1948). *Bulletin de la Société générale suisse d'histoire,* 9–11.

Perrenoud, P. (1976), De quelques apports piagétiens à une sociologie de la pratique. *Cahiers Vilfredo Pareto. Revue européenne des sciences sociales,* 38–39, 451–470.

Perret-Clermont, A.-N. (1996), Piaget parmi ses aînés et ses pairs, in J.-M. Barrelet and A.-N. Perret-Clermont (eds), *Jean Piaget et Neuchâtel. L'apprenti et le savant*. Lausanne: Editions Payot, pp. 255–286.

Peters, R.S. (1966), *Ethik und Erziehung*. Düsseldorf: Schwann 1972.

Peters, R.S. (1978), Die Beziehung zwischen Piagets und Freuds Entwicklungstheorien, in G. Steiner (ed.), *Die Psychologie des 20. Jahrhunderts, VII. Piaget und die Folgen*. Zürich: Kindler, pp. 385–400.

Peterson, J. (1929), Review: "The Child's Conception of the World". *The American Journal of Psychology*, 41, 481–483.

Pfister, O. (1920), Jean Piaget, la psychanalyse et la pédagogie. *Imago* 6, 294–295.

Pfister, O. (1922), *Die Liebe des Kindes und ihre Fehlentwicklungen. Ein Buch für Eltern und Berufserzieher*. Bern: Bircher.

Pinard, A., and Laurendeau, M. (1964), A scale of mental development based on the theory of Piaget: description of a project, in I.J. Athey and D.O. Rubadeau (eds), *Educational Implications of Piaget's Theory*. Waltham: Ginn, 1970, pp. 307–317.

Pinard, A., and Laurendeau, M. (1969), Stage in Piaget's cognitive developmental theory: exegesis of a concept, in D. Elkind and J.H. Flavell (eds), *Studies in Cognitive Development*. London: Oxford University Press, pp. 121–170.

Polya, G. (1954), *Mathematics and Plausible Reasoning*. Princeton: Princton University Press.

Pope, M., and Denicolo, P.M. (2001), *Transformative Education: Personal Construct Approaches to Practice and Research*. London: Whurr.

Povey, R.M., and Hill, E. (1975), Can pre-school children form concepts? *Educational Research*, 17, 180–192.

Pulaski, M.A.S. (1971), *Piaget. Eine Einführung in seine Theorien und sein Werk*. Frankfurt: Fischer 1978.

Quine, W.V.O. (1943), Notes on existence and necessity. *Journal of Symbolic Logic*, 8, 45–47.

Rabaud, E. (1911), *Le transformisme et l'expérience*. Paris: Alcan.

Rauh, H. (2002), Vorgeburtliche Entwicklung und frühe Kindheit, in R. Oerter and L. Montada (eds), *Entwicklungspsychologie*. Weinheim: Psychologie Verlags Union, pp. 131–208.

Rawls, J. (1971), *A Theory of Justice*. Cambridge: Harvard University Press.

Resnick, L.B. (1987), Learning in school and out. *Educational Researcher*, 16, 13–20.

Reusser, K. (2006), Jean Piagets Theorie der Entwicklung des Erkennens, in W. Schneider and F. Wilkening (eds), *Enzyklopädie der Psychologie. Entwicklungspsychologie, I*. Göttingen: Hogrefe, pp. 91–189.

Reymond, A. (1918), A propos d'une "recherche". *La semaine littéraire*, 550–551.

Reymond, A. (1929), Transcendance et Immanence. *Cahiers protestants*, 13: 161–170, 331–333.

Reymond, A. (1931), La pensée philosophique en Suisse romande de 1900 à nos jours. *Revue de théologie et de philosophie*, 19, 364–377.

Reymond, A. (1942), *Philosophie spiritualiste*. Paris: Rouge/Vrin.

Ribeaupierre, A. de (1997), Les modèles néo-piagétiens: quoi de nouveau? *Psychologie Française*, 42, 9–21.

Richebächer, S. (2005), *Sabina Spielrein. "Eine fast grausame Liebe zur Wissenschaft"*. Zürich: Dörlemann.

Riegel, K.F. (1973), Dialectic operations: the final period of cognitive development. *Human Development*, 16, 346–370.

Rijsman, J. (1996), Le panorama intellectuell et technologique de la scène piagétienne, in J.-M. Barrelet and A.-N. Perret-Clermont (eds), *Jean Piaget et Neuchâtel. L'apprenti et le savant*. Lausanne: Editions Payot, pp. 145–164.

Robert-Grandpierre, C. (1996), Grandchamp et Pierre Bovet, in J.-M. Barrelet and A.-N. Perret-Clermont (eds), *Jean Piaget et Neuchâtel. L'apprenti et le savant*. Lausanne: Editions Payot, pp. 121–130.

Rogoff, B. (1993), Children's guided participation and participatory appropriation in sociocultural activity, in R.H. Wozniak and K.W. Fischer (eds), *Development in Context: Acting and Thinking in Specific Environments*. Hillsdale: Erlbaum, pp. 121–154.

Rolland, R. (1903–12), *Jean-Christoph*. Paris: Ollendorf.

Ros, A. (1994), "Wirklichkeit" und "Konstruktion", in G. Rusch and S.J. Schmidt (eds), *Piaget und der Radikale Konstruktivismus. DELFIN*. Frankfurt: Suhrkamp, pp. 139–213.

Rose, S.A., and Ruff, H.A. (1987), Cross-modal abilities in human infants, in J.D. Osofsky (ed.), *Handbook of Infant Development*. New York: Wiley, pp. 318–362.

Rossello, P. (1943), *Les précurseurs du Bureau international d'éducation. Un aspect inédit de l'histoire de l'éducation et des institutions internationales*. Genève: BIE.

Roszkowski, W. (1913), A propos des Limnées de la faune profonde du lac Léman. *Zoologischer Anzeiger*, 43, 88–90.

Rotman, B. (1977), *Jean Piaget: Psychologist of the Real*. Ithaca: Cornell.

Rousseau, J.-J. (1762/1966), *Emile ou l'éducation*. Paris: Garnier Flammarion.

Russell, J. (1983), Cognitive structures and verbalized beliefs, in S. Modgil, C. Modgil and G. Brown (eds), *Jean Piaget, an Interdisciplinary Critique*. London: Routledge & Kegan Paul, pp. 122–136.

Sabatier, A. (1897), *Esquisse d'une philosophie de la religion d'après la psychologie et l'histoire*. Paris: Fischbacher.

Sandler, A. (1975), Comments on the significance of Piaget's work for psychoanaysis. *International Review of Psycho-Analysis*, 2, 365–377.

Saussure, F. de (1916), *Grundfragen der allgemeinen Sprachwissenschaft*. Berlin: De Gruyter 1967.

Schaer, J.-P. (1996), Les études à l'Université de Neuchâtel, in J.-M. Barrelet and A.-N. Perret-Clermont (eds), *Jean Piaget et Neuchâtel. L'apprenti et le savant*. Lausanne: Editions Payot, pp. 67–80.

Schaffer, H.R. (1989), Joint involvement episodes as context for cognitive development, in H. Daniels (ed.), *An Introduction to Vygotsky*. London: Routledge 1996, pp. 251–280.

Schaller-Jeanneret, A.-F. (1996), Les premières étapes de la formation intellectuelle, in J.-M. Barrelet and A.-N. Perret-Clermont (eds), *Jean Piaget et Neuchâtel. L'apprenti et le savant*. Lausanne: Editions Payot, pp. 51–66.

Scheffler, I. (1985), *Of Human Potential. An Essay in the Philosophy of Education*. Boston: Routledge & Kegan Paul.

Schepeler, E.M. (1993), Jean Piaget's experiences on the couch: some clues to a mystery. *International Journal of Psycho-Analysis*, 74, 255–273.

Schneider, H. (1981), *Die Theorie Piagets: ein Paradigma für die Psychoanalyse?* Bern: Huber.

Schurz, G. (1985), Denken, Sprache und Erziehung. Die aktuelle Piaget-Kontroverse. *Zeitschrift für Semiotik*, 7, 335–366.

Schwarz, M. (1996), *Einführung in die Kognitive Linguistik*. Tübingen: Francke.

Schwebel, M., and Raph, J. (1973), *Piaget in the Classroom*. New York: Basic Books.

Scribner, S. (1984), Denkweisen und Sprechweisen, in T. Schöfthaler and D. Goldschmidt (eds), *Soziale Struktur und Vernunft. Jean Piagets Modell entwickelten Denkens in der Diskussion kulturvergleichender Forschung*. Frankfurt: Suhrkamp, pp. 311–335.

Sebesta, R.T. (1996), *Concepts of Programming Languages*. Menlo Park: Addison-Wesley.

Seiler, T.B. (1973), Die Bereichsspezifität formaler Denkstrukturen—Konsequenzen für den pädagogischen Prozess, in K. Frey and M. Lang (eds), *Kognitionspsycholgie und naturwissenschaftlicher Unterricht*. Bern: Huber, pp. 249–283.

Sennett, R. (1977/1983), *Verfall und Ende des öffentlichen Lebens. Die Tyrannei der Intimität*. Frankfurt: Fischer.

Sève, L. (1971), Sur le structuralisme. *Nouvelle Revue Internationale*, 154, 204–221 and 155, 195–208.

Shultz, T.R., Wells, D., and Sarda, M. (1980), Development of the ability to distinguish intended actions from mistakes, reflexes, and passive movements. *British Journal of Social and Clinical Psychology*, 19, 301–310.

Siebert, H. (2003), *Pädagogischer Konstruktivismus. Lernen als Konstruktion von Wirklichkeit.* Neuwied: Luchterhand.

Siegler, R.S. (1991), *Children's Thinking.* Englewood Cliffs: Prentice Hall.

Siegler, R.S., and Opfer, J.E. (2003), Development of numerical estimation: evidence for multiple representations of number. *Psychological Science,* 14, 237–243.

Sigel, I.W. (1969), The Piagetian system and the world of education, in D. Elkind and J. Flavell (eds), *Studies in Cognitive Development: Essays in Honour of Jean Piaget.* New York, Oxford University Press.

Sinclair, H., and Kamii, C. (1970), Some implications of Piaget's theory for teaching young children. *School Review (Chicago),* 78, 169–183.

Skinner, B.F. (1980), *Notebooks.* Englewood Cliffs: Prentice-Hall.

Slama-Cazacu, T. (1961/1977), *Dialogue in Children.* The Hague: Mouton.

Smedslund, J. (1955), *Multiple Probability Learning.* Oslo: Akad. Forlag.

Smedslund, J. (1961), The acquisition of conservation of substances and weight in children. *Scandinavian Journal of Psychology,* 2, 11–20, 71–87, 153–160, 203–210.

Smedslund, J. (1966), Les origines sociales de la décentration, in F. Bresson and H. Montmollin (eds), *Psychologie et épistémologie génétiques. Thèmes piagétiens.* Paris: Dunod, pp. 159–167.

Smetana, J.G. (1981), Preschool children's conceptions of moral and social rules. *Child Development,* 52, 1333–1336.

Smith, H.B. (1937), *Growing Minds. An Introduction to Educational Psychology.* London: University of London Press.

Smith, L. (2000), *A Brief Biography of Jean Piaget,* www.piaget.org/aboutPiaget.html.

Smith, R.B. (1933), Review of "The Moral Judgment of the Child". *Progressive Education,* 10, 237–238.

Smock, Ch. D. (1981), Constructivism and educational practices. In I.E. Sigel, D.M. Brodinsky and R.M. Golinkoff (eds), *New Directions in Piagetian Theory and Practice.* Hillsdale: Erlbaum, pp. 51–69.

Sodian, B. (2002), Entwicklung begrifflichen Wissens, in R. Oerter and L. Montada (eds), *Entwicklungspsychologie.* Weinheim: Psychologie Verlags Union, pp. 443–468.

Spelke, E.S. (2000), Core knowledge. *American Psychologist,* 55, 1233–1243.

Spelke, E.S., Breinlinger, K., Macomber, J., and Jacobson, K. (1992), Origins of knowledge. *Psychological Review,* 99, 605–632.

Spelke, E.S., Kattz, G., Purcell, S.E., Ehrlich, S.M., and Breinlinger, K. (1994), Early knowledge of object motion: continuity and inertia. *Cognition,* 51, 131–176.

Spencer, H. (1863/1877), *Les principes de biologie*. Paris: Germer Baillière.

Spielrein, S. (1923), Die Zeit im unterschwelligen Seelenleben. *Imago* 9, 300–317.

Sprinthall, R., and Sprinthall, N. (1974), *Educational Psychology: A Developmental Approach*. Reading: Addison-Wesley.

Starkey, P., and Cooper, R.G. (1980), Perception of number by human infants. *Science*, 210, 1033–1035.

Steeg, F.H. (1996), *Lernen und Auslese im Schulsystem am Beispiel der "Rechenschwäche". Mehrebenenanalyse der Funktionen unseres Bildungssystems und Versuch einer ideologiekritischen Folgerung auf didaktische Ansätze und praktische Umsetzungen*. Frankfurt: Lang.

Steiner, G. (ed.) (1978), *Die Psychologie des 20. Jahrhunderts, VII. Piaget und die Folgen*. Zürich: Kindler.

Stern, C., and Stern, W. (1907/1928), *Die Kindersprache. Eine psychologische und sprachtheoretische Untersuchung*. Leipzig: Barth.

Stern, D.N. (1985), *The Interpersonal World of the Infant—A View from Psychoanalysis and Developmental Psychology*. New York: Basic Books.

Stern, W. (1914/1927), *Psychologie der frühen Kindheit*. Leipzig: Quelle und Meier.

Sternberg, R.J. (1977), *Intelligence, Information, Processing and Analogical Reasoning*. Hove: Erlbaum.

Stock, R. (1979), Dix ans au sein de l'unesco, in B. Suchodolski (ed.), *Le Bureau International d'éducation au service du mouvement éducatif*. Paris: UNESCO, pp. 117–127.

Strauss, S., and Rimalt, J. (1974), The effects of organizational disquilibrium training on structural elaboration. *Developmental Psychology*, 10, 526–533.

Streib, H. (2001), Faith development research revisited: the religious styles perspectives. *International Journal for the Psychology of Religion*, 11, 143–158.

Sund, R. (1976), *Piaget for Educators*. Columbus: Merril.

Sutherland, P. (1992), *Cognitive Development Today: Piaget and His Critics*. London: Chapman.

Sutton-Smith, B. (1966/1970), Piaget on play: a critique, in I.J. Athey and D.O. Rubadeau (eds), *Educational Implications of Piaget's Theory*. Waltham: Ginn, pp. 139–148.

Swanson, G.E. (1967), *Religion and Regime: A Sociological Account of the Reformation*. Ann Arbor: University of Michigan Press.

Tanner, J.M., and Inhelder, B. (1960), (eds), *Discussions on Child Development: a Consideration of the Biological, Psychological, and Cultural Approaches to the Understanding of Human Development and Behaviour, IV*. London: Tavistock.

Tarpley, W.G., and Chaitkin, A. (1992), *George Bush. The Unauthorized Biography*. Washington D.C.: Executive Intelligence Review, www.tarpley.net/bushb.htm.

Thomann, C. (1996), L'engagement chrétien et social, in J.-M. Barrelet and A.-N. Perret-Clermont (eds), *Jean Piaget et Neuchâtel. L'apprenti et le savant*. Lausanne: Editions Payot, pp. 111–119.

Tolman, E.C. (1932), *Purposive Behavior in Animals and Men*. New York: Appleton-Century-Crofts.

Trevarthen, C. (1979), Communication and cooperation in early infancy: a description of primary intersubjectivity, in M. Bullowa (ed.), *Before Speech: The Beginning of Interpersonal Communication* Cambridge: Cambridge University Press pp. 321–348.

Tribolet, M. de (1996), Arthur Piaget (1865–1952): portrait intellectuel et moral du père de Jean Piaget, in J.-M. Barrelet and A.-N. Perret-Clermont (eds), *Jean Piaget et Neuchâtel. L'apprenti et le savant*. Lausanne: Editions Payot, pp. 39–50.

Tröhler, D. (2005), *Langue* as Homeland: The Genevan reception of pragmatism, in T. S. Popkewitz (ed.), *Inventing the Modern Self and John Dewey. Modernities and the Traveling of Pragmatism in Education*. New York: Palgrave Macmillan, pp. 61–83.

Tryphon, A., Parrat-Dayan, S., and Volkmann-Raue, S. (1996), La récéption de l'oeuvre de Piaget dans le milieu psychologique germanophone des années 1920–1930. *Archives de psychologie*, 64, 83–108.

Tudge, J.R.H., and Winterhoff, P.A. (1993), Vygotsky, Piaget, and Bandura: perspectives on the relations between the social world and cognitive development, in P. Lloyd and C. Fernyhough (eds), *Lev Vygotsky. Critical Assessments*. London: Routledge 1999, pp. 311–338.

Turiel, E. (1974), Conflict and transition in adolescent moral development. *Child Development*, 45, 14–29.

Turiel, E. (1983), *The Development of Social Knowledge. Morality and Convention*. New York: Cambridge University Press.

Uzgiris, I.C., and Hunt, J. McV. (1970), Attentional preferences and experience. *Journal of Genetic Psychology*, 117, 109–121.

Van der Veer, R. (1996), La réception des premières idées de Jean Piaget en Union soviétique, in J.-M. Barrelet and A.-N. Perret-Clermont (eds), *Jean Piaget et Neuchâtel. L'apprenti et le savant*. Lausanne: Editions Payot pp. 213–232.

Venn, C., and Walkerdine, V. (1978), The acquisition and production of knowledge: Piaget's theory reconsidered. *Ideology and Consciousness*, 3, 67–94.

Vidal, F. (1986), Jean Piaget et la psychanalyse. Premières rencontres. *Le Bloc-notes de la psychanalyse*, 6: 171–189.

Vidal, F. (1988), L'Institut Rousseau au temps des passions. *Education et Recherche*, 10, 60–81.

Vidal, F. (1989), Freud und Piaget Jean, "Enkel" von Sigmund Freud, in B. Nitzschke (ed.), *Freud und die akademische Psychologie. Beiträge zu einer historischen Kontroverse*. München: PVU, pp. 162–184.

Vidal, F. (1992), Jean Piaget's Early Critique of Mendelism: "La notion de l'espèce suivant l'école mendélienne" (a 1913 Manuscript). *History and Philosophy of the Life Sciences*, 14, 113–135.

Vidal, F. (1993), "Les mystères de la douleur divine". Une "prière" du jeune Jean Piaget pour l'année 1916. *Revue de Théologie et de Philosophie*, 126, 112–118.

Vidal, F. (1994a), *Piaget before Piaget*. Cambridge, MA: Harvard University Press.

Vidal, F. (1994b), La place de la psychologie dans l'orde des sciences. *Revue de synthèse*, 3–4, 327–354.

Vidal, F. (1996), Jean Piaget, "Ami de la nature", in J.-M. Barrelet and A.-N. Perret-Clermont (eds), *Jean Piaget et Neuchâtel. L'apprenti et le savant*. Lausanne: Editions Payot, pp. 95–109.

Vidal, F. (1997), L'éducation nouvelle et l'esprit de Genève. Une utopie politico-pédagogique des années 1920. *Equinoxe. Revue de Sciences humaines*, 17, 81–98.

Vidal, F. (1998), Immanence, affectivité et démocracie dans "Le jugement moral chez l'enfant"'. *Bulletin de psychologie*, 51, 585–597.

Vidal, F. (1999), La vanité de la nomenclature et autres inédits de jeunesse de Jean Piaget, www.piaget.org/piaget.

Vidal, F. (2001), Sabina Spielrein, Jean Piaget—going their own ways. *Journal of Analytical Psychology*, 46, 139–153.

Vidal, F., and Parot, F. (1996), Ignace Meyerson et Jean Piaget: une amitié dans l'histoire, in F. Parot (ed.), *Pour une psychologie historique. Ecrits en hommage à Ignace Meyerson*. Paris: PUF, pp. 61–73.

Völzing, P.-L. (1982), *Kinder argumentieren. Die Ontogenese argumentativer Fähigkeiten*. Paderborn: Schöningh.

Vonèche, J., and Bovet, M. (1982), Training research and cognitive development. What do Piagetians want to accomplish? In S. Mogdil and C. Mogdil (eds), *Jean Piaget. Consensus and Controversy*. London: Holt, Rinehart & Winston, pp. 83–94.

Vygotsky, L.S. (1932), Piaget's theory of the child's language and thought, in *Rech i myshlenie rebenka*. Moscow-Leningrad: Uchpedgiz, pp. 3–54, www.marxists.org/archive/vygotsky/index.htm.

Vygotsky, L.S. (1934/2002), *Denken und Sprechen. Psychologische Untersuchungen*. Weinheim: Beltz.

Waddington, C.H. (1975), *The Evolution of an Evolutionist*. Edinburgh: Edinburgh University Press.

Wagner-Egelhaaf, M. (2000), *Autobiographie*. Stuttgart: Metzler.

Wallon, H. (1925), *L'enfant turbulent*. Paris: Alcan.

Wallon, H. (1927), Compte rendu de J. Piaget: "La représentation du monde chez l'enfant" et "La causalité physique chez l'enfant". *Année psychologique*, 28, 399–401.

Wallon, H. (1942), *De l'acte à la pensée. Essai de psychologie comparée*. Paris: Flammarion.

Wallon, H. (1947), L'Etude psychologique et sociologique de l'enfant. *Cahiers Internationaux de Sociologie*, 3, 3–23.

Warden, C.J. (1931), Review of the child's conception of physical causality. *The Pedagogical Seminary and Journal of Genetic Psychology*, 29, 296–298.

Watt, J. (1989), *Individualism and Educational Theory*. Dordrecht: Kluwer.

Wavre, R. (1937), Gustave Juvet, le mathématicien et l'ami, in *A la mémoire de Gustave Juvet, 1896–1936*. Lausanne: Université de Lausanne, pp. 20–36.

Weber, L. (1971), *The English Infant School and Informal Education*. Englewood Cliffs: Prentice-Hall.

Weber, M. (1905/1972), Die protestantische Ethik und der Geist des Kapitalismus, in *Gesammelte Schriften zur Religionssoziologie, Vol. 1*. Tübingen: Mohr-Siebeck, pp. 17–206.

Weikart, D.P., Rogers, L., Adcock, C., and McClelland, D. (1971), *The Cognitively Oriented Curriculum. A Framework for Preschool Teachers*. Urbana: Eric Naaeyc.

Weindling, P. (2005), 'Un internationaliste visionnaire confronté aux réalités de la guerre froide: John W. Thonpson et le programme de l'UNESCO pour l'Allemagne 1945–1955, in *60 aus l'histoire de l'PUNESCO. Actes du collogues internationales, 16–18 November 2005*. Paris: UNESCO, pp. 253–61.

Weinert, F.E., and Kluwe, R.H. (eds) (1983/1987), *Metacognition, Motivation and Understanding*. Hillsdale: Erlbaum.

Wellman, H.M., and Estes, D. (1986), Early understanding of mental enteties: a reexamination of childhood realism. *Child Development*, 57, 910–923.

Wellman, H.M., and Gelman, S.A. (1998), Knowledge acquisition in foundational domains, in D. Kuhn and R.S. Siegler (eds), *Handbook of Child Psychology, II*. New York: Wiley, pp. 523–573.

Wells, G.C. (1981), *Learning through Interaction*. Cambridge: Cambridge University Press.

Werner, E.E. (1979), *Cross-Cultural Child Development*. Belmont: Wadsworth.

Wetzel, F.G. (1978), Elemente des Rationalismus in der Erkenntnistheorie
Jean Piagets, in G. Steiner (ed.), *Die Psychologie des 20. Jahrhunderts, VII.
Piaget und die Folgen*. Zürich: Kindler, pp. 41–63.

Whitbourne, S.K., and Weinstock, C.S. (1979), *Die mittlere Lebenss-
panne. Entwicklungspsychologie des Erwachsenenalters*. München: Urban &
Schwarzenberg 1982.

Wiggershaus, R. (1986), *Die Frankfurter Schule. Geschichte—Theoretische
Entwicklung—Politische Bedeutung*. München: Hanser 1987.

Wilden, A. (1972), System and Structure. Essays in Communication and
Exchange. London: Tavistock 1980.

Wilkening, F. (1981), Integration velocity, time, and distance information:
a developmental study. *Cognitive Psychology*, 13, 231–247.

Wilkening, F., and Krist, H. (2002), Entwicklung der Wahrnehmung und
Psychomotorik, in R. Oerter and L. Montada (eds), *Entwicklungspsychologie*. Weinheim: Psychologie Verlags Union, pp. 395–417.

Wimmer, H., and Perner, J. (1983), Beliefs about beliefs. Representation and
constraining function of wrong beliefs in young children's understanding
of deception. *Cognition*, 13, 103–128.

Wittmann, E. (1982), *Mathematisches Denken bei Vor- und Grundschulkindern*.
Braunschweig: Vieweg.

Wolff, P.H. (1960), *The Developmental Psychologies of Jean Piaget and Psychoanalysis*. New York: International Universities Press.

Xypas, C. (1997), Le projet moral et éducatif de Jean Piaget,
http://pst.chez.tiscali.fr/svtiufm/educmora.htm.

Xypas, C. (2001), *L'autre Piaget. Cheminement intellectuel d'un éducateur
d'humanité*. Paris: L'Harmattan.

Youniss, J. (1994), *Soziale Konstruktion und psychische Entwicklung*. Frankfurt:
Suhrkamp.

Zazzo, R. (1988), *Où en est la psychologie de l'enfant?* Paris: Gallimard.

Zimmer, D.E. (1986), *So kommt der Mensch zur Sprache. Über Spracherwerb,
Sprachentstehung, Sprache und Denken*. Zürich: Haffmanns.

Zittoun, T., Perret-Clermont, A.-N., and Barrelet, J.-M. (1996), Introduction,
in J.-M. Barrelet and A.-N. Perret-Clermont (eds), *Jean Piaget et Neuchâtel.
L'apprenti et le savant*. Lausanne: Editions Payot, pp. 133–143.

Name Index

Abele, Jean 259
Ach, Narziss 75
Adler, Alfred 54, 56–7
Aebli, Hans 257–8
Agassiz, Louis 15
Almie, Millie 245
Anderson, Allen 237
Antipoff, Hélène 97, 246
Apostel, Leo 221
Aristotle 90, 189, 223–4
Ashby, William Ross 214
Audemars, Mina 66
Augustine, Aurelius 40
Ausubel, David 245

Bachelard, Gaston 224
Bachelard, Suzanne 223
Bacon, Francis 140, 152
Baden-Powell, Robert 137
Bain, Alexander 86
Baldwin, James Mark 76, 80, 85,
    112, 141, 159, 164–5, 167,
    169–70, 221–2, 230, 245,
    255
Bandura, Albert 254
Barth, Karl 99
Bateson, Gregory 239
Baudouin, Charles 68
Baumgarten, Franziska 90–1
Bedot, Maurice 18–9, 51
Belnap, Nuel 237
Benrubi, Isaak 231
Bergson, Henri 19–21, 23, 27–9, 33,
    37, 41, 43, 54, 73, 129, 134,

136, 141, 155, 164, 169, 175,
    184, 199, 226–7, 231, 250
Berkeley, George 102
Bernard, Claude 214
Bersot, Henri 9
Bertalanffy, Ludwig van 212, 229
Besseige, P.-H. 88
Beth, Evert 200, 221
Bidell, Thomas 264
Binet, Alfred 56, 63, 66–7, 87, 141,
    167
Blanc, Henri 22
Bleuler, Eugen 52, 54–5, 64, 68, 77,
    92
Blondel, Charles 82, 88, 126, 223
Blonsky, Pavel 87
Bonnet, Gabriel 142
Bourdieu, Pierre 258
Bourjade, Jean 88, 90, 223
Boutroux, Pierre 28, 224
Bovet, Magalie 215, 248–9
Bovet, Pierre 16, 21, 28, 30, 49, 52,
    56, 58, 65, 67–9, 71–4, 77, 86,
    97, 100, 112, 128–31, 134, 136,
    139, 141–3, 148, 155, 169, 189,
    238
Bower, Thomas G. 265
Bowlby, John 212
Brainerd, Charles 258
Bréhier, Emile 229
Brentano, Franz 75, 231
Broadbent, Donald E. 254
Brouwer, Luitzen 192, 226
Bruner, Jerome 245, 265

Brunschvicg, Léon 56, 73, 79, 81,
    84–5, 87, 97, 99, 101–3, 119,
    185, 189, 192, 222, 226
Bryant, Peter 236
Bühler, Charlotte 77, 89, 91, 178,
    204
Bühler, Karl 77, 141, 184, 239
Burger, Daniel 71
Burger, Jean–Daniel 102
Burt, Cyril 58, 63
Bush, Prescott 239
Butts, Marie 129

Calvin, Jean 40
Cannon, Walter B. 214, 229
Cantor, George 192
Carey, Susan 264
Caruso, Igor 125
Case, Robbie 263
Castellion, Sébastien 40
Cellérier, Guy 154
Chamay, André 96
Châteney, Gaston and Blanche 96
Chomsky, Noam 211
Claparède, Edouard 50, 64–70, 73,
    79, 82, 87, 119, 129–30, 135–6,
    141, 143, 148, 152, 155, 166–7,
    171, 189, 205–6, 238
Claparède, Jean–Louis 129
Compayré, Gabriel 80
Comenius, Amos 140, 152
Comte, Auguste 26, 28
Cope, Edward D. 157
Cornut, Samuel 20, 26–7, 31, 39
Cousinet, Roger 79
Couturat, Louis 63

Darwin, Charles 20, 33, 48
Davy, George 125
Decroly, Ovide 66–7, 130, 134,
    141
Degand, Julia 67

Delachaux, Théodore 16
Delacroix, Henri 56, 87–8, 90, 177,
    223
Demolin, Edmond 129
Descartes, René 43, 224
Descoeudres, Alice 67, 114
DeVries, Rheta 257
Dewey, John xi, 129, 134, 141, 167,
    245, 255
Dillon, Clarence 239
Donaldson, Margaret 236
Dottrens, Robert 128–9, 136,
    142–3, 148
Driesch, Hans 225
Dumas, George 64
Durkheim, Emile 28, 46, 100, 102,
    109–12, 116, 119–20, 138–9,
    183
Dux, Günter 258,

Ehrenfeld, Christian von 184
Einstein, Albert 129, 151, 199, 222,
    232
Elkind, David 255
Empedocles 90
Erikson, Erik 212, 254–5
Euler, Leonard 198
Evans, Luther 148

Fauconnet, Paul 120
Febvre, Lucien 148
Ferrière, Adolphe 49, 65–6, 91, 129,
    134–6, 141, 155, 167
Fichte, Johann Gottlieb 196
Fischer, Kurt 263–4
Fiske, John 166
Flavell, John H. 245
Fleck, Ludwik 258
Flournoy, Henri 69
Flournoy, Théodore 30, 46, 52–3,
    56, 65, 67–8, 72–3, 136, 141
Fodor, Jerry A. 264

Foerster, Friedrich W. 114
Foerster, Heinz von 237, 264
Forel, François-Alphonse 16
Foucault, Michel 229–30, 254
Fouillée, Alfred 28, 32, 41, 166, 175
Fowler, James 255
Freinet, Célestin 67
Freire, Paolo 246
Freud, Sigmund 45, 52, 55–7,
    69–70, 72, 77, 93–4, 178, 208,
    215, 243, 245, 254, 256
Fröbel, Friedrich 140
Fuhrmann, Otto 16–19, 22, 50–1

Galparin, Peter 246
Gandillac, Maurice de 229
Garcia, Rolando 237
Giroud, Aline 67
Glasersfeld, Ernst von 264
Goblot, Edmond 56, 74, 226
Godet, Paul 13–18, 30
Godet, Pierre 97
Goebbels, Joseph 119
Goethe, Johann Wolfgang 209
Goldman, Ronald 255
Goldmann, Lucien 126, 229
Goldschmidt, Richard 158
Goodenough, Florence 244
Gréco, Pierre 221
Grize, Jean–Blaise 221
Groos, Karl 76, 177, 179
Grünbaum, Abraham 89, 95
Guillaume, Paul 177
Guyau, Jean-Marie 28, 44

Habermas, Jürgen 259
Hall, G. Stanley 65, 76, 80, 87, 141,
    245
Hargreaves, Ronald 212
Harpe, Jean de la 97, 99, 128
Harriman, W. Averell 239
Hazlitt, Victoria 91

Hegel, Georg W.F. 130–1
Herbart, Johann Friedrich 140, 164
Hilbert, David 192
Høffding, Harald 87, 225
Horkheimer, Max 121
Hubendick, Bengt 59
Humbert-Droz, Jules 11
Hunt, J. McVicker 245
Huxley, Julian 212

Inhelder, Bärbel 189–90, 198, 200,
    204, 215, 234, 244, 248, 256
Isaacs, Nathan 245
Isaacs, Susan 89–91, 125, 245

Jacobson, Roman 229
James, William 21, 28, 87, 134, 141,
    153, 164, 184, 206, 245
Janet, Pierre 28, 56–7, 64, 70, 76,
    79, 82, 105, 141, 156, 167, 175,
    181, 189–93, 205–6, 208–9,
    216, 222, 226
Jaroshevsky, Mikhail 125
Jaurès, Jean 47
Jeannet, Pierre 39
Jéquier, Robert 71
Johnson–Laird, Phillip 263
Jonckheere, Tobie 130
Jung, Carl Gustav 52–3, 56–7, 68,
    180, 245
Junod, Charles-Daniel 25–6
Juvet, Gustave 16, 21, 29, 192

Kamii, Constance 257
Kant, Immanuel 28, 45, 74, 83, 89,
    98, 103, 117, 121, 155, 197,
    222–3
Katz, David & Rosa 89
Kay, Alan 259
Kelly, George 264
Kerschensteiner, Georg 134
Kilpatrick, William H. 129

Klein, Felix 192, 203
Kleint, Boris 90
Koffka, Kurt 185, 188
Kohlberg, Lawrence 254–5
Köhler, Wolfgang 185, 187
Koyré, Alexandre 224
Kropotkin, Peter 48
Kuenburg, Max von 90
Külpe, Oskar 75
Kuhn, Thomas S. 258, 264
Kussmaul, Adolf 168

Lachelier, Jules 28
Lacroix, Jean 233
Lafendel, Louise 66
Lalande, André 28, 56, 64, 77, 83,
    85, 97, 231
Lambercier, Marc 185
Larguier de Bancel, Jean 216
Le Dantec, Félix 21, 28, 43–4, 164–5
Legrand Roy, Eugène 16
Lenin 47
Leontjey, Alexej 92
Leuzinger–Schuler, A. 89
Lévi-Strauss, Claude 229–30
Lévy-Bruhl, Lucien 80–1, 119
Lewin, Kurt 187, 229
Lipps, Gotthold F. 52
Löbisch, Johann Elias 168
Locke, John 194, 196
Loosli, Carl–Albert 16
Lorenz, Konrad 212
Luquet, Georges-Henri 76, 179
Luria, Alexander 92–3

Mach, Ernst 184
Maheu, René 153
Maine de Biran, Pierre 155
Malche, Albert 128–9
Malebranche, Nicolas de 101
Malrieu, Philippe 204–5
Malvaux, Pierre 259

Marion, Henri 134
Markman, Ellen M. 236
Marx, Karl 126
Maturana, Humberto 264
Mauriac, François 151
Mauss, Marcel 126, 223, 229
Mayo, Elton 125
M'Bow, Amadou-Mahtar 256
McCulloch, Warren 210
Mead, George Herbert 255
Mead, Margaret 212, 217
Meili, Richard 97, 187, 189
Mendel, Gregor Johann 22–3
Merleau-Ponty, Maurice 204, 231
Meyer, Edith 198
Meyerson, Emile 97, 190, 226, 234
Meyerson, Ignace 64, 87, 92, 95,
    146–7, 169, 222
Meyhoffer, Paul 66
Miéville, Henri-Louis 231
Monod, Jacques 161
Monod, Wilfred 31, 34
Montessori, Maria 66, 134, 141,
    148
Mott, John 30
Mozart, Wolfgang A. 238
Muchow, Martha 89–90
Munari, Alberto 252
Murchison, Carl 244
Murray, E. 87
Murray, Henry A. 245
Mussard, Jules 67

Neisser, Ulrich 254
Nietzsche, Friedrich 117
Noelting, Gérard 215
Nunn, Percy 130

Ochs, René 154
Oevermann, Ulrich 258
Oléron, Pierre 181
Oppenheimer, Robert 151,

Ormian, Heinrich J. 201
Oser, Fritz 255

Papert, Seymour 221, 259, 263
Pâris, Gaston 7
Parkhurst, Helen 141
Pascal, Blaise 38
Pascual-Leone, Juan 263
Pauli, Laurent 148
Pavlov, Ivan 171, 245
Paulsen, Wilhelm 67
Pérez, Bernard 75, 177
Pettavel, Paul 34, 37, 47, 49, 71
Périnet, Gérôme 137
Pestalozzi, Johann H. 140
Peterson, Joseph 90
Pfister, Oskar 52–3, 57–8, 68
Piaget, Arthur 5–10, 11, 35–7, 50–1
Piaget, Frédéric 5–6
Piaget, Jacqueline 96, 133, 156, 169, 171–4, 177–8, 180–1
Piaget, Laurent 2, 96, 138, 146, 172–3
Piaget, Lucienne 96, 173–4
Piaget-Vauthier, Madeleine 5
Piaget-Burger, Marthe 5, 9, 26, 35, 71
Piaget-Jackson, Rebecca-Suzanne 5, 7, 9–11, 25–6, 35, 47, 52–3, 71
Piaget-Châteney, Valentine 96, 138, 146
Piéron, Henri 56, 87, 147, 189
Pitts, Walter 210
Plato 90, 197, 223
Plotin 37
Poincaré, Henri 192, 209
Pope, Maureen 264
Preyer, Wilhelm 75–6
Prigogine, Ilya 236–7
Proust, Marcel 151
Pythagoras 90

Quine, William V.O. 221

Rabaud, Etienne 22, 157
Ramuz, Charles F. 151
Rasmussen, Vilhelm 80
Rauh, Frédéric 74
Rawls, John 259
Renan, Ernest 79
Rey, André 189
Reymond, Arnold 28–30, 49–50, 72–3, 97, 102, 109, 231
Ribot, Théodule 28, 64, 75–6
Rockcastle, John 245
Ricoeur, Paul 223
Rignano, Eugenio 185, 226
Ripple, Richard 245
Rolland, Romain 38–9, 48, 53
Roller, Samuel 148
Romanes, George 75
Romy, Marcel 21
Rorty, Richard 253
Roszkowski, Waclaw 22–4, 50
Rossello, Pedro 129–30, 146, 153
Rossetti, Etienne 21
Roth, Gerhard 264
Rotten, Elisabeth 67, 129
Rousseau, Jean-Jacques xii, 32, 38, 46, 84, 133, 137, 140, 161,166, 182–3, 250
Rubinstein, Sergej 125, 228
Russell, Bertrand 189
Ruyssen, Théodore 74

Sabatier, Auguste 26, 28, 33, 40, 59
Saussure, Ferdinand de 176, 229
Saussure, Reymond de 71, 238
Schleiermacher, Friedrich 26
Schneider, Ernst 68
Sève, Lucien 215
Siebert, Horst 265
Siegler, Robert 263

Simon, Théodore 56, 58, 64, 66–7, 167
Sinclair, Hermina 215
Skinner, Burrus F. 254
Smedslund, Jan 217
Socrates 140
Spearman, Charles 55
Spelke, Liz 244, 264
Spencer, Herbert 28, 43–4, 134, 164, 193, 231
Spielrein, Sabina 68–71, 199, 239
Spitz, René 147, 207
Steinthal, Heymann 164
Stern, Clara 76–7, 88–9, 167, 181
Stern, William 77, 79, 88–9, 167, 177, 181, 188
Sternberg, Richard 263
Stirner, Max 117
Streib, Heinz 255
Sully, James 75–6, 80, 87
Swanson, Guy 255
Szeminska, Alina 132, 187, 239
Szuman, Stefan 169

Tagore, Rabindranath 67
Taine, Hippolyte 75
Tarde, Gabriel 28, 46, 109, 213–14
Terman, Lewis 245
Thomas, Albert 129
Thorndike, Edward 129, 245
Tiedemann, Dietrich 168
Tolman, Edward 254
Tolstoy, Leon 39, 48
Torrès-Bodet, Jaime 148

Varela, Francisco 264
Vauthier, Louis 35
Vinet, Alexandre 96
Vonèche, Jacques 234, 246
Vygotski, Lev 92–4, 125, 233, 263, 265

Waddington, Conrad 158, 259
Wagner, Moritz 22
Wallon, Henri 88, 90, 155, 167, 169, 182–3, 189, 204–5, 239
Warden, C. J. 91
Washburne, Carlton 134, 141
Wavre, Rolin 21, 29, 143
Weikart, David 245, 257
Weil-Sandler, Anne-Marie 149
Wertheimer, Max 185, 192
Westermarck, Edward 206
Whitehead, Alfred 189
Wiener, Norbert 214
Wilker, Karl 67
Wolf, Käthe 146
Wolff, Caspar Friedrich 161
Wreschner, Arthur 52

Xypas, Constantin 154, 239

Youniss, James 265
Yung, Emile 18–19, 22–3

Zacharias, Jerome 245
Zazzo, René 212

Subject Index

abstraction 70, 150, 164, 168, 184,
    196–7, 210, 235, 237, 250
    reflecting 85, 214, 229, 253
accommodation 75, 85, 159, 164–7,
    178, 184, 190, 206, 208, 212–3,
    235, 250, 253
action 32, 37–8, 42, 45, 53, 75–6, 82,
    98, 101, 113, 119, 127, 136,
    170–86, 194–5, 209, 228, 235,
    238, 247, 250, 252
active school 134–41, 143, 149–50,
    155
activity 38, 66, 75, 77, 99, 101, 105,
    107, 119, 123, 163–7, 175,
    181–4, 207, 225–6, 250
    and adaptation 20–1, 156–9
    and learning 131, 134–41, 215,
    256–7
    perceptive 174, 185
adaptation 20–1, 44, 51, 55, 74,
    76–8, 82–5, 93, 105–6, 156–68,
    178–9, 182, 212, 231, 250
adolescence (see puberty) 24–7,
    34–5, 39, 74, 100, 115, 120,
    133, 149, 201–4, 218, 248, 251
affectivity 53, 74, 84, 100, 107, 112,
    116–17, 119, 122, 149, 177,
    193, 204–10, 256
animism 72, 79–80, 86, 95, 218
anticipation 174, 176, 180, 186,
    213
apriorism 88, 185, 222–3, 226, 228
art 45, 150, 153 , 178, 211, 233, 238
artificialism 79, 81, 84, 86–8, 95

assimilation 44, 83, 86–7, 163–7,
    170–1, 178, 184, 190, 206,
    212–3, 217, 228, 231, 235, 250
    genetic 158–9
    reciprocal 77, 208, 213
autism 52–55, 57, 68, 70, 74, 78, 88,
    92–4, 114, 125, 165, 169, 176,
    179, 239
autonomy 28, 35, 100, 104, 112–21,
    123–5, 132, 140–2, 155, 165–6,
    170, 252, 255

behavior 80, 100, 105, 110, 119,
    126, 157–60, 162, 165–8,
    192–3, 205–6, 208, 210, 212–4,
    228, 231, 264
    of children 76, 89, 113–14, 156,
    172, 175, 177, 180, 182
    educational 10, 95, 134
    moral 5, 114–19
behaviorism 245, 254, 256
biology 14–24, 29, 41, 50–1, 55, 89,
    115, 156–62, 166, 193, 211,
    214–5, 220, 225, 229, 231, 246,
    258–9
biometrics 51–2, 55, 156

categories 20, 29, 80, 85, 87, 169,
    175, 191, 196, 198, 215, 222–3,
    250
causality 63, 70, 76, 80–1, 84–7, 93,
    169, 172–5, 199, 202, 210, 215,
    228, 234, 247
chance 160–1, 201–2, 222, 247

childhood 9–10, 30, 56, 77, 90, 98, 118, 120, 145
Christianity 15, 25–7, 30–40, 43, 46–8, 101, 106, 112, 123, 233
class/classification 20, 29, 63–4, 111, 181, 187–9, 193, 195, 213–4, 223, 237, 250, 257
consciousness 20, 37–8, 42–3, 48, 57, 74–5, 82, 84, 92, 106–7, 110–11, 169, 208–10, 243
  collective 109–12
  grasp of 82, 92, 101, 105, 119, 176–7, 198
  moral 33, 113–9
conservation (see permanency) 190, 217, 248–9, 251
constraint 10, 88, 100–1, 109, 112–24, 166, 181, 251, 253
constructivism 38, 70, 83–5, 99, 104–7, 125, 127, 163, 169, 175, 184, 192, 197–8, 222–3, 225–30, 233, 251, 253, 256–7, 263–5
contradiction 53, 82, 126, 151, 155, 166–7, 194, 201, 213–14, 250, 256
cooperation 47, 88–9, 113–14, 116–23, 132–5, 137, 151, 155, 179, 194–5, 220, 247, 265
coordination 75, 79, 83, 86, 165, 170–3, 178, 192–6, 199–200, 212–3, 218, 227, 229, 237, 246
correspondence
  cognitif 78, 80, 87, 99, 104, 118–19, 123, 140, 188, 195, 223, 227, 231, 236–7
  moral 102–3, 113, 121
  social 33, 48, 126, 142
creativity 19–20, 27, 33, 38, 103, 132, 150, 173, 178, 235, 257
curriculum 257
cybernetics 214–15, 229

darwinism 20–22, 33, 48, 51, 151, 161, 211
décalage (displacement) 175, 190
decentration 82, 108, 124, 149, 187, 201, 231, 247, 265
deduction 43, 79, 86, 167, 191, 194–5, 201, 216, 221, 224, 236
democracy 11, 31, 48, 119–21, 252
  and school 66, 141–2, 147
determinism 107, 161, 245
dialectic 122, 126, 230–1, 236, 248
didactics 66, 134, 150–1, 155, 257–8, 265
differentiation
  cognitive 80, 96, 103, 165–6, 170–1, 176, 188, 195–6, 199, 201, 213–14, 218, 227, 236, 247, 264
  social 100, 102, 110, 120, 123, 224
discipline 33, 54, 106, 111, 115–16, 121–2, 128, 132, 142, 208
  scientific 1, 41, 152–3, 198, 220–1, 229–31, 244, 251, 253, 258
dogmatism 25–6, 28–9, 32–3, 40–1, 53, 81, 99, 101, 120, 122
drawings 76, 79, 179, 198
dreams 10, 49, 52–3, 70, 78, 80, 180
duration 19, 28, 199–200
dynamism 74, 86, 194, 198

education
  aims 132
  authoritarian 89, 120, 123–4
  effects 101, 106, 120
  family 86, 110–1, 116
  moral 47, 123, 137
  own children 133, 138
  pre-school 257
  principles 46, 133–6, 140, 150–3

progressive/new xi–xii, 65–7, 123–4, 128–32, 135, 140–2, 154–5, 245
political 141–2, 145, 149
problems 57, 116, 132, 136, 138–9
religious 10, 26, 37, 72, 81
school 140, 150–2, 257
sexual 137–8
system 146, 154
traditional 124, 136, 147
egocentrism 70, 73–4, 77–9, 82–96, 105–6, 116, 119, 122, 127, 137, 149, 165, 168, 198, 247
egoism 33, 42, 44–5, 48, 53–4, 111, 117, 139, 252
empiricism 87, 185, 190–1, 211, 224–8, 252
epigenesis 158, 161
epistemology 84–7, 191, 220–33, 252–3, 164–5
errors
logical 63, 75, 88, 109
pedagogical 136–7
equality 33, 47, 118, 120–1, 133–4, 139, 141–2, 183
equilibration 158, 212–7, 250
equilibrium
biological 41–3, 158–9, 166, 212, 214
logical 42, 54, 64, 82–3, 194, 208, 250
philosophy of 43–8, 167, 193, 213
psychological 41, 53–4, 74, 165–6, 184–6, 205
and religion 42, 45–6, 53–4, 103
moral 44–6, 85, 110–2
social 41, 45–7, 111, 114
ethics 8, 45–6, 102–3
evolution 14, 19–24, 26, 33, 55, 157–62, 193, 215

experience
cognitive 74, 79, 83–4, 87, 90–3, 99, 105, 135, 195–7, 211–12
logical 195–7, 211–12
moral 74, 116–8
mystical 37, 41–2, 45–6, 53, 103, 107
physical 195–7, 211–12
practical 142, 170–4
psychoanalytical 55, 68–9, 71
religious 28, 46, 53, 72–3, 103
scientific 90, 225–6, 228
social 106, 114, 212
experiments 232
in biology 22–3, 98, 156–7
in pedagogy 141, 144, 148, 152
in psychology 43, 63, 67, 78–82, 87, 91–2, 125, 144, 174, 187–90, 198–9, 202, 207, 209, 246, 251–2

fact 223, 226–7
faith 25–6, 31–9, 42–3, 46, 73, 100–3, 107, 255
and science 30, 40–2, 47
family 5–10, 35, 110–11, 138, 149, 194
feelings 8–10, 45–6, 57, 72, 80, 100–1, 103, 116–17, 120, 152, 180, 205–8, 221
finalism 79–81, 95, 102, 161, 253
function
biological 74, 82
cognitive 88, 159, 164–5, 167, 170, 191, 215
moral 106, 118
symbolic/semiotic 78, 176–81, 183, 237
functionalism 70, 88, 164, 228–9, 264

generalization 70, 79, 91, 163, 170–1, 196, 226, 235, 237
Geneva xi–xii, 5, 7, 18, 29, 46, 64–72, 79, 96–7, 109, 122, 128–30, 142, 148–9, 157, 187, 190, 209, 218, 220, 234, 238, 239, 245, 256
geometry 198–9, 223
genotype 55, 158–9
Gestalt 169, 184–7, 229
group
    cognitive 163, 192, 250
    learning 131, 139, 141, 251, 256
    mathematical 188, 192, 202–3
    social 100, 107, 121, 252
grouping 146, 185, 188, 192–4, 198–200, 203, 237

habits 95, 156, 164, 170–1
heredity 22–3, 51, 55, 156–7, 211, 215, 224
heteronomy 10, 113–14, 117–18, 123–4, 133, 139, 251
holism 1, 231, 243
homeostasis 158, 214–5
historiography 7, 47, 140–2, 253
history 32, 34, 90, 98, 126–7, 149–50, 198, 221–5, 230–1, 236, 249, 253, 254, 258
humanities 150
hypothesis 14, 135, 167, 191, 195, 201, 221, 223, 264

idea 29–30, 54, 75, 83, 126, 127, 196, 223, 238
    collective 122, 126, 137
    history of 1, 72–3, 266
    metaphysical 32–4, 38–9, 107
    moral 114–18
ideal
    cognitive 34, 41–8, 98–9, 102–4, 106–7, 120, 166, 186, 197, 201

    moral 34, 43–6, 103, 106–7, 111–14, 120, 137, 206
    pedagogical 46, 128
    political 47–8, 121
    social 103, 111–12, 126, 206
    teacher 151–2
idealism 31–4, 41, 85, 99, 102, 121, 164, 167, 223–5, 227–8, 231, 253
ideology 122, 126–7, 247
illusions 78, 89, 105, 152, 186
image
    mental 70, 76, 78, 80, 172, 174–80, 184, 186–7, 215
    psychological 10, 37–8, 45, 53
    visual 79, 83, 184
imagination 76, 84, 101, 178 246
imitation 44, 76, 82–3, 86, 105, 115, 165, 170, 173–4, 177–9, 181–2, 186–7, 215, 246, 253, 265
implication 79, 83, 202, 210, 224, 237
immanentism 73, 86, 100–4, 107, 114, 117–18, 123, 126, 135, 161, 165, 197, 215, 219, 222, 230, 255
individualism 39, 46, 110–11, 158, 182, 245, 265
individuality 45, 105, 107, 109, 219
individualization 102, 110, 123, 127, 141, 224
induction 43, 79, 150
INRC 203
instincts 21, 33, 49, 56, 76–7, 106, 163, 167, 182, 193, 197, 205, 211
intelligence 68, 172–3
    development 75, 82, 88, 103, 163, 169–70, 173, 175–7, 181, 183, 187, 193, 205–7, 230–1

function 19, 119, 149, 164, 166–7, 172, 182, 184, 195, 197, 203, 205–7, 215
    test 56, 58, 63
International Bureau of Education (IBE) 129–31, 141–2, 145–51, 153–55, 256
intention 75, 80, 95, 114, 118, 172–3, 205, 247, 255
interaction
    biological 22, 44, 157, 159
    psychological 82–4, 163, 170, 193, 207, 212, 218, 226–8, 231, 237
    social 75, 87, 89, 110, 114–15, 126, 182–3, 265
interiorization 177, 187, 189, 195, 216
internalization 100, 111, 170, 174, 183, 186, 194, 224
introspection 20, 82
intuition 20, 38, 54, 140, 187–90, 192, 194, 198–200, 226, 247, 264–5
isomorphism (see parallelism) 159, 185, 189, 193, 195, 207, 210, 227, 235, 253

Jean-Jacques Rousseau Institute (JJRI) 28–9, 52, 64–9, 71, 73–4, 77, 96–7, 114, 128–31, 139, 141–8, 154, 169, 189–90, 198, 200, 234, 244
judgment 73–4, 102
    cognitive 82
    moral 119, 123–4, 194, 206, 251, 254–5
justice 32–3, 101, 107, 114–15, 117, 123, 133, 141, 206

knowledge 19, 27, 72, 159–60, 185–6, 193, 197, 221, 226, 228, 263
    acquisition of 134, 136, 140–1, 159, 216, 264
    and faith 42
    construction of 104, 169–70, 196–7, 209, 211, 223–4, 226, 235
    intuitive 38
    moral 252
    pedagogical 151–2
    scientific 20, 75, 93–4, 222–5, 232, 253
    self 36, 105
    spontaneous 91–3, 140, 250

lamarckism 14, 20–1, 23, 157, 211
language
    and thought 75–8, 84, 95, 111, 176–7, 180, 217–8, 250
    development 67, 78, 82–4, 89, 180–1, 183–4, 250
    learning 150, 176, 206, 211, 265
    teaching 139, 150
Lausanne 5, 22, 68, 96–7, 109
laws
    biological 22–3, 41–2, 156, 158
    juridical 121, 127, 145, 153
    psychological 23, 43–4, 54, 73–4, 119, 135, 163, 171, 184, 192–3, 197, 212, 218, 223, 228–31, 252
    scientific 20, 41–2, 85–6, 99–100, 202, 209, 212, 222, 253
    social 114
learning 76
    and development 93, 140, 158, 165–6, 197, 215–18, 263–5
    and language 78, 83, 119, 150, 211
    in school 134–7, 141–2, 147, 256–8

logic 29, 41, 63, 70, 72–6, 79, 82–96,
  100–1, 104, 111, 116, 119, 167,
  184, 189, 192–6, 200–3,
  213–14, 219, 221, 223, 230,
  232, 239, 248–51, 259
  intensional 237
  of action 82, 95, 101, 169, 175,
  181
love 37, 45, 48, 72, 74, 100–1, 103,
  107, 112, 117, 210

magic 68, 70, 78, 81, 85, 112, 137,
  172
malacology 9, 18–19, 50,
  59
mathematics 29, 41, 149, 191–8,
  202–4, 211, 214–15, 223,
  225–7, 229, 236, 250, 253, 259
  didactics 150, 257
marxism 126, 204, 233, 239
materialism 21, 41, 126
maturation 19, 89–90, 158, 161,
  210–11, 217, 250
meaning 79, 176, 178, 181, 186,
  209, 236–7
measurement 19, 157, 195, 199,
  200, 202
memory 20, 103, 175, 215–6,
  263–4
metaphysics 20–1, 26–7, 32–5, 38,
  40–1, 43, 46–8, 50, 53, 93, 99,
  104, 109, 118, 161, 199, 204,
  221, 232, 266
method
  axiomatic 191, 221
  classification 9, 14, 16–8, 20,
  22–3, 29, 51–2, 55, 63–4, 67,
  77, 90, 167
  clinical 63–4, 74–6, 87–8, 90–2,
  125, 190, 251–2
  critical 190–1
  deductive 191, 221

historical–critical 7, 73, 221, 223,
  253
  genetic 76, 98, 104, 221
  regressive 168
  test 56, 58, 63–4, 66–7, 74, 89–91,
  125, 172, 187, 191, 198, 202,
  239, 249, 251, 256
methodology 68, 91, 134, 191
mind = intelligence 36, 75–6, 79,
  99, 102–3, 106–7, 115–16, 118,
  121, 166, 193, 197, 204, 224–7,
  231, 264–5
mollusks 14, 16–20, 22, 51, 55, 59,
  81, 98, 156–7, 159
monism 231, 253
morality
  and adolescence 10, 31, 42, 49,
  72
  and protestantism 5–6, 26, 32–4,
  40–1, 46, 72, 100–8
  and science 15, 34, 40, 43–6, 48,
  68, 72, 99
  and society 47–8, 110–12,
  119–23, 206–7
  development of 33, 80, 86, 100,
  102–3, 113–27, 206–7, 210,
  251–2, 254–5
  education of 15, 57, 112, 116–17,
  133–4, 139, 151, 155, 265
  philosophy of 29–34, 45, 74,
  101–8, 117–19, 125
motivation 85, 136, 178, 204–6,
  252
movement 169–73, 176, 192,
  199–200, 209, 223, 247, 250
mutationism 20–3, 157, 159, 161
mysticism 37, 40, 45, 53–4, 57, 71,
  103, 107, 118, 120, 137

nationalism 33, 39, 47–8, 121, 127,
  130
natural history 13–5, 20

necessity 74, 79–80, 83, 118, 132, 160, 195, 201–2, 208, 210, 214, 222, 235–6
needs (children) 78, 84, 93, 113, 117, 135, 142, 166, 193
Neuchâtel 5–7, 15, 18, 51, 97–8, 109, 128, 156, 192
neurology 169, 210, 213, 264
newborns 114, 168–71, 184, 246
nominalism 20, 28–9, 44, 50, 109
norms 73, 100–7, 116–18, 122–3, 132, 155, 195, 206, 223, 236
numbers 64, 67, 76, 150, 188–90, 195–6, 229, 247, 249

obedience 100, 117, 139, 251
objectivity 46, 72–4, 80, 83–6, 93, 95, 101, 104–5, 114, 118–19, 124–5, 138, 152, 169, 173, 186, 189, 201, 223, 227–8, 252, 255, 258
observation 63, 66–8, 75–7, 96, 98, 113, 156, 168–9, 182, 226
order 17
    arrangement 188, 196–7
    instruct 95, 100, 112–4, 183
    moral 126, 137
    social 32, 41, 117, 127
organization
    biological 43–5, 159–61
    cognitive 38, 90, 92, 104, 163–6, 168, 170, 192, 197, 206, 223, 231
    self- 214
    social 109–10
operations 82, 07, 119, 168, 186, 189, 192–4, 214, 235–6, 247–50
    and affectivity 205–7
    and language 181, 200, 211
    and perception 185–6
    attributed/applied 234–5

concret 186, 194–202, 223–4, 237, 247–9, 257, 263
    formal 87, 200–4, 210, 218, 222–4, 227, 236, 247–8
    infralogical 195, 198
    logico-mathematical 29, 195, 198, 215
    scientific 127, 221
orthodoxy 36, 48, 99
orthogenesis 85

pacifism 11, 31, 39, 47, 123, 131, 142, 145
parallelism (see isomorphism)
    affective – cognitive 205–7, 210
    individual – science 223–4, 253
    individual – society 28, 46, 110,126
    intellectual – moral 74, 103, 119, 252
    intellectual – motor 74
    mechanic – psychological 43
    ontogenetic – phylogenetic 76, 90
    psychological – physical 210, 250
    realism – idealism 99
    reality – construction 85, 87
    reality – necessity – possibility 236
    space – time 173, 199
    subject – object 209
parents 10, 36, 56, 72, 81, 86, 89, 100–1, 115–16, 118, 124, 133–4, 138, 149, 183, 252
Paris xi, 5, 7, 9, 29, 55–8, 67, 122, 131–2, 147, 189, 192, 216
participation 80–1, 90, 95
pedagogy 46, 67, 123, 128–55, 245, 256–8, 265–6
    and psychology 56–8, 152–4
    experimental 56, 65–6, 76, 152
    history 1, 140–1

perception 19, 75, 83, 99, 105, 167–9, 175–7, 179, 184–6, 198, 205, 209, 211, 226, 243
permanency (see conservation) 169, 172, 175, 185, 190, 198, 201, 247
personality 35, 44, 46, 53–7, 71, 104–8, 112, 117, 123, 149, 151–2, 165, 204, 206, 264
phenocopy 158–9, 162
phenomenism 79–81, 85–6, 172, 223
phenomenology 204, 226
phenotype 51, 55, 156, 158–9
philosophy 19–21, 24, 27–30, 32, 34–5, 41, 43–5, 48–50, 73, 97–8, 102, 109, 150, 221, 231–3, 243, 253, 258–9
physics 41, 85–6, 150, 202, 225–9, 264–5
play 8, 70, 76, 113, 121, 136, 177–80, 252–3
positivism 20–1, 47, 52, 85, 90, 197, 233, 253
possibility 74, 80, 167, 201–4, 228, 234–6, 246
pragmatism 21, 28, 41, 98, 167, 215, 226
probability 43, 201–2
progress 26, 28, 31–4, 65, 76, 81, 103, 106, 112, 115–19, 122, 128, 131, 135, 141, 158, 161, 223–5, 231–2
proportions 201–3, 244, 247
protestantism xi, 7–8, 10, 25–6, 30–1, 40, 42, 45, 52, 72, 99, 102, 104, 107, 151, 245
psychoanalysis 8, 10, 46, 52–8, 68–72, 92, 125, 204, 208, 239, 256

psychologism 46, 55, 152, 156–62, 223
psychology 41, 143, 152–3, 163, 210, 225, 254–6
    experimental 63, 65–7, 76, 148, 152, 155, 234, 244
    genetic 85, 98, 104, 126, 140, 153, 155, 215, 245–6
    religious 43, 46, 52, 72–4, 103, 123, 255
    social 46, 95, 110–24, 183
puberty (see adolescence) 15, 25–39, 100–1, 204
punishment 10, 57, 114, 124, 138–9, 255

quality 20, 43–4, 53, 72, 95, 118, 163–4, 167–8, 189, 222, 230, 248
quantity 43, 53, 164, 189–90, 193, 200, 202, 222–3, 244

rationalism 107, 118, 185, 230, 233
rationality (see reason) 9, 53, 73, 109, 116, 188, 222–3
reactions 91, 158, 163, 170–1, 184, 205–6, 213–4
    circular 170–1, 173, 193
realism 29, 76, 79–80, 85–6, 92, 99, 104, 109, 114, 120, 164, 166–7, 179, 224–8, 231, 253
reality
    and religion 33–4, 38, 46, 73, 101, 103, 106–7
    children's 72, 74, 78–80, 85, 87, 93, 178–9
    construction of 19–20, 41–2, 76, 83–7, 90, 99, 103, 150, 163, 166, 169, 186, 192, 197, 201, 208, 226–8, 230–2, 235–6, 246–7, 253

ontological 84–5, 102–3, 109, 197, 227, 253

reason (see rationality) 38, 45, 53, 57, 63, 73–4, 82–7, 91, 98–107, 111–12, 117, 120, 135, 166–7, 194, 203, 205, 222–3, 236, 246
constituting/constituted 85

reciprocity 44, 79, 83–4, 101, 104–5, 113–14, 117–18, 126, 133, 139, 141, 145, 155, 192, 203, 206, 213

recognition 38, 53, 99, 163, 170, 215, 236, 251

reductionism 232, 244, 246

reflexes 76, 156–7, 170–1, 184, 205

regulation 82, 158–9, 175, 178, 193, 208, 213, 218, 225, 227
affective 205–6
auto–/self- 163, 166, 214–15, 229–30, 253

relations 63, 111, 184, 187–90, 194–5, 199, 203, 210, 221–3, 229

relationship
parent-child 9, 10, 81, 86, 89, 112–16, 133
peer 133–4
social 110, 112–14, 118, 123, 125, 127, 131, 182, 192, 207

relativism 85, 124, 222, 226

relativity 83, 85, 167, 200, 222, 232

religion 1, 8, 10, 25–8, 30–5, 37–9, 42, 45–6, 52–3, 72–3, 99–103, 119,123, 204, 233, 255

representation 19, 84, 166, 174–81, 183, 186–7, 194, 209, 212, 227, 231, 247, 250, 253, 263, 265

repression 28, 56–8, 208, 215

research 73, 98, 103, 123, 225, 252
in biology 51, 55, 156, 163

in pedagogy 130–1, 143–4
in philosophy 40, 43, 47, 49
in psychology 65, 67, 75–7, 87, 89, 92, 104, 114, 143–5, 163, 168–9, 187, 189, 191, 198, 200, 215, 217, 220–2, 234, 246, 251–2, 254
in sociology 125
pupil's 134–6, 151
teacher's 152–3

respect 8, 37, 100, 106, 110, 112–13, 116–25, 132–4, 137, 151, 165–6, 183, 206

reversibility 74, 82–3, 166, 174, 185–6, 189, 192–4, 200, 203, 213–14, 237

rhythm 82, 119, 170, 193

rule 29, 34, 79, 100, 105–6, 110–17, 120–1, 123, 126–7, 141, 178–9, 190, 206, 251–3, 258

sanction 114, 141, 178–9, 251, 255

schema 83, 86–7, 95, 105, 125, 163–6, 168–75, 177–8, 181, 184, 187, 198, 205–9, 213–15, 217, 235–6

school 11, 89–90, 131
experimental 65–6, 128–9, 134–8, 140–2, 149, 245, 257
public 111, 136–7, 149, 258
reform 66, 128–31, 143, 147, 151, 153–4
system 58–9, 136, 146

science 14–19, 22–5, 41, 43, 46, 85, 98–100, 127, 152, 156, 220–3, 225, 231–3, 253
and religion 26, 30, 34, 40–2, 46–7, 73, 99, 101–3, 204
history of 87, 90, 98, 198, 223–4, 232, 236
teaching 136, 150, 245, 257

sedum 157

selection 20, 158–60

self 49, 53–4, 57, 100–1, 103–8, 112, 116, 125, 132, 150, 155, 168, 170, 178, 180, 201, 206, 208, 221, 253

self-government 131, 141–2, 147

self-organization 38, 107, 161, 163, 166, 170, 214–15, 229–30

seriation 188, 192, 200, 257

sexuality 36, 45, 52, 56, 96, 137–8, 245

sign 80–1, 84, 126, 176–81, 186, 196, 209

sociability 88, 114, 171, 182

social change 65, 100, 103, 110–12, 120–1, 128, 132

social factor 86–7, 89, 94, 115, 125, 142, 149, 182–3, 194, 212–13, 218, 224, 251

socialization 56, 70, 77–8, 80, 82–4, 89, 93, 105–6, 113–20, 123, 135, 155, 176, 179, 182–3, 194, 218

socialism 6, 11, 31, 47–8

society 31–2, 34, 40–1, 46–8, 100–2, 109–12, 117, 119–20, 123, 126, 141, 145, 151, 183, 223, 249

sociocentrism 122–3, 127, 149

sociology 41, 97–8, 100, 109, 125–7, 139, 229–30, 254, 258–9

solipsism (see autism) 86, 113, 115, 168–9

space 172–5, 198–9, 247

species 18, 20, 22–3, 29, 51, 59, 81, 157, 214

speech 10, 68, 165, 176, 178, 181
    egocentric 92

speed 199–200, 223, 247, 259

stages 26, 64, 68, 70, 74, 76–8, 81–3, 89–91, 119, 125, 167–207, 213, 217–18, 223–4, 236–7, 246–9, 252–3, 255–6, 263–4
    affective 205–7
    and teaching 140–1
    moral 113–14, 125, 133, 254–5
    of concrete operations 194–202, 206, 218, 223, 234, 237
    of formal operations 74, 86, 200–4, 206, 208, 210, 218, 222, 224, 227
    preoperational 81, 126, 175–93, 198, 223, 237, 249
    sensori-motor 115, 168–75, 205
    transition 210, 213, 248, 264

structuralism 176, 228–31, 258

structures 87, 90, 114–15, 122, 126, 158–9, 163–8, 181, 185, 198, 201, 210–18, 225–30, 235–7, 248–50, 253, 264–5
    affective 206–7
    and function 88, 133, 164, 167, 183, 231
    and language 176, 181, 211
    figurative 185–7, 196
    logico-mathematical 185, 194–7, 206, 211–12, 214, 216, 225, 227–8, 231, 249, 262
    normative 105–6
    of-the-whole 44, 185, 193–4
    operative 92, 168, 186, 189, 193, 196, 211, 228, 263

students group ACSE 30–2, 34, 41, 46–8, 73, 97, 99

subject 73, 77, 80, 95–6, 163, 169, 196, 209, 217, 222–3, 225–9, 235
    study 136, 142, 149–50, 152, 225, 257

symbol 20, 26, 32, 38–9, 46, 53, 57, 63, 73, 101–12, 113, 119,

122–3, 126–7, 168, 174–87,
193–4, 200–1, 215, 230
symbolic thinking 70–1, 122,
124, 176–87, 253, 265
symbolic play 89, 177–9
syncretism 79, 97, 184

taxonomy (see classification) 14,
22, 167
teacher 11, 57, 116, 124, 130, 143,
211
and students 133, 137, 140, 142
function 134, 140, 147, 150–1,
258, 264
material 135, 150, 245
personality 151–2
training 65–6, 128, 144, 149–53,
246
teaching 66, 72, 97, 109, 130,
135–42, 147, 149–50, 217, 234,
256–8
language 84, 150
methods 134–7, 140–2, 147, 150,
256, 265
peace 131, 145
subjects 150
teleology (see finalism) 20, 161,
250, 253
thought 10, 109, 147, 150, 159–60,
248
and action 76, 82, 86, 119,
175–6, 184, 235
and perception 99,176, 179, 185,
187, 226, 248
and reality 85, 93, 99, 102, 163,
184, 209, 230
autistic 53–4, 57, 68, 70, 78, 92–3,
165, 176
autonomous 35–6, 40, 204
child 68, 70, 84–5, 88, 90, 92, 105,
132–3, 243, 249

concrete 168, 194–200, 230, 257
development 73–4, 160, 163, 166,
168–9, 175, 216–19, 222,
230–1, 237, 265
egocentric 53, 77–93, 106, 116,
122, 125, 127, 165, 247
formal 80, 200–4, 231
intuitive 20, 187–191
logico-mathematical 29, 192,
194–7
normative 57, 72, 100–4, 106,
122–3, 166
operational 74, 127, 191–204,
248–9
pre-operational 126, 176–89
religious 38, 73, 101–3, 160
representational 19, 166, 174–84,
187, 194, 263, 265
scientific 53, 73, 104, 127, 197,
222, 224–5, 230
sensori-motor 75, 127, 174, 182
symbolic 70–1, 122, 127, 174,
176–83, 253
verbal 83–4, 91, 119, 216–17
time (see duration) 19–20, 85, 126,
173, 175, 198–200, 222
topology 198, 223
totality 44, 109–10, 193–5, 213, 221,
224
transcendence 32, 38, 46, 73, 81,
86, 99–104, 107, 117, 123–4,
200, 221, 223, 251
transduction 79
truth 7–8, 30, 42, 72, 85, 137, 153
religious 36–8, 73, 101
normative 78, 105, 111, 181
scientific 87, 191, 202, 228, 232

unconscious 28, 52–4, 56–8, 71, 93,
106, 180, 208–10
UNESCO 130, 148–9, 153–4, 256

universality 1, 73, 90, 104, 217–18, 222, 225, 229–30, 235, 249, 253
universalism 100, 103, 117–18, 135, 155, 231, 253, 255
universals 29, 43
universe 20, 26–7, 32, 37, 99, 103, 106, 160, 170
university 147, 149, 152

values 7, 30, 32, 39, 41–2, 45–6, 57, 72–4, 83–5, 100, 102–3, 106–8, 111–12, 115, 118, 126, 151, 160, 193, 204, 206–7, 209–10, 232, 254

verbalism 124, 137, 150
vitalism 19–21, 250

war 11, 31–4, 36, 41, 47–8, 76, 121, 145–50
weight 190, 195, 202–3, 217
will 43, 45–6, 55, 96, 102, 115, 122, 138, 155, 205–6
women 9, 33, 96, 127
work 7–9, 11, 17, 37, 111, 127, 148, 228, 238–9, 251

Zurich 52–6